THE REALITY OF FOREIGN AID

The Reality of Foreign Aid

Willard L. Thorp

Published for the
COUNCIL ON FOREIGN RELATIONS
by

PRAEGER PUBLISHERS
New York · Washington · London

PRAEGER PUBLISHERS
111 Fourth Avenue, New York, N.Y. 10003, U.S.A.
5, Cromwell Place, London S.W.7, England

Published in the United States of America in 1971
by Praeger Publishers, Inc.

Library of Congress Catalog Card Number: 70–121720

For a partial list of Council publications, see pages 369–70.

Printed in the United States of America

To Clarice,
my partner in development

Contents

List of Tables

Preface

That in this productive twentieth century billions of people remain hungry, sick, unable to read, and enduring life at the lowest survival level cannot but be deeply disturbing. How to deal with the poverty problem in a well-to-do country has proved to be no simple matter—and the difficulties are greatly compounded when nations try to carry on programs of assistance reaching into the less-developed countries.

In its first major stage, foreign aid had seemed to be a relatively easy and uncomplicated operation. In the 1940s, I had been responsible for the Post-UNRRA Relief Program and the so-called Interim Aid Program, which were to be followed by the European Recovery Program. The essential difference between the supplying countries (United States and Canada) and the recipients was in the presence or absence of war devastation rather than in cultures, engineering and management competence, and effective government services. New social and economic blueprints were not needed. The physical requirements for reconstruction were fairly obvious, although there were problems in obtaining certain products such as textiles or electrical machinery for shipment abroad, because of the accumulated demand at home. The recipients participated in developing a rational allocation among themselves of the resources that were provided. And most important, there was little disagreement between the executive branch and Congress.

Several years later, when I presented President Truman's Point IV Program to Congress, some of the special difficulties in carrying out a "cooperative program for aid in the development of economically underdeveloped countries" were spelled out in some detail: unstable political and economic conditions in the less-developed countries, the absence of a theory of growth, the limited availability of appropriate personnel and capital, and the organizational difficulties of setting up and maintaining programs of so many types in so many areas. Much of the presentation at that stage had to do with describing the need for technical assistance, supported by illustrations of scattered projects in the past. It was assumed that the International Bank for Reconstruction and Development, the Export-Import Bank, and a revived flow of private foreign investment would take care of the capital requirements. The Point IV presentation was cautious, insisting that it was to be an "evolutionary program," undertaking "exploratory and experimental operations in some areas to gain new experience," and, as a result of experience, probably "requiring continual adjustment in the methods of approach."

This book is intended to review the unexpected difficulties that emerged as the richer countries tried to give effective aid to the less-developed countries. There was no problem of gross requirements, because the possible uses for capital and technical assistance proved to be enormous. Neither recipients nor suppliers were properly organized for the task. Many of the recipients were struggling with problems of infant vitality and newly acquired sovereignty. Part of the difficulty was that neither history nor social science was prepared to give much direction as to how evolutionary change at a revolutionary pace can be encouraged and development accelerated. And new multilateral institutions were themselves in the process of development. Part of the trouble was that the objectives were never clear and expectations were too great on all sides.

For nearly five years (1962–67) I was chairman of the Development Assistance Committee of the Organization for Economic Cooperation and Development (OECD), the place where those providing aid meet. I made many visits to the capitals of the committee's members, and became more and more impressed with the tremendous progress made in twenty years toward more effective aid policies and arrangements. The less-developed countries, with exceptions of course, are making wiser use of their own and contributed resources and are increasingly establishing priorities within a rational program. To be sure, economic progress seems to be more rapid than social change, and the development of political institutions representing the public interest is slowest of all, but progress in each of these areas is not unrelated to the others. So far as the developed countries are concerned, most have improved their systems of management and have built up an administrative group with virtually professional standing. And the problems of strategy and tactics are being studied by social scientists as never before.

It is this learning process that is important and about which this book is written. It is focused primarily on the policies and activities of the developed countries, because these are the subjects with which I am most familiar. Special attention is paid to the United States not only because its program has been by far the largest but also because it has been the most open, fully documented, and widely discussed of all. And at the moment (1970) it is the one with the least certain future. While this book, then, is largely centered on the learning process on the part of aid-suppliers, a parallel book would undoubtedly demonstrate a parallel growth in sophistication among the less-developed countries, though any such report would be hard to write, because of the number of countries involved and their heterogeneity.

In any extensive consideration of foreign aid, one must deal with a wide-ranging series of questions—why? what? how? when? how much? to whom? how long?—as well as the operational issues of management structure, arrangements, terms and conditions, controls, and evaluation. I think that they are all in this book, but none are strictly independent subjects. "How long" depends on "how much," and "to whom" depends on "why." The first four chapters provide a general setting with respect to the development problem and the history of foreign aid. Two chapters then discuss the two main types of contribution that can be made from abroad—knowledge and capital. Five chapters deal with operational policy choices, and two raise internal and external governmental problems. And, finally, other ways of helping beyond conventional foreign aid are discussed.

Two organizations have made this book possible, although its beginnings should be credited to my years in the Department of State. The Development Assistance Committee of the OECD not only educated me during the years when I served as its chairman, but it is the source of so much of the data in this book that due acknowledgment at each point would be tiresome indeed. The second organization is the Council on Foreign Relations, which provided the time, encouragement, and supporting facilities needed for such an enterprise. Of particular assistance was the study group under the chairmanship of Lloyd Reynolds, which spent many hours discussing the policy issues raised herein. Its other members were William J. Barnds, David E. Bell, Paul

Clark, Frank M. Coffin, William Diebold, Jr., Isaiah Frank, Ernest Gross, Isador Lubin, Leo Model, Lloyd N. Morrisett, F. Taylor Ostrander, Jr., Gustav Ranis, William D. Rogers, Seymour J. Rubin, Helena Stalson, Kenneth W. Thompson, Robert W. Valkenier, and C. Tyler Wood. Although this group raised many helpful and clarifying points that were incorporated in the manuscript, the responsibility for what finally appears within these covers is entirely mine.

WILLARD L. THORP

Amherst, Massachusetts
August, 1970

THE REALITY OF FOREIGN AID

1 · Setback in Foreign Aid

Foreign economic aid to less-developed countries is no small operation. It approximated $13 billion in 1968, with virtually all countries in the world involved in sending or receiving it. The outflow of public and private assistance from twenty-five non-Communist countries averages about $20 per year per person. For the less-developed countries, the inflow is equal to about one-third of their total import bill and about one-fourth of the amount invested with their boundaries, including expenditures for replacement. Nor is the flow only one of resources. Essential to development is the transmission of knowledge and experience from the more-developed world through various forms of technical cooperation.

The international flow of assistance for development is not new. Historically it took place largely through private ventures, missionary activity, and migration. The new element today is the active participation by governments in the support of areas for which they have no direct political responsibility—less-developed areas which have profited but little from the great political, social, and economic transformation of the Western world in the last two centuries.

The various national assistance programs were not the result of central policy-planning efforts, although most countries have reviewed and modified their policies and procedures frequently. For some, like the United Kingdom and France, the problem has been to shift from treating these areas authoritarianly as colonies to recognizing them as sovereign powers. For others, like the Scandinavian countries, there was little background or experience in dealing with less-developed areas. For most, including the United States, foreign aid has meant many things involving such activities as missionary enterprises, disaster relief, general postwar rehabilitation, aid to refugees, defense support, market expansion, foreign investments, political intervention, cultural extension, multilateralism, and development aid to poor countries.

Simply to speak of social and economic development is to make no distinctions among a wide variety of situations. The less-developed countries are large and small, old and new, rich and poor in physical resources. They differ in customs, traditions, religions, sense of unity, and character of leadership. Some are already well along the road to development, while others have hardly started. The process of giving assistance to them raises many difficult policy issues for the developed countries, ranging from the direct questions of how, where, how much, and on what terms, through the less evident issues created by national sensitivities and pride of sovereignty, to the uncomfortable uncertainties about the development process itself.

Each supplier country has worked out its own set of answers, but they all have tended to move in one general direction. The members of the Development Assistance Committee (DAC) [1] agreed in 1961 in the Resolution on the Common Aid Effort "to secure an expansion of the aggregate volume of resources made available to less-developed countries and to improve their effectiveness." The record of official disbursements for economic assistance to less-developed countries by the sixteen DAC members, given in Table 1, shows a rising total. Yearly figures vary considerably, but the first five years of the 1960s averaged 47 per cent above the last five years of the 1950s. And the more recent figures for 1967 and 1968 are another 16 per cent higher, although most of the increase is due to higher prices. The picture of growth would be more striking if the rapidly increasing outflow to the less-developed countries from the multilateral agencies were added.[2] This record of official aid indicates national policy as expressed in government action. However, government programs are only part of the actual flow of resources over and above the exchanges of trade. Unfortunately, data are not available for contributions made by voluntary agencies, but the total flow of private investment and credit from the sixteen countries reached $5.7 billion in 1968, bringing the total flow from DAC members

TABLE 1

FLOWS OF NET OFFICIAL RESOURCES FROM DAC MEMBERS [a]
TO LESS-DEVELOPED COUNTRIES AND MULTILATERAL AGENCIES,
1956–68
(*$ Million*)

| Country | Annual Averages | | 1966 | 1967 | 1968 |
	1956–60	1961–65			
Australia	47	93	128	167	157
Austria	2	13	33	27	28
Belgium	49	83	81	99	93
Canada	61	93	212	213	214
Denmark	6	10	26	28	29
France	807	871	745	826	855
Germany	274	484	486	547	595
Italy	94	86	115	156	150
Japan	128	225	466	583	659
Netherlands	36	56	94	114	134
Norway	6	13	13	16	23
Portugal	12	44	24	47	35
Sweden	9	24	57	60	71
Switzerland	11	9	3	4	19
United Kingdom	300	453	526	498	428
United States	2,321	3,551	3,660	3,723	3,605
Total	4,161	6,108	6,669	7,106	7,095

[a] The Commission of the European Economic Communities is also a member. Flows to it rather than from it are included in this table under the country of source. In general, the EEC is treated for statistical purposes as a multilateral agency.
Source: Development Assistance Committee, OECD.

up to $13.0 billion. A still larger figure would be shown if assistance programs covering military supplies were added, but this activity is not included in "economic assistance."

The record of the total flow of assistance is best shown by estimates of the amount received each year by the less-developed countries. The chart on page 6, based on figures given in detail in Table 13, shows the annual receipts of assistance by less-

developed countries from both official and private sources, including assistance given by the Communist countries but excluding contributions by voluntary (nonprofit), private agencies. The
estimates are made according to current statistical practices. As
the chart makes clear, the total flow of aid to less-developed
countries increased in each of the ten years except 1962, when
the private flow was sharply reduced, and the level for 1968 was
considerably above that for any previous year.

FOREIGN AID RECEIVED BY LESS-DEVELOPED COUNTRIES, 1959–68

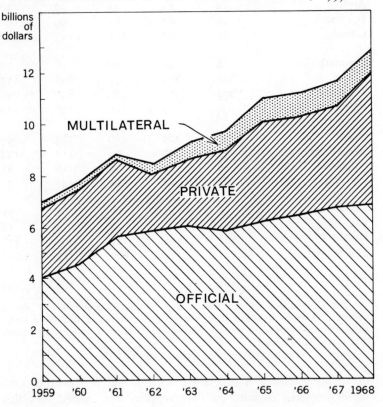

Where then is the setback? The answer is: in the United
States. Even so, it is clearly inaccurate to talk about a decline in
American foreign aid as something that has happened. Much of
the economic assistance, here recorded as "disbursements," is re-

lated to relatively long-term projects so that a considerable part
of the flow for any one year reflects projects approved and funds
set aside in earlier years. As a result, there is such an accumulated pipeline (work in progress already funded from past appropriations) that a reduction in new funds appropriated may not
be reflected in a significant reduction in the flow of aid for several years.

The disturbing point is that in the United States the appropriations of *new* funds have been declining since 1965. No other
donor has a comparable record in cutting back its appropriations
for economic assistance to the less-developed countries during
this recent period. In fact, since 1967 at least a half-dozen developed countries have set themselves specific targets for stepping up
their aid. Canada, Denmark, and Norway have set dates when
their official disbursements and private transfers are to reach 1
per cent of national income. The Netherlands and Germany,
whose official and private flows already exceed 1 per cent of national income, have set themselves targets for covering the 1 per
cent by official aid appropriations. Sweden has set itself an even
higher target for official aid appropriations, 1 per cent of gross
national product. To achieve the indicated targets, the increases
in economic assistance will have to be over 20 per cent per year
for Canada, Denmark, Norway, and Sweden, 25 per cent for the
Netherlands, and 11 per cent for Germany. Since these increases
are expected to be on a regular basis, the larger appropriations
will soon be reflected in parallel increases in disbursements. The
schedule for all six countries amounts to an average increase of
about $200 million per year over the next four years. More im-
portant, however, is their demonstration of their attitude toward
foreign aid.[3] Elsewhere, public leaders and groups in the legislatures are demanding that their governments do more to increase
their assistance efforts.

But the prospects for rapid growth in official aid totals seem
less bright as one goes up the scale from small to large supplier
country. The four largest programs have increased by about 50
per cent since the late 1950s, while the programs of the twelve
smaller suppliers have more than trebled. France's official program was at its peak in 1962. It declined for four years, largely
because of reductions in aid to Algeria, but turned up again in
1967. The German program has been rising at about 10 per cent

per year since 1964. Britain's disbursements for economic aid reached a new peak in 1966 but fell back in 1967 and 1968, reflecting new efforts to deal with its imbalance of payments. However, the Labor government's White Paper on future public expenditures forecasted an average annual rate of increase of 6.8 per cent in overseas aid for the next three years, while the Minister for Overseas Development announced in Parliament at the end of 1969 that Britain expected to reach the 1 per cent target "not much later than the target date of 1975." American official aid appears to have reached a peak in disbursements in 1967, and appropriations for economic assistance to less-developed countries have been setting a new low each year since 1965. In contrast, Japan's Finance Minister announced in February 1970, that further increases in his country's aid program would bring it up to $1.4 billion in 1970, making Japan the second largest donor in the world. Already by 1968 it had moved up to third place.

*   *   *

Except for the United States, no country has constant, acrimonious public debates about its foreign aid program. In other political systems the policies and allocation of funds are largely made within the executive branch of the government and ratified by the various parliaments. Such discussion of foreign aid as does take place in most countries is generally a questioning of why the program is not larger.

In the United States the executive branch proposes but the Congress disposes of the level of aid and often of policy issues in the foreign assistance field. Parts of the American program—for example, the Food for Freedom program (PL 480) and the activities of the Export-Import Bank—do not come up for detailed review every year. However, the Congress expresses its attitude toward the total effort with considerable thoroughness during the annual authorization and appropriation of funds under the Act for International Development. This is the part of the total aid activity which receives by far the most publicity.

Since 1965, the proposals for foreign aid put forward by the President have met with more and more difficulty in Congress. In 1968, long before the bill for Fiscal Year 1968–69 reached the floor of Congress in early July, it was common talk that the aid program was in trouble. Even its continuance was seriously challenged. After twenty years of repetitive congressional debate of rat-holes, dictatorships, corruption, balance of payments, the threat of Communism, the brotherhood of man, and the responsibilities of global leadership, a new emphasis was quickly apparent. By July the size of the 1967–68 government deficit and the prospect of a similar red ink figure in 1968–69 had stirred the fiscal Cassandras in and out of Congress to predictions of imminent financial disaster. More and more members of Congress came to believe that the reduction of the threatening deficit was of overriding importance, whether by increasing taxes or by curtailing expenditures or both. At the same time, many were taking a fresh look at priorities among claims on the budget in a country of rising violence in the cities, unsolved racial problems, lagging development in education, new health commitments, and a foreign policy which received little enthusiastic support.

The economy drive and the sense of rising domestic requirements apparently dominated the annual discussion of the Act for International Development by the committees considering authorization. As a result, their recommendations in both the House and Senate called for unprecedented cuts from the program proposed by the administration, already the lowest request in years. A small group in each body objected to such drastic reductions, but the habitual opponents were joined by a large middle group, which, though not opposed to aid as such, felt that considerations of debt, deficit, war, the dollar, inflation, and urgent domestic needs left only a low priority for foreign aid.

A proposal by the leading congressional critics for a "moratorium," whereby the program might continue using obligated but unspent funds from earlier appropriations but would receive no new funds except for a few items such as administration, was soundly defeated. In the process of authorization, amendments from the floor proposing increases in particular items were consistently voted down while further reductions were accepted, setting the final authorizations considerably below the committee recommendations in both the House and Senate. A further drastic cut was made in the appropriation process. The record of the downhill course of economic aid in the Act for International Development in 1968 and 1969 is shown in Table 2. These figures include economic and military assistance and administration costs handled by AID.

TABLE 2

Steps in U.S. Economic Aid (AID) Authorization and
Appropriation, 1968–69 and 1969–70
($ *Million*)

	1968–69	1969–70
President's Request	2,958.4	2,630.4
Authorization:		
House Foreign Affairs Committee		
Recommendation	2,359.6	2,189.4
House Bill	1,988.8	2,193.9
Senate Foreign Relations Committee		
Recommendation	1,940.8	1,967.7
Senate Bill	1,940.8	1,967.7
Conference Committee Recommendation		
and Final Authorization	1,969.0	1,969.5
Appropriation:		
House Appropriations Committee		
Recommendation	1,619.1	1,599.4
House Bill	1,619.1	1,649.4
Senate Appropriations Committee		
Recommendation	1,932.4	2,131.5 [a]
Senate Bill	1,932.4	2,026.9
Conference Committee Recommendation		
and Final Appropriation	1,755.6	1,812.4 [b]

Note: Expenditures requiring local currency are not included.
[a] Reported by the Committee with the understanding that individual items would not exceed authorized amounts.
[b] The Conference Committee's initial recommendation of $1,866.9 was rejected by the Senate.
Source: House and Senate Committee Reports on Foreign Aid Authorization Bills, Fiscal Years 1969, 1970; *Congressional Record*, December 9, 1969, and January 27, 1970.

The President's request for $420 million for military assistance in 1968, already a substantial cut from earlier years, was reduced to $375 million in the authorization bill, which remained unchanged in the final appropriation.

From a high point of $3.9 billion in 1962 and 1963, aid appropriations were cut by more than half by 1969 and 1970. The low priority of foreign assistance and even of multilateralism was further indicated when the Congress failed to act during the 1968 session on the President's request to provide $480 million over three years as the U.S. share in replenishing the funds of the

International Development Association (IDA), the soft-loan agency in the World Bank group.

Although the dominant issue in the 1968 debate on foreign aid was the belief that federal expenditures must be substantially reduced, other issues were raised. The aid program was described as a wasteful and futile effort to buy the friendship of other nations; as supporting dictatorships; as not making any real contribution to the less-developed countries; as subject to mismanagement, lacking in competence and zeal; as a give-away program tending to reduce the sense of responsibility on the part of the recipient; as serving the interest of the recipient rather than the United States; as failing to use multilateral channels; as containing too large a grant element; and as contrary to the principle that "charity should begin at home."

Behind the scenes and only indirectly related to foreign aid was the Vietnam war and general uneasiness concerning the obligations of the United States throughout the world. Since foreign policy does not often come up for congressional action, the foreign aid legislation offered a symbolic opportunity to react to the existing foreign policy posture by expressing a desire for the United States to reduce its international responsibilities.

The supporters of foreign aid marshalled a host of counter arguments. Aid was a constructive element in foreign policy with political and economic benefits both at home and abroad. Family planning and food production were areas where it was particularly important to maintain the existing encouraging momentum. Sustained economic development would reduce international and internal strife. Commitments had been made to Latin America which could not be carried out under the reduced program. Other donor countries, pressed by the United States in the past to increase their activity, might also follow the U.S. lead downwards. The U.S. already had a big stake in the less developed countries. If there are defects in program management, they should be corrected rather than used as the reason for attacking foreign aid as such. One difficulty, supporters granted, had been an over-expectation of quick results, but the real benefits would be long range and indirect in nature, for the objectives were peace, security, and a decent life within a stronger world community of nations.

So far as public reaction was concerned, support had been presented at the hearings by repeat performances of various church, labor, and citizens organizations. However, the drive to cut the aid program gained considerable support from the answers to questionnaires sent by various congressmen to their constituents. Most questionnaires listed about a dozen items in the budget in general terms—national defense, public roads, poverty program, aid to education, health program, postal service, and the like— and asked which should be cut most severely. For most respondents, foreign aid headed the list when compared with domestic programs. To be sure, in one instance where foreign aid was presented in its most favorable light with the question, "Do you support an expanded U.S. program to help willing underdeveloped countries implement birth control programs and increase agricultural output to meet the imminent threat of a world food shortage?" the answer was "Yes" by 81 per cent. But when the same respondents chose from the list of possible programs to be cut, foreign aid still was their leading candidate for reduced spending.

Not all members of Congress and few citizens' groups were happy with the final result of the congressional action. The Senate Committee on Foreign Relations, which had recommended in the authorization process a figure well above the final settlement, criticized the proliferation of aid programs and cited the fiscal and balance-of-payments crises, but then said, "When some of these more urgent problems have been solved, the committee will be disposed to look once again with favor on an expanded, reorganized, and reordered foreign aid program." [4] Nevertheless, the conclusion seems evident that the United States, once the leader in building up a common effort among the richer countries to provide assistance generously, is the one donor country in the world where the official foreign aid program is in serious trouble.

Although the action on the Act for International Development in 1968 came as a shock to many of its supporters, the record of assistance in recent years suggests that this was no sudden development. Appropriations for foreign economic assistance, omitting the items of military assistance and defense support, fell to their lowest level in 1955 ($360 million), rose to a new high for 1962–63 ($2,210 million), and fell steadily thereafter to $1,015 for 1968–69. The drop in that portion of military assistance which is provided under the Act has been even greater. Other elements in the total program have also declined—for example, the

Food for Freedom program. The activities of the Export-Import Bank related to less-developed countries have, however, increased, and $4.5 billion was added to its statutory lending authority in 1968.

On the basis of disbursements as a percentage of gross national product, the economic assistance provided by the United States in all its official programs gave it a ranking of third in 1964, but only seventh in 1968, among the sixteen members of the Development Assistance Committee. When public and private assistance are combined, it stood in sixth place in 1964 and thirteenth in 1968. The record of American economic assistance hardly justifies the oft-repeated charge that the other advanced nations are not bearing their fair share.

* * *

The situation showed little improvement in 1969. In May 1969, President Nixon sent his first foreign aid message to Congress with proposals for Fiscal Year 1970. He himself described it as "the lowest proposed since the program began. But it is about $900 million more than was appropriated last year. I consider it necessary to meet essential requirements now, and to maintain a base for future action." Clearly, this was primarily a holding action, although increased emphasis on technical assistance was proposed as well as a new agency to promote private investment in the less-developed countries.

The message suggested that in developing his program, the President would be aided by a "comprehensive review" to be undertaken by a task force of private citizens and by the recommendations of the internationally sponsored Commission on International Development under the chairmanship of Lester Pearson. These two study groups follow an honorable tradition. Judge Frank Coffin reported in 1964 that in this field there already had been eight Presidential Committees, four special studies originated by the Congress, and at least three by the executive branch.[5] Since then, there has been a continuing President's General Advisory Committee and a Presidential Task Force, not to mention a series of limited advisory groups. This listing does not, of course, include the many studies and recommendations by international agencies and private organizations.

The President's message did not indicate any real new drive to change the trend in U.S. aid. Such reactions as have come from

Congress have indicated that in the present state of foreign affairs and of domestic demands, the President's request will be cut
substantially. In sharp contrast, it was reported on the same day
as the President's message that Canada would increase its aid by
17 per cent over the previous year even though the over-all Canadian budget was generally regarded as representing a year of au-
sterity.

Although committee hearings were held earlier, the authorization debate did not begin until November and final action on
the authorization was not taken until December 19. The appropriation was taken up immediately but, despite Senator Mc-
Gee's appeal to the Senate that "we hold our noses and adopt the
conference report," it was rejected just before the Christmas adjournment because of disagreement over the inclusion of $54.5
million for Taiwan in the military assistance title of the bill. On
Senate insistence, this item was finally omitted, and the final appropriation included $1,462 million for economic aid and $350
million for military assistance. Although there was a slight increase in economic assistance, the level for the last two fiscal
years, $1,756 and $1,812 million, is less than half the amounts
appropriated for the first three years of the 1960s, which averaged
$4,080 million. These are the figures which best indicate the at-
titude of Congress, although total foreign aid disbursements include funds for the Food for Freedom program, the Export-
Import Bank, the Peace Corps, and special appropriations for
international agencies.

The 1969 debates on the floor of Congress were more limited
than usual, most congressmen evidently feeling that they were
considering an interim proposal, with President Nixon yet to
come forward with a really revised program. While a few new
derogatory adjectives were added, such as mindless and obsolete,
more time was devoted to the question of whether or not to
earmark military assistance to South Korea and Taiwan and certain special help to Israel ($20 million for a prototype desalting
plant and $5 million for Hadassah's health work in Israel) than
to any basic policy issues. Congress did establish the Inter-American Social Development Institute "to stimulate people-to-people
channels for aid" and the Overseas Private Investment Corporation. More important, the authorization legislation was made to
apply for two years. The unprecedented extension was justified on
the basis of the difficulty of approving a completely new aid pro-

gram when the Peterson Report was not yet completed and the coming year included an election campaign. Some supported the idea because it would hold the program to its present low level at least for the duration of the present Congress.

Since authorization legislation is not needed for Fiscal Year 1970–71, the President's proposals for that year start their course in the House Appropriations Committee. Dr. Hannah, head of Agency for International Development (AID), in appearing before the committee, described the proposed program as a holding operation, with no significant effort to implement the recommendation of the Peterson Task Force that the downward trend of our development assistance should be reversed.

This is clearly shown in the government budget request for the fiscal year 1970–71 (see Table 3).

TABLE 3

U. S. Outlays for International Affairs and Finance Programs, 1968–69 to 1970–71

(*$ Million*)

	1968–69 Actual	1969–70 Estimate	1970–71 Estimate
AID Development loans	540	458	427
Technical cooperation	198	178	181
Alliance for Progress	374	371	366
Supporting assistance	474	461	513
Contingencies and other	346	293	235
Subtotal	1,931	1,761	1,720
Food for Peace	975	971	852
International financial institutions	121	256	335
Export-Import Bank	246	600	195
Peace Corps	105	102	100
Overseas Private Investment Corp.	—	—	–16
Other	18	25	24
Total	3,396	3,715	3,210

Source: *The Budget of the United States Government—Fiscal Year 1971.* Washington, 1970.

The record of declining outlays by AID results largely from reduced appropriations in 1969 and 1970 and from the request for budget authority for AID to undertake new obligations in 1970–

71 which is $403 million below the 1970 budget recommendation. Since it would be unprecedented if the Congress actually appropriated the full amount requested by the President for 1970–71, the probability is that the decline in outlays will be even greater than is shown in Table 3.

Because of the two-year authorization, neither the Senate nor House foreign affairs committee reviewed the 1970–71 AID request. (The only program requiring authorization was the Peace Corps.) The report of the Appropriations Committee was considered by the House on June 4, 1970, and passed after two hours of debate. It reduced the total by about 10 per cent below the figure for 1969–70. It showed special dislike toward the multilateral agencies, not merely reducing their funds, ostensibly on the basis of the Jackson Report, but including a requirement that they permit GAO auditing and present a justification to Congress. Finally, a parliamentary principle was made operative—that while limitations could be stated in an appropriations act, it could not contain "legislation." As a result, a number of policy items which have been in the Appropriations Act for years were thrown out on a point of order, provisions such as that disapproving of the admission of Communist China to the United Nations, as well as new proposals such as one denying aid to any country not endeavoring to control the trade in narcotics with the United States. While action could not be taken on the Peace Corps request, the House Appropriations Committee indicated that it would propose a reduction to $80 million.

* * *

While each government supplying aid has had to work out its internal problems of priority and procedure—some with much more difficulty than others—the weather forecast for foreign assistance, as described by the recipients, is not entirely fair and pleasant. The Decade of Development is "now beginning to be called the Decade of Discouragement, or worse still, the Decade of Disappointment. Neither the developed nor the developing nations could be assigned exclusive responsibility." [6]

It is not difficult to summarize the oratory of the second United Nations Conference on Trade and Development (UNCTAD II) at New Delhi, that convocation in early 1968 of all developed and less-developed countries. The less-developed countries were vigorously critical of the behavior of the suppliers, and vice versa. In advance, President Boumedienne keynoted the preparatory meeting of the less-developed countries at Algiers in 1967 with the charge that "Europe and the U.S. have plundered the natural wealth of the Third World. . . . We should consider whatever contribution the industrialized countries make as a simple restitution of a tiny part of the debt the Western countries contracted by their odious exploitation." Habit Theam of Senegal described the deterioration of the terms of trade as "a plundering of countries that produce primary products by those who sell them manufactured goods." And Peru's José Antonio Encinas del Pando explained that "we came here because the haves won't let us into the twentieth century."

Many further points aimed more directly at possible policy changes were made. Representatives of the less-developed countries charged that, while the flow of assistance is substantial, it is still far below the 1 per cent of the donors' national income, to which all had previously agreed. The trade of the poor countries, faced with various barriers, is lagging behind the growth of trade among the rich countries; even in the trade which they do have, their selling prices have declined relative to the prices of the things they buy. The debt burden, tied aid, and rising prices reduce the flow of real aid; and the procedures for providing aid are so cumbersome that they not only create delays but also stand in the way of many worthy projects. They regret that the rich countries, despite growing affluence, are preoccupied with inflationary and budgetary pressures and with protecting their payments or reserve positions. At the U.N. Economic and Social Council, on July 8, 1968, U Thant cautioned against "prosperous provincialism" in international life, and Raul Prebisch, after visiting many capitals, noted that the development effort is plagued by the expanding prosperity in the rich countries which "tends to form an attitude of detachment, if not indifference, to the well-being of others."

Such a simple explanation may be questioned, especially since "expanding prosperity" is hardly a new phenomenon. But regardless of the causes, it is true that so far as the United States is concerned, domestic problems of race, poverty, inflation, and urban decay are absorbing popular and governmental attention as never before, and this shift is not hidden from the less-developed countries.

A somewhat less emotional but nevertheless strong criticism of present assistance efforts, directed at the industrialized countries but particularly the United States, was approved by the Special Latin American Cordinating Committee (CECLA) in May 1969 and presented to President Nixon. It argued that American investments were taking more out of Latin America than they were putting in and that only the concessionary part of loans should be regarded as assistance. The committee asked for much more aid on more favorable terms, including non-tying to American products, and for greater access to the American market; and it complained about red-tape.

The rich countries are also finding fault with the performance of the recipients, and their criticisms are many and sharp. In New Delhi, they pointed out that since economic development is internal to a country, outside assistance can only be useful when it is aiding a significant national effort. The recipients, it was charged, are inflation-prone; they waste their own inadequate savings; and they have ineffective tax systems, extensive corruption, bad systems of land tenure, excessive social security programs, and confused and incompetent administrative structures. They put obstacles in the way of flows of private capital; they spend much too much on present and prospective military ventures; and their five-year plans are fanciful, aimed at justifying increases in aid. Even within the development process their sense of priorities is wrong in that they want large industrial complexes although none of the prerequisites are present.

A more balanced analysis is presented by the Commission on International Development of which Lester Pearson was chairman.[7] It recognizes the deteriorating climate of opinion in both developed and less-developed countries; but it concludes that the record of two decades proves that rapid economic development is feasible, given adequate effort and sound policies, and that such policies have become much clearer as the result of experience. It makes a large number of constructive proposals, of which perhaps the most important is that the multilateral agencies should play an increasing part in the total effort.

The multilateral agencies themselves are not free from internal and external criticism. Sir Robert Jackson's report on the capacity of the United Nations development system is highly critical of the operational and administrative machinery operating without any comprehensive and coordinated development policy.

Further dissatisfaction is suggested by the fact that the member governments have established the Administrative Management Service within the U.N. Secretariat to make a detailed and continuing review of the use of manpower and resources within the offices covered by the U.N. budget.

With the air filled with charges and counter-charges, it is amazing that so much is nonetheless being accomplished in the less-developed world. As in the world of politics, words are louder and less meaningful than events. The basic facts are that the flow of aid has been growing both in scale and in effectiveness. There is no supplier country whose aid program resembles at all closely the pattern of five years ago, for operations have become much more pragmatic and professional. While governments are generally slow learners, both they and the individuals concerned are much more aware of the possible and the impossible, of the wide variety of political and economic circumstances with which they must deal, and of the significance of various sector priorities in plans and programming. Although there undoubtedly is much room for improvement, there are many success stories. The estimated rate of growth in gross national product for all less-developed countries for 1960 through 1969 averaged 5.7 per cent per year, slightly better than the record for the developed countries. It is an unfortunate paradox that economic assistance to the poor countries should be called into question at the very time that both suppliers and recipients are using their resources more effectively, and when many essential programs and projects have been started and are in process of achieving a momentum of their own.

Foreign economic assistance is a complex process with many suppliers and many recipients, public and private flows, bilateral and multilateral arrangements, and a wide variety of types and forms of assistance provided under an equally wide variety of terms and conditions. In all these aspects, changes are taking place and more are to be expected. To have a competent judgment of the whole foreign aid process, one must look at the underlying conditions in the poor countries and then at the ways and means whereby the developed can best assist the less developed. When one has considered these matters, the basic question of whether to reduce or expand the program can be better answered.

2 · The Political Condition of the Poor Countries

Since the end of World War II the international political structure has been completely recast. The United States has become deeply involved throughout the world, while Russia has become the other superpower. Western Europe has embarked on new experiments in cooperation and partial integration. And nearly all the colonies that made up the great empires only a few decades ago have become independent.

The drama of newly achieved political independence tends to obscure the fact that not all less-developed countries are former colonies. In Asia, Thailand was not part of an empire. In Africa, Ethiopia and Liberia have always been independent. Although the countries of the Near East have been subject to foreign control most of them have had some decades of independence, and the most recent breaks with empires (or mandates) were those of Syria and Lebanon in 1943 and Israel in 1948. The countries of Latin America, except for a few areas on the north coast and among the Caribbean islands, have ruled themselves for more than a century.

For the rest of the less-developed world, independence has been a very recent political development. During the twenty-five years to 1968, 66 new states were born: 15 became independent in the late 1940s, mostly in Asia and the Middle East; 7 more were added in the 1950s; and 44 in the 1960s, mostly in Africa. The arrangement for flying national flags at the United Nations has had to be continually enlarged, which is merely symbolic of the many more important international institutional changes necessitated by the increase in numbers. In size, these new countries range from India, seventh largest country in the world in area and second in population, down to Nauru, a Pacific island of only 8 square miles. Together, these 66 new states cover about one-fourth of the land area of the world, and include about 40 per cent of the world's population.

Before World War II there were few colonies where the demand for self-rule was pressing. The League of Nations devised the mandate system to deal with situations where countries needed preparation to "stand by themselves under the strenuous conditions of the modern world," but it was little used. Much the same tutelary procedure was later established under the United Nations through the device of "trust territories."

After the war, however, with India as the exemplar, the insistence on instant independence in colony after colony was so strong that almost all countries skipped any intermediate stage. In fact, the United Nations became one of the major forces in the drive to break up the empires, regardless of the degree of preparedness for independence. Abetted by liberals in many countries, who were not alert to the new problems being created, colony after colony achieved independence with surprising speed, though a few "over-seas territories" still remain.

* * *

Technically, what shifted was the location of ultimate political responsibility. As colonies, the new nations may have had elements of self-rule, but the metropolitan power was in control of key phases of their life. With independence, a new native government had to establish new political, economic, and social institutions. It had to keep order in spite of many divisive forces—tribal, religious, linguistic, regional—which had been kept submerged by the former overlord. It had to manage its own financial affairs. It was now required to develop its own policies at home as well as a pattern for relations with other countries, and it had to participate as a full member in various international organizations with which it was unfamiliar but which prestige required it to join. And it had to find leaders skillful enough to transform support for the negative objective of throwing out the foreign power into a more positive consensus for creating a unified and progressing nation. There was no simple or standard way to meet these necessities. Great differences in size, per capita income, education, and experience made for varied political patterns.

While the original aim was to get rid of the foreign presence and control, this was hardly a constructive objective except in terms of the Marxist notion that improvement would automatically follow because the imperial power had presumably held back the colony's development and exploited its resources. In fact, liberation provided no new resources but put unanticipated burdens on the new nation. It had to develop and support an expanded governmental structure, including new military and international cadres. The higher and sometimes even the lower posts in the civil service had been held by persons in the colonial service of the metropolitan power. In some cases, the existing judicial establishment was entirely foreign; in others, the government-owned utilities were operated entirely by foreign specialists.

During the nineteenth century and at least the first third of the twentieth, the overseas empires seemed to be permanent features of the world political structure. While the nature and sense of responsibility accepted by the metropolitan power varied from time to time and place to place, its thrust seems to have been primarily to maintain order and to facilitate private trade and investment within the empire. To be sure, various private groups showed their concern for the native populations through providing scattered missionary, educational, and health services. There was little public education and often the attempt was made to preserve the native institutions and way of life with a minimum of change. In most instances, there was a slowly growing native elite and some degree of local participation in government. The British colonies, for example, ranged from those largely self-governing, such as Jamaica, to those without any legislature where the British-appointed governor ruled by ukase as in Cyprus.

Most people in the developed countries have certain tests of "good government." They oppose one-party systems and dictatorships. They feel that a functioning constitution is necessary to protect individual rights and set limits on government action. They regard popular elections as the correct way to choose one's political leaders and are shocked by coups d'état and revolutions. While some of the new states are making a major effort to follow this pattern, many of them meet none of these criteria and are far from having anything which might be called a democratic government. Tribal government was usually based on quite different principles and practices. Nor was colonialism a condition which encouraged concepts of individual and disciplined political responsibility. The haranguing for independence did not encourage orderly opposition but often led to the idea that political ends were to be achieved through sabotage and violence.

Government in many countries tends to be more a matter of choosing among personalities than among principles. While there may be elections, the dominance of a single party is likely to make the process one of ratification rather than of choice. To be sure, the one-party system is usually not as monolithic as it appears. Divisions on policy or leadership are not necessarily eliminated within the state but are merely shifted to within the party, and popular support moves directly to this or that leader. Such a situation invites intrigue and the use of corruption as political means for obtaining support—President Obregon spoke of the "silver cannon-balls" he used against rebellious generals,[1] and similar weapons are equally effective against civilians in opposition. Nevertheless, for a new country with no political traditions and little national loyalty, it is not surprising that varied forms of individual political leadership should emerge.

In much of the developed world there is a distrust of military men in government, even though it is not unusual for generals to become heads of state. However, in the less-developed world they rise to power more often, either because the civilian government is unable to maintain order and this is their specialty, or because they believe that they can set the country on a better course. A hopeful analysis of this state of affairs is presented in the Rockefeller Report[2] which suggests that in the past most army officers came from the landowner class and the military was a conservative force resistant to change. More recently, however, the situation has changed and ambitious sons of the working classes have entered the military to seek an education and the opportunity for advancement. As a result,

> a new type of military man is coming to the fore and often becoming a major force for constructive social change in the American republics. . . . The danger for the new military is that it may become isolated from the people with authoritarianism turning into a means to suppress rather than eliminate the build-up of social and political tension.

The report also notes a similar development within the business community where long-established vested interests and practices are yielding to new, young management—a promising and constructive force necessary to the process of change because of the technical, managerial, and marketing requirements of modern industry.

Undoubtedly, these are sweeping generalizations, and the record has yet to be written. Nevertheless, it may be true that the military man is better educated, more sensitive to problems of organization, and more concerned about the future of his country. But he does come out of an authoritarian and specialized environment which is hardly the ideal for social development.

* * *

In the period of empires, there was no great push for economic development. A few persons were fully educated and frequently participated in the colonial civil service, which often disqualified them for later service under their own government. Some roads and hospitals were built, and there was some modern development in central cities. Since a group of foreigners was in residence, certain facilities such as electricity or modern housing were constructed, at least for their enclave.

One cannot be very critical of the lack of any sense of urgency in the economic and social development of the colonies since the postulates underlying government activity within the advanced countries were not very different. While the development of Western Europe and North America were of concern to theorists in the seventeenth and eighteenth centuries (note the Mercantilists and *The Wealth of Nations*), the nineteenth believed in laissez-faire and the idea that economic and social development is spontaneous and autonomous. Government did provide some roads and facilities for general education, but even such public and quasi-monopolistic services as power, transportation, and communication were developed largely by private entrepreneurs. Economists talked of equilibrium and employment rather than of growth. It is small wonder that the colonies often were relatively untouched except for their usefulness as exporters of raw materials and tropical products.

The early years of the twentieth century saw a gradual drift toward more and more government intervention, centered largely on specific weaknesses in the so-called capitalistic system. The Great Depression of the 1930s, when the fear of persistent stagnation was prevalent, led to special concern with full employment and stabilization. More recently the problem of the rate of growth has moved to the forefront. The widespread interest in comparing various national growth rates, especially those of the United States and the Soviet Union after World War II, added another dimension. And the relatively new statistical measures of production, prices, employment, and the various elements in the gross national product have made possible more sophisticated economic analyses of stability and growth.

Modern governments no longer are permitted to let nature take its course; more and more they have come to accept responsibility for maintaining growth rates. Thus the governments of the developed countries in the OECD set themselves a 50 per cent growth target for the decade of the 1960s, a bit less than the U.N. Development Decade target of an annual growth rate of 5 per cent.

Growth is an even more important test for the governments in the less-developed countries. Because independence was expected to lead quickly to general improvement, the new political leaders were most sanguine about the future and not shy in making promises. But the expectations they raised ran sooner or later into the hard facts of reality. To a considerable degree, changes of leadership in many of the new governments result from the inability of any particular set of incumbents to meet popular demands for specific improvements or a generally higher level of living. Often the threatened disorders or lagging pace of development have been such that they could apparently be dealt with only by a military take-over.

The demand for development is not limited to the former colonies, but is now general throughout the less-developed world. Many Latin American countries had long been dominated by small elite groups for whom life was relatively abundant. With a very few exceptions, the frequent government change-overs were reflections of personalities rather than fundamental policy changes. However, these countries also have been caught up in a changed world in which governments are held responsible by their citizens for seeing that rapid economic and social development is achieved.

* * *

The need for action may seem clear enough, but the political obstacles are tremendous. Each country represents a special case, and consequently generalizations tend to oversimplify reality.

Nevertheless, for most of the less-developed countries, the concept of national loyalty is yet to be developed. The family, the tribe, the language or religious group, the region, all take precedence over the "nation." So long as there was some distant but mighty power keeping peace among the different subgroups, they seemed to live together in relative peace and quiet. Take away that overseer and powerful centrifugal forces may be released, such as have plagued India, Indonesia, Rwanda and Burundi, Congo, Nigeria, and others.

Perhaps the greatest threat to political effectiveness in some countries is in the strength of tribalism. In much of Africa, regardless of whether or not there was a metropolitan power, the people have been accustomed to rule by tribal chiefs. The familiar illustrations of Nigeria and Zambia are not unique. These tribal groupings have become political units evident in elections, if any, in legislatures, and in schisms. It is the hope of national political leaders that the central government can bring enough benefits to the smaller units to build up loyalty to the nation, but this requires political skill and effective management at the center as well as a period of time perhaps spanning several generations.

In the few cases where independence was achieved only after a major struggle, the common enemy and the common effort created some cohesion. Historically, new nations have usually been through strife and sacrifice, but many of today's nations underwent no armed struggle at all. Nationalism seems to be strongest when aimed at something foreign. "Africa for the Africans" is no short-run slogan. Late in 1968, both Ghana and Kenya took action intended to remove wholesale and retail trade from the hands of foreigners even if they were citizens, the vacuum thus created to be filled by Africans. However, the effort to reduce the foreign presence does not necessarily have much internal cohesive quality. In some cases, the internal divisive force is the familiar one between the states and a federal government and may take a violent form as in the Congo and Nigeria. Or it may merely be a major nuisance; for example, India's food problem is made more difficult by the fact that some Indian states are deficit and others are surplus food producers which resist orders of the central government to share.

That the nation should take precedence in loyalty over constituent groups is a condition not easily or quickly achieved. The many conflicting interests in less-developed countries are real and persistent. They may appear politically in the form of multiparty systems or of many ambitious competing politicians with their personal supporters. As a result, coalitions may be necessary wherein the controlling group must devote most of its time and energy to staying on top. Under such conditions, and even more so in a new country where competing leaders are not widely known, it is not surprising that the processes for establishing and maintaining leadership are relatively unstable. At worst, the absence of a tradition of national unity may lead to internal disorder. At best, it creates difficulty for geographically scattered programs involving local community action such as education or rural development.

A second obstacle to political development is that national boundaries were usually drawn in colonial times from simple maps without any effort to build on a more rational basis. They were arbitrary straight lines, or they followed rivers though the river valley was the natural unit and the boundaries might better have been based on watersheds. Many of the areas are too small in population or too poor in resources to take advantage of modern methods of production. The only hope for such nonviable countries is for them to minimize their boundaries and to function as part of some larger unit. As colonies, they were part of a much larger whole; they had no other international relations of their own and therefore no experience in dealing with their neighbors or of expanding their markets except with the metropolitan power.

The loss of the economic advantage of being within an empire has been eased in many cases either by a continuation of the favorable tariff treatment or by a very gradual shift to the full status of a foreign trading partner. The former colonies of the Common Market countries were given associated member status, and the free entry for their products which they formerly had with a single metropolitan power was now extended to all six members of the European Economic Community. Using the alternative method, the United States, upon granting independence to the Philippines, scheduled a slow increase over twenty years that brought the tariff on Philippine goods up to the level applied to all foreign countries.

A third obstacle to a stable political regime, especially in countries which have been independent for some years, often is the presence of powerful forces in the country which are resistant to change—groups which are satisfied with life as it is for them. These may be the persons at the top; they may be institutions satisfied with the status quo rather than open to change. Such groupings may encompass wide differences, as in Latin America, where the elite and the peasants represent two quite different ways of life yet combine in resistance to change.

The less-developed countries are not new in the sense that North America was virgin land and a new society in the eighteenth century. They have deeply inbred habits of behavior and social and economic patterns unrelated to and probably antagonistic to development. The cow in India, the prolonged ceremonies in the East Indies, communal ownership of property, a disregard for truth-telling and for time commitments suggest only a few of the intransigent difficulties facing a new government wishing to change an old world. While old institutions create problems because of their durability, new ones cannot be effectively established overnight but must grow and develop over time. Yet "modernization" depends on these institutions.

A fourth complication is pressure from sympathetic or ambitious advisers. As part of an empire, all necessary contacts were with the metropolitan power and deliberately limited in other directions; for example, American private investment was not usually permitted in the French colonies. Even the independent countries often were contained in rather clear "spheres of interest." These pre-independence relationships are still strong, though sometimes strained in periods of difficulty. Belgium and France have very close relations with their former colonies in Africa; the Dutch have headed the Consultative Group for Indonesia; and the British Commonwealth has expanded to include most of the former British colonies. The experience of Mali is rather unusual by contrast, in that it withdrew from the Franc Zone in 1960 and rejected French military assistance and advisers, as well as various cooperation agreements, in order to pursue an independent course.

At any rate, the "age of development" did open up the borders, bringing numerous advisers from the United Nations and its specialized agencies, who did not always agree as to a scale of priorities. Private entrepreneurs appeared with a wide variety of suggestions and offers. And official representatives of the various developed countries, including the European Communist nations and Mainland China, were eager to promote their own political and economic prescriptions. Nor were decisions easy to make on solely technical grounds, since the advice was often coupled with competing promises of assistance in one form or another. As always, the new governments were tempted to use the "bread and circuses" technique, emphasizing conspicuous construction for short-run prestige effect. In addition, it seemed easy to win support by new programs of income distribution which, when added to investment programs, inevitably led to inflation. Not surprisingly, the new governments have not always seemed to make decisions based on some long-term, objective, rational system of priorities.

Perhaps most difficult of all the obstacles faced by the governments of the less-developed countries are the magnitude and basic nature of the changes necessary, and the scarcity of trained personnel and material resources to bring them about. In the poorer countries, the experience of government personnel has been limited to carrying out the operations necessary to maintain the government and provide a modicum of economic and social services, while often the key posts were held by foreigners. Consequently, the native members of the civil service had little experience in handling complex policy problems, whereas the problems of development require long-range policies and programs of quite a different sort. The wonder is that these governments have managed to do as well as they have, considering that they must contend with the tremendous assistance of old social and economic habits and institutions created centuries ago in a quite different context.

* * *

All these difficulties create a basic political problem for the poorer nations which might be summarized in an Index of Discontent:

$$\text{Discontent} = \frac{\text{Expectations}}{\text{Realization}}$$

The problem of any government is to find some middle course which will break through quiescence, inertia, and elite protectionism but still keep the index below a boiling point at which there will be revolutionary action of some sort. Undoubtedly, the less-developed world expected that somehow it could rapidly bridge the gap to much higher levels of living. But economic growth is a slow process at best, and the expectations include not only such economic goods as food and shelter, but also education, better health, and social mobility. The numerator has a basic tendency to outpace the denominator and the index races upward.

It may be that so-called democratic government is not well suited for such a state of affairs with the added interplay of internal divisive forces, and that under such conditions order can only be maintained by force. Hence, it is not surprising that frequently one-party systems and so-called strong men have taken over or that those in power are forced to rely on control of the press and to declare states of emergency. Often, the threat or fact of disorder leads to a take-over by the military, whose profession gives them the means and the authority required for handling disturbances and providing some security of person and property.

It would be unrealistic to argue that all insurgency, violent rebellion, or threatened violence is wrong. There may be times when this is the only way to break out of confinement or even to settle an internal disagreement. Progress involves change, and stability may be nothing but stagnation in the face of rising discontent. However, there is a relationship between political stability and economic and social development, although the latter is so subject to other influences that one cannot generalize about it with any certainty. It was the survival problem of the political leaders in the poor countries which led Secretary Rusk to warn the House Foreign Affairs Committee on May 2, 1968, that deep cuts in the foreign aid request could result in violent revolutions in underdeveloped countries and the overthrow of moderate leaders. The alternative, as he saw it, is between moderate leaders who are committed to orderly economic and social progress and promoters of violent revolution.

> But leaders who believe in peaceful progress cannot be expected to endure unless they produce results—unless their peoples receive tangible economic and social benefits. . . . They can have no hope of success, no matter how great their efforts, without adequate assistance from the wealthy nations of the world.[3]

While his remarks may only slightly overstate the influence of economic stagnation on political survival, the opposite is certainly not true. Tangible economic and social benefits will not assure the continuance in power of moderate political leadership. Too

many factors enter into political stability for any one to be controlling.

*   *   *

It is doubtful that outside governments can do very much to influence directly the shape of the political scene in the developing
world. The central feature of the independence movement was
political. Independence meant quite simply the absence of control by an outside power. Such diverse problems as creating an
appropriate political structure, including ways and means for
coping with internal differences, selecting executives rather than
rebels as leaders, building efficient administrative cadres, and finding an acceptable balance in the perennial conflict between government and individual rights can only be accomplished from
within, and then only over a long period of trial and error in
building a national tradition. The record of political instability
will not soon improve. For many countries, it is not at all clear
yet which type of government structure can help them most
through the establishment and development periods.

This does not mean that the rich countries should pass by on
the other side, nor that they should enforce a political pattern
with tanks as the U.S.S.R. did in Czechoslovakia. It does mean
that there are raw nerves exposed—that those providing assistance
must recognize the many difficulties and hazards and must carry
out their various missions sympathetically and sensitively. Although the main thrust of foreign aid will necessarily be in support of social and economic progress, outside assistance can be of
some help in the political field, for example, in the improvement
of administrative processes such as collecting taxes, setting up
budgetary and statistical systems, and designing civil service structures. In this sort of endeavor, there has been notable progress—
not universal, but sufficiently widespread to be encouraging—
which stems largely from substantial improvements in the quality,
training, and experience of government officials. Economic planning is an established and sometimes effective government function. Government operation in the less-developed countries is
coming to be based more on considered policy choices than on
personal impulse. Greater emphasis is placed on long-range projects in education and agricultural production rather than on
those with short-run payoffs like stadiums and presidential
palaces. And some changes in political leadership (for example, in

Ghana and Indonesia), have resulted in more weight being given to the basic requirements for development. It may even be that somewhat more sober views are now held about the rate of progress which is attainable. Nevertheless, one must expect that political growing pains will be indicated in many different ways for a long time in the future.

The growing subsurface ferment in the less-developed countries is related to a greater awareness that the locus of final authority no longer is far away overseas, and that the redress of grievances lies closer at hand. Varying greatly from country to country, the forces of change are being strengthened by education, improved transportation and communication, growing trade unions and cooperatives, rising incomes, and the emergence of a middle class. With these, as well as in their absence, come inevitable strains and political uncertainties. While foreign economic aid may accelerate the process of change somewhat, the underlying conditions make certain there will be a long political record of trial and error and of shifting leadership. With the pursuit of political independence and the break-up of empires occurring so recently in the past, it seems clear that attempts from the outside to influence the political situation in a less-developed country are likely not only to fail but also to damage working relations aimed at social and economic development.

3· The Economic and Social Condition of the Poor Countries

Despite their many geographical, political, and cultural differences, what the less-developed countries have in common, whether recently independent or not, is that they are poor. There is no clear demarcation between the more developed and the less developed; but using the conventional classification (see Appendix), the contrast in their economic level for 1968 is shown in Table 4.

TABLE 4

PER CAPITA INCOME, DEVELOPED AND LESS-DEVELOPED COUNTRIES, 1968 [a]

	Population mid-1968 (Million)	GNP ($ Billion)	Per Capita GNP ($)
Developed countries	648	1,699	1,622
Less-developed countries [b]	1,695	342	202

[a] The Communist countries are omitted.
[b] Cuba and Yugoslavia are omitted.
Source: AID, *Reports Control No. 137.* Washington, March 27, 1970.

These general averages conceal even wider differences between the richest and the poorest. The unweighted average per capita income for the five countries with the highest per capita income (United States, Kuwait, Sweden, Canada, and Switzerland) was $3,543, while the poorest five (Rwanda, Malawi, Upper Volta, Burundi, and Mali) averaged $50. The estimates for 1968 in-

33

clude 22 countries with an average per capita income of less than $100 per year and 43 under $200. To be sure, there is some extreme poverty in every country, but the difference is that poverty is the rule rather than the exception in the less-developed countries.

Because of different living requirements and the fact that the exchange rates which must be used in reducing all figures to dollars do not accurately reflect price differences and relative purchasing power, numerical comparisons of this sort should never be regarded as in anyway exact. Averages give no indication as to the distribution of income. Furthermore, the average level is affected by the extent to which work is done in the home and group activities take nonmonetary forms.

For many countries, the necessary underlying statistical information is extremely deficient. The totals for national income are usually built from a number of separate estimates, each of which is unsatisfactory in its own way. The measurement of agricultural acreage and yield per acre are seldom made by a reliable method; manufacturing information is likely to come from a fixed sample and so would respond slowly to new industries; construction refers chiefly to public works; and the contribution from services is often an arm-chair guess.

While income estimates may be rather wide of the real level, their biases tend to persist so that they are more likely to be closer to the mark in recording growth, especially over a period of several years. The data are of less value for inter-country comparison. However, no matter how much one argues about the statistics and allows for the fact that tropical living reduces the expense of housing, clothing, and food, the contrast with the developed countries in level of living is perfectly clear.

The real meaning of these figures is not in the numbers themselves but that they represent the omnipresence of illiteracy and ignorance, the widespread incidence of disease, the lack of decent housing, and the barest minimum of consumer goods which will permit human survival. It is these basic conditions of life which make them the less-developed countries.

* * *

Coupled with poverty itself are a number of widespread conditions which greatly aggravate the situation. The most important is the world trend toward lower death rates as a result of gains in sanitation and preventive medicine, improved medical care, and the virtual elimination of major epidemics. At the same time, high birth rates are being maintained with a consequent rapid increase in population. This in turn adds to the national requirements for food, clothing, education, and housing, so that increased national output is only partially reflected in increased per capita income.

A second complicating factor in most of the less-developed countries is the rapid growth of cities. In the developed countries, the urban problem tends to be a compound of inner-city decay, transportation difficulties, pollution, insufficient taxes, etc. In the less-developed countries, the trouble is sheer inadequacy. A tidal wave of people has come from the rural areas to the cities in the hope that they will find a better life there. Thus, Cairo is larger than Chicago; São Paulo, Calcutta, and Jakarta have more inhabitants than Los Angeles, Leningrad, or Paris. City living requires many more special facilities than life in the country, and the decent absorption of 100,000 persons into a city is possible only at tremendous cost, effort, and organization. Furthermore, urban life requires more market-economy products and more cash income. Urban growth in the last two decades has far exceeded the possibilities for city employment and put an impossible burden on housing, water supply, gas and electricity, transportation, schools, hospitals, and so on. Economic planning has all too often concentrated on over-all production capacity, leaving urban policy to be handled by the cities themselves. This universal situation is a reflection of population increases plus the failure of the rural areas to provide an attractive existence for their young people.

The combination of population growth and the flow to the cities has created a tremendous unemployment problem, the result of what Secretary-General U Thant has referred to as "exploding cities in exploding economies." A recent OAS Secretariat study indicated that one-fourth of the total Latin-American work force was underemployed or unemployed in 1960, and that the situation had deteriorated further by 1969.[1] One can hazard a guess that the condition is even worse in the more crowded countries of Asia, and such levels of unemployment cannot help but produce major social and political problems. The situation is even more ominous when one realizes that half the population in the less-developed countries is under twenty years of age, and they are already demanding work or relief.

Another interacting difficulty is the dominance of agriculture in most of the poor countries. In fact, one significant feature of a developing country is a gradual shift in economic composition, with agriculture slowly declining in relative importance and industry, construction, and the services increasing. Because of their dependence on agriculture and hence on the availability of water, the economies of many of the less-developed countries are particularly susceptible to weather conditions. The importance of the monsoon to India has been fully publicized. Another illustration is the drought in Chile in 1967–68, officially classified as the "worst in two centuries," which created serious food shortages because of reduced herds and crop shortfalls. As a result, the rising import bill for food, already heavy, cut into the foreign exchange available for economic development. The water shortage paralyzed hydroelectric generating stations. Relief programs put heavier demands on government revenues, already reduced by decreased production.

Weather is not the only disruptive force. Since agricultural and mineral products are often sold on the world markets, fluctuations in world price have a direct effect on the import or export situation. A natural product can be displaced by new products such as synthetic rubber or textiles or new processes such as the production of nitrogen from the air rather than nitrate rock. Good fortune can also strike. The discovery of oil transformed Libya from an area of little promise into one with rapid growth prospects. Newly found Algerian natural gas is being sold not only to France, Spain, and Italy, but even to Canada, and shipments to the United States are scheduled to begin in 1973 after special tankers have been built. In the Sahara Desert, Mauritania has found copper and yttrium (a mineral used in color television tubes).

Another condition varying widely from country to country is the potential for economic production. This is in part a matter of a country's natural resources, but is also related to the size of the market in which it can sell. Many of the less-developed countries have small populations which, when combined with low per capita incomes, offer very limited opportunities for production on a scale necessary to achieve low unit costs. Estimates of population in mid-1967 for 95 less-developed countries which AID made indicate the restricted size of many national markets.

Population	Number of Countries
Under 1 million	14
1 to 2.5 million	16
2.5 to 5.0 million	25
5.0 to 10.0 million	13
Over 10.0 million	27
	95

Since these tend to be areas where families are relatively large, the use of the family as the consumption unit would reduce the national market to something like one-fifth the figures shown in the table.

Another indication of the limited nature of demand in these countries is shown by the fact that while six metropolitan areas within the United States had total incomes larger than either Boston or the State of Connecticut in 1967, only India, Brazil and Mexico of all the less-developed countries reached a similar level of income for the entire country.

Small markets mean that exports will be required to achieve the requisite scale of production and imports will be needed to satisfy demands which cannot be efficiently met locally. Obviously, then, economic growth in most areas is closely associated with expansion in foreign trade. In this connection, countries seeking new markets are fortunate in that the revolution in transportation, especially for those with access to the ocean, has greatly reduced distance as a barrier to trade. It is said that U.S. coal can be shipped from Norfolk, Virginia, to Japan at less cost than from Norfolk to Pittsburgh. However, breaking into export markets meets other obstacles which are extremely difficult to overcome.

In addition to these limiting economic factors, note must be taken of the endlessly varied traditions and customs which, however suitable for the status quo, are obstacles to change or the efficient use of resources. Systems of land tenure may have kept land idle in large estates or led to its fragmentation into absurdly small plots. The "sacred cow" is no mere literary invention, but a costly luxury for India. The personification of natural objects may prevent their use for production; frequent holidays and prolonged social celebrations interfere with productivity; a fatalistic belief in predestination can weaken present ambition and concern about the future. And the whole group of habits necessary to group employment, such as being on time, obeying instructions, and keeping the machine oiled, may never have been developed.

TABLE 5

YEAR-TO-YEAR CHANGE IN GROSS NATIONAL PRODUCT
(CONSTANT DOLLARS), 1964–68

Country	Per Cent Change from Preceding Year				
	1964	1965	1966	1967	1968
Cyprus	−7.4	19.9	8.7	12.4	4.9
Israel	10.2	8.2	0.8	2.8	14.0
India [a]	7.1	−3.8	1.5	10.5	4.2
Morocco	1.0	1.7	−1.8	8.4	12.0

[a] Fiscal year beginning April 1.

Source: Statistics and Reports Division, AID, *Gross National Product.* RC-W-138. Washington, April 25, 1969.

For those whose lives are on a precarious subsistence level, the resistance to change may sometimes be not so much a rigidity based on tradition as an unwillingness to take any added risks. Complications such as these are better described by a broader more accurate phrase: *social and* economic development.

Some of these factors show directly in the statistics of growth while others are persisting difficulties. Short-run changes up or down may reflect the fortunes of a single export industry or non-economic factors such as the weather, military activity, or political disturbance: The point is illustrated more specifically in Table 5 by four examples where one can see how wide these annual changes can be as a result of internal unrest (Cyprus), war (Israel), weather (India), or new discoveries (Morocco). Nor can stability of growth rates over longer periods be counted on. Half of the twenty-five less-developed countries whose 1955–60 annual growth rate for gross national product was above 5 per cent averaged below 5 per cent in the succeeding five years. Occasionally, growth actually stops. Between 1961 and 1969, a negative growth rate has appeared only 23 times for non-Communist less-developed countries. Among the developed countries during the same period, only Luxembourg and Iceland reported any year-to-year declines.

It is important to note that development activities can proceed even during times of special trouble and falling GNP. Construction of new industries in India continued in spite of the failure of the monsoon. The IBRD announced a loan on November 13, 1968, to the Federal Republic of Nigeria to finance the completion of the Kainji multipurpose project for electric power, river transportation, and irrigation. Despite war and civil disturbances, the project, whose first IBRD loan was made in July 1964, is on schedule. The operations in Latin America of American *servicios* (joint projects usually in health, education, or agriculture) were never interrupted by the frequent political coups and counter-coups during the 1930s and 1940s.

* * *

One cannot avoid being puzzled about the persisting poverty in the less-developed world in view of the fact that the last three hundred years have seen an extraordinary extension of man's capacities—to make his voice heard even from the moon, to move earth by the ton rather than the shovelful, to travel faster than the speed of sound, to see microscopic bits of matter, to control indoor temperature, and to carry out the most complicated calculations. The technological revolution has provided goods and services of which man hardly even dreamed in the past.

Obviously, the benefits of this changed world have not been shared equally. Historians, and anthropologists, and biologists have put forward many explanations for the tremendous differences in development between Northern Europe and North America, and almost all of the rest of the world. Why should some countries have been geared to change and others to immobility?

Some have blamed the difference on climate, arguing that the weather changes in the temperate zone stimulate energy and vitality. Others suggest that the Protestant religion encouraged the "capitalistic" virtues of independence and thrift. Recent studies have elevated the extent and character of Western education to an important position among the explanations. Still others cite the importance of export trade, not only because of the contacts which it creates but also because it provides a flow of cash income.

Why the West developed as it did is not as important as the fact that so-called modernization was so little contagious. However, one merely needs to recall how comparatively recent has been the development of modern communication and transportation to realize that whole masses of people were isolated even in descriptive knowledge from anything other than their own immediate world. In the last analysis, the breakdown of this isolation was a prerequisite for a high index of discontent.

So far as the developed countries are concerned, their history has made it clear that economic growth is self-perpetuating. John Maynard Keynes once said that the economic problem (man satisfying his wants) would solve itself in one hundred years through the beneficent operation of scientific research with the resulting new technologies, plus the compound rate of interest, by which he meant the increase in the supply of capital at a geometric rate. [2] To these built-in forces, one might add the gains from improved management, the development of skilled manpower, various aspects of fiscal and monetary policy, and the pressure of competition.

So far as the poor countries are concerned, their poverty is the core in a number of overlapping vicious circles. Such income as there is must go for subsistence so there can be little saving, little education, little improvement in productivity, and as a result of each, continued poverty. Governments cannot place much of a tax burden upon persons at the subsistence level and thus cannot gather domestic resources on any considerable scale for the purposes of economic development. Even where there would seem to be the opportunity to collect revenue, the tax apparatus is not likely to be very efficient, with smuggling of imports and concealed capital exports frequent methods of escape. A poor country cannot afford education or health facilities, and ignorance and ill-health maintain the poverty levels. With such a low level of spending, markets are small and scattered and therefore the economies of large-scale production and distribution are unavailable. Basic facilities such as roads, electric power, and schools may be nonexistent. Industry may still be in the handicraft stage. Compounding the lack of skilled manpower, is a low rate of savings and investment and a scarcity of foreign earnings. As already pointed out, existing institutions tend to be adjusted to maintaining the status quo rather than to inviting the hazards of change.

The vicious circles that make it difficult to break out of the restraints of poverty are no mere theoretical constructs. They are clearly evident from a broad comparison of the growth rates of the poor countries themselves. While there are many exceptions to the rule, the tendency is for the poorest countries to have the worst current growth record. Increases of 5 per cent or more per year (1960–66) were shown by only one-third of the countries with per capita incomes below $300, by 6 out of 10 with incomes between $300 and $600, and by 6 out of 7 with per capita incomes over $600. To be sure, a handful of very poor but high aid-receiving countries—Taiwan, Jordan, Korea, and Thailand—have higher growth rates than most developed countries, but these are exceptional cases. Looking at the total record, one finds a widening gap among the less-developed countries, with the poorest making the least progress.

While poverty reflects shortages in the so-called economic factors of production or their ineffective use, there are important preconditions for achieving a satisfactory rate of economic progress which lie outside the field of economics and which are matters of quality rather than quantity. These include such necessities as a government willing and determined to overcome customs and traditions which limit growth; an effective public administration; a dynamic managerial and administrating class with scope in which to operate; an accepted judicial system; a strong drive for increasing agricultural productivity; a banking system capable of channeling internal savings into productive investment; and a desire for learning and a competent educational system able to provide trained manpower. In short, the creation of the necessary institutions is an integral part of the process of development. Likewise, the over-all result of progress should be more than a higher economic level of living. It should bring about a stronger and more stable nation and widespread improvement in the quality of life, measured in such intangibles as health, education, and individual opportunity.

* * *

One measure of progress, unfortunately often suggested, is the "closing of the gap" between per capita income in the richer and the poorer countries. The gap is usually measured in dollar terms, and because of the different levels already existing, this particular gap will inevitably grow wider for many years to come. Thus, using the 1968 figures given above ($2,622 average annual income per capita in the richer countries and 202 in the less-developed), a per capita rate of growth by the developed countries of 5 per cent (the average for the preceding five years) would mean about $131 per capita per year for the rich countries. To keep the so-called gap from widening would then require the per capita income in poor countries to grow by 65 per cent per year. And one can be very skeptical of the possibility of finding in the entire world sufficient raw materials, including substitutes, to supply everyone with the quantity and variety of goods now consumed in the richer countries.

While the concept of the gap may be useful as a reminder of the great distance between poverty and affluence, its reduction should be neither the test of success nor its widening an augury of failure. It measures the evidence of progress in the poor countries against the growth in the rich countries. Despite the obstacles to development they face, many of the less-developed countries are making valiant efforts to move ahead, and it is much more meaningful to measure their progress against their own situation.

The United Nations suggested possible development targets for the United Nations Development Decade of the 1960s. It set as its "main economic objective . . . to create conditions in which the national incomes of the developing countries not only will be increasing by 5 per cent yearly by 1970, but will also continue to expand at this annual rate thereafter." (The Alliance for Progress set as its goal a growth of 2.5 per cent per capita per year.) In addition, there were many more specialized targets for the Decade, ranging from the percentages of children to be in primary schools by 1970 (70 per cent in Africa, 50 per cent in Asia, and 100 per cent in Latin America) to a minimum of one physician per 10,000 population, an annual rate of 5 million new dwellings each in both urban areas and rural areas, and at least ten copies of a daily newspaper, five radio sets and two cinema seats for every 100 inhabitants in each country. If the purpose of the targets is to stimulate action by providing operational objectives, these specific objectives are probably much more effective than any abstraction such as the gross national product.

However useful such quantitative goals may be, one needs to consider also what the quality of the education may be, the medical facilities available to the physician, the utilities in the communities where the new houses are built, and the uses to which the expanded means of communication are put. In terms of people, the distribution of additional income may be as important as its rate of growth. Nor are social conditions separate from economic. Community development, training, and health all contribute to economic productivity. Finally, there is the basic attitude towards change. In view of the existence of religious, cultural, and political institutions which strongly maintain and defend tradition and established practice, one measure of development is how receptive a society is to the introduction of new ways of doing things.

Another frequently discussed goal, not directly related to general growth, is that the poorer countries should become self-sufficient, a phrase which does not imply autarchy but rather the ability to finance foreign requirements either through foreign-exchange earnings, nonconcessionary borrowings, or private foreign investment. According to this measure, the United States regards Mexico, Taiwan, and Iran as having moved recently to self-support and no longer needing concessionary aid. The Australian government, in announcing a five-year program based on a World Bank survey to develop Papua-New Guinea, stated that the basic aim was to double the export earnings of the Territory by 1972–73 and make the economy self-sufficient by 1980. The planners in India and Pakistan are already talking about when they can end the flow of aid, though their requirements for assistance are expected to be substantial in the interim period. However, this test of the ending of aid carries with it no standard of the level or quality of living and thus can hardly be taken as a measure of economic and social development.

* * *

The published news from the less-developed world gives the impression of wide areas of unrest and instability. One hears of the diversion of much-needed resources to the competitive building of military strength or to foolish investment in status symbols like airlines or elaborate government buildings. But these reports are unrepresentative, for many countries are in fact making quiet progress in building and strengthening their national life.

Using figures of gross national product at constant prices as estimated by AID, the less-developed countries advanced during the five-year period 1963–68 at an average rate of 5.3 per cent annually, and for 1968 and 1969 reached 6.1 and 6.7 per cent, respectively. Over the five-year period, 26 of the 43 countries for which data are available met the United Nations target of a 5 per cent growth rate. Ten countries exceeded 7 per cent for the five years, led by Libya, Taiwan, Korea, Iran, and Thailand. Encouraging as this record is, one should bear in mind that the largest number of countries for which data are not available are in Africa, where the growth rates appear to be relatively low.

As already pointed out, numbers are inadequate to measure either how poor the less-developed countries are or how much progress is actually being made. However, there is considerable testimony from experts close to the situation in various countries. Mr. Morarji Desai, Indian Minister of Finance, in taking stock of past achievements at the end of 1968, suggested certain aspects of Indian development which justified the hope that the pace of development would accelerate. "The advent of the 'green revolution' with diverse agro-industries, a widening network of infrastructure, growth in small- and medium-scale industries backed by major industrial complexes have made it possible to hope that the extreme rigors of poverty and want need not prevail for many more decades." [3] Already, India is ranked as the ninth industrial nation in the world, shipping steel cables and agricultural implements to the United States, railroad equipment and electrical machinery to Latin America, and freight cars to the Soviet Union. Both its rate of saving and the level of taxation have increased in the last decade. However, the uncertainties of progress are evident in the same report which suggests that the momentum of growth at the end of 1968 contrasted sharply with the pessimistic outlook a mere 24 months earlier.

From the other side of the globe, Filipo Herrera, president of the Inter-American Development Bank, recently reported proudly that in less than 20 years the gross national product of Latin America had doubled, the output of steel and electric power had risen fourfold, industrial growth rate had been maintained at 6 per cent per year and agricultural output at 4 per cent, thus exceeding population growth. He noted that university and primary enrollment increased 80 per cent and secondary enrollment 140 per cent between 1960 and 1966. Water and sewage systems now serviced 110 million persons instead of 60 million. Central government tax collections had risen 40 per cent since 1960, and countries long afflicted by inflation, such as Brazil, Chile, and Colombia, had put stabilization programs into effect. Finally, he emphasized the marked strengthening of the institutional framework for development. [4]

Herrera's figures are very impressive, but any report of progress depends upon the starting point which is selected. That $1.3 billion has been invested in water supply and sewage disposal projects in Latin America since 1960 also requires the comment that this significant achievement is nevertheless running far behind the goal established in the Charter of the Alliance for Progress. Nor does the statement reflect the discouraging report by the U.N. Economic Commission for Latin America that the region has plunged deeply into foreign debt, that it has lost ground in world trade, and that 40 per cent of Latin America's economically available manpower is unemployed, underemployed, "or employed in what are to all intents and purposes unproductive services." Half of this "unemployment equivalent" is in agriculture.[5] The report declares that, in ECLA's judgment, the required changes in the institutions and in the basic structural conditions needed for stable economic and social progress are moving slowly.

From the masses of data and comment, the conclusion is clear that nearly all the poor countries are making progress, not only in the cold statistics of national income, but also in many other areas which are worthy ends in themselves and clearly bear on productivity, such as the elimination of malaria, the spread of family planning, greatly increased educational efforts, reforms in tax collection methods, better statistical records, the greater use of commercial fertilizer, improved capacity to handle tourist trade, and increased exports of manufactured goods with better export standards. The planning process has left the area of complete fantasy and is beginning to have some influence in establishing priorities. Nevertheless, progress is slow: a great deal remains to be done, the index of popular discontent is high, and the level of living is still distressingly low for hundreds of millions of people.

In viewing the conditions of urban poverty, rural unemployment and subsistence farming, continued rapid population increases, little industrial modernization, drastic inequalities in income, lack of skills and middle-class services, and the poverty of life itself, one can easily be discouraged about the possibility of real economic and social betterment. But if one looks at change rather than at the present level, there can be little doubt that progress is being made in many fields and that the changes taking place will have a cumulative effect on the whole economic and social structure.

4 · The Growth of Foreign Aid

During the nineteenth and early twentieth centuries, the flow of goods and services between the rich and the poor countries was substantial. Nearly all of the flow was in trade and private investment, with the emphasis being placed on transactions which provided their own profitability. In the empires, various services were provided by the metropolitan powers, ranging from troops acting as constabulary to agricultural research stations. The British government tried to make each colony balance its current budget with current tax revenues (as distinct from its capital budget), while the French government seems to have been more willing to grant subsidies for the current budget. There was a considerable outflow of private capital from the rich countries, which, however, was more likely to be related to some mining or agricultural venture than to infrastructure requirements. The flows to the independent countries of Latin America were entirely in the form of private capital.

During the 1920s, there was a boom in private investment abroad through the sale of foreign securities in the richer countries. However, the depression in the 1930s ended the flow, and many of the securities went into default.

The situation began to change in the 1940s. Recognizing the virtual disappearance of private foreign investment and the urgent need for capital transfers, the Bretton Woods Conference in 1944 set up the International Bank for Reconstruction and Development (IBRD or World Bank), using the backing provided by its members to obtain private capital for relending to governments. The United States, which had been providing military and civilian assistance to its allies under lend-lease, extended relief and rehabilitation assistance after the war under various appropriations which finally culminated in the Marshall Plan. During the war, the colonial powers had not fully paid for assistance from outlying territories, and an appreciable part of American postwar aid flowed through the immediate European recipient to less-developed areas.

The growing interest in economic development as a goal in itself was early evident in the United Nations. In the first General Assembly, members were urged to give aid to the war-devastated areas. However, within two years, the Assembly passed a parallel resolution urging that aid be given the less-developed countries. At the time, foreign assistance seemed to be a relatively simple matter. The less-developed countries needed to be provided with technical assistance and foreign capital to help them build their own capacity to produce.

The rich countries have become involved in giving assistance to less-developed countries at different times and by different routes. In the breakup of empires the initial capital and personnel requirements were met to a large extent by the former metropolitan powers. While the idea of separation frequently was associated with a throw-the-foreigners-out policy, independence was often negotiated rather than seized, and the metropolitan powers usually committed themselves to providing substantial amounts of assistance in the short-run future. Perhaps the most interesting arrangement is that whereby the European Economic Community established the former colonies of its six members as associate members, granting them not only trade preferences but a substantial amount of economic assistance through the specially created European Development Fund.

* * *

Because of the size and leadership position of the United States, its record in providing aid is of special importance. Until 1940, American assistance to less-developed countries was almost entirely a private matter. Many nonprofit organizations contributed to activities such as schools and universities, hospitals, and agricultural experiment stations and demonstration farms; industrial enterprises to the application of their special knowledge; and private experts and firms to a wide variety of specific projects. There was little nonprivate aid to foreign students coming to the developing countries.

Before 1940, the U.S. government was a party to this process only on a restricted scale. Various departments of the government had carried out some programs in less-developed countries in a quiet way. The Department of Agriculture operated research and experiment stations in several Latin American countries. Other government agencies lent employees for brief periods. For example, the Library of Congress helped several countries set up proper cataloguing systems. U.S. responsibility for Puerto Rico, the Virgin Islands, and the Philippines provided some limited experience with development problems, especially in public administration, education, and road-building.

To give added substance to the "good neighbor policy," which President Roosevelt had announced in general terms in 1933, the flow of technical assistance of all kinds through government agencies was regularized. In 1939 it was put under the Interdepartmental Committee on Scientific and Cultural Cooperation. In addition to the provision of experts, a number of cultural centers and schools were supported and the exchange of students and teachers was encouraged. Thus, before the war there were various small technical assistance projects involving little expenditure and not set in any general framework related to the broader problems of economic and social development planning.

In 1942, the Institute of Inter-American Affairs was established, bringing the United States more into an operational than an advisory capacity. Under executive agreements, joint operations, called *servicios*, were organized in many Latin American countries in agriculture, health, and education. In nearly all cases, the director and chief technicians were American, and the United States contributed largely to the operating budgets. Again, there was no effort to review a country's total requirements; work in the three fields stood on its own feet as worthy of U.S. support.

By stretching a point, one can find further scattered evidence of official American economic assistance to foreign countries even before World War II. The Export-Import Bank, established in 1934 to finance trade with Russia, soon made loans of $60 million to the Argentine government for industrial and agricultural development, $20 million to Brazil for a steel mill, and $25 million to China in 1938 largely for the "Burma Road." Assistant Secretary of State Sumner Welles justified them, in terms which sound familiar today, as leading to social progress and political stability, contributing to the growth of true democracy, increasing the probability of political and military security, and providing a greater demand and increased purchasing power for United States exports.

World War II shifted attention away from the less-developed countries to the allies, with the lend-lease programs supplying them with civilian goods as well as military supplies. These were gifts to the extent that they were used up during the war, while shipments made after the armistice were put on a very soft-loan basis. However, assistance did not end with the war. The initial United Nations Relief and Rehabilitation Administration (UNRRA) program for postwar relief and reconstruction, based on contributions of 1 per cent per year of national income, lasted two years and was followed by a number of special annual appropriations involving such varied geographic areas as the Philippines, Greece and Turkey, Britain, and categories as post-UNRRA foreign relief, refugee aid, and funds for the various new United Nations agencies. At the same time, the Export-Import Bank made large loans, particularly to France, and the Army appropriation included funds for "government and relief in occupied areas" (GARIOA).

Each of these expenditures had its own imperative justification, and they varied widely in their terms and in the manner of their administration. Congress became increasingly restless with such fragmentation. The demand grew rapidly for a consolidated program rather than a continuing series of separate requests. At the same time, the unprecedented extent of war destruction in Europe was becoming clearer, with consequent economic stagnation within each country and foreign economic relations restricted by the loss of the means whereby it had earned foreign exchange in the past. Furthermore, the bilateral approach to postwar assistance ran into increasing difficulty because each European nation was unable to define its requirements without some estimate of the related progress to be expected of its trading partners. These circumstances led to the formulation of a multinational program, centering on European recovery. It constituted in 1948 the first generalized American foreign-aid authorization bill —which took form as the European Recovery Program.

In 1949, while the Marshall Plan (as it is more commonly known) was still in the beginning stages, President Truman announced another program, Point IV, in his inaugural address. It complemented the earlier emphasis on import requirements for Europe by enunciating a policy of assistance, particularly technical assistance, to the less-developed countries. A year later, Congress made this national policy in the Act for International Development of 1950: "It is declared to be the policy of the United States to aid the efforts of economically underdeveloped areas to develop their resources and improve their working and living conditions by encouraging the exchange of technical knowledge and skills and the flow of investment capital."

The creation of NATO and the outbreak of the Korean War led to a shift away from economic aid to a large increase in military assistance intended to build up international security arrangements. Foreign aid appropriations, mostly for military assistance, skyrocketed to more than $7.5 billion and $7.3 billion in 1950–51 and 1951–52, but was still regarded as a temporary program. And then the end of the reconstruction crisis in Europe, the Korean armistice, the completion of the initial NATO build-up, the death of Stalin, and reduced East-West tensions coincided with the victory of the Republican party on an economy platform. Consequently, when the Mutual Security Act was extended in 1953, Congress stipulated that economic aid was to end within 24 months and military aid within 36. In that same year, however, a new aid program was started based on the utilization of surplus agricultural products. The death notice for aid did not stick. With the help of the cautious recommendations of the Randall Committee, the 1954 Act, like that of 1950 which established the Point IV program, made clear that foreign aid was not just a temporary postwar phenomenon but should be regarded as a permanent feature of U.S. foreign policy.

During the Eisenhower period, efforts to economize and concern for collective security largely dominated aid activity. The program was given considerable assistance indirectly by various actions of the Communist countries, including the launching of their own aid programs. To be sure, renewal of the Act each year incurred congressional thunder and lightning, and the administration's proposals were cut in the complex process of authorization and appropriation by about one-fifth on the average, the largest cut being 28 per cent in 1958.

In the years of the lowest Mutual Security Act appropriations, 1954–55 and 1955–56, military assistance averaged $1,508 million, defense support $715 million, and economic assistance only $520 million. The military assistance went largely to Europe to build up NATO. Some of the defense support, however, could be classified as economic assistance since it went for road-building, airport construction, and other uses beneficial to the civilian economy, mostly in countries on the Communist perimeter.

After the low-point in appropriations for economic assistance in 1954–55, the amount set for this purpose began to rise while the amounts for military assistance and defense support declined. By 1960–61, the appropriation for economic assistance had grown to $1,310 million, and was nearly equalled by the amount obligated under the Food for Freedom Act.

Upon taking office, President Kennedy enthusiastically endorsed foreign aid, asking for "a major economic assistance effort by the free industrialized nations." He proposed that Congress replace the 10-year-old Mutual Security Act with new legislation separating military from nonmilitary aid programs and focussing on assistance to less-developed countries. The resulting Foreign Assistance Act of 1961 establishing the Agency for International Development (AID) is still the basic legislation, though considerably amended. The economic assistance appropriation increased by 50 per cent over the next two years. More funds were voted to transfer food under PL 480. The amounts for military assistance were sharply reduced. In addition, as part of the fresh approach, the Peace Corps was established. Outside as well as inside the United States, 1961 was an extraordinary year. The International Development Association (IDA) had just been established; the Alliance for Progress was formed; the first pre-investment survey by the United Nations Special Fund was completed; and OECD's Development Assistance Committee (DAC), described in Chapter 13, began to take shape.

President Kennedy's fresh initiative pushed the AID appropriation for economic and supporting assistance to $2,915 million for 1961–62, including a supplementary appropriation to launch the Alliance for Progress. Although this was the largest appropriation since the days of the Marshall Plan, it proved to be a peak rather than a new plateau. The record since then is shown in Table 6.

TABLE 6

U.S. APPROPRIATIONS FOR ECONOMIC AID AND SUPPORTING
ASSISTANCE, FISCAL YEARS 1961–62 TO 1969–70
($ *Million*)

	1961–62	1963–64	1965–66	1967–68	1968–69	1969–70
Bilateral loans [b]	1,688	1,197	1,053	824	555	638
Technical assistance	322	235	277	260	248	248
International organizations [c]	154	116	145	130	138	105
Administration	51	53	57	59	54	55
Contingency and other	276	64	246	23	20	23
Supporting assistance	425	333	684	600	365	395
Total	2,915 [a]	1,998	2,463	1,896	1,381	1,462

[a] Includes a supplementary appropriation to implement U.S. commitments
agreed to under the Act of Bogotá.
[b] Includes grants to Social Progress Trust Fund for relending.
[c] Does not include separate appropriations for international banks.
Source: AID *Reports.*

In 1963, a committee headed by General Lucius D. Clay unexpectedly suggested that the program should be tightened, a
euphemism for "reduced," and as a result, President Kennedy
lowered his request to Congress. Nevertheless, Congress made a
record cut, finally bringing the economic and supporting assistance appropriations for 1963–64 to slightly less than $2 billion.
Increases in supporting assistance advanced the totals to nearly
$2.5 billion for 1965–66, but then the downhill slide began.

The drastic cut in the appropriation for economic aid and supporting assistance for 1968–69 to $1,381 million and the slight in-
crease to $1,462 million for 1969–70 have been described in Chap-
ter 1. The decline was moderated somewhat by a sizable amount
($375 million) of reappropriated funds, de-obligations (the re-
lease for other use of funds previously appropriated and committed), and recoveries which were available for new commitment.

Other U.S. aid channels have not followed quite such a downhill course. The Food for Freedom program reached a peak in 1966 because of huge shipments to India but has since declined. New loans made by the Export-Import Bank increased sharply in 1967. On the other hand, the amount for military assistance which has been included under another title in the same Act since the beginning of NATO has been greatly reduced. While it was $1.6 billion in 1961–62, only $375 million was appropriated for this purpose in 1968–69 and $350 million in 1969–70, largely as the result of a redistribution of responsibility between the Defense Department and AID.

As already noted in Chapter 1, President Nixon, in his message to Congress on foreign aid, May 28, 1969, requested an appropriation of $2,210 million for economic assistance, $75 million to be added to the reserves backing guarantees related to private investment, and $375 million for military assistance. He also indicated his hope that $20 million would be appropriated for the ordinary capital of the Asian Development Bank, $25 million for its special fund, and $300 million for the fund for special operations of the Inter-American Development Bank. It was clearly an interim action, indicating that the Administration will not take a final position on foreign aid until a later date.

* * *

The prolonged annual public discussion of foreign aid usually centers about the appropriation under the Foreign Assistance Act, although in recent years it has been the source of only about one-half of official foreign aid. At present, economic foreign assistance is made up chiefly of appropriations to the Agency for International Development, Public Law 480 (Food for Freedom), the Peace Corps, and credits extended by the Export-Import Bank. Special appropriations are made from time to time for international agencies, such as IDA, IDB, and the Social Progress Trust Fund (for Latin America).

The flow of economic assistance can be monitored at several different points. First in the time sequence are the amounts set in the budget request by the President and in both the authorization and the appropriation by Congress. Next came the "commitment" figures, which represent funds obligated by the appropriate executive agency for specific purposes. Commitments go into the "pipeline" and may be spent almost immediately or, depending on the character of the project, remain unspent for several years. For one reason or another a commitment may never be carried out, in which case the funds become de-obligated and may be recommitted. Last in the process are the "disbursement" figures when payment is made. Since in a large project there may be progress payments, even the disbursement figure does not quite represent completed activity. However, disbursement figures are the most accurate as to the actual assistance provided and have a clear meaning for all programs. They are the most comparable record among the aid-supplying countries. Their weakness is that they reflect programs and intentions which were agreed upon at some previous time rather than indicate the current attitude toward assistance programs.

Both commitments and disbursement data are given in Table 7 for all U.S. assistance programs in 1967 and 1968. One problem in recording the various stages in the United States is that budget and appropriations data are on a fiscal-year basis, while commitments and disbursements data, as reported to DAC, are on a calendar-year basis.

The largest part of the sums appropriated under the Act for

TABLE 7

U.S. ECONOMIC ASSISTANCE TO LESS-DEVELOPED COUNTRIES:
OFFICIAL COMMITMENTS AND DISBURSEMENTS, 1967 AND 1968
($ *Million*)

	Commitments		Disbursements	
	1967	1968	1967	1968
Foreign Assistance Act (AID)[a]	2,259	2,324	2,177	1,948
P.L. 480	1,498	1,038	1,093	1,061
Export-Import Bank	914	741	481	635
Peace Corps	104	110	108	110
Multilateral Contributions [b]	694	444	310	252
Other	52	113	51	92
Total, gross	5,520	4,770	4,221	4,098
Amortization [c]	—	—	498	493
Total, net	5,520	4,770	3,723	3,605

[a] Including assistance through the Social Progress Trust Fund.

[b] Of which AID contributed $111 million in 1967 and $110 million in 1968 as commitments, and $103 million in 1967 and $112 million in 1968 as disbursements. Nearly all the balance represents special appropriations.

[c] Including recoveries on local-currency assistance.

Source: AID.

International Development is devoted to the establishment and execution of bilateral economic programs, although AID is also responsible for the U.S. contribution to a number of smaller multilateral agencies such as the United Nations Children Fund (UNICEF), the United Nations Refugee Works Agency (UNRWA), the United Nations Development Program (UNDP), and the Indus Basin Development Fund.

The statistics given in Table 7 do not include the amount for military assistance administered by the Defense Department ($375 million appropriated for 1968–69), most of which goes to Greece, Iran, Korea, Jordan, Laos, Taiwan, and Turkey. They do include, however, supporting assistance ($385 million) which is administered by AID and used either to finance projects for counterinsurgency, security, or related purposes, or to make funds available for defense budgets through providing commodities which can be sold for local currency. Of the balance, some small amounts were earmarked in 1968–69, such as $50 million for assistance to family-planning programs and $15 million for American schools and hospitals abroad, but the bulk of the funds is available as low-interest loans or as grants for technical assistance. AID also carries out a number of activities intended to encourage foreign private investment in the less-developed countries, such as making pre-investment surveys and providing guarantee programs against various kinds of risk.

The Agricultural Trade and Development Act of 1954 (PL 480) established a program to use American agricultural surpluses (the limitation to surpluses was dropped later) for assistance either on a grant basis or as a sale for local currency. In 1966, in view of the rapid disappearance of surpluses, Congress required a transition over five years from local currency to concessional dollar sales, except in cases of emergency relief. The authorizing act, now popularly known as the Food for Freedom Act, was extended in 1968 to December 1970, with authorizations for annual sales of $1.9 billion and donations of $600 million. The program is operated by the Department of Agriculture. While deliveries in 1968 were slightly less than in 1967, new commitments were considerably lower because of substantially improved crop conditions in many countries, particularly in South Asia. New sales agreements with India and Pakistan dropped from $682 million to $184 million, and the only country to show a marked increase was Indonesia.

Since an important objective of the Export-Import Bank is to promote American exports, it is actively involved in helping to finance American investment and trade with the less-developed countries. The bank has an independent board of directors and obtains new funds from the Treasury. In March 1968 its life was extended to June 30, 1973, and its lending authority was increased to $13.5 billion. In addition, the Export Expansion Facility was established, authorizing the Bank to support up to $500 million of export transactions which may not fully meet its usual test of reasonable assurance of repayment. In 1968, its disbursements to less-developed countries for economic purposes constituted 42 per cent of its total activity and more than half of that was to Latin America. The increase in disbursements in 1968 reflected the record level of new commitments made in 1967. Interest rates and maturities for Export-Import Bank credits are somewhat flexible. While interest generally was at 6 per cent in 1968, one loan was made to Indonesia at 3 per cent.

The Peace Corps, discussed in Chapter 5, is established under a separate authorization and has its own administration. Unlike AID, it is not limited as to the number of countries in which it can operate (see Chapter 8) and has volunteers in about 60 nations.

Assistance almost never has taken the form of payments of cash except for various appropriations to international agencies, and even there the dollar commitment is often tied to the purchase of American goods and services. (The outstanding exception to giving aid in legal tender was a Congress-initiated appropriation intended to provide military aid to China in 1948.) The aid flow to the recipient consists of services and goods with the U.S. government paying the supplier, usually an American enterprise or individual. Technical assistance is the lesser part of the total; it pays for sending persons abroad to teach and train, act as advisors, or perform needed services or for bringing students or trainees to the United States (see Chapter 5). The greater part of aid takes the form of actual goods—a cement plant or a shipload of wheat, a fleet of trucks or road-building equipment. Sometimes the aid functions in two steps—for example, wheat shipped under PL 480 may be sold by the local government to its people and the proceeds then used to pay workers on a new irrigation project.

The American aid program has been subject not only to change in structure but also to shifting emphasis within the organizational framework. Thus, in an appearance before the Senate Committee on Foreign Relations on July 14, 1969, Secretary Rogers said that, pending a full-scale review, greater stress would be placed on four aspects of the foreign aid programs:

1. We will increase the opportunities for private enterprise and private initiative to apply those vast resources and energies to the work of development.
2. We will emphasize the transfer of American knowledge and skills through technical assistance.
3. We will increase our support for multilateral aid programs and our efforts to coordinate our aid with other donors.
4. We will continue to place the highest priority on food production and reduction of population growth.[1]

Although merely an interim statement, it indicates that emphasis can and does change from time to time.

* * *

The assistance of other countries to the less-developed world has not had quite the checkered career described above for the United States. For the former colonial powers, there already were civil servants familiar with overseas problems as well as budgetary items allocated for aid. On the other hand, Canada, Austria, Norway, and Sweden, never having possessed colonies, had to start at the beginning, as did postwar Germany and Japan. The limited connections of the United States with less-developed countries had not created an experienced bureaucracy.

Each supplier had its own management problems—the former metropolitan powers had to adjust to the fact that their erstwhile colonies were now foreign countries, while others had to devise new policy and operating machinery. New ministries were created, such as the British Ministry of Overseas Development, the German Ministry for Economic Cooperation, and the Dutch Minister Without Portfolio, and new agencies have been established, such as the Swedish International Development Authority or the Japanese Overseas Economic Cooperation Fund.

The annual totals for net official disbursements for economic assistance which the sixteen members of the Development Assistance Committee (DAC) have made from 1956 to date are given in Table 8.

TABLE 8

NET OFFICIAL DISBURSEMENTS TO LESS-DEVELOPED COUNTRIES
AND MULTILATERAL AGENCIES, DAC MEMBERS, 1956–68
($ *Million*)

1956	3,263
1957	3,858
1958	4,389
1959	4,328
1960 [a]	4,965
1961	6,143
1962	6,035
1963	6,076
1964	5,942
1965	6,314
1966	6,669
1967	7,106
1968	7,095

[a] Revised figures for Japan included, beginning 1960, but not before.
Source: Development Assistance Committee, OECD.

These figures show annual disbursements to carry out projects
and programs which may have been funded and started months
or even years before, minus amortization received during the year
on past loans. Changes in appropriations policy, either up or
down, will have a delayed impact on the record of disbursements.
No great weight should be put on year-to-year differences since
these can be caused by chance variations in the flows around the
year-end. Nevertheless, the trend is clear: a rapid rise to 1961, a
plateau and even a slight decline to 1964, and a further rise since
then. However, one should keep in mind that this was a period of
rising prices so that figures in current dollars, as these are, overstate the flow of real goods and services.

The record for individual countries has varied widely since
1956. At that time such countries as Austria and the Scandinavian nations provided little assistance other than relatively generous support to the multilateral agencies. In a comparison of the
net official disbursements in 1956 with those in 1968, the programs of the United States and France are much less dominant
(see Table 9).

When the records of individual countries are compared, the actual size does not represent the relative effort put forward because

TABLE 9

RELATIVE SHARES OF NET OFFICIAL ASSISTANCE, LEADING DAC
MEMBERS, 1956 AND 1968
(*Per Cent*)

Country	1956	1968
United States	61.5	50.8
France	19.8	12.0
United Kingdom	6.3	6.0
Germany	4.3	8.4
Japan	2.2	9.3
Other DAC members	5.9 [a]	13.5 [b]
Total	100.0	100.0

[a] Countries exceeding 1 per cent were Australia, Italy, and Netherlands.
[b] Countries exceeding 1 per cent were Australia, Belgium, Canada, Italy, Netherlands and Sweden.
Source: Development Assistance Committee, OECD.

the countries vary greatly in size. Furthermore, percentages of increase depend upon the level at which the calculation started.
Thus the fact that the official Austrian program was 18 times
larger in 1968 than in 1956 is merely a reflection that it was almost nonexistent in the earlier period. Therefore, in order to provide more meaningful comparisons, Table 10 presents the percentage of its gross national product that each country's official
economic assistance constitutes. Even so, the figures are open to
important qualification since they fail to allow for differences in
the quality of aid, particularly whether it is in the form of grants
or loans, whether it is tied or not, how much is multilateral, how
much technical assistance, and how much would be added if
private flows were included. Two-year averages are used to avoid
single-year fluctuations.

From 1960–61 to 1967–68, eight countries increased their official aid more rapidly than the rise in their gross national product,
but not one of the "big four" is included although each of them
was near or above the general average. Total aid in the two years
1967–68 would have had to be 32 per cent, or $2,200 million
higher, merely to have kept pace with the growth in gross national
product since the beginning of the decade. An interesting tendency is clearly evident—that the countries' percentages scatter
much more widely in the earlier period; or, to put it another way,

the high percentages have fallen and the low have risen. This suggests some recognition of a common responsibility to give aid and a rough effort to share more equally the burden of economic assistance.

Another fact demonstrated in Table 10 is that, using gross national product as a measure of capacity to give assistance, the United States is not the leader: over the six years, it fell from fifth to ninth place. All the evidence points to its being even lower on the list when 1969 and 1970 data are available. By analogy with the progressive tax principle that the rich should contribute more than their proportionate share, the scale of the American aid program is even less impressive.

TABLE 10

Official Economic Assistance as Percentages of Gross National Product, DAC Members, Two-Year Averages, 1960–61 and 1967–68
(*Per Cent of GNP*)

Country	1960–61	1967–68
Australia	0.41	0.60
Austria	0.02	0.25
Belgium	0.82	0.48
Canada	0.19	0.36
Denmark	0.11	0.23
France	1.40	0.70
Germany	0.63	0.45
Italy	0.26	0.21
Japan	0.38	0.48
Netherlands	0.38	0.51
Norway	0.20	0.22
Portugal	1.55	0.85
Sweden	0.06	0.27
Switzerland	0.14	0.07
United Kingdom	0.58	0.44
United States	0.60	0.44
Total	0.59	0.44

Source: Development Assistance Committee, OECD.

* * *

In addition to official assistance by governments, there are substantial private flows, which are discussed in some detail in Chapter 11. These activities contribute to the development of poor countries by providing capital, technical skill, and management for new economic activities, by adding to employment and providing manpower training, by increasing the government's tax base and revenues, and by demonstrating what is meant by "modernization." In resource terms, they take goods and services away from the supplying country just as does official assistance.

In addition to the activities of business enterprises, there are the private contributions of foundations, churches, and other voluntary agencies, which are probably the most eligible of all flows to be regarded as aid. However, no figures are available for this sort of assistance from most countries. Furthermore, they would probably not be comparable with the other data since such agencies often provide services at costs well below the going rates. For the United States alone, these contributions are roughly estimated by the government at about $750 million per year. To a large extent, these activities provide either technical assistance or relief goods for consumers.

Before World War II, foreign private investments and export credits were the main sources of foreign capital available to less-developed countries, and the flow has again become substantial. Figures for private capital exports are derived largely from balance-of-payments data, sometimes supplemented by questionnaires, and the statistics are subject to many uncertainties. Where recipient countries belong to the currency area of the capital-exporting country (for example, Belgium, France, and Portugal), such transactions are not recorded in the balance of payments. Similarly, the capital flows of multinational corporations, most important of which are the international oil companies, are often difficult to determine. The total private flow for all DAC members, distinguished by its wide year-by-year fluctuations, is shown in Table 11.

The figures for private capital flow include new direct investment and re-invested earnings (49 per cent in 1967–68), purchase of foreign securities (16 per cent) and of securities of multilateral agencies (9 per cent), and net increases in export credits for longer than one year (26 per cent). The three years, 1965–67, had seemed to establish a plateau higher than ever before, but 1968 showed a new peak substantially above any year for which the

TABLE 11

PRIVATE CAPITAL FLOWS (INCLUDING THE OIL INDUSTRY) FROM
DAC MEMBERS TO LESS-DEVELOPED COUNTRIES AND
MULTILATERAL AGENCIES, 1956–68

Year	Total	Oil Industry [a]
1956	2,998	820
1957	3,779	1,359
1958	2,917	685
1959	2,829	748
1960	3,150	564
1961	3,106	716
1962	2,453	323
1963	2,557	401
1964	3,200	532
1965	4,174	907
1966	3,841	604
1967	4,241	700
1968	5,867	[b]

[a] Net new direct investment plus re-invested earnings.
[b] Not available.
Source: Development Assistance Committee, OECD.

record is available. The figures for oil investment are given separately to show that this industry does not dominate the scene, although it did exceed one-third in 1957, reflecting the effect of the Suez crisis.

Recently, high interest rates in the industrialized countries, efforts to restrict credit expansion to reduce inflation, and balance-of-payment problems might have been expected to curtail the private flow. In fact, quite the opposite seems to have happened. Eleven of the sixteen DAC members reached new highs for private outflows to less-developed countries in 1968. Of the remaining five, Italy and Sweden had only exceeded their 1968 figure once before, while the United Kingdom made the poorest showing with a decline each year since 1965. The United States outflow, which had increased in 1967, reached a new peak in 1968, probably because the control program which was established to improve the balance of payments was less stringent on flows to the developing countries, and because many enterprises financed new foreign investment by selling American securities in the European dollar market. The German private outflow doubled in 1967 and almost doubled again in 1968.

As in the case of official outlays, the economic significance of the private outflow to the economies of the developed countries is best indicated by comparing it with the gross national product, as given in Table 12.

TABLE 12

PRIVATE CAPITAL FLOWS AS PERCENTAGES OF GROSS NATIONAL
PRODUCT OF DAC MEMBERS, TWO-YEAR AVERAGES,
1960–61 AND 1967–68
(*Per Cent of GNP*)

Country	1960–61	1967–68
Australia	a	0.11
Austria	0.18	0.30
Belgium	0.65	0.52
Canada	0.13	0.13
Denmark	0.46	0.17
France	0.74	0.47
Germany	0.34	0.65
Italy	0.52	0.36
Japan	0.27	0.23
Netherlands	1.48	0.53
Norway	0.18	0.28
Portugal	a	0.48
Sweden	0.31	0.24
Switzerland	1.87	1.06
United Kingdom	0.61	0.32
United States	0.21	0.25
Total	0.34	0.32

a Not available.
Source: Development Assistance Committee, OECD.

The private capital flows of the supplier countries vary much more than their official assistance. The outflows from Australia, Canada, Japan, and the Scandinavian countries are very small fractions of their gross national products. The highest rank goes to Switzerland, which probably reflects its role as a financial center rather than as an original source of savings. Germany's rapid rise to second place probably resulted from its balance-of-payments position. The United States, on the other hand, ranks eleventh on the basis of the 1967–68 record. While its share of the total official flow for 1968 was 50.8 per cent, it provided only 35.3 per cent of the private flow. As in the case of official aid, the extent of the scatter among the percentages was appreciably less in 1967–68 than in the earlier period.

Compared with official assistance, which reflects a deliberate national policy choice, the private flow is the result of separate decisions by thousands of individuals. Although governments have the power to stop the private flow, there is little they can do to bring it about. In general, the governments in the rich countries either take a neutral position or encourage the expansion of private foreign investment by tax measures, guarantee schemes, bilateral treaties, and various indirect forms of assistance to the potential investor. The poor countries have feared private foreign investment for various reasons, epitomized in the term "neocolonialism." Despite their political anti-foreign protests about neocolonialism, most of the poor countries have tried to attract private foreign capital, although many of them do worry about it as threatening their independence. Their growing groups of businessmen naturally fear more expert competition inside the wall of tariff protection. Nevertheless, the higher figures of the last several years would seem to reflect more recognition on both sides of the mutual advantages in a greater flow of private capital.

*   *   *

Another major source of economic assistance not included in the standard statistics presented up to this point is the Communist "bloc" of countries. Soon after the importance of United States economic aid to the less-developed countries became apparent, the Soviet Union followed suit. The Marxist theory that revolution would only come after a considerable period of industrialization and class struggle provided no guidance to policy in a country's earlier stages. Even so, the Soviet Union had already found it necessary to give aid to the "bloc" countries, but had kept economic relations with other countries, developed or less developed, to a minimum.

It was not until two years after Stalin's death that credit agreemeets with less-developed countries were signed in any considerable volume. Whether the objective was political or economic or even personal one cannot say, but it began in 1955 when Khrushchev and Bulganin visited India and Burma. The Soviet bloc then moved to work more closely with a selected group of countries, giving aid on a large scale to India, the United Arab Republic, and Indonesia, and also with some other smaller countries. The stress was on basic industrial projects, government-owned and operated. There has been a bias in favor of the spectacular and visible, i.e. stadiums in Indonesia, Guinea, and Mali, the Aswan Dam in Egypt, the Bokaro steel plant in India, or, recently, the agreement to build a 335-mile broad-gauge railway to link Baghdad with the sea. In addition, there has been substantial military assistance, earlier to Indonesia, and later to the Arab countries.

Soviet economic aid almost always has taken the form of specific projects on a loan basis with low interest rates. The size of its combined economic and military credits make repayment uncertain in Egypt, Cuba, Guinea, and Indonesia. Seldom has there been any common effort with Western countries. The exception most often cited is Afghanistan, where the economic missions of the United States and the U.S.S.R. have offices in the same building and where American- and Russian-built roads form a single system. In Ghana, sugar production is being aided by both the United States and Poland.

Khrushchev's enthusiasm was not fully transferred along with his power to Brezhnev and Kosygin, partly because aid programs did not seem to captivate the recipients. The temporary Soviet competition with Chinese aid in Africa was no longer as vital. Nor did the anti-imperialism argument seem to bring the revolutionary new states into the socialist orbit. The annual level of offers by Communist countries, including mainland China, probably reached the high point between $1.2 billion and $1.5 billion in the years 1964–66; it fell to $400 million in 1967 and rose again to more than $700 million in 1968. The OECD Secretariat estimates the 1968 commitments to have been divided among $307 million by the U.S.S.R., $361 million by the Eastern European countries, and $56 million by China.

In the aid of Communist countries, the delay between commitments and disbursements has been unusually long, due in part to the dominance in its structure of projects of heavy industry and infrastructure. Actual disbursements have been well under one half billion dollars annually since 1960, and were probably at their highest during 1962–64. These figures do not include military assistance, which has been estimated at $5.5 billion since 1954. Aid to Cuba, which received $1.9 billion, is not included in these estimates since it is regarded as a member of the Communist bloc.[2]

Mainland China has also provided economic assistance though not as yet on a very large scale, total expenditures to 1968 being estimated at $175 million. Since 1964, when two-thirds of its aid commitments were with newly independent African countries, its actual performance has been severely cut back. Some of this may have reflected internal difficulties; but China's political activity in the less-developed countries was evidently a bit too heavy-handed, since five of them expelled Chinese diplomats or severed relations with Peking.

More recently, there is evidence of a new Chinese effort in Africa. In Tanzania in the summer of 1968, there were 1,000 mainland Chinese technicians preparing for the construction of the 1,100-mile railroad connecting Zambia's copper area with Dar es Salaam. Mainland China also has undertaken to construct a Mali-Guinea railroad. China has given Pakistan a long-term interest-free loan to be used in the construction of a giant engineering complex.

Aid has been caught up in the Soviet-China rivalry for leadership of the world Communist movement. Each has charged the other with attempting, through its aid programs, to control important sectors of the economy of various countries in order to exert influence in their domestic and foreign policies.

* * *

Some of the more advanced among the less-developed countries are extending assistance to other countries. Many of them, such as Israel with as many as 400–500 experts abroad at any one time, have provided technical assistance in fields in which they have special expertise. The countries in the Colombo Plan and in the Organization of American States are active in providing technical assistance to each other. In addition, there are growing amounts of bilatral lending and export credits. The largest tender in the group is undoubtedly Kuwait, whose Kuwait Development Fund is making commitments at a rate exceeding $200 million per year.

mostly for infrastructure projects. India and the United Arab Republic have both extended export credits to neighboring countries. Similarly, Argentina, Brazil, Mexico and Venezuela have increasingly extended export credits to other Latin American countries, assisted in some cases by the Inter-American Development Bank. All these countries contribute to the various international agencies. Kuwait and Saudi Arabia have purchased bonds of the World Bank group ($13.8 million and $15 million, respectively) while Israel recently bought $3 million of IDB bonds. The Vatican, among other forms of assistance, has also established an IDB trust fund.

While one cannot expect large sums to be provided by the less-developed countries, except in an exceptional case like Kuwait, the extent to which many of them can contribute technical assistance is very promising. Their knowledge and experience in certain fields may be more germane to the problems of lesser developed countries, and therefore more effective, than the technical assistance of an advanced industrial country. Although a country like Taiwan has made small capital grants in Chad and Sierra Leone, it has 600 experts, mostly agricultural, active in 19 African countries.

* * *

Little mention has been made of the multilateral agencies for the simple reason that they are channels rather than sources of assistance. They obtain their funds either from governments or from private sources. Nevertheless, they are clearly a part of the growing structure of economic assistance to poor countries, and their activities are discussed in detail in Chapter 9.

Discussions of the growth of aid are complicated by the fact that the financial contributions made available to multilateral aid agencies in any given year may be more or less than their disbursements of assistance to less-developed countries. The problem is made even more troublesome by the fact that the less-developed countries contribute to these agencies, some of which may also give loans or technical assistance to the developed countries (for example, IBRD loans to Australia or Norway). Thus there are different totals for economic assistance given and economic assistance received. What matters, however, is the flow that actually reaches the less-developed countries, which is estimated in Table 13.

TABLE 13

ESTIMATED RECEIPTS [a] OF NET FINANCING OF LESS-DEVELOPED COUNTRIES FROM ALL SOURCES, 1959–68
($ Million)

Source	1959 [b]	1960	1961	1962	1963	1964	1965	1966	1967	1968
DAC members, official bilateral [c]	3,978	4,364	5,392	5,509	5,711	5,562	5,866	6,139	6,370	6,436
Other industrial countries [d]	6	6	5	6	7	11	9	10	15	20
Centrally planned countries [e]	160	200	300	400	375	375	325	350	350	325
Multilateral agencies	261	284	252	410	653	790	892	895	1,041	814
Private bilateral [c]	2,615	2,945	3,016	2,214	2,590	3,059	3,926	3,826	3,935	5,262
Total	7,020	7,799	8,965	8,538	9,336	9,798	11,018	11,220	11,711	12,858

[a] On net disbursements basis. Does not include activities of voluntary agencies.
[b] Partly estimated.
[c] Bilateral only.
[d] Finland, New Zealand, South Africa.
[e] Very rough estimates, not including assistance to Cuba and Yugoslavia.
Source: Based on data from the Development Assistance Committee, OECD.

While this one table summarizes the growth of aid to a point sufficient to demonstrate that it is an important flow both in terms of out-payments by the rich countries and additions to the resources of the poor countries, it does not begin to suggest the wide variety of problems involved in carrying out such a complex process. The possible combinations of supplier and recipient, the uses to which the assistance should be put, the terms and conditions of each arrangement, the needs and possibilities of coordination, the place and form of the multilateral agencies—problems such as these are implicit in the process and provide the subjects for the following chapters.

5 · The Transmission of Knowledge

Perhaps the greatest contribution that the developed world can make to the less-developed countries is to pass along its knowledge and experience. Machinery can be replaced, but the knowledge of how to build it and when and how to use it is the product of centuries of accumulated trial and error. What is required is not only the skills of the trained engineer but also the common knowledge of the unskilled worker. Most African children do not play with nuts and bolts, wheels or mechanical toys; they do not grow up in homes where complicated products are commonplace. They are completely ignorant of the dangers of electricity or the operation of the gasoline engine. One of the first great problems of the early Soviet tractor stations was to convince the workers of the necessity of proper lubrication, something known to every youngster who lives in a mechanized part of the world.

The transmission of knowledge, usually called technical assistance, is not merely a matter of technology in the narrow sense, but includes managerial and administrative skills and arrangements. The technical knowledge required for operating a shoe factory is specific and exact, defined primarily by the product and the process. Related problems of manpower training, appropriate methods of compensation, and efficient marketing leave more room for judgment. The knowledge required for setting up a tax system involves a much wider basis. In any case, knowledge and experience often must be adapted to the particular culture in which they are to be used. Workers may prefer to sit cross-legged, or the water needed for a process may require special treatment. The most skilled census-taker in the West would need all his ingenuity to take a census in India or Chad.

In the broader questions of economic and social policy and the creation of new institutions, the basic preconditions underlying either the Western or the so-called centrally planned societies are almost never present in a less-developed country. New approaches must be fitted to differences in scales of values. The incentives which the adviser is accustomed to use may not be appealing, and there are likely to be unexpected taboos or traditional inhibitions which must somehow be avoided.

The recognized importance of technical assistance is indicated by the numbers involved. With considerable ingenuity and uncertainty, Angus Maddison produced an estimate in 1965 that the supply of foreign manpower engaged in providing technical assistance to less-developed countries totaled about 260,000 persons.[1] This includes 80,000 operational and advisory personnel in DAC-member technical assistance programs (the 1968 figure is 87,000), 8,000 in United Nations programs, 9,000 needed in connection with official assistance capital projects, and 10,000-12,000, from Communist countries. He subtotals these figures, a bit inexactly, to equal 105,000 persons with official bilateral or multilateral affiliation. To this he adds 155,000 persons in nonofficial categories. Maddison's figures do not include members of the various national peace corps and other volunteer groups.

This estimate relates to people active in the less-developed countries. The transmission of knowledge also takes place in the developed countries, where students and observers of all kinds are found in substantial numbers. Finally, one should add the movement of experts back and forth to and from the less-developed countries themselves.

It should not be assumed that knowledge and experience are transmitted only through people. Thus the absence of libraries and the scarcity of books and magazines represent another handicap. While some effort has been made to fill this gap, it still remains a serious deficiency in many countries, particularly when one is trying to find out a technical detail, or the experience of other countries with this or that policy problem.

The process of providing technical assistance to a less-developed country involves a number of steps—agreeing on the project, finding competent personnel to carry it out, and assuring through on-the-spot arrangements that an actual transfer takes place. Technical assistance may be an essential part of some larger project, as when a new agricultural experiment station is set up in a country having a shortage in agricultural research personnel. In the 1940s and 1950s, technical assistance was largely in the form of separate, limited, unrelated projects resulting from requests originating in some government department, frequently encouraged by an outside agency. Often it was of relatively short duration. More recently, there has been growing interest in substituting for such a collection of widely scattered short-run projects a large-scale and more continuous operation in the form of a regional program, combining capital and technical assistance. Often this starts with a pre-investment project. Thus instead of providing teachers here and there, though this may be necessary at the start, the emphasis is on building a whole school system—teacher training, school buildings and equipment, and administrative machinery. It might associate a public health center, a new road, and a shoe factory with the educational effort. Not only does consolidation reduce the complexity of administration and permit various economies of scale, but the cumulative process of several developmental activities in a community or region seems to be more effective in breaking through various resistances than the same amount of effort fragmented over a wider area.

The type of technical assistance needed is related to the stage of development of the recipient country. In general, the countries which are making the least progress in development are those which have very low incomes and high illiteracy rates. This condition often is associated with such factors as location, climate, lack of natural resources, character of social and political organization, and scattered population. Such subsistence conditions create a mutually re-enforcing resistance to change. Here the requirement is not so much for capital as for the application of knowledge to find how best to break the social and economic paralysis. The more primitive countries need technical assistance to begin to understand their possibilities, to formulate requests for assistance, and to start the long course of training their own manpower. Such basic needs are reflected in the fact that Africa, which receives about one-quarter of the total flow of bilateral economic assistance, absorbs more than one-half the volume of technical assistance.

It is difficult to make any over-all judgment as to the contribution made to development by many different people doing many different things in many different places. The large number in the private category are presumably regarded by their employers as worth at least their cost. Much of the official assistance ends in a specific product—a survey of mineral resources or a program to develop tourism. Like all advice, the measure should not be how much is given, but how much is taken and, in technical assistance, how much takes effect after the donor departs. Usually the adviser has an "opposite number" or one or more assistants who are expected to take over whatever continuing responsibility there may be. In any event, the indispensable nature of technical assistance would seem to be demonstrated by the fact that the requests by the less-developed countries for this kind of help have steadily expanded.

* * *

From the very beginning, the transmission of knowledge and skills was an important part of programs of development assistance. It was the key element in President Truman's Point IV proposal in 1949. The United Nations specialized agencies send out experts, hold seminars, and prepare many detailed reports. In 1949, parallel to the Point IV program in the United States, the U.N. Expanded Program was established whereby a central fund was contributed to on a voluntary basis by various governments and allocated among requests from less-developed countries, the project then being carried out by the appropriate U.N. agency. Later, this activity was supplemented by the U.N. Special Fund, which provided capital sums in large part for pre-investment projects such as research agencies, experiment stations, and the like. The two were merged into the United Nations Development Program (UNDP) on January 1, 1966, but are still dependent upon annual pledges. The sad story of the recent delay in U.S. pledging is given in Chapter 9.

A much larger program of technical assistance is carried out by various countries on a bilateral basis, as is shown in Table 14.
The bilateral programs of technical assistance have increased more rapidly than capital flows, disbursements have doubled since 1962 and comprised 20.0 per cent of all official net aid in 1968 as compared with 12.4 per cent in 1962. Since the number of students and trainees officially financed rose by about 60 per cent, and the number of experts and volunteers by 30 per cent, the much higher rate of growth in disbursements is obviously the result of general increases in salaries, wages, and travel costs, the upgrading of the positions held and the quality of personnel de-

TABLE 14

Technical Assistance Commitments and Disbursements,
DAC Members, 1962–68
($ Million)

Year	Commitments [a]	Disbursements
1962	858	748
1963	955	873
1964	1,098	951
1965	1,206	1,053
1966	1,422	1,235
1967	1,637	1,330
1968	1,673	1,492

[a] Disbursements where commitments were not available.
Source: Development Assistance Committee, OECD.

manded, and the increasing provision of necessary demonstration
supplies and equipment. The specialized agencies, often operating in behalf of the United Nations Development Fund, have
also expanded rapidly.

The technical assistance programs of donor countries differ
considerably. Belgium, Denmark, and France each provided more
than 50 per cent of its official net bilateral assistance in this
fashion in 1968, while Australia, Japan, and Italy had relatively
the smallest programs. The United States's disbursements, rising
substantially in 1968, were 19.6 per cent of its official bilateral
aid, compared with the average for all other DAC members of
26.2 per cent.

Some of the smaller donor countries offer specialized skills, as
reflected in the type of assistance requested from them—Austria
and Switzerland in high-altitude farming and hotel operation,
Norway in fishing, Japan in rice-growing, Israel in poultry-farm-
ing, and the like. In general, smaller donors prefer to channel a
substantial part of their technical assistance through multilateral
agencies, whereas large donors are more likely to build up their
own bilateral programs.

The bilateral disbursement of the United States for technical
cooperation, including the Peace Corps, in 1968 was $657 mil-
lion, about twice the level of 1962. Its contribution to the United
Nations Development Program had increased by 34 per cent.
The proposed AID technical assistance program for 1967–68 in-

cluded small increases, but the sweeping cuts by Congress in 1968 did not exempt technical assistance. The final AID appropriation for 1968–69 was $386 million, of which $138 million was for international agencies like the United Nations Development Program and the Children's Fund. The congressional debates included few criticisms of this part of the program and much favorable comment, and efforts on the floor of the House of Representatives to cut the figure even more were defeated.

In his message to Congress in May 1969, President Nixon proposed "a strong new emphasis on technical assistance" by means of a two-year funding authorization, a new Technical Assistance Bureau within AID, and a request for an appropriation of $463 million, the only item for which more was asked than President Johnson had requested in 1968–69. About one-fourth of the proposed total would go to multilateral organizations, another fourth to the Alliance for Progress for use in Latin America, and one-half for what is called "world-wide."

Congress did not spend much time debating this item in 1969. The amount fixed in the authorization in the Act for International Development to cover the two years 1969–70 and 1970–71 was $396.9 million. The final appropriation for 1969–70 was $353.25 million, of which $105 million was earmarked for the various U.N. agencies. This was an apparent reduction from the previous year, but in reality consists primarily of the shifting of the two items of U.N. aid to Arab refugees and support for the

TABLE 15

TECHNICAL ASSISTANCE COMMITMENTS AND DISBURSEMENTS,
UNITED STATES, 1962–68 [a]
(*$ Million*)

Year	Commitments	Disbursements
1962	413	331
1963	424	368
1964	433	377
1965	466	424
1966	634	535
1967	725	564
1968	709	657

[a] Including loans for technical assistance
Source: Development Assistance Committee, OECD.

U.N. force in Cyprus from economic aid to the support assistance title.

The AID appropriations record is quite incomplete in depicting the U.S. disbursements for technical assistance. The disbursements as reported to DAC in recent years, not including contributions to multilateral agencies, are given in Table 15. In short, technical assistance has grown substantially during the last decade.

*   *   *

There are two main channels for passing along skills and knowledge. One channel sends advisers, trainers, and demonstrators to the less-developed country; the other brings students and trainees from the less-developed country to some more advanced country. For the newly independent countries, there was no alternative to keeping some foreigners in the country to carry on the more complicated activities related to power systems, port equipment, banks, etc. In most African countries the number of foreigners is probably greater ten years after independence than before. It was impossible to realize the idea of complete independence. For example, the Cypriot constitution declares that all government posts be occupied 70 per cent by Greeks and 30 per cent by Turks. This left no spaces for any other nationalities so the government had to contract with rather than employ foreign experts to keep the power plants running.

As it became more and more apparent that outside experts were needed, the poor countries turned to the United Nations agencies and to individual governments with their requests for assistance. For statistical purposes, persons thus provided are classified as operational personnel, advisers, and volunteers. Operational personnel form a category of considerable importance in the French and British and to a lesser extent, in the Australian, Belgian, and German programs. They usually fill posts for which no citizen is as yet qualified, such as being in charge of a power plant, running a hospital, or taking a census. Often the arrangement stipulates that the supplying government supplement the local salary. As might be expected, the number of foreign operating personnel in government service in fields other than education who receive some support from developed governments, reported as 19,927 in 1968, is slowly declining as the training process provides replacements. Most developed governments restrict their civil service to citizens, and one can expect that the less-developed countries will eventually be able to operate on the same basis. Perhaps there will be an intermediate stage, in which such foreigners as are needed will be employed by and fully compensated for by the host government.

The 18,992 persons classified as advisers in fields other than education do not have direct operating responsibility, but are associated with some government activity in a planning or consulting capacity. In many cases, the line between the two categories is not very clear.

Individuals active in education are not included in either of the above categories, although 4,345 educational administrators and 2,470 educational advisers were reported, as well as 37,718 teachers, mostly from France in former French colonies. In total, therefore, over 40 per cent of all personnel engaged in technical assistance is in the field of education. The volunteer category includes activities like the Peace Corps, operated by a government, but with the individual usually paid little more than subsistence. Within this group of 25,555 persons, 45 per cent are teachers.

The United States technical assistance program does not explicitly provide for operational personnel, but includes about one-half of all non-educational advisers under DAC bilateral programs. Between 1965 and 1968, Americans so engaged increased from 6,726 to 9,896, a fourth of whom were in Vietnam. The leading areas of activity for advisers financed by DAC members are agriculture, public administration, public utilities, and industry. Recent years have seen a substantial increase of American advisers in the agricultural, public administration, and health fields, with reduced numbers in power, industry, and trade. In the volunteer category, about three-fourths of the persons involved are from the United States.

Worthy of more than a passing reference under the heading of advisers is the International Executive Service Corps. This is a private undertaking, though financed in part by AID, which arranges for experienced businessmen, often retired, to undertake short-term assignments to advise enterprises in the poorer countries which have requested assistance on management and technical problems. IESC has 3,800 volunteers on its roster. In 1967, 519 requests were received from businesses in 43 countries and 300 projects were completed. The local business pays a fee based on local practice.

There are a number of ways to improve the method by which experts are provided. The first is through a better coordination of the request process. Ideally, this should be done by the less-developed country itself, determining priorities and selecting the most likely suppliers. Because of the strategic position of advisers, however, competition among suppliers as well as the enthusiasm of specialists have prevented an orderly allocation of the scarce supply, nor has this been helped by the frequent lack of co-ordination among the various elements within the requesting government. Some progress has taken place in bringing more order into this field through the appointment by the UNDP of Resident Representatives to individual less-developed countries to represent the many agencies within the U.N. group, though this has neither entirely eliminated competition among the special-ized agencies nor covered the bilateral programs.

The DAC has strongly supported the development of local co-ordinating machinery. One major difficulty is that in many less-developed countries only the United States and the United Na-tions have full-time aid specialists, so that the representation of other donors in any effort at coordination may be very uneven. While much can be done on an informal basis, especially where the number of donors is few, there is machinery for more gen-eral consultation in about fifteen countries where the consortia and consultative groups exist. However, they are chiefly con-cerned with capital requirements, seldom meet in the recipient country, and usually do not concern themselves with individual projects. Nevertheless, they should at least make certain that there is an orderly procedure whereby the great number of small technical assistance projects are coordinated.

In the last analysis, the best agency to coordinate technical as-sistance proposals and projects is the government of the less-developed country itself. This depends on how sophisticated the government may be, and particularly on the ability, location, and prestige of its planning board. But if it realizes that the receipt and utilization of technical assistance is both a responsibility and a cost, it may be more selective in its requests.

Another wasteful factor which could be eliminated through coordination is inadequate record-keeping of the entire technical assistance effort. At present there frequently is considerable du-plication over time—in effect, a lack of coordination with the past. Cases have been found where as many as a dozen experts have followed one another in reviewing and reporting on a single problem like tourism. A few less-developed countries now publish regular reports on technical assistance activity, a project very much to be encouraged.

* * *

Although the process of providing technical assistance is clearly a long-run activity, and good experts are in short supply, little effort has been made to build up a permanent corps of experts for this purpose, except in the secretariats of the United Nations agencies. It frequently happens that there are shortages in the same fields in the developed countries at the same time that overseas requests are being made. Nowhere are there surpluses of doctors, dentists, teachers, veterinarians, or geologists. The fact that the Swiss may rate high in hotel management does not necessarily mean that they have hotel managers who are willing and suited to serve in a distant less-developed country. And the group of older people with experience gained in the various colonial services is rapidly disappearing. Most experts are already employed and may not be enthusiastic about short-run assignments in less-developed areas. They may not know the language; they may know their technology only as a part of an advanced society; they may not be natural teachers or have the necessary patience; and they may have any number of personal reasons restricting their mobility. The right experts for a specific foreign assignment are hard to find, and there have been many failures.

Several countries, particularly the Federal Republic of Germany and the United Kingdom, have made serious efforts to improve the supply situation. They have not only made this work more attractive in levels of pay plus fringe benefits, but have also moved in the direction of establishing a permanent corps of experts within the government itself or through cooperative arrangements with universities. French teachers serving in Africa receive the same benefits, such as seniority and retirement rights, as do those in the home country. Although the United States government often uses its own employees in short-run cases, it contracts out many of the projects to appropriate intermediaries, such as universities or private consulting firms. While this passes the recruitment problem on to some private agency, it still remains true that there are serious international shortages which need to be dealt with on a long-term basis. To some extent, the

U.N. specialized agencies have built up permanent staffs, which are, however, connected with their regular budget activities; thus most of the projects which these agencies carry out for the U.N. Development Program are done with individuals specially employed for the job.

One way of easing the supply problem is to try to hold down the outflow of trained personnel from the less-developed countries. The number sent overseas for education, with its encouragement of permanent migration, might be reduced by establishing and strengthening universities in the area, and by providing more teacher-trainers rather than teachers. A reduced staffing of international agencies by nationals of less-developed countries could also help.

There should be ways of reducing the number of sterile cases. In part, the suppliers are guilty here by seldom providing a long enough period to permit the expert to remain on the spot. He may be needed not only for the planning stage but also for a prolonged period of explanation and support. All too often there is no follow-up, and the enthusiasm engendered by the expert gradually disappears with his departure, and no one is on the spot who can answer unexpected questions. It also is important that the recipient country feel more responsibility for the project. Although frequently necessary and sometimes appropriate, technical assistance is too often on a grant basis. To be sure, the host country sometimes bears part of the local costs, but in many cases it might do much more. Certainly, for development and training purposes the project should involve as much local participation as possible. It might increase the chance that the expert will be fully utilized and his advice followed if the less-developed country had more of a stake in it. After all, the costs involved are usually relatively small.

* * *

Finding the right expert is only the beginning of the process. The administrative detail in working out each individual arrangement at home and abroad is horrendous. It seems much easier to arrange to send $100 million of inert wheat to India than two lively experts on agricultural credit with continuing problems during their stay. The situation is aggravated by the fact that experts from different aid-suppliers and U.N. agencies may come under different arrangements in the same country concerning such touchy subjects as diplomatic privileges and basic compensation. It is an unfortunate fact that the various suppliers and recipients of technical assistance have never been able to agree on some set of uniform conditions relating to the treatment of visiting experts.

It is difficult to compare costs by source since national programs are not always comparable, different types of supporting expenditure may be included under the general heading, and certain fringe benefits (diplomatic privileges, for example) vary according to national arrangements. Nevertheless, it is evident that in general, both the salary level and the standard of living in the United States makes an American adviser more expensive than one from some other donor country. While he may also be relatively more productive, the opposite may be true. Possibly, on a comparative advantage basis, more actual technical assistance might be provided to the less-developed countries if the United States were to make the same expenditures available to finance experts from other countries. Indirectly, this is what happens when increased support is given to the multilateral agencies.

* * *

While small groups of volunteers have worked in less-developed countries under private auspices for many years, the United States Peace Corps, initiated in 1961, is the first case of volunteer activity to be sponsored by any government. Since then, nearly all of the developed countries have established volunteer programs. In 1968, 25,555 volunteers served abroad under government programs. Each DAC member, except Italy and Portugal, reported some such activity, although the United States was responsible for more than two-thirds of the total. Many young Belgians and Frenchmen are in a somewhat similar program as an alternative to military service. The number of young Germans working voluntarily as development assistants has reached 2,005 under the German Development Service, and German church institutions and private organizations have an equal number serving abroad. It is interesting that a parallel development has taken place in several less-developed countries (e.g., Iran), where skilled volunteers have been mobilized for service within their own country.

The response to the activities of these volunteers in the host countries has been generally favorable. At the end of 1969, U.S. Peace Corps volunteers were active in 58 countries, with 10,151 volunteers. Furthermore, many countries have asked for larger groups. Occasionally, volunteers have had to suffer for some political difficulty between the supplying and host countries, but the actual cases of dissatisfaction with their performance or behavior have been amazingly few. Quite as important as their on-the-job usefulness is the fact that the various Peace Corps operations provide an outlet for young people interested in international affairs and in the problems of the poor countries. On their return home, they enlarge the small group in each advanced country of persons with actual experience abroad. Most of them either become teachers or enter government service. Despite the recent reductions in appropriations for foreign aid in the United States, the administration's request for the Peace Corps has been only slightly reduced. The final appropriations have been: 1967–68, $107.5 million; 1968–69, $102.8 million; 1969–70, $98.45 million.

The original idea of the volunteer services was to enlist young people, often with very little specialized skill other than that automatically acquired by living in a modernized society. However, a gradual shift has taken place, recognized first by the European organizations, toward the use of individuals of various ages with some special training and skill. This trend has meant an increase in the average age and somewhat more difficult problems of recruitment and assignment, but it also seems to reflect the wishes of many of the host countries.

*   *   *

The other general approach to the transmission of knowledge is to bring individuals for study or training to the more advanced country. Over 39,100 students and 34,900 trainees from developing countries were financed by DAC countries in 1968, nearly double the number reported in 1962. Increasingly, the students are postgraduates, about half of them in science, education, and medicine. The trainees are a more varied group of persons. They are most likely to be employed in industry, public utilities, social services, and labor relations. A small but increasing amount of assistance is being given by DAC countries for study in neighboring less-developed countries.

The above figures are far below the total numbers of foreign students who come to the DAC countries. While there are many private sources of aid and some grants by the governments of less-developed countries themselves, the bulk of the foreign students in the Western countries are self-financed, except for the inherent subsidy given to all students in most educational institutions.

In 1968, the U.S. financed, in whole or in part, 11,027 foreign students who came to the United States—one-third each from Africa and from Asia, 24 per cent from the Americas, and 6 per cent from Europe, mostly Turkey. At the same time, 1,484 persons were given aid to study in other countries, most of whom went to the American University in Beirut. In addition 6,406 trainees came to the U.S. and 1,809 were helped to go to other countries.

As one might expect, their fields of interest differ markedly from those of American students, reflecting the general emphasis within the American aid program on public administration and economic planning, education, and agriculture. The areas which seem particularly under-represented are those of health and medicine, and such general service fields as trade, banking, insurance, and tourism. The importance of distribution and of service industries increases with economic development, but even the shift from subsistence to market economies opens up important areas for technological transfer.

The bringing of students to the richer countries has raised a number of troublesome questions. Educational institutions in advanced countries have not been geared to the life, habits, or needs of the less-developed countries. Training in a modern big-city hospital may not be wholly appropriate to the condition to which the student returns. And life in the developed countries often so attracts students that they find ways of extending their stay abroad, thus destroying the intent to build up manpower in the less-developed countries for which their grants were given.

Migration has always been a primary way in which knowledge and experience have been transmitted. In the colonial era, many Europeans settled in foreign countries; Chinese moved into Southeast Asia, Indians into East Africa, and Near-Easterners and Jews to trading posts everywhere. All made major contributions to the development of their new homes. An effort to maintain this kind of flow from Europe today is carried on by the Intergovernmental Committee for European Migration (ICEM), which arranges for the migration of some 1,500 skilled Europeans per year to Latin-American countries. But migration also involves the flow of ambitious manpower. There can be no doubt of the serious ness of the present "brain drain" whereby promising young persons from the less-developed countries are tempted to migrate to the developed countries. Today the "import" of doctors and nurses from less-developed countries to the United States has helped greatly to meet a serious domestic shortage. However, what is gain to the United States is probably a much greater loss to the less-developed country.

Efforts have been made to meet this problem by putting the emphasis of study away from home more on postgraduate work, exacting commitments to return, and developing special curricula in certain universities. A better long-run solution is to provide higher education, in all but highly specialized fields, in the less-developed countries themselves, perhaps on a regional basis. The educational process can then focus on the manpower needs of the area. In the short run, the provision of new facilities and faculty is much more costly than transporting and maintaining students abroad; but once an institution is established, the foreign-exchange cost will drop and the educational output should be more relevant to the needs of the less-developed countries.

The real costs of servicing foreign students are considerably more than the amounts paid out as foreign aid, particularly in view of the skyrocketing costs entailed by the explosion in higher education in the developed countries themselves. They have never included in their reports to the DAC any allocation of direct government and other aid to their own educational institutions, which help carry all students, foreign or domestic. Special concern is shown for the basic problem of educational adjustment by the provision in the AID legislation authorizing up to $10 million for assistance to research and educational institutions in the United States "for the purpose of strengthening their capacity to develop and carry out programs concerned with the economic and social development of less-developed countries." [2]

Whatever the administrative burdens involved in the use of experts, they exist in perhaps a more exaggerated form with respect to student grants. The process of selecting from among potential grantees those who can benefit from Western university exposure, although they may have had a completely different preparation from Western students, is so difficult that many host countries have left the choice essentially to the local authorities. Since a number of Western countries are interested, problems of allocation arise. And again, the fact that the terms of the grants given by different countries vary adds another distortion to the selection process. There are private organizations, such as the African-American Institute and colleges and universities offering special scholarships, which have devised effective methods for selecting those to whom assistance is to be given; but much remains to be done to organize better selection procedures on a wider international basis. While useful efforts have been made to help the visitor to benefit fully from his stay in the host country through better orientation and travel plans, a greater investment in such activities would increase the return on the entire effort.

* * *

The process of the transmission of knowledge not only involves getting it across borders but also disseminating it within the less-developed country. It is not enough for a foreigner to come to a country and perform a particular task. The important thing is to have training take place which makes it quite unnecessary to import the foreign expert. In the Western world, education has held a primary position in the concept of national development, be it political, economic, or social. For economic objectives, expenditures on education and training may clearly be considered an investment increasing the capacity for productive work, though such investment is not recorded in the usual estimates of national savings or of national wealth. While a large part of the specialized training required by modern industry is provided on the job, formal and usually public education provides the basic skills and concepts that are essential.

In reviewing the world scene today, it is apparent that trouble is fairly universal in the educational world. A crisis is rapidly approaching, if it has not already arrived, created by an explosive demand for education, an acute scarcity of resources, and a raging rejection of present educational procedures, given the tendency of educational systems to resist change and adaptation to their changing environment and its needs. In the developed countries a number of years in school has become a standard requirement for all, and the current problems seem to be how to mix general cultural education and vocational training, how many should continue for longer periods in "institutions of higher learning," and just what should they do once they are there. In the less-developed countries, despite a remarkable rate of expansion in enrollments, the problem of basic literacy is far from being solved. The possibility of making much progress is aggravated by the fact that they start with grossly underdeveloped educational systems plus high birth rates and a high proportion of children to total population, a multitude of competing demands on low national incomes, a relatively high unit cost of education (teachers are often highly paid), and an incomplete, inefficient, and often irrelevant educational process both in curriculum and structure.[3] UNESCO reports that in 35 African countries, enrollments in primary and secondary schools, though increasing, are not keeping pace with population growth.

Historically, the educational process of the West tended to be transplanted into these areas on a limited scale with little adaptation. The scattered efforts of private philanthropic and church groups resembled those at home, and the metropolitan powers merely exported their home curricula, materials, and procedures. Nor was there any attempt to spread education very widely. Today, three out of five adults in the less-developed countries do not have the simplest ability to read and write, and elementary schooling has become a high priority item in many national budgets. On the average, sums allocated to education by the less-developed countries increased by 12.5 per cent per year in the 1960s and grew even more rapidly in the 1950s when the base was lower.

Since nearly all leaders were educated in developed countries, their initial efforts were to expand along familiar lines. Even within such limits, given the fact that everything cannot be done at once, certain policy choices immediately appeared: Should universal literacy be the primary objective, or should there be a planned pyramid with proportionate expansion at all levels? Prospects for universal literacy are indeed dim. The initial desire for schooling may fade in the light of a curriculum often not related to the student's present or future and under the pressures on him to contribute to his support. It is not unusual in a less-developed country that 60 out of 100 children in the age group might start school and only 6 effectively complete the primary course.

Although general education must be a domestic process, there is wide room for foreign assistance, both technical and material. Much more can be done through teachers, teacher-trainers, educational advisers, counterpart funds, and foreign supplies. In 1966 the DAC members' aid to education (excluding other forms of technical assistance which might be called educational in the generic sense) was about $600 million through official bilateral channels, with an added $140 million from multilateral agencies, and about $250 million from private voluntary agencies and business enterprises. In total, it came to about $1 billion.

The pattern of assistance varied among donors: France contributes thousands of school-teachers to French-speaking Africa; Germany has set up many vocational schools. American aid emphasizes improvement and expansion of high school and college-level systems of vocational education and teacher-training. At least half the Peace Corps is engaged in teaching at sub-college levels. Both the World Bank and the Inter-American Development Bank have made loans for specific educational projects. Philip Coombs has estimated that 10 to 20 per cent of the total $1 billion granted to the less-developed countries as aid to education goes into scholarships and fellowships; another 20 to 30 per cent goes for "hardware" such as buildings and equipment, and a remaining 60 to 70 per cent is accounted for by personnel, teachers, administrators, and advisers.

The part which foreign aid can and does play in building up the educational process in less-developed countries has gone through an evolutionary cycle. In recognition of the "brain drain" and the fact that university curricula in advanced countries were not always appropriate, much more emphasis is now being placed on building up universities within the less-developed countries, with foreign study provided only for highly specialized or postgraduate work. This shift has required substantial initial investments in buildings, books, and equipment, and in sending advanced teachers for at least some years.

A second shift in emphasis is to engage in teacher-training rather than direct teaching. While there seems to be no reduction in the demand for foreign teachers in the less-developed countries, it is obvious that efforts to increase the spread of literacy must be based upon a corps of native teachers. Worldwide, 240,000 classrooms have been built and some 400,000 teachers have been trained with AID help. Despite the extensive efforts in many less-developed countries, there is a shortage of teachers, and this has led to the greater use of mechanical aids, such as television.

Finally, in half-a-dozen countries but particularly in the United States, many universities are now sharing the responsibility for assisting specific educational institutions in less-developed countries. With AID support, nine leading American technical schools have helped create an Institute of Technology at Kanpur in India. The Agricultural University of West Pakistan is being assisted through Washington State University. Southern Illinois University is active in Afghanistan, and Hampton Institute in Sierra Leone. In all, 123 American universities and colleges have AID contracts to carry out various projects in less-developed countries, though not all are in the educational field *per se.*

There can be no question but that manpower development must have a high priority in any long-term program of economic and social development, a priority it clearly receives in many less-developed countries. The average national expenditure for education among Latin American countries in 1968 was 4.5 per cent of gross national product. Furthermore, out of recent experience have come notable efforts to improve quality by educational planning, developing more relevant curricula, improving administration, and trying to bring the levels of education into better balance. In earlier days, education in the French colonies was a copy of that in France itself. This has now been abandoned and much more appropriate curricula and time periods have been developed by French advisors in the same areas. To be sure, the benefits of even the most effective educational system appear only slowly but current progress is an encouraging sign of advance even though it is not registered immediately on the indicators.

Undoubtedly, there is room for much more substantial foreign support in the development of new educational institutions and methods. The United States, which provides about one-half of the total foreign aid given by DAC members, gives less than one-third of the total going to education, and is likely to fall still lower because of reduced appropriations. AID committed $189 million to education in 1966–67, $199 million in 1967–68, and had proposed, before the cut, that it commit $252 million in 1969, the bulk of which would pay for the overseas services of American educational experts.

Educational assistance is clearly an activity with a very great multiplier effect, and its cutback means a much greater loss than the immediate budgetary cost. An encouraging sign, however, is that the World Bank is now showing considerably more interest in this field. For example, a recent World Bank loan to Malaysia will provide $8.8 million, about half the total cost, for a program of school construction and equipping of vocational, secondary, technical, and agricultural schools in Malaysia. In addition to the World Bank contribution, experienced teachers for the agricultural and technical schools and overseas fellowships for teacher-training will be financed by the government and by bilateral aid. The project was prepared under the World Bank/UNESCO Cooperative Program, and others like it are contemplated.

Since the less-developed countries must build an integrated and balanced educational system, special problems are created for them when there are several different suppliers accustomed to quite different educational patterns. Former colonies usually follow in the footsteps of their metropolitan power, but as new states they will not long reproduce faithfully any of the Western prototypes, but rather develop approaches more suitable to their own requirements. An indication of the search for better answers is the establishment of new agencies in addition to UNESCO, such as the International Institute for Educational Planning, the Council of New Educational Technologies, the Center for Educational Research and Innovation, and the various United Nations Training Centres.

It is dangerous to suggest that any particular form of assistance should receive priority. Because the requirements of each less-developed country vary, it is tempting to speak in the broadest terms of the need for technical assistance and for capital. Since projects requiring capital are more glamorous and administratively easier to carry out, producing tangible results that can be readily examined by evaluators, they are likely to be preferred by both supplier and recipient. Furthermore, in the context of foreign aid, education is generally regarded as a factor in development rather than as an end in itself. That it releases potentialities in the individual, that it encourages social mobility, that it broadens horizons, and that it permits more intelligent political participation are all values which more than justify the increased emphasis given to it.

It is a truism that every less-developed country has a shortage of competent manpower, from the policy-maker at the top to the unskilled worker at the bottom. The transmission and dissemination of knowledge thus become key requirements. The shortages in the possible carriers are so great that there must be a much more careful examination of ways and means; the central problem, the experts are agreed, is how to adjust more effectively a limited supply to a boundless need.

New research in the education field can help in finding ways to use resources more efficiently, and many of the less-developed countries are beginning to project their manpower requirements for the future. There will need to be a closely knit, coordinated, and much larger international effort to provide the assistance which the expanded educational systems will inevitably require.

*   *   *

An effective technical assistance program has a multiplier effect on the use of capital, which, in turn, requires added training and skills. In a direct way, technical assistance serves to develop plans, programs, and projects where capital investment can be effective and catalytic. Not only does the expansion of an educational system through teacher-training require buildings, books, and supplies, but it also encourages printing and publishing. In the United Kingdom, there is one copy of a daily newspaper for every two persons, in Africa one for every 100. More doctors mean more hospitals and equipment. There is nothing surprising about this snowball effect. Economists have long demonstrated that the satisfaction of one want usually has a multiplier effect on demand. This human characteristic is at the heart of the process of growth and development.

6 · The Transfer of Capital

The transmission of knowledge, essential as it is, is only part of the assistance which can be offered by the rich countries. While a man's human abilities can be increased by education and training, his productivity can be greatly expanded by giving him tools and machinery. For many reasons, the pre-modern society saves and invests little. Of the many factors contributing to modern economic growth with its high and sustained rate of increase in real product per capita, a key requirement is an unprecedented high level in the proportion of savings and investment to national product.[1] Many of the other requisites are internal, such as changes in the structures of production and consumption, appropriate government activities, new methods of economic organization, and extended manpower training. However, the supply of capital can be supplemented from outside.

The effectiveness of added capital is related to a country's stage of development. At any moment of time, there is a condition called "absorptive capacity," which reflects the limitations set by other factors of production: appropriately skilled manpower, energy, raw materials, managerial capacity, marketing feasibility. Limitations may also result from the absence of related institutional factors such as law and order or banking facilities. The process of development might thus be described as raising the level of absorptive capacity—the ability to use manpower and capital more effectively. While the ability to increase domestic capital formation (savings) increases as the GNP increases, the opportunities for its use should expand even more rapidly.

91

The actual contribution which capital makes in a particular country at a particular time cannot be determined by some generalized concept like a capital-output ratio whereby, say, two additional units of capital will increase output by one unit per year. The productivity of capital, if one can calculate it at all, differs widely in agriculture, electric power, textile products, roads, and education, and among the subgroups under these general headings. Furthermore, in terms of development, the valuation of results cannot stop with the specific project but must consider its impact on other sectors in the society and on the long-run as well as the short-run consequences. However, since capital is a scarce commodity and most less-developed countries do not have developed capital markets which can carry out the allocating function, their economic policy choices are largely related to the supply and use of capital.

The capital required for development purposes in any less-developed country comes chiefly from its own savings. Despite their poverty, the less-developed countries usually manage to do some saving and investment, including government spending for capital projects. A tabulation made by the United Nations for 1962–64 showed that for 36 poorer countries for which data were available, the median percentage of gross domestic saving compared with gross domestic product was 12 per cent, although there were wide variations.[2] The parallel figure for the rich countries would be at least 20 per cent.

Kuznets' study of capital formation verifies the relationship between per capita income and capital formation, namely, that richer people save more.[3] He also finds a marked association between industrial structure and capital formation, i.e., savings rates are higher in the more industrialized countries. The analysis is complicated by the fact that the two variables—per capita income and degree of industrialization—are themselves closely related. For most poorer countries, being neither well-to-do nor industrialized, a significant share of domestic investment is financed through foreign funds.

At first, the function of assistance provided from abroad was thought of only as meeting foreign requirements over and above those which the recipient could meet from its own foreign earnings—in other words, to meet a foreign-exchange gap. However, it is now recognized that the gap may be a domestic one where domestic savings are less than investment; again, this difference can be met by foreign assistance which, by adding to total resources available, makes the larger investment possible.

* * *

In providing capital assistance through official channels, the usual procedure is for an agreement to be reached between the supplier and the recipient whereby the supplier will finance the provision of certain goods or services to the less-developed country. The agreement may be for part of the total needed for some project or for a completed plant. It may involve a number of different participants. Although the needed goods are sometimes obtained from a third country, most assistance comes from the supplying country itself.

The supplying government, if it is a Western country, is usually neither producer, shipper, nor installer of the items involved. It finances but frequently does not purchase. Instead, it authorizes the recipient government to procure, which in turn usually places the order with an importer, engineering firm, or contractor. The funds might be handled through commitments against which banks would issue credit, through progress payments, or through reimbursement procedures. In some instances, particularly when multilateral agencies are involved, the project may be put up for international bidding. In any event, nearly all foreign assistance given by the rich countries is actually carried out through private business channels. In the United States, farmers are the principal domestic beneficiaries, but many manufacturers are also involved, such as the makers of fertilizer, steel, and machinery. American engineering firms build power plants, dams, and irrigation projects all over the world with the help of American assistance payments.

In the less-developed country, some of the products involved are directly used by public authorities—medicines, public buildings, equipment for publicly owned industry, school equipment—but some of them pass into private hands either for cash or credit. Wheat is sent to India not because Indians cannot afford to buy it with rupees but because India does not have the foreign exchange to pay for it in a foreign market. The consumer pays in local currency. This procedure produces income for the receiving government, giving it additional funds to spend, and the results can be inflationary. The situation first arose in the Marshall Plan arrangements. In order to control inflationary pressures, the concept of counterpart funds was invented whereby the European governments agreed to put such receipts in a special account of which some fraction was available to the U.S. government for its use abroad, and the remainder was used to finance local programs agreed to by both governments. The same idea, with variations, has been carried over into present-day assistance operations.

Since more than 40 per cent of official bilateral aid generates counterpart funds,[4] it is obvious that how and when this local currency is released is exceedingly important. The funds might be used for fighting inflation by keeping that amount of money out of circulation, for pump-priming by putting it in circulation, for budget-balancing, for paying local costs on long-term investment projects, for supporting or endowing social institutions—the possibilities are many. The degree of control which the original supplier actually has over the funds varies according to the agreement with the recipient government. Since the sums are large in a few cases, there has been a tendency for them to accumulate, thereby having an impact on the over-all financial situation. Here the timing of counterpart releases or withholdings may have a significant effect. Thus, an original transaction can persist almost indefinitely in its influence on the development process. On the other hand, a sensitive recipient country may feel that this procedure enables the supplier to exert too much influence over its domestic program.

* * *

The initial aid transaction can take a number of different forms. In 1968 the DAC members as a whole made 50 per cent of their official commitments to less-developed countries and multilateral organizations in the form of grants, capital subscriptions, and "grant-like contributions." The last category consists chiefly of U.S. food aid but also involves transactions where repayment for commodities or the servicing of loans is in local currency rather than the suppliers' and is then used in accordance with an agreement between the two countries. This does not exhaust the categorization of aid, for there are loans, which can be subdivided by interest rate, maturity, and length of grace period into soft loans and hard loans. There also are export credits and long-term investments. One form used in private financing, the income bond—a security which is excused from its service payments under certain unfavorable conditions—was somewhat recognizable in the Anglo-American loan of 1946, but seems not to have been explored for less-developed-country financing, though something of the sort might be appropriate.

Official bilateral flows to less-developed countries have always had a high proportion of grants. The Marshall Plan was based on the fact that the European allies had exhausted their holdings and earning capacity of foreign exchange during the war. For the first year assistance was divided into about $5 billion in grants and $1 billion in loans, and about the same proportion continued through the three following years.

For the DAC members taken together, the percentage of new commitments that include grants and grant-like contributions has been falling since those early days. It was between 70 and 80 per cent at the outset but fell rapidly in the early 1960s, not so much because of a reduction in grants but rather that the increase in volume was chiefly in the form of loans. The record for the five years 1964–68 is given in Table 16, which also divides loans into soft loans, measured both by interest rate and maturity, and those which are harder.

TABLE 16

COMMITMENTS TO LESS-DEVELOPED COUNTRIES AS GRANTS OR LOANS, DAC MEMBERS, 1964–68

(*Per Cent*)

Year	Grants	Soft Loans		Other Loans	
		3% or less	25 years or more	over 3%	under 25 years
1964	60.2	23.9	24.5	15.9	15.3
1965	60.9	17.5	15.1	21.6	24.0
1966	62.2	23.1	19.0	14.7	18.8
1967	56.1	22.1	20.4	21.8	23.5
1968	51.4	29.6	26.2	19.0	22.4

Source: Development Assistance Committee, OECD.

The record for grants clearly shows a decided decline, but the division of the remainder between soft and hard loans has no clear trend, although it is probably true that the percentage of soft loans is increasing.

Actually, the internal variations between soft and hard loans are largely the result of annual shifts in the records of the major donors. So far as the United States is concerned, in recent times, Congress has steadily pressed to reduce the amount of assistance in the form of grants. In 1958, a substantial part of the appropriation was put in the Development Loan Fund, which could accept repayment in local currencies. A further important step aimed at reducing the proportion of grants in U.S. assistance was the establishment of new requirements for food assistance under PL 480, which established a five-year transition period that began in 1967 to increase the use of dollar-repayable loans, on the theory that days of surplus were over and there should be no substantial difference between the treatment of food commodities and other forms of aid, except in cases of famine. The general attitude of Congress toward grants is indicated by Section 634(e) in the Act which instructs the President to include in his recommendations to Congress each year "a specific plan for each country receiving bilateral grant economic assistance whereby, wherever practicable, such grant economic assistance shall be progressively reduced and eventually terminated." U.S. technical assistance and contributions to multilateral agencies, however, continue to be provided on a grant basis.

The record of the commitments of DAC members with respect to grants is given in Table 17. These figures are percentages of commitments rather than disbursements, since that gives a clearer indication of current policy. If disbursements figures were used, loans would be included whose terms were fixed half-a-dozen years before. For smaller programs, the percentages may be markedly affected by individual loan commitments entered into during any one year. Austria is the only country which shows a steady increase in the percentage of grants and has climbed up to the average. Canada has also improved its position. Australia, with 100 per cent in each year, and Belgium and Norway, always above 92 per cent, could hardly be expected to improve their performance. The United States, however, has dropped steadily lower from 65 per cent in grants in 1962 to only 45 per cent in 1968. The decline is largely the result of the gradual shift from grant-like contributions to soft loans with respect to food aid.

Loans vary as to interest rate, maturity date, and grace period. Their only common characteristic is that they must be repaid. Canada and Sweden provide 50-year interest-free loans; the

TABLE 17

GRANTS AND GRANT-LIKE CONTRIBUTIONS AS PERCENTAGES OF TOTAL
OFFICIAL COMMITMENTS BY DAC MEMBERS, 1964–68
(*Per Cent*)

Country	1964	1965	1966	1967	1968
Australia	100	100	100	100	100
Belgium	97	98	94	94	95
Norway	95	96	100	100	92
Canada	51	54	77	48	75
Sweden	80	89	71	84	75
Switzerland	68	78	65	100	73
France	80	80	83	74	72
Japan	51	37	42	38	62
Denmark	77	70	62	64	57
Netherlands	75	71	76	72	52
Austria	21	14	24	29	51
United Kingdom	54	55	50	57	46
United States	58	62	61	56	45
Germany	50	43	42	34	38
Italy	54	21	13	12	25
Portugal	18	29	23	19	21
All DAC countries	60.2	60.9	62.2	56.1	51.4

Source: Development Assistance Committee, OECD.

United Kingdom and Denmark provide 25-year interest-free loans. In 1965, DAC recommended that the norm for official development loans be 3 per cent interest, 25 years maturity, and a 7-year grace period, which are the terms most commonly stipulated at present. In some cases, a project is financed by "mixed" credits; France, for example, may combine soft official credits with private export credits.

The countries whose terms were hardest in 1968, taking the proportion of grants into account, were Portugal, Italy, and Germany. The United States, which once had been the leader in the softness of its terms, was tied with Norway for eleventh place in terms of the extent to which commitments were either completely on a grant basis or involved a grant element by extending loans on better than commercial terms.

One result of the extension of loans is that the less-developed countries have gone more and more into debt. The rapid growth of public debt is demonstrated by estimates made by the World Bank of outstanding public and publicly guaranteed external debt for 79 less-developed countries. The record since 1961 is shown in Table 18.

TABLE 18

EXTERNAL PUBLIC DEBT OUTSTANDING OF SEVENTY-NINE
LESS-DEVELOPED COUNTRIES
(*$ Billion*)

Region	Dec. 31 1961	Dec. 31 1965	June 30, 1968 Total	Disbursed	Undisbursed
Africa	3.3	6.6	8.0	6.6	1.3
Southern Europe [a]	2.3	4.1	5.1	3.8	1.3
East Asia	2.2	3.9	5.6	4.3	1.4
Middle East	1.4	2.4	3.6	2.4	1.3
South Asia [b]	3.6	7.8	10.4	7.9	2.5
Western Hemisphere [c]	8.8	12.2	14.8	11.0	3.7
Total	21.6	37.1	47.5	36.0	11.5

[a] Includes private debt of Yugoslavia.
[b] Does not include suppliers' credits of India.
[c] Includes private debt of Brazil.
Source: World Bank, *Annual Report 1969.*

In every area except the Western Hemisphere, where the debt already was large, the external public debt has more than doubled since 1961. There is no year in which there has been a net reduction in debt in any of the areas. Seven countries (India, Pakistan, Argentina, Brazil, Chile, Colombia, and Mexico) account for nearly one-half the total.

Similarly, debt service, i.e., interest and amortization, have increased and now exceed $4 billion per year. However, payments have not grown as fast as debt, being 10.7 per cent of principal outstanding in 1961 and 8.5 per cent in 1969. A rough guess on the sources of the loans would indicate that one-half has come from individual governments, one-fourth from multilateral agencies, and the remaining fourth from export, credits and other private arrangements. The receipt of debt payments would not follow the same pattern, a much larger share being taken by suppliers' credits and private loans where interest rates are higher and maturities much shorter.

* * *

Since the use of credit is a normal operation in the economic world, a rise in the volume of debt outstanding is not in itself alarming; in fact, it represents an aspect of growth whereby capital is transferred temporarily from owners to users for a charge. Presumably, it increases productivity and earning power on the part of the borrower sufficiently to meet the service charges with something left over.

However, foreign borrowing raises a special difficulty—it must be serviced in foreign exchange. The use of the capital may take care of that problem, as in the development of a mineral resource for export. However, when its use is more clearly and narrowly domestic, it may not even provide a domestically produced economic product, as is the case with the import of food or the development of an educational facility. If the borrowed capital is used in building a power plant, it would presumably increase the national income and eventually lead to various increases in output, but it would not contribute automatically to making the necessary foreign payments. Thus the capacity to service the loan is not related so much to the loan's productivity as to the prospective condition of the general balance of payments.

Both the amount of debt and the burden of debt service are unevenly distributed among the less-developed countries, in part because a number of the newer countries have not yet had time to accumulate past borrowings. However, the transfer problem is very serious for some countries. According to the World Bank, interest and amortization on external official debt exceeded 20 per cent of commodity exports in Argentina, Brazil, India, Mali, Mexico, Tunisia, Uruguay, and Yugoslavia.[5] This does not take into account service payments on private unguaranteed debt.

Those who argue in favor of using loans rather than grants give two reasons: one is to reduce the apparent burden on the lender by requiring interest payments and the return of principal; the second is that recipients will consider more carefully the use of borrowed money than of gifts. Once the latter may have been true, but since no country has enough capital to meet all demands, priorities must be established. In most cases, a recipient would prefer a grant as less burdensome; but with economic planning generally established in the less-developed countries, the recipient is unlikely to make any distinction in the actual use of funds according to their terms. Interestingly, suppliers seem to be more willing to provide food or technical assistance in grant form than other items.

Another frequent argument is that since loans are the normal procedure for obtaining capital assistance, loans will put an end to the psychological difficulties created by charity. But the loans proposed—usually quite soft in their terms—are even then not commercial. And loans in place of grants prolong the period when assistance will be required, since part of the future assistance often must be used to service former loans. Some supplier countries, it is argued, cannot afford to give grants, though they can manage to make loans; but the immediate outpayment is the same, whether a loan or a grant.

It has been suggested that the cost of foreign aid might be made clearer to taxpayers in supplier countries if loans were made at the same level of interest the national treasury pays in borrowing funds and that if the recipient country cannot afford it, aid should then provide a subsidy to meet the cost of borrowing. This is primarily a matter of bookkeeping which, however, raises procedural problems about the assurance of the subsidy.

The loan element in the lend-lease settlements and the Marshall Plan probably would have been much higher had not the fiasco of the World War I debts been clearly in mind, with its insoluble transfer problems. The present situation, in which accelerated debt service on the various obligations of European countries has been of substantial assistance to the unexpectedly weak U.S. balance of payments, has suggested to some that the same future advantage might come from loans to less-developed countries, but they forget how widely different the two situations are.

Actually, there is little justification for the increased use of loans. The necessity for assistance programs is created by the inability of a less-developed country to pay for the foreign component of its development needs. The development process is no short-run emergency matter, and no one expects this condition in international payments between the developed and the less-developed countries to change very rapidly. To the extent that assistance is obtained at anything less than commercial costs, the pressure on foreign payments is reduced. The assistance is less than it appears to be when it establishes obligations for future payments. To be sure, it presumably adds to the country's productivity; but if part of its future product must be used for payments, the rate of growth will be less or the amount of aid required will be more. Furthermore, one country's exports (payments) are another country's imports (receipts). To increase imports into the richer countries, thus making payments possible, is not always an easy problem to deal with, because of its distorting effect on established industries and employment. That the increasing debt burden will require increased levels of assistance in the future, if there is no major increase in the trade flow from borrower to lender, will be discussed more specifically in Chapter 11.

* * *

The foregoing discussion has dealt primarily with official transfers of capital, but private investment is also an extremely important channel (which will be discussed in detail in Chapter 10). In functional terms, private capital makes the same kind of contribution as does official capital, although it may provide management and other skills at the same time. It involves not only different incentives but a different institutional background. In 1967 and 1968, about one-half of such aid consisted of new direct investment and re-invested earnings. The remainder was more or less equally divided between portfolio investments, including the private purchase of bonds of multilateral agencies, and export credits.

Because government policy is usually involved, special attention should be given at this point to the problems created by export credits. All developed countries make special efforts to promote their exports and usually have government agencies to guarantee or insure export credits, which have been initially financed by the exporter or by commercial banks. Export credit has the same basis as domestic commercial credit, namely, that the purchaser needs time to complete his use or resale of the product before payment. Thus a purchaser of raw cotton would pay off his debt with the proceeds of the sale of the textile products made from it. At present, the use of export credits has extended far beyond this original, short-term commercial use. The rich countries have expanded export credits not only on the basis of commercial motivation but also as a way of supplementing limited aid resources. Less-developed countries also use this form of borrowing to supplement other sources of foreign capital and even to circumvent the necessity of dealing with governments and international agencies.

The recent expansion in export credits of more than 5-year maturity is clearly shown in Table 19, in which the difference between credits maturing and new credits extended, i.e., the increase in the amount of export credit outstanding, is given for 1965–68.

TABLE 19

ANNUAL NET INCREASE IN PRIVATE EXPORT CREDITS OF MORE
THAN 5-YEAR MATURITY DAC MEMBERS, 1965–68
($ *Million*)

1965	750.1
1966	1,107.3
1967	978.9
1968	1,470.3

Source: Development Assistance Committee, OECD.

For many years, the major exporting countries tried to limit the offer of export credit on unusually favorable terms as a form of competitive selling. They agreed under the so-called Berne Union rules to maintain a five-year limit on maturities "except for exceptional cases." However, the 1960s have seen the exceptional cases become the rule. While the volume of the shorter-term export credits showed little change, export credits with maturities over five years have grown very rapidly.

Since the new credits in every year have exceeded the amount paid off, a substantial revolving fund must have accumulated, which may be as large as $10 billion. The gross flow each year, obviously much larger than the increase, plays an important part in determining what imports are available through private channels to the less-developed countries and to which countries. This fact alone raises development problems, especially where the activity of private lenders and borrowers results in substantial trade and subsequent payments for nonpriority items.

The problem created by the expansion of export credits is not only in the nature of the flow of goods which results but also in the subsequent necessity for payment. Export credits carry high interest rates and a relatively short term. While there are some less-developed countries with little external debt, others are having difficulty in meeting current obligations. Most of the recent cases of defaults in payments can be blamed largely on imports financed with export credits, and usually the analysis of the situation has disclosed that the debts outstanding are much larger than either the lenders or the borrower realized.

This situation creates a sharp policy clash within the exporting countries because export credits and development loans are always handled by two different agencies. The promotion of exports has strong business support, and international action on export credits in the past has been aimed primarily at limiting "unfair competition" by agreement not to lower interest rates or lengthen the maturity. On the other hand, these same countries are committed, in providing aid for economic development, to low interest rates and longer terms in order to reduce the growth of heavy external-debt-servicing. The problem is complicated by the fact that governments seeking to make a good record in economic assistance to less-developed countries can use export credit guarantees as a way of increasing the volume of financing without an immediate burden on the government budget.

Several attempts have been made in the OECD to find a way of distinguishing between commercial and developmental credits, but the two so overlap and interlock that no satisfactory solution has been found. The staff of the World Bank, examining the problem for UNCTAD, suggested that there is room for marked improvement in the collection of information, the administration of external debt by individual developing countries, the coordination of creditor practices and policies, and better international coordination with respect to the financial burdens of individual debtor countries. In the meantime, the situation continues where the benefits of softer official loans by the developed countries may be more than offset by expanded, high-cost export credits.

* * *

One other complication in considering the flow of capital to the less-developed countries is the counterflow from them to the economically advanced areas. It is not surprising that a resident in a less-developed country who may accumulate savings should decide to invest them in an organized capital market in another country, or even to place them there merely for safekeeping. This is particularly easy to do if one is in the export business. In some cases, the counterflow undoubtedly consists of "flight capital," as happened in Cyprus and Algeria. Efforts to control such outflows by regulation have had little success. Nor is it clear that if it had been possible to prevent funds from moving abroad, they would necessarily have become available for investment in economic projects of importance for development.

It is essential to create conditions in less-developed countries that will convert domestic savings into investment. This involves not merely some promise of financial and political stability but institutions which can act as financial intermediaries. Such evidence as there is, and it is unusually unsatisfactory, suggests that the demand for higher consumption levels and the importance of small-scale agriculture in the gross national product have worked against much increase in the percentages of gross domestic product which have gone into capital formation.

*   *   *

Another important policy issue has recently arisen concerning the general form of capital assistance. The DAC analysis of bilateral commitments in 1967 and 1968 shows that 30 per cent were for specific projects, 19 per cent for technical assistance, 23 per cent for nonproject assistance (i.e., foreign exchange available for use at the recipient's discretion within certain limitations of tying to purchases from the supplying country), 17 per cent as export credits, and 11 per cent as other contributions. On the other hand, commitments by multilateral agencies were 83 per cent for capital projects and 15 per cent for technical assistance.

Where nonproject assistance is supplied as a means of supporting certain policies of the recipient, it is sometimes called "program aid." During the 1960s it has exceeded the flow of project financing in bilateral commitments, although the fact that almost all multilateral assistance is on a project basis tends to make the totals more or less equal. The growth of nonproject aid is the result of several different conditions. The first is the food deficits in many less-developed countries, so that 18.6 per cent of all bilateral commitments in 1967 consisted of food aid from Australia, Canada, and the United States. In addition, the concentration on investment in projects sometimes failed to take into account the future requirements for spare parts and imported materials; consequently, further assistance in the form of imports has been necessary so that the new industrial plant can operate more nearly at capacity. (This phenomenon was important in the Marshall Plan, where some limited strategic assistance often energized otherwise idle productive capacity.) An interesting aspect of non-project loans resulting from the variety of goods imported is their tendency to assist the small and newly established businessman. The Indian government, for example, often sells the imports on a first-come first-served basis to whomever has rupees, and as a result a larger proportion goes to very small entrepreneurs.

Nonproject aid has also been provided in circumstances where the limited taxing power of a poor country makes it difficult for the government to meet all the local costs of its development program. If it can import goods and sell them locally, it can then use the local currency for development purposes. In other cases, assistance has gone frankly for budget support. For many years, France gave such assistance to its former colonies, while trying at the same time to build up more normal government revenues. The United States has included a separate item in its assistance program called "supporting assistance," provided primarily to build the defensive strength of less-developed countries on the Communist perimeter. It is separate from military assistance and, by supplying goods which the recipient can sell, usually results in providing budgetary assistance to the local government. The intention most often is to help meet defense costs beyond a country's immediate economic capacity. During the last several years, over 90 per cent of "supporting assistance" in the budget has gone to Vietnam, Korea, Laos, and Thailand.

As the less-developed countries become more skilled in their planning and administration and as consultation develops through such media as consortia and consultative groups (discussed in Chapter 13), foreign assistance is being brought into a more effective relationship with local needs and plans. Nonproject assistance is often used to provide encouragement and support for objectives agreed upon by suppliers and recipients. Desirable programs—a family planning program, a reduction in tariffs, or a change in the exchange rate—may be made possible if some assistance is available. No project like a dam, power plant, or port improvement can provide much local currency in the short run. The result of using assistance to finance noncapital imports has been much greater flexibility in the uses for which the assistance can be made available.

The program approach has come under attack because of its political implications and possible side-effects.[6] The argument runs that since program aid requires the recipient to give priority to selected development ends and thus presumably to change its central policies at the cost of some domestic group, it creates local political strains. Inevitably, there are difficulties in agreeing on what are the right policies and then on carrying out any agreement in an uncertain world. Failure to meet commitments can damage the relation between supplier and recipient; and finally, the chance that there may be "arm-twisting," or charges of the same, brings unpredictable consequences.

Although it has always been recognized that the less-developed country might fail to carry out its promised program, it now is evident that the developed country may also meet difficulties. For example, India and some Latin American countries have undertaken certain programs in the expectation of adequate foreign support, with the United States the major source; but the Congressional cuts threaten to make it impossible for the United States to carry out its share of the program. If the downward adjustment were in new projects, the Congressional action, however disappointing to the recipients, would be less likely to bring charges of American failure to play its part in programs whose initiation it had encouraged.

The criticisms of program aid are not exclusively directed at the form of assistance, for serious problems can and do arise when aid takes project form. It is also directed at the extent and manner by which suppliers concern themselves with the performance of the recipient. To be sure, more and more governments in the Third World are becoming capable of recognizing the problems in handling their savings and foreign funds and welcome the support of the IMF, IBRD, or individual supplier governments to carry out programs which are far from the bread-and-circus variety. The cost of materials and equipment has mounted, as have the administrative burdens of project aid. Program aid should not be discarded, but the criticisms should be accepted as fair warning that the proper course is consultation rather than imposition. Although this is a highly sensitive area, proper cooperation can nevertheless be of great benefit to supplier and to recipient.

It is somewhat misleading to assume that the character of foreign assistance can actually direct the capital-use pattern in the recipient country. For example, if a country has matched up its requirements from abroad and its resources for payment, it can usually manage to import the full list no matter which items are provided through foreign assistance simply by adjusting the expenditures of its own earned foreign exchange accordingly. To be sure, its preferences on strictly economic criteria may be altered if it is offered specific items on a concessionary basis. The supplier can be certain that the country gets whatever the item financed by concessionary assistance may be—but perhaps the recipient would otherwise have purchased it and some other item could have been omitted. The economist's concept of the margin is useful here: it is the marginal item which is likely to be displaced. As a result, unless there is some idea of the general plans, policies, and priorities of the country, it is difficult to be certain that a particular project, judged by itself, should be given priority or that it represents the addition which the foreign assistance is intended to make in the economy. If the supplier had full confidence in the planners and political leaders in the country, which is seldom the case, or if there were so perfect a market structure that the marginal concept would really work, which it does not even in the rich countries, assistance might be given quite blindly. But, in the absence of these assurances, those giving assistance have a responsibility to work with the country in order best to coordinate its foreign and domestic resources. By looking at the total picture, a judgment can be made, limited though it may be, as to whether or not the resources available are being used to their best advantage.

At any rate, the $60 billion of net official economic assistance which the rich countries have provided in the ten years, 1959–68, plus the $35 billion from the private sector, represent a massive flow of goods and services to the less-developed countries. There is no way of adding them together to see what this really means except in terms of money. In terms of social and economic development in the less-developed countries, the effect of this flow cannot be separated from the efforts of the recipients themselves. Nevertheless, one can see a tremendous development of basic infrastructure—roads, electric power plants, water supply, hospitals, and educational facilities. Much has been learned by both suppliers and recipients about the obstacles to rapid growth, the many difficult policy choices that must be made, and ways and means of making the whole process more effective. The number of cases of poor performance seems to be diminishing and the relative successes to be increasing with the accumulation of experience. And the cases of most rapid growth are those where either there have been massive inflows of foreign capital or where the development of natural resources has made possible large domestic savings and investment.

7 · For What Uses?

Economic development in the less-developed countries only became a self-conscious operation after World War II. While social scientists had long discussed the importance of the basic factors of production and the general conditions which encouraged economic growth, such as laissez-faire, competition, and free trade, they had concluded that supply and demand operating in a competitive market could best determine the structure of each national economy so as to achieve the optimum satisfaction of wants. This analysis, perhaps appropriate to public policy for the advanced economies, gave only limited guidance to the planners in the less-developed countries where markets were also less developed, or to those countries providing foreign assistance.

A thoroughly underdeveloped country would consist of separate communities connected, if at all, by primitive roads or trails. Power would be provided by man or animal; production would be limited to handicrafts. Modernization may have started in some areas, either around ports or centers of special natural resources, but much of the country and the population would still be living under relatively primitive conditions.

In such circumstances, the development problem is not to meet a few outstanding requirements, but to deal with a multitude of essential needs with the limited and inadequate resources at hand. The selection of priorities is made by the less-developed country, subject to the many political restraints which surround any budget-making process. There are pressures for higher wages for civil servants, for an expanded military posture, for television, for increased social security benefits, for new public buildings—in sum, for many purposes not directly associated with economic development.

While foreign assistance can be allocated for a particular use, its ultimate effect may be manifested in a totally different area of the economy. Thus the economic assistance which went to Indonesia in the early 1960s was clearly intended for specific economic purposes, but actually released Indonesia's resources for use in building its military machine. Nevertheless, in project aid one can be certain of the immediate uses to which foreign assistance is put. Given the basic conditions of under-development, it is not surprising that foreign assistance tended to concentrate on obvious infrastructure requirements on the assumption that these were the prerequisites to development. In addition, such projects were sometimes justified as preparing the way for foreign private investment. Thus, for example, loans made by IBRD to the less-developed countries during its first fifteen years of operation, 1946–61, were 75 per cent in the areas of transportation (roads, railroads, port improvements, airports) and electric power. The emphasis on transportation (41.3 per cent of all IBRD loans in the earlier period) was based on the reasonable assumption that ways and means of increasing the flow of people and goods and reducing travel time within countries were primary economic and political requirements.

In the advanced countries, where history has seen the gradual growth of roads, railroads, airlines, and modern highway systems crowded with automobiles and trucks, it is hard to realize that many less-developed countries have hardly begun the process and that in vast areas the human being, donkey, camel, and bullock are still the primary means of transport. Yet the ability to move people and goods is essential to nearly every aspect of economic and social development. Not only are the costs of building a transport system enormous, but there are many difficult decisions to be made—which routes shall be developed first; how to allocate between main highways, feeder roads, railroads, waterways; what kinds of roads should be built; what organizational and administrative machinery is required; and in the field of foreign aid, how can assistance best be provided for an activity whose costs are very largely those of local labor and local materials.[1]

The expansion of electric power (33.6 per cent of IBRD loans) has been brought about in a few cases by the opportunities provided by favorable hydroelectric sites for industrial use, but more often the justification was its crucial importance in modern life, making economic and social change possible and inevitable. It has been assumed that little money could be raised for transportation and power through private investment. During the three years from July 1966–June 1969, electric power continued to take up one-third of the Bank's new loans, but aid to transportation fell to 25 per cent as loans for agricultural and industrial purposes increased. The loans to industry were largely funds advanced to national development finance companies, which then made loans to local industrial borrowers.

With the advent of IDA, which can make soft loans, it was possible for the World Bank group to extend credits to very poor countries. The leading sector in IDA's loans during the three years July 1966–June 1969 has been industry (mostly industrial imports for India), taking up about 45 per cent of all new loans. Transportation covered 20 per cent, agriculture 17 per cent, and education about 9 per cent.

As might be expected, the uses to which bilateral assistance have been put vary tremendously. In recent years, where project financing has been involved, somewhat more than two-fifths of the total has been devoted to economic infrastructure with at least another 10 per cent for social and administrative purposes. Slightly more than one quarter has gone to industry and mining, and 10 per cent to agricultural projects.

Any effort to categorize the flow of capital raises many difficulties. Some projects are difficult to classify; for example, investments in roads and fertilizer plants may really be directed at agriculture. Electric power may be required for industrial development. Furthermore, about one-half of all bilateral assistance is not related directly to capital projects but consists of more general imports, especially food. In the last analysis, because of the possible redistribution of other resources, aid may contribute to growth anywhere in the economy.

If the sectoral allocation of technical assistance is included, the emphasis would appear in quite different terms, although most of the allocations might be regarded as infrastructure. When the Expanded Program for Technical Assistance (EPTA) was first approved in the Economic and Social Council of the United Nations, specific allocations were made of the first $10 million and of $7 million of the second $10 million (the remainder to be allocated by the Technical Assistance Board) as follows:[2]

	Per Cent
Food and Agriculture Organization	29
United Nations Secretariat	23
World Health Organization	22
United Nations Educational Scientific and Cultural Organization	14
International Labour Organization	11
International Civil Aviation Organization	1
	100

The allocation to the Secretariat was for subjects not covered by any specialized agency, ranging from demography to community development and from industrial production problems to public administration.

Ten years later when expenditures were close to $30 million, the allocations were in the same order with the ranking unchanged, although the three leaders had smaller percentages, UNESCO and ICAO had increased their shares, and the International Telecommunications Union, the World Meteorological Organization, and the International Atomic Energy Agency had been added.

More recently, the consolidated EPTA and U.N. Special Fund has given special emphasis to what it calls "pre-investment projects." What this means is shown by the 104 new projects approved early in 1969. The greatest number of projects (42) are to bring into operation national training institutes for technical training and advanced education; nearly as many projects (37) consist of surveys and feasibility studies for the development of natural resources; 22 projects will establish or strengthen applied research services for agriculture and industry; and 3 are for economic development planning. From the time the U.N. Special Fund became operative in 1960 to the end of 1968, UNDP had approved 1,025 pre-investment projects at a total initial cost on its part of $1,003 million and on the part of the recipients of $1,438 million. Subsequent investments by governments and private enterprises in the projects which have been studied have been much larger.

* * *

A persistent theme of the last two decades has been the ambition of the less-developed countries to industrialize. It was their belief that the manufacturing industries of the rich countries were the fabulous producers which provided the goods necessary for the higher standard of living. Their own development, largely related to supplying raw materials, seemed to hold little promise because of the inelasticity of demand for such products. Nor were traditional occupations likely to provide much additional employment for growing populations; hence, new activities, preferably industrial, were necessary. Furthermore, Karl Marx and the historians had plotted the progress of nations as moving from the agricultural to the industrial state, though without any very detailed blueprint. Finally, the sort of industry dreamed about—steel mills, machine tool factories, petrochemical plants—were all fairly large-scale projects. Technically and administratively, they were much easier to handle, both by supplier and recipient, than the equivalent in a much larger number of small-scale projects. Since the international credit institutions and bilateral programs found it very difficult to make judgments about and deal administratively with small local projects, they gradually came to handle this phase of development through intermediate credit institutions, usually in the form of national development banks.

The effort to develop industry is also bound up with the necessity for each less-developed country to reduce its import bill and increase foreign earnings in order to lessen dependence on foreign assistance. Traditionally, the less-developed countries have supplied primary products to the advanced countries—tropical agricultural products, petroleum, and minerals. The world demand for such goods, however, has not expanded as rapidly as the world demand for manufactured goods, and the much greater production of synthetic substitutes and the increased element of fabrication in more and more complex products have reduced the proportional requirement for imported raw materials. Thus the less-developed countries try to substitute their own manufactures for goods traditionally imported, often with the aid of infant-industry protection, or turn to manufacturing products in which they believe they can show a comparative advantage for export. Unless they can increase their exports (or earn foreign exchange through tourism and other invisible exports), either their economic growth will be retarded or the volume of aid to them will have to be substantially greater and last longer.

There are many examples of success in developing modern industry in less-developed countries. Historically, the record of Japan is perhaps the most impressive. Brazil's capital goods industry, India's iron and steel products, and Mexico's advance to the point where manufactures constitute over 25 per cent of total output are all demonstrations of what is possible. In the summer of 1969, Mr. N. J. Kamath of India's Ministry of Industrial Development reported, after a visit to Japan, that the Japanese authorities were willing to increase the quota for Indian-made sewing machines and watch components. In the private sector he found "Japanese firms interested in India's light machine tools and simple type spindles as they are finding it uneconomic to manufacture these items in Japan." [3]

The problem of industrial development is more difficult for many of the smaller countries whose own markets are very limited by the number of consumers and the level of income. Their hope lies in foreign markets, but that is more easily said than done. They must produce goods which will attract foreign buyers and meet such requirements as standard sizes and proper packaging. They must overcome the costs of transportation and of intermediaries. And finally, they must face barriers in foreign markets that are intended to protect the domestic producer and prevent or at least restrict foreign goods from entering.

Since industry is a general term covering a great many products and processes, the less-developed country is faced with the problem of whom to contact for the kind of highly specialized assistance needed. Despite the ubiquity of the commercial representatives of the larger industrial powers, their character as salesmen makes them suspect. Because the specialized agencies of the United Nations, as originally established, included no organization concerned with industry, responsibility for that area fell to the general Secretariat, a fact which the less-developed countries regarded as an unfortunate makeshift in the U.N. structure. As a result of their insistence, the United Nations Industrial Development Organization (UNIDO) was established. UNIDO and the Inter-American Export Promotion Center hope to close the gap by making information available on suppliers, prices, quality, and delivery terms of industrial equipment, by establishing a roster of industrial consultants according to their specialized skills, and by operating an industrial service geared to solve specific industrial problems. This will be helpful to those who know what questions to ask. Where production already exists—furniture, pottery, metal work, shoemaking, and all the rest—there is still no simple way to obtain information on improved techniques although international business and trade associations are already providing technical assistance in some cases.

A growing volume of foreign capital has been moving directly into industry in the less-developed countries, usually bringing along experience and skill, and the U.S. government has done what it could to encourage private flows (see Chapter 10). However, AID's direct assistance in support of specific industrial projects has been declining, except for the recent development of so-called Cooley loans; that is, lending local currencies available as counterpart funds to American enterprises. On the other hand, the Export-Import Bank is heavily engaged in industrial development by supplying loan funds for projects involving American exports.

* * *

With a greater appreciation in the 1960s of the complexity of the growth process, the notion of economic development has been expanded into the broader concept of *social and* economic development. To be sure, health and education have always ranked high in technical assistance, but new emphasis has been placed on the special problems of rural community development, the rapid expansion of cities and of housing needs, and the improvement of essential government services relating to social security and welfare. Much of this activity requires relatively little foreign aid, except for technical assistance and possible budgetary help from the local currency, mobilized by program loans.

To a considerable degree, work in the social field involves institution-building. Governments and private groups have contributed to the development of cooperatives. In Latin America, between 1962 and 1966, such organizations grew from 16,800 with 5.7 million members to 26,000 with 8.7 million members, and the number of credit unions doubled during the same period. In several countries the scale of employment has grown to the point where labor unions are being formed, another area which has received assistance from the more advanced countries.

Recognition was accorded the area of social development, as distinct from the economic, when the United States in 1961 set up the Social Progress Trust Fund. Under an agreement with the Inter-American Development Bank, which was to act as administrator, $525 million was made available for use in Latin America. The original fund was virtually all committed by the end of 1965 in long-term, low-interest loans for land settlement and improved land use, housing for low-income groups, water supply and sewage facilities, and higher education. Since 1965, the IADB has continued making loans from its Fund for Special Operations, contributed to by the 20 member countries.

*   *   *

Another shift in emphasis has taken place since the mid-1960s. AID has set the expansion of food production and the lowering of birth rates in the less-developed countries as its highest priorities, presumably because of the threat to human survival from population increases that exceed the growth in the available food supply. Not all other donor countries reflect this assessment in their assistance programs, nor does giving priority to these two objectives undercut the importance of other fields of development. The need for better educated and trained manpower has also been given more and more attention.

Until the mid-1960s, agricultural development had a very low priority in the planning of the less-developed countries. Agriculture was often caught in a trap wherein land ownership was either held in estates that were too large or fragmented in plots that were too small; farm workers were sluggish and inefficient because they were badly fed and ill; the returns were insufficient to provide funds for investment; and there was no procedure whereby new methods could be developed or transmitted to the farmer. Industrialization was believed to be the engine of growth, and agriculture represented a lower form of economic activity. To be sure, any cash export crop such as citrus fruit or cocoa was regarded as being of strategic importance for economic growth, although there was a natural tendency to overexpand production and the erratic swings in the world prices of such commodities made planning difficult.

The new interest in agriculture was the reaction to a number of converging situations. Convincing statistics were brought forward by many experts emulating Malthus and pointing out that world population was growing at a faster rate than world food production and that there no longer were large, fertile, and adjacent areas awaiting the plow. While per capita food production in the less-developed countries was up 2 per cent in 1967 and 1968 over 1957–59, it was lower than in the early years of the decade.[4] Two consecutive monsoon failures in India produced a massive food shortage which threatened to exhaust India's supply of foreign exchange and thus wreck its development plan. And, finally, the accumulated wheat surplus in the hands of the major producers had been exhausted.

The picture is even more disturbing when looking to the future, since undernourishment is already widespread either because of an actual lack of sufficient food or because of poor nutrition. The situation is aggravated by the high rates of population growth, which are steadily expanding the number of consumers and by the tendency for a substantial part of any increases in per capita incomes to be spent for food. The threat of world-wide hunger is very real indeed.

There are two different approaches to the problem. The first is to handle present production less wastefully. Under this heading come a variety of actions from pest, disease, and weed control to improved shipping and storage facilities. Most of these improvements are desirable but require capital and in any event cannot increase the supply beyond the amount produced.

A much more promising, and open-ended approach is to increase the yield per acre. The differences in yield among countries appear to be surprisingly wide. The former, simple explanation that it was the result of differences in soil and methods of cultivation has now given way to the recognition of a wide variety of factors, ranging from government price policy and land tenure to water supply and farm practices.

After years of lagging agricultural growth, extraordinary increases in the yields of wheat and rice in Asia since 1967 suggest that an agricultural revolution may be taking place. Lester R. Brown reports that

> The 1968 Pakistan wheat harvest was up 37 per cent over the previous record, possibly an increase without precedent in any major country. India's wheat crop this year [1968] was up 35 per cent over the previous record; its total food grain harvest up 12 per cent. Ceylon's rice crop has increased 34 per cent during the past two years. The Philippines, with two consecutive dramatic gains in its rice crop, has apparently ended half a century of dependence on rice imports.[5]

At the core of this "green revolution" are the new cereal varieties, developed largely through the work of the Rockefeller and Ford Foundations. In contrast to the old varieties, the new require much more water and fertilizer, which must be carefully applied in precise amounts at specified stages in the growth cycle; but their shorter stalks are early maturing, hardier, and can be planted year round. Thus not only can two and three crops be harvested annually, but the yield is also often double that of crops planted with the old seeds. The new cultivation practices, being more sophisticated than the traditional ones, call for innovative change and enterprise on the part of farmers. This, as well as the breakthrough itself, has made it possible to bring into use various other agricultural improvements in farm management, irrigation methods, deep wells and pumps, more mechanized operations, and pest and disease control, which, though long known, have not been previously subject to a comparable push.

As the use of the new high-yield cereal varieties spreads and encouraging developments continue, a brief sigh of relief may be permitted. Yet while the promise of rapidly expanding food supplies should not be minimized, unsuspected diseases and pests afflicting the new strains may yet appear. More importantly, the up-trends that are forecast may not be able to keep pace indefinitely with projected demand if the world's population continues to grow at present rates.

The new technology will flourish best in a setting of relevant major economic, social, and political change in developing countries. It will, in turn, cause change. In some cases, price policy, intended to ease the problems of city dwellers, has taken away the farmer's incentive and must be revised. While the effort to improve the efficiency of farm operations must be given high priority, activities that directly support production, such as agricultural credit, transportation, storage facilities and marketing arrangements are required, as well as the balanced growth that will provide incentive goods and a rising effective demand.

To bring the new technology into widespread use is particularly difficult because it must be transmitted to millions of farmers widely dispersed in thousands upon thousands of villages. By comparison, setting up a steel mill is relatively easy, requiring but a few hundred persons to build it and the training of a few hundred more to operate it. In addition, the supplies of fertilizer, water, pumping equipment and other machinery must be greatly expanded. (Within eight years the consumption of fertilizer in India increased sixfold to 1,750 thousand tons nutrient content in 1968 despite complaints about its high cost and inefficient distribution.) The agricultural revolution thus involves huge capital investment, not to mention expanded extension services.

Greater research activity is needed to make further improvements in the new wheat and rice varieties, especially to adapt them to different ecological conditions. (The miracle rice is highly successful in West Pakistan, but in East Pakistan it has been attacked by a virus disease and bacterial blight.) Since there are many other agricultural products where little progress to improve yield has been made as yet, particularly for products raised in the tropics, concentrated research efforts already started in several international centers are sorely needed and may bring results comparable to those of the new wheat and rice strains. Already, in El Salvador a new dry bean variety has been developed whose yield is three times that of the old kinds. The use of oilseed proteins for human consumption is being actively studied, and in Latin America extensive marketing tests are being made of several different low-cost soft drinks high in protein and vitamin content.

Agriculture, more than most industries, is clearly dependent upon the internal resources and organization of a country, and only by its own efforts can a less-developed country significantly improve agricultural productivity. Nonetheless, foreign assistance not only has created the opportunity but must continue to play an important part in carrying forward the new agriculture. For example, in building up their own fertilizer industries, developing countries will have to secure from abroad new fertilizer plants, spare parts, certain raw materials, and also the initial capital. The water requirements call for pump wells, irrigation systems, and the like. Other needed products like insecticides will have to be imported as well. If the over-all result is a major change in farm output and income, it will mean development far beyond the narrow bounds of agriculture. Not only will agriculture require various inputs that can be supplied domestically, but since the bulk of the population lives in the countryside, improved rural conditions will be reflected in higher incomes and greater demand for consumer goods, thereby contributing to industrial development.

While the public discussion of the general problem has centered largely on Asia, the backwardness of agriculture is a general phenomenon in less-developed countries. Except for 1966 and 1968, well over one-half of American exports of wheat under concessional programs have gone to countries other than India and

Pakistan. For example, in 1969–70 Turkey will require the import of 850,000 metric tons of wheat. In fiscal year 1968–69, American sales agreements under PL 480 payable in foreign currency were made with 5 less-developed countries, soft-loan agreements repayable in dollars with an additional 17 countries, 5 countries were added under disaster relief and other emergency assistance, and still 3 more in the child feeding program, bringing the total number of countries involved to 30. In addition, under the aegis of the World Food Program, American foodstuffs went to 41 countries.

* * *

The greater interest in food and agriculture is seen in the assistance programs of the DAC members. Food itself has constituted an important part of their economic aid, the total thus provided having risen to a peak of $1,494 million in 1964, or 27 per cent of all official bilateral assistance. Since then it declined to $1,115 million, or 18 per cent in 1967; the amount provided on a grant or grant-like basis was cut in half while the amount provided on a loan basis increased. The bulk of these food shipments has come from the United States.

To be sure, the farmers in the developed world could produce much more food than their governments will permit. Despite restrictive controls of one kind or another on production, the world has possessed surpluses of wheat, rice, and other products until recently. Where there were price-support programs, as in the United States, it was relatively simple with the supply at hand to alleviate conditions of food shortage in many less-developed countries. As the surpluses became exhausted, the United States somewhat modified its domestic programs aimed at restricting production. The world wheat picture changed dramatically in 1968–69, with production higher than ever before and surpluses beginning to build up again. World trade in wheat dropped about 10 per cent, largely as the result of reduced shipments to India and Pakistan because of their increased yields. As a result, wheat stocks on April 1, 1969, in the five main exporting countries, were 600 million bushels higher than one year previously. The problem would not exist if it were easy to get the products from where they are produced to where they are needed. Here again, the obstacles are the transfer problem and poverty conditions.

While the use of aid to provide food is an immediate necessity, building up food production is the long-run requirement. It has frequently been argued that the provision of food aid has taken the pressure off the need to develop local agriculture, and the United States now links the provision of food aid to programs for agricultural improvement. So far as capital projects are concerned, bilateral assistance commitments directly related to agriculture were about $200 million per year in 1967 and 1968. The IBRD and IDA show growing interest with new loans as follows: $87 million to 10 countries in 1966–67, $172 million to 12 countries in 1967–68, and $367 million to 24 countries in 1968–69, for fertilizer plants, water control, rural roads, and other related activities.

In 1966, agriculture was declared to be one of the three priority areas for the U.S. development assistance program, along with health and education. As a result, AID committed $569 million for agricultural assistance in 1968 and, before the drastic congressional cuts, had planned to commit about $800 million for this purpose in 1969. Much the largest part was earmarked for fertilizers and their manufacture. In addition, since 1960 some 4,000 Asian agriculturists have been trained under American auspices. The sort of operation involved is illustrated by the case of Kenya, where a composite effort by the U. S. Department of Agriculture, the Kenyan Ministry of Agriculture, and a commercial African seed company devised a complete program to introduce the use of new seeds with recommendations for cultural practices, which resulted in doubling and trebling the yields of maize.[6]

The United Kingdom, Italy, Japan, and the Scandinavian countries have devoted a larger share of their assistance to agriculture than the United States has. However, the new phase will have much higher capital requirements than in earlier years. Some of the need is being met by foreign private investment. It is most unfortunate that the cut in American assistance and the long delay in replenishing IDA are likely to bear heavily on the emerging possibility for rapid and substantial progress.

The new agriculture raises many problems beyond the immediate ones of supplying the requisite inputs, the necessary facilities for storage and transport, and essential extension work. It may create new class distinctions among farmers, with the progressive farmers becoming much richer while the smaller, poorer and less venturesome ones fall farther behind. It may create a rural elite with new political strength. It may raise serious problems of price policy, or cause a complete revision of existing trade channels. It may provide a new market for consumer goods which will require a balancing development in industry. And the possibility of mul- tiple cropping may conflict with weather conditions and with man-made holiday and ceremonial schedules. Thus, the new agri- culture may prove to be much more than a "green revolution," as it introduces extensive change in social and political structures and in international relations.[7]

* * *

Perhaps more important than increasing the food supply is the long-run problem of population.[8] Even if some unknown force should completely stop all reproduction on the globe so that there would be no births though deaths would continue, the normal growth to adulthood of those under 15, who comprise one-third of existing population, would add much more to demand over the next twenty years than mortality would reduce it. More realistic assumptions made by the United Nations Population Commis- sion, which assume a gradual reduction of 50 per cent in fertility in the less-developed areas and a lesser decline in the developed countries where the birth rate is already lower, suggest that world population, estimated at 2,998 million in 1960 will be 4,554 mil- lion in 1980 and 6,726 million in the year 2,000, with most of the increase in the less-developed countries. It has been optimistically estimated that an additional energetic world-wide effort by gov- ernments and international agencies to reduce fertility beyond that needed to bring about the 50 per cent reduction might fur- ther reduce the estimated population at the end of the century by one billion. However, even 5.7 billion individuals would be nearly double the number of persons alive in 1960.

While there may be infinite quibbles about estimating future population figures, the narrow differences among demographers do not challenge the main implication of their projections. Two other recent statistical exercises brought the population projection into sharper focus. One was the lagging rate of growth in agri- cultural production, so that the long discredited Malthusian pre- diction of inevitable world famine conditions suddenly seemed real. The second was the sad fact that the rate of economic growth of the less-developed countries was substantially reduced in its effect, when spread over a larger and larger population.

The impact of population growth is far more than merely a matter of food. Each new person adds a burden on national resources—dwellings, schools, clothing, etc.—and, as an adult, may not be able to make an equivalent contribution to the national income. The great efforts to expand education in the less-developed countries have not reduced the number of illiterates because of population growth. Slums cannot be emptied despite vast housing projects, and the birth rate in rural areas leads to further migration to the cities. At the present time, average economic growth rates of about 5 per cent in both developed and less-developed countries are reduced to 3.6 and 2.5 per cent, respectively, when put on a per capita basis. The result of such meager progress for the individual in the less-developed countries may be not just starvation, disease, and ignorance, but growing discontent and dissatisfaction with the forces of order and discipline.

One other aspect of the population explosion, of which people are becoming aware, is its effect on the quality of life itself. Whether it is the limitations on world resources, the growing traffic problem on highways, the difficulty of finding uncrowded recreational areas, or the growing pollution of air, water, and quiet, the trouble stems basically from increasing numbers.

For reasons largely related to religion and social tradition, plus a widespread belief that a larger population gave a nation greater strength, governments in the past became involved in population problems, if at all, through legislation restricting information on contraception and prohibiting abortion. The new prospects for some limitation on population growth reflect the discovery that a substantial majority of women in all societies and cultures want to limit their child-bearing, the realization that population growth retards per capita betterment, the development of new contraceptive methods, and the adoption by some governments of programs to promote family planning. An effective program of family planning cannot be established overnight, but recent efforts in India and Pakistan are already beginning to show results. In South Korea and Taiwan, it is estimated that more than 25 per cent of the women of child-bearing age are now either sterilized or practicing modern and highly effective methods of contraception. In fact, in Taiwan, the birth rate has fallen from over 40 per 1,000 population per year to below 30. The outstanding case is that of Singapore, where the annual rate of population growth has fallen since 1957 from 44 per 1,000 to 15, which is generally attributed to the widespread acceptance of family planning methods. By the middle of 1969, 28 countries in the less-developed world had instituted official family planning policies.

While the basis of any program must be the use of techniques directly limiting family size, there are a variety of influences (some of which can be shaped by government policy) that affect the desire for numerous children. The conditions of urban life are less conducive to large families than those of rural life. Education tends to increase the sense of parental responsibility. There is a close relationship between higher income levels and family size. A large proportion of women in the working force is another deterrent, and reduced dependence on the family as the only source of old-age security makes children less necessary as insurance. Instead of encouraging large families through family allowances, bonuses may be given to men and women coming to birth-control clinics, and privileges such as free delivery at child-birth, free schooling, and tax deductions or family allowances may be taken away after some stated number of children.

The greatest difficulty in carrying out a national family program is that, like agriculture, it involves individuals dispersed throughout the country. The organizational requirement for an effectively functioning program to reach all families is tremendous. Clinics must be established in all the villages, which require a large number of specially trained personnel; educational material must be prepared; and a broad popular understanding and acceptance of family planning must be created.

Most of the outside assistance has been given in the past by private agencies and foundations, especially the International Planned Parenthood Federation, the Population Council, and the Ford and Rockefeller Foundations, the first two of which have frequently had direct financial support from governments. Aid was devoted chiefly to technical research, building local family planning organizations, improving demographic work, and carrying on various limited local experiments. The remarkable research progress made during the last decade clearly makes family planning a practical program. Nevertheless, available methods are not fully satisfactory, and further research is perhaps the most important immediate requirement.

For a long time the only government directly engaged in operational family-planning projects in less-developed countries was Sweden, and its record goes back only to 1958. It was not until

1964 that other countries began to provide such aid, particularly the United States and the United Kingdom.

In 1967 the Congress added Title X to the Foreign Assistance Act under the heading "Programs Relating to Population Growth." It was declared to be the sense of the Congress that voluntary family planning programs to provide knowledge and medical facilities "can make a substantial contribution to improve health, family stability, greater individual opportunity, economic development, a sufficiency of food, and a higher standard of living." Except for a restriction against programs involving coercion, the authority was very broad. In discussing this provision, the Senate Committee on Foreign Relations noted that the amount "is a floor, not a ceiling. The committee hopes the AID will divert even more funds to population programs if it becomes feasible to do so. If population problems are not solved, the economic development efforts of AID are doomed to failure."

In 1967 U.S. commitments were $4 million; in 1968 the Congress specifically earmarked $35 million for family planning programs and made available an even greater amount of counterpart funds. Assistance was provided to 25 countries, including major aid for programs in India, Korea, Pakistan, and the Philippines. In the appropriation for 1969–70, the Congress set aside $75 million for this purpose, with an authorization for $100 million in 1970–71.

In July 1969, President Nixon sent a message to Congress in which he stated that he had asked all the relevant agencies to give population and family planning high priority for attention, personnel, research, and funding within the aid programs. He also proposed the creation by Congress of a Commission on Population Growth and the American Future, and increased activity in research, training, and family services within the United States.

Other countries are also active in this field but to a much lesser degree, although Sweden is still one of the leaders. Commitments made by DAC members in 1968 were estimated by the OECD Development Center to be $80 million, and $105 million in 1969, although actual disbursements may not have been more than $40 million.

Assistance has taken the form of help in training personnel and setting up demonstration projects, in providing contraceptive devices and factories for making them, in contributing transport and other equipment, and in helping to finance the rapidly rising administrative costs of the whole enterprise. Thus far, the amounts of assistance which actually could be used have not been great and those programs probably will never be a heavy drain on foreign aid funds.

Not all of the developed countries are committed to family planning, while some of the less-developed simply do not approve, or feel that it is a racist plot to weaken them. Many of the African countries do not acknowledge the existence of population pressure, and some Latin American countries face political difficulties in this connection. The disaffection of some members prevented the United Nations from moving into the field except by way of demography; however, in December 1966, the General Assembly reversed its former position of noninvolvement and opened the door for a cautious program. This did not lead to much action, and in 1968 the Secretary-General established a Population Trust Fund to which countries might make contributions. It has a staff of population program officers who assist less-developed countries in determining their population problems and assistance needs. A recent study, given specific endorsement by President Nixon in his message to Congress, has suggested that, in order to obtain strong central coordination and direction, a Commissioner for Population be appointed to have the central role in planning and coordinating assistance in this field by the United Nations and the specialized agencies, and that the target for the Population Trust Fund be $100 million per year, developed over a three-year period.

The U.N. Trust Fund for Population Problems, supported largely by the United States, is administered by the United Nations Development Program, which established the director, as proposed. The basic intention of this suggestion was to avoid the delaying influence of bureaucratic confusion and competition by centralizing the responsibility for family planning in one office. However, the vested interests were successful and the proposal was supplanted by an agreement whereby the Fund, like other U.N. activities, is subject to policy participation by various agencies such as the Economic and Social Council, Population Commission, Population Division in the U.N. Secretariat, UNESCO, World Health Organization, and the regional commissions. In addition, the IBRD has announced its willingness to finance projects associated with family-planning programs.

Probably no other expenditure can have as great an impact on the level of living, for it is in per capita terms that the standard is measured. If reduced fertility can lower the increase in population by one billion in thirty years, it will occur largely in the less-developed countries, and might amount to as much as a 25 per cent increase in the average per capita income. It seems obvious, therefore, that the industrialized countries should do all that they can by word and deed to encourage and support these new and rapidly growing efforts.

* * *

A general review such as this is likely to lose sight of the wide differences among the less-developed countries and the fact that the strategic requirements for development vary not only among them but from time to time in each country. At one time, it was widely argued that unbalanced programs were the most effective stimulant to development since advances in one sector made advances necessary elsewhere. But it was equally possible that the lagging sectors would hold back the prospective advance. Some have argued that development stems from the availability of electric power, while others regard expanding exports as the key to economic growth.

Probably each of these and other theories is true at some time in some country. The real point is that social and economic development encompass so many elements in a country's life that no pattern of growth is universal. The variety of uses to which foreign assistance is put is itself an indication of a pragmatic approach, whereby a country tries on a case-by-case basis to make the best possible use of the limited resources available.

8 · To Which Countries?

For some of the richer countries, the choice of where to send bilateral financial assistance is largely a reflection of historical, political, and cultural ties with certain less-developed countries. One might have expected that former colonies would have a special resentment against their former rulers, but this has not proved to be the case. Habits of taste and familiarity with products and trademarks, plus long-established trade channels and monetary links, do not change when a new national flag is raised. Indeed, at the time of separation, commitments have often been entered into for future assistance. Thus the British, on announcing their intention to withdraw from the Far East, promised Singapore £50 million and Malaysia £25 million over the next five years to ease the transition.

An examination of the trade patterns of a number of ex-colonies before and after independence shows that, although usually a wider spread in the sources of imports develops, partly because there are now various suppliers of economic assistance, the former metropolitan power is likely to continue to be the chief purchaser of the less-developed country's products. Continuation of trade with the former power is encouraged by efforts to avoid an abrupt erection of trade barriers upon independence, since presumably none existed within the empire. Thus, when the Philippines became independent, the United States agreed to increase tariffs on Philippine goods to the level of foreign countries gradually over a twenty-year period. The arrangements between the Common Market and its associated members (former colonies) also prevented the sudden shift from no tariff to the

128

tariffs levied against foreign countries. In the case of the United Kingdom, those ex-colonies which joined the Commonwealth obtained special trade preferences.

In addition to economic ties, other forces tended to maintain the special relationship. Buyers in the colonial areas were familiar with business and commercial practices in the metropole and vice versa. Often many personal links persisted, for higher education was usually provided in the metropole while many of its colonial officers became deeply attached to the country in which they served. Familiarity with people and with problems also makes setting up and operating assistance programs easier on both sides. It is not surprising, therefore, to find that most British, French, Belgian, and Dutch aid goes to former parts of their empires. Italy has maintained a special interest in Somalia. And most assistance to Latin America comes from the United States.

As a further factor, there are less-developed overseas areas which are still dependencies. If colonies had been listed as recipients of assistance only when they became independent, the amount of foreign aid would have seemed to increase tremendously in the 1960s. The inclusion or exclusion of aid flows to overseas territories in the statistical records is a matter which each donor country has decided according to the nature of the political arrangements and the way appropriations are handled. The United States, for example, does not include flows to Puerto Rico, most of which are indirect, but does include aid to its Trust Territory in the Pacific covering the Caroline, Marshall, and Mariana Islands except Guam. If Denmark included its assistance to Greenland, it would significantly raise its ranking. Australia gives two-thirds of its aid to Papua and New Guinea; France about one-third to its overseas departments and territories; about 40 per cent of Netherlands aid in 1964–66 went to Dutch overseas territories; the United Kingdom gives about 8 per cent to its diminishing list of outlying areas. Portugal is a special case in which all of its foreign aid goes to its overseas territories, in spite of insisting in various international forums that they are politically integrated with Portugal and that hence there are no plans for their independence. On a per capita basis, bilateral aid received by overseas dependencies averaged $16.66 per person in 1966–68 as compared with the over-all average of $3.68. The highest was $162.81 per capita for the French overseas departments and territories. All such cases of overseas territories accounted for 7.1

per cent of the total net official flow in 1967 recorded in DAC statistics.

The patterns of the past are somewhat less important for the United States, Germany, and a number of the smaller nations. The multilateral agencies, which have a world-wide membership, are virtually compelled to be global in dispensing their assistance, and the strictly regional agencies like the Inter-American Development Bank must not play favorites within their areas.

Whether or not there are historical reasons controlling the distribution of aid, geographic patterns once established tend to change relatively slowly for operating reasons as well as political considerations. Many projects and programs take years to complete, and the working relationships established over the period tend to generate further flows. As a matter of fact, unless a country is increasing the amount of its assistance, it usually has little leeway for any rapid and considerable revision of its geographical pattern. A measure of the extent of this inertia is given in the 1969 DAC Chairman's Report. Correlation coefficients calculated on the basis of aid flows to recipients over successive years for the period 1960 to 1968 were always very high, the lowest being 0.92 for 1960 and 1961, advancing to 0.98 for 1964 and 1965, and 0.97 in the later years. Thus there is very little change from year to year in the total country pattern.

While the American program is truly world-wide, with the number of potential recipients increasing as new countries are born, there has been a tendency in recent years for the bulk of the total distributed by AID to become more and more concentrated. Of all bilateral programs planned for 1968–69, three-fifths of the official assistance goes to eleven countries, called "development-emphasis countries," whose status can be roughly described as follows: (a) building up momentum (Morocco, Congo-Kinshasa, Indonesia); (b) in midstream (India, Pakistan, Chile, Colombia, Tunisia, Ghana); and (c) in transition to self-sustaining development (Turkey and Korea). One-fifth of all aid is for Vietnam, Laos, and Thailand, and the remaining one-fifth is for all the other less-developed countries. Other elements in the U.S. program, such as the Food for Peace program, the loans by the Export-Import Bank, and the Peace Corps show a much greater scattering among countries.

Most other bilateral suppliers are more concentrated geographically than the United States in their distribution of assistance. Both France and the United Kingdom have expressed the desire to broaden their distributions but the special claims have prevented them from accomplishing much in this respect while the so-called Franc Area and the Commonwealth still dominate their programs. For the smaller supplier countries, there has been a tendency toward greater concentration on fewer recipients because of their smaller diplomatic apparatus and the difficulty of administering assistance effectively in widely scattered areas. In addition, it is generally recognized that significant changes are more likely to take place as the result of cumulative interacting forces rather than a minor contribution here and there. The Netherlands has the policy of concentrating its assistance, other than that for its dependencies, in countries for which there are consortia or consultative groups, thus benefiting from the special activity of the managing agency. The multilateral agencies, on the other hand, have built-in pressures for almost universal distribution.

The trend in the United States toward geographical concentration of AID programs was reinforced in the Foreign Assistance Act of 1966, which set specific limitations on the number of countries other than members of the Alliance for Progress to receive aid—although the President might, and did, exceed these limits if he determines that it is in the national interest to do so.

There can be no doubt that the almost global character of the United States program has tended to disperse energy and interest, while adding to the problems of administration. Nevertheless, the problem of development is global and the United States is not operating on a limited sphere-of-interest basis. Its preferences should be indicated more by relative amounts than exclusions. In 1961–62 there were new AID loans and authorizations to 81 less-developed countries, and other assistance programs brought the number up to 88. For 1965–66, the AID total was reduced to 72 countries, but other assistance programs, particularly Food for Freedom, increased the number to 89. Although the largest number of countries were in Africa, half of them had net obligations and loan authorizations in 1966 of less than $1.3 million each, often in the technical assistance category.

While the non-AID programs continue their relatively wide geographical distribution, the number of countries receiving offi-

TABLE 20

Bilateral Country Programs of the United States,
Fiscal Years 1966–67 to 1969–70
(*Number of Countries*)

	1966–67	1967–68	1968–69	1969–70
Technical assistance	65	60	53	42
Development loans	38	27	25	31
Supporting assistance	16	12	9	7
Africa	33	29	21	12
Non-Africa	41	35	34	33
Total countries involved	74	64	55	45

Source: AID.

cial U.S. aid in bilateral programs decreased rapidly in the last half of the 1960s (See Table 20). The increased concentration is clearly evident, though it is in large part the result of reduced programs in Africa, and of technical assistance activity. While the presentation of the 1970–71 program noted a reduction of only two countries in the total list, it stressed the increased concentration of most of the assistance in a few countries (98 per cent of supporting assistance to 3 countries, 83 per cent of country program funds to 8 countries). The technical assistance program has been reduced since 1967 outside of Latin America from 45 to 22 countries.

The imposition of number-of-country limits on AID programs by Congress might have made it necessary for the Agency to concentrate its development loan efforts on larger countries, except for special cases such as Korea and Vietnam. However, since the Agency itself is operating at present well within the numerical limits, the congressional set of numbers would not appear to be restricting its activities. Nevertheless, it is important to keep in mind that, unfortunately, a large number of small countries do exist. Individually they may not be economically or politically important, but the quantity of aid which they could absorb would not be large. Fortunately, the U.S. program includes a limited appropriation called the Self Help Fund which ambassadors may draw upon in very small sums. Thus in a country where there is no American aid program as such, it is still possible to make a slight demonstration of American interest and concern in its development. It would be a move in the right direction if the ceilings for this particular purpose were somewhat higher.

* * *

There are cases where the allocation of assistance has been explicitly related to some political objective. Assistance given other less-developed countries by Taiwan, plus the irritating behavior of the Communist Chinese in some of their assistance efforts, have increased the opposition in the United Nations to the admission of mainland China. The Federal Republic of Germany, under the so-called Hallstein doctrine, formerly did not provide aid to countries that recognized East Germany. Israel and Taiwan have built up friendly relations with a number of African countries by means of technical assistance. In addition to such general policies there are many instances where assistance from one country to another is affected by a changed political situation. Indonesia is a clear example. Western aid, which had been sizable, was largely withdrawn when Sukarno not only spent heavily on expanding the military but also permitted destructive attacks on Western embassies, libraries, and private property. When Sukarno was deposed, the new government changed the country's political orientation; after a test-period, Western countries renewed the flow of assistance.

A more detailed picture of the variety of elements which may enter into country allocations can be seen from the record of the United States, where more is known about the process than in other donor countries because of the public debate each year on the program. Since the very start, Congress has been concerned with the allocation of aid among countries. Beginning with the Marshall Plan, it has always required a detailed description of prospective country programs. Although the proposals are not binding, it is expected by the Congress that there will be little deviation from the presentation. In the case of Latin America, because of the special nature of the Alliance for Progress, the Congress allocates a lump sum for a geographic region, but here also prospective country allocations are required. The approval of U.S. membership and the appropriation of funds for the regional banks are the only other instances of legislative action related to a region.

That the appropriation should take the form of firm country

allocations has seldom been seriously suggested. In the absence of an enormous staff, Congress would have to rely in any event upon the executive branch and would have to freeze the pattern many months before the programs were to begin. The present leverage for negotiations involving domestic policies would be weakened, and recipients would feel that the fixed amounts were theirs as a matter of right. Thus when Congress, unbidden by the executive, added to the Marshall Plan appropriation a special sum of $50 million for Spain, the Spanish Ambassador called immediately at the Department of State to find out where he should go to collect the money. It was only after considerable difficulty that he was persuaded to discuss how the funds were to be used. Given the number of potential recipients, the variety of programs, the lack of technical knowledge and immediate political interest in most of the country details, and the great sensitivity on the part of individual recipients, it is not surprising that Congress has expressed itself on this subject more in general policy terms than in specific recommendations.

In 1968 and in later debates, this tendency showed itself in a general disposition to continue pressure on the administration to hold down the number of aid-receivers. Except in a few Committee discussions, individual cases were usually not cited to challenge or defend specific allocations, and in general debate the aim was largely to assert the strength or weakness of the program, as illustrated in the following exchange on the Alliance for Progress:

> Mr. Gross: Despite all this looting of the U.S. Treasury, there are just as many military supported dictators and oligarchies—just as many peons and peasants in Latin America as there were when this program was launched. . . .
>
> Mr. Gonzalez: Over the past 7 years, Latin America, with sustained assistance from the United States, has gone far toward realizing the goals of the Alliance for Progress. Advances over a broad front, including economic growth, improved social justice and greater political stability, have been substantiated. . . . Trust, confidence, and mutual respect . . . have been generated between the United States and its southern neighbors.[1]

India was even more frequently commented on than the Alliance for Progress. Some resented India's position on Vietnam or felt that economic development there was a hopeless effort. Others cited India as giving remarkable evidence of achievement, stressing particularly the possible breakthrough in agricultural production, fertilizer use, and family planning. From time to time, general references to Israel, Nigeria, Guinea, Uganda, Pakistan, Liberia, and Egypt appeared in the debate.

The problem with respect to naming individual countries in the legislation came up in 1969 in the debates over the military aid appropriation, when the House proposed to earmark funds for aircraft for Korea and Taiwan. Among the elements contributing to the ultimate defeat of the proposals was the fact that Congress had never specified recipients by name in general-category appropriations. To be sure, since the administration presents its detailed program to the Committees and the Committees are critical of shifts which have not been discussed in advance, the administration is not entirely free to make changes even within the legislative generalities. In the particular case noted above, it is clearly expected that the Korean aircraft will be included in the allocation of military aid, while the needs of Taiwan are being taken care of in another way by the Department of Defense.

Congress, however, frequently considers prohibitions of one kind or other on economic assistance. Those actions are taken on the grounds that, as supplier, the United States is free to select the recipients of its assistance and that aid should be withheld from some countries for policy reasons. Thus in the 1968 debates, various amendments were proposed that would tighten restrictions on aid to Cuba or to countries trading with Cuba, that requested the President to negotiate with Israel concerning Phantom planes or as an alternative that, pending an arms agreement with the U.S.S.R., it is the sense of the Congress that Israel be provided with an adequate deterrent force; that Jordan be included in the prohibition on granting aid to the U.A.R.; and that would remove the power of the President to waive the restriction on aid to Communist countries (a 1962 action) until the release of the *Pueblo* crew. Other proposed restrictions (discussed in Chapter 13) were not aimed so much at specific countries as at various forms of behavior.

Proposals of this kind have been made each year according to the temper of the time. Some of them are rejected, some are framed as "the sense of the Congress," some as requests that the President act in one way or another, some as requirements but allowing exceptions where the President feels that it is in the national interest, and some as firm requirements permitting no exceptions.

Beginning with the rewritten Act of 1961, prohibitions against providing assistance to specific countries, which stem from political reasons, were included in the authorization or in the appropriations act as follows and continued in subsequent years unless otherwise noted:

1961. Cuba.
Countries dominated or controlled by the international Communist movement.
1962. Eighteen Communist countries were listed by name.
1963. Indonesia, unless the President finds national interest. (Prohibition withdrawn in 1966.)
1965. North Vietnam.
1965. United Arab Republic, unless the President finds national interest. (Food sales had been restricted in the Agricultural Trade Development and Assistance Act of 1954.)

Under the heading of political action might also be included the 1967 statement that "it is the sense of the Congress that in any case in which any foreign country has severed diplomatic relations with the United States, the President should suspend assistance."

The Act also contains some general though not always clear political provisions. Thus in 1962 Congress stated that great attention should be given to those countries whose views on the world crisis coincide with those of the United States and which do not, as a result of assistance, divert their own economic resources to military or propaganda efforts directed against the United States.

*   *   *

It has sometimes been suggested that, as a general principle, assistance by DAC members should be withdrawn from countries which receive aid from Communist countries. Efforts should be made to discourage countries from accepting Soviet aid on the grounds that it represented a dangerous foot in the door, admitting propaganda and subversion and that Soviet aid in programming might not result in a wise use of resources. The statistical record might lead to the conclusion that Soviet aid was responsible for the withdrawal of Western aid from the United Arab Republic and Indonesia. In the U.A.R. case, the Western reduction of aid came in 1955 with Egypt's purchases of Soviet bloc military hardware and pledging of Egyptian exports as payment, the Aswan Dam contretemps, and the nationalization of the Suez Canal Company. In the case of Indonesia, there was a similar pattern in the military field plus a series of specific provocations. So far as India is concerned, the other country receiving substantial aid from Eastern Europe, the flow of Western aid has never been halted because of any flows of Soviet assistance. (Once it was stopped briefly as part of the effort to stop India-Pakistan hostilities.)

The Communist countries, it soon became evident, did not need to provide aid to the less-developed countries in order to have easy access, and the experts sent to carry out particular projects tended to form an isolated enclave rather than a humming propaganda hive. Withdrawal of Western aid would leave the country fully exposed to Communist political pressure without the defense of an alternative source of assistance. At UNCTAD, both developed and less-developed countries complained about the limited aid and trade policies of the Communist countries. Much more unfortunate has been the Communist willingness to provide large amounts of military hardware which have then required local resources and energy that could better be applied to economic development.

In general, it can be said that Communist economic assistance, except for that provided by the mainland Chinese, should not be opposed but rather welcomed as sharing in the development costs. Where Western aid has been reduced or stopped, it has been for much broader reasons of political alienation.

An attempt to establish aid policy that debarred Communist assistance would impose a political condition which the so-called neutralist countries would find very difficult to accept. Furthermore, it would imply that the Western nations were ready to meet fully the needs of the country involved. It is much wiser to keep channels open, being ready to provide a backstop for a country whenever it might feel that Communist pressure on its policies were excessive. The latter policy would weaken any attempt by Communist countries to use aid as a means of political pressure, nor would it require firm commitment from the West.

In a real sense, this was the position taken by the Western Powers in the Yugoslav case; by standing ready to give aid they gave Yugoslavia freedom of choice. What, then, might be regarded as political tests for denying aid to a less-developed country? As already pointed out in Chapter 2, many of these countries do not have, and probably cannot have, a so-called democratic government, which makes that an unreasonable requirement. Even destructive mob action cannot always be blamed on the government, for anti-American demonstrations may be the operation of individuals in the hope that the U.S. government will over-react. However, suppliers can hardly be expected to provide added resources to a country that is continually provocative and antagonistic. As this is not an easy formula to apply, suppliers tend to base their judgment upon various specific actions that a less-developed country might take, which indicate policy decisions. A number of such actions are listed in the aid legislation of the United States (see Chapter 13); although they are not always presented so explicitly by other supplier countries, they play an inevitable part in their foreign relations.

* * *

With the various bilateral donors being influenced by such a wide variety of special considerations and the multilateral agencies under pressure to recognize the needs of all their members, it might be expected that the resulting geographical distribution of the total aid would be globally unsystematic, though defensible on the part of each supplier. Actually, there has been surprisingly little critical analysis of assistance allocations by governments, in part because each supplier has its own preferred distribution and most recipients would distrust any effort to set agreed allocations as a device to keep down the total.

There are two further reasons why there has been so little discussion of the over-all aid distribution pattern: the picture of the actual distribution is not very distinct nor is there any agreement on what a proper basis should be. Since the problem relates in part to the ability to obtain foreign goods, intercountry comparisons would require data on the foreign exchange available to each country from its own sources and as well as data on assistance from all sources—bilateral, multilateral, and private—and then allowances would have to be made for qualitative differences and for outstanding obligations. Some African officials have complained that too much aid was going to India and that the United States was not giving sufficient recognition to African needs. Similarly, Latin Americans complained that too much European aid was going to Africa. The picture is likely to be confused by such shifts as occurred in Western European financial aid to Latin America during the 1960s, which declined sharply in the early years of the decade but recovered somewhat after 1966. At the same time, there has been substantial European participation in technical assistance and in scholarships. Obviously, any judgment concerning the distribution of aid must take all flows into account.

For the period 1965–67 a little less than one-half the total of official bilateral and multilateral aid went to Asia, and its share declined only insignificantly in 1968. India, Pakistan, Vietnam, and Korea were the four countries in the world with the largest total receipts. Africa received somewhat less than one-quarter, of which two-thirds went to countries south of the Sahara. Latin America absorbed about one-sixth in 1965–67, and a somewhat larger share in 1968. The less-developed countries of Europe, principally Greece, Spain, Turkey, and Yugoslavia, received between 5 and 6 per cent of the total flow. The flow of private capital was just the reverse, with Latin America leading and Africa second in total receipts. In his address at the Annual Meeting of the World Bank Group in September 1968, Mr. Mc-Namara suggested that while assistance to Asia still needed to be increased, the Group should give more attention to Latin America and Africa. A year later he reported that this geographical shift in emphasis was well under way.

Such studies as have been made have found little correlation between the present geographical pattern of assistance and various characteristics of the recipients. Nor is it at all clear what criteria should be used in examining the geographical pattern. Because, obviously, the amount of assistance must have some general relation to the size of the country, one approach has been to measure assistance received on a per capita basis, the implication being that there ought to be a more-or-less equal distribution according to population. That there is some relationship between population and aid has been indicated by various statistical analyses of the distribution of aid. The analyses usually end up with a formula which adds a related population-figure to a constant. Thus a recent DAC calculation,[2] covering the period 1960–67 and based on an average annual net bilateral official flow of $5.2 billion to 102 developing countries, showed that if each country were allowed $21.3 million plus $2 per head on its

1965 population, the result would have a correlation of 0.88 with the actual distribution. Over the period, the constant tended to shrink and size to become somewhat more important.

The apparent fit of this general formula is really only a demonstration that larger countries, size being measured by population, tend to get more assistance. In fact, aid on a per capita basis varies widely among recipients. Table 21 shows how the ten largest recipients fared in 1966–68. Countries which receive the

TABLE 21

OFFICIAL BILATERAL (DAC) AND MULTILATERAL ASSISTANCE TO
TEN LARGEST RECIPIENTS ON PER CAPITA BASIS, 1966–68

Country	Annual Average Net Receipts ($ million)	Population (million)	Per Capita Assistance ($)
India	1,191	514	2.3
Pakistan	480	121	4.0
Vietnam	467	17	27.5
Korea	253	30	8.5
Indonesia	207	110	1.9
Brazil	205	86	2.4
Turkey	204	33	6.2
Chile	145	9	16.3
Colombia	126	19	6.6
Mexico	117	46	2.6
Total, 10 largest recipients	3,395	885	3.8
Total, all less-developed countries	7,067	1,673	4.2

Source: Development Assistance Committee, OECD.

larger flows of assistance are on the list not merely because of their size, but because many of them are special cases; Vietnam, Korea, Chile, and Colombia are all relatively small countries. Furthermore, the very size of the assistance programs to large countries is a handicap. For example, to bring the largest program, that of India, up to the present average per capita level would require it to receive another $800 million annually. Given the many differences among the less-developed countries and the forms of assistance, it would be a very naïve goal to try to equalize assistance on a per capita basis, although such an approach does make a kind of adjustment for size and points out the exceptional cases.

The inverse relationship of assistance to size is much clearer. The tendency for small countries, measured by population, to receive relatively more aid might be expected not only because they are much less able to be self-sufficient but also because many projects such as power plants or improved harbors have a minimum size. Undoubtedly the political pressure on the multilateral agencies to serve all their members also has a bearing. No matter which test is applied for measuring aid—population, the percentage of imports, or the percentage of gross domestic product —small countries dominate the top rankings, as Table 22 shows.

TABLE 22

THE TEN LEADING COUNTRIES IN NET OFFICIAL BILATERAL AND MULTILATERAL AID RECEIPTS PER CAPITA AND PERCENTAGE OF IMPORTS AND GDP, 1966–68

Country	Aid Per Capita ($)	Aid as Percentage of Imports of Goods and Services		Aid as Percentage of Gross Domestic Product	
Malta	53.8	Laos	217.8	Laos	34.9
Liberia	31.6	Afghanistan	71.6	So. Vietnam	20.3
				Congo	
Israel	30.7	Rwanda	67.9	(Braz.)	16.4
Congo					
(Braz.)	27.7	So. Vietnam	54.3	Liberia	15.0
So. Vietnam	27.5	Mali	53.2	Somalia	14.2
Gabon	26.9	Upper Volta	53.2	Jordan	11.8
Jordan	25.9	Niger	50.7	Malawi	11.0
Laos	24.4	Chad	50.2	Malta	10.3
Guyana	19.4	India	43.8	Rwanda	10.0
Tunisia	18.3	Dahomey	39.9	Dahomey	9.0
All less-developed countries	4.2		15.3		2.7

Source: Development Assistance Committee, OECD.

Except for India in ninth place in the imports ranking, no large country appears on any list, and Guyana, ninth in per capita ranking, is the only country in the Western Hemisphere. Although the table does not show that the distribution of aid gives proper weight to small countries, it does show that many of them are well above the average, no matter what measure is used.

*   *   *

In a review of the geographical distribution of aid, it would seem reasonable to argue that aid should be related to need and that countries with the lowest per capita income should be given priority. But here the problem of absorptive capacity arises because of the lack of infrastructure and trained manpower and an under-developed civil service. Something has blocked economic development in these poorer countries, making it doubtful that an injection of large amounts of foreign capital would break the barriers. At their stage of development, technical assistance, which is a much less costly form of aid, may be of greater help. However, of the ten countries highest on the list for technical assistance received per capita, six (Jordan, Tunisia, Gabon, Liberia, Zambia, and Vietnam) were also on the corresponding list for capital assistance. As might be expected, official assistance seems to pay more attention to the poverty criterion, whereas private flows go to the more advanced of the less-developed countries. Compared with the flow to the much poorer countries in Asia and Africa, less official assistance from all DAC members is going to the relatively rich countries of Latin America and the Mediterranean area; but private flows are largest to Latin America, with Africa in second place. Of course, there is wide divergence in both forms of assistance among individual countries.

Any evaluation of the weight given to "need" by comparing per capita income with aid flows runs into two difficulties. The first is that the relative amount of foreign exchange which less-developed countries earn varies according to their natural resources, and this affects their need for foreign assistance. Second, the average level does not reflect the distribution of income, which in turn bears on the extent of poverty. Even the developed countries have limited statistics on this subject, while almost nothing is known about income distribution in the less-developed countries. Furthermore, the situation is not assistance that seems in the first instance to benefit those with higher income may actually reach the very poor. Although some well-to-do group may be sponsoring a new fertilizer plant, the result is to increase the farmers' productivity, ease food shortages in the cities, and increase government revenues.

One explicit policy statement on the subject of geographical aid allocation was made by Felipe Herrera, President of the Inter-American Development Bank, when he said that, by the end of 1967,

> the bank had provided, in per capita terms, about twice as much financing to the less developed countries [within Latin America] as to the intermediate and large countries. Analysis of our loans to the "less developed countries" shows they were made at far lower average interest rates, on longer terms, and that they were for larger amounts, in proportion to the local counterpart funds, than were applicable to loans to the other member countries. . . . It also is to be noted that this approach is used not only toward those countries classified as relatively less developed but also toward certain depressed areas within those countries which on the whole show a greater progress or a higher degree of development— areas like the Brazilian northeast, certain provinces in Argentina, the extreme northern and southern parts of Chile, and the *Sierra* and the mountains in Peru.[3]

In the consensus of Viña del Mar, drawn up by the Latin American countries in 1969, they agreed that priority should be given to "the relatively less developed in the region."

Actually, the poverty test is probably applied less often to the quantity of aid than to the terms on which it is extended. As general policy, the United Kingdom gives its interest-free loans to the poorer countries. France, though perhaps for other reasons, gives its grant funds almost entirely to its former colonies and present overseas territories but makes loans to other and usually richer less-developed countries. The World Bank Group has limited its allocations of soft-loan funds from IDA to countries whose per capita income is below the $250 per capita level. Since most donors provide technical assistance on a grant basis and such assistance is appropriately a higher proportion of the aid given the poorest countries (except for India, Pakistan, and the Middle East), they also receive a kind of unplanned preference in terms of payment requirements.

Still another way of giving special help to "the least advanced of the developing countries" was proposed at UNCTAD II, namely that they should be given trade preferences of especially long duration. The question of how to define the countries to be included in this special category was put off by suggesting that the decision be made on a case-by-case basis.

It has been urged that special support should be given the poorest countries to improve their public services, particularly in education and health, and that an international agency should be created to operate such a scheme.[4] While there is much to be said for being specially concerned about the poorest countries, it is not clear that emphasis should be limited to education and health—public administration, road-building, and road-maintenance might equally well be strategic areas of extra attention. Nor is it clear that some new agency is required. It might be more effective to insist that the existing agencies give more attention to the poorest countries.

* * *

For a period in the early 1960s, the United States claimed to give priority to countries that were approaching the point where they would no longer need concessionary aid—a kind of poverty test in reverse, measured in terms of foreign-exchange earnings. Presumably this would speed up the process of reducing the number of recipients and, incidentally, permit talk of "success" in Marshall Plan terms. Self-sufficiency in this context has no reference to the country's achievement of some target level of per capita income, but rather to a healthy balance-of-payments position in which the country can either earn its way directly with current foreign-exchange earnings or borrow on commercial terms. The test for aid allocation would be the prospective success of expanding a country's earnings of foreign exchange through commodity exports or services like tourism. Thus Taiwan is regarded as no longer needing aid, although its per capita income is estimated at $250 per year. Iran also was regarded as having achieved self-support in 1968 when the U.S. AID mission there was formally closed. Although its per capita income was estimated to be $280 in 1968, its growth rate in terms of gross national product had averaged 10.4 per cent for the 1965-68 period, and its petroleum resources gave it a strong foreign-exchange position.

There is little evidence that this principle has had any important general effect on allocation, except for the terminal point of cut-off. If it had, it would imply giving less aid to the countries which are making the least progress and thus tend to stretch out even farther their approach to the goal of self-sufficiency. Of course, self-support is a much desired goal for countries to reach, but it is not clear that special priority should be given to those who are near it.

* * *

In 1961, a new emphasis on the performance of the less-developed country, "self-help," appeared in the Charter of Punta del Este, a multilateral instrument of which nearly all the signatories were less-developed countries. At the same time, the United States introduced the test of "self-help" among the criteria set up in the Foreign Assistance Act of 1961 as follows:

> The effectiveness with which the country is using its own resources to promote economic and social development.
> The importance to the United States of strengthening the country, its economy, its political structure, and its social institutions.
> The availability of assistance from other sources.[5]

Since then, American representatives have strongly emphasized to other recipients and to suppliers that assistance should be related to sound self-help measures. In fact, in AID's presentation to Congress in 1968, it described recipient performance as "the first object of AID attention in planning a program of U.S. assistance." However, this relates only to the AID program; the PL 480 aid and Export-Import Bank loans are not subject to these same criteria. More centralized programming of the various U.S. programs would greatly increase their total effectiveness.

AID does not measure self-help solely on a quantitative basis but argues that it must be "of the right kind," referring to such elements as "attention given to higher food production, efforts made to create a favorable climate for private enterprise and investment, establishment of sound priorities, and the extent of economic, social and political reform." In actual operation this test varies from situation to situation and is not subject to simple statistical verification. In a small country receiving a technical assistance grant, it may mean merely the assurance by the country of meeting the complementary local requirements for the project. In the case of big and complex programs like those of India or Brazil, it requires a detailed consideration of how the foreign assistance will be related to domestic policies and programs, and vice versa.

In the last analysis, self-help or performance can best be judged by persons informed about all aspects of the less-developed country's behavior. In assessing performance, the short run may give different answers from the long run. Also, the secondary benefits and the effect on such unmeasurable elements as institutional structure should be taken into account. Obviously, there are limits at any time as to what amounts of aid a country can use effectively. Presumably the experts know not only how much reliance can be placed on an imperfect statistical record but much more about the basic policies in effect, the efforts being made, and the obstacles encountered. They must be able to evaluate the extent by which outside assistance can support and strengthen the country's own efforts. Where there are consortia or consultative groups, the sponsoring agency is responsible for giving the expert advice. In other cases, the supplier government must build up and maintain a staff of persons who can make these judgments. Focused primarily on the efforts made by the less-developed country, these judgments are important not only for allocation purposes, but also for the pattern of assistance, so that foreign resources can reinforce domestic efforts.

*   *   *

Even if individual suppliers should deal wisely with the problem of allocation from their separate points of view, the sum of their independent efforts would not necessarily make a satisfactory total distribution. The foregoing summary of the random forces at work and the difficulty of finding reasonable tests with which to judge country allocation do not mean, however, that the distribution is completely arbitrary. Despite the many special cases, countries do give weight to such broad tests as need and performance. The increasing amount of discussion among suppliers concerning general principles and specific situations is reducing the extent to which conflicting actions may be taken. The fact that consortia, consultative groups, or CIAP reviews exist for most of the larger recipients introduces the possibility of comparison on relatively comparable bases. Finally, the fact that there is such a wide gap between the limited supply of assistance and the many opportunities for its effective use means that there is little likelihood of any recipient getting too much assistance. It is more probable that it will get too little.

* * *

Recent policy declarations of the United States concerning assistance to Africa have highlighted another development which bears on the allocation problem, namely greater reliance on regional projects and regional agencies. As has been pointed out, national boundaries are often chance products of history. With the process of independence not yet completed, Africa has over 40 countries with boundaries that are, for the most part, not based upon social, economic, or ethnic considerations. While many of them include a large land mass, their populations are relatively small. Lines of communication run to the sea. Historically, neighbors had little economic or political contact except where there was a common metropolitan power, and even then it was often very limited.

So long as empires existed, active regional organizations with broad coverage were limited largely to the Western Hemisphere. Various conferences were held by the Latin American countries prior to 1889, the beginning of an organizational period when not only the Pan-American Union (later the Organization of American States) but also many narrowly specialized agencies were formed. Within the United Nations system, regional commissions have been established for Europe, Latin America, Asia and the Far East, Africa, and a more limited regional operation in the Middle East under the guise of an Economic and Social Office in Beirut. Another early effort to exchange information about national plans and to arrange technical assistance was the Colombo Plan, which grew out of the 1950 meeting of the Foreign Ministers of the British Commonwealth. Active largely as discussion centers, these various organizations also provide technical assistance.

Various efforts have been made among the African countries to establish regional groupings. To some extent they have developed common plans which help in the allocation of aid. The recent establishment by the IBRD of a Consultative Group for Kenya, Uganda and Tanzania is the first effort in the aid coordination field since the Marshall Plan to bring more than one recipient into a common discussion of assistance with suppliers, although this is hardly new since the three countries had a Common Services Organization in their colonial days.

Regionalism is not limited to Africa. In Latin America, the Inter-American Committee for the Alliance for Progress is an invaluable institution in which the member countries examine each other's needs, policies, and programs. The Central American Common Market is sufficiently unified so that the CIAP examines the development needs of the five countries together. Five countries with the help of the Inter-American Development Bank are jointly developing the Rio de la Plata basin. The Regional Cooperation for Development Agreement involving Iran, Pakistan, and Turkey provides another vehicle for consultation in many fields and has already approved some fifty regional industrial projects.

This recent emphasis on regionalism holds much promise not only in the effort to reduce the enormous web of possible bilateral relationships but also to distribute assistance on a somewhat more rational basis. There often are development projects which necessarily involve more than one recipient, particularly the development of transportation facilities which cross national boundaries like the Pan-American Highway and the TVA-style development of river basins like those relating to the Indus, the Mekong, and the Rio de la Plata. Other regional projects make sense where some product or service is needed but no single country in the area is large enough to justify it, such as a regional university.

Of growing importance are the regional development institutions, among which the Inter-American Development Bank, the Asian Development Bank, and the African Development Bank are the leaders. The multilateral and regional agencies are in an excellent position to view the total picture and could make corrections with their own resources for gaps in the over-all assistance pattern resulting from the unrelated and differently valued bilateral programs. However, if regional institutions are to substitute for bilateral arrangements, there must be less emphasis on the project approach so favored by banks, since program loans may sometimes be the assistance that is more needed. There will also have to be much stronger financial backing and support for such agencies than has yet been in evidence. Otherwise, the talk about the regional approach may turn out to be merely an excuse for reduced assistance.

9 · More Multilateralism?

International institutions play a highly important role in economic assistance, but their existence raises a variety of policy problems for the rich countries. By no means uniform, the agencies have differing memberships, varied organizational structures, different means of financing, separate secretariats, and operate in more or less different spheres.

The United Nations General Assembly, the U.N. Economic and Social Council, the United Nations regional commissions, and more recently the UNCTAD are forums of prolonged debate among rich and poor on various issues of aid policy. It could not be otherwise in the United Nations, since about four-fifths of its members qualify as less-developed countries and development is their main interest. The resolution in the First General Assembly urging that assistance be given to war-devastated areas was soon displaced by an oft-repeated appeal for help to less-developed countries. No recent United Nations General Assembly has adjourned without enacting, after prolonged discussion, a series of resolutions with elaborate "whereases" bearing upon economic and social development. The procedure is followed in most of the specialized agencies.

* * *

In the hope of giving more concentrated attention to development problems, the United Nations Conference on Trade and Development (UNCTAD) was created and held its first conference in Geneva in 1964 and its second in New Delhi in early 1968. The first Conference enacted a large number of recommendations, not always unanimously, some of which were plainly hortatory while others provided for studies and reports on various subjects. During the interval between conferences, there was considerable secretariat activity and a number of intergovernmental committee and subcommittee meetings.

UNCTAD II was a massive affair with some two thousand delegates from 132 countries, a larger membership than the United Nations itself because of the inclusion of such jurisdictions as the Papal See and Liechtenstein. Unfortunately, such publicity as there was concerning the meeting stressed political gestures rather than the substantive discussions. Thus, there were walk-outs when the representative of South Africa spoke, considerable sound and fury when the U.S.S.R. demanded a seat for East Germany, a prolonged controversy over the political difficulty of fitting Cuba and Israel into the recognized regional blocs, and more excitement when the U.S.S.R. attempted to refer the *Pueblo* incident to the Maritime Committee for review. However, the diplomatic community has come to recognize the necessity for home consumption of these inevitable irrelevant interruptions. They prolonged rather than prevented the debates on substance.

The second conference is often referred to as a failure because on the record it actually accomplished very little. There were hundreds of hours of speeches, and it is always possible that some of them must have clarified the issues, though they also may have hardened positions. As to actual achievement, undoubtedly the expectations of the secretariat and the less-developed countries were too high. Only certain limited accomplishments are possible in such a huge conference. There can be an exchange of views intended to increase the recognition of different points of view and narrow the areas of difference. Machinery for study, negotiation, and recommendation on specific problems can be set in motion. And there can be ratification of an agreement generally reached beforehand.

However, such an assemblage cannot possibly negotiate the details of new trade arrangements, nor can it do anything to enforce aid commitments. As to the first, the conference urged the members to support and give effect to the trade principles that were adopted at UNCTAD I. Beyond that, it did move the trade problem along by establishing a Special Committee on Preferences to develop a proposal for action. As to the second, it raised the aid target by substituting gross national product for national income in the denominator of the 1 per cent calculation, but nothing happened to make the target more controlling. Many other subjects were discussed at the conference, resulting most often in that face-saving device—the call for further study.

UNCTAD II was oratorically much less violent than the first meeting. Although the conference itself may have been a loss on any cost-benefit calculation, the period between the two conferences probably was a plus. In preparation, both the rich and the poor countries reviewed their problems and policies in the search for demands and concessions that might reasonably be made. The DAC and the Trade Committee of the OECD held many meetings trying to develop common positions on the various agenda items, as did the various continental blocs of less-developed countries. Furthermore, a number of committees met from time to time during the interim between UNCTAD I and UNCTAD II with smaller memberships and somewhat more fruitful discussions.

It is doubtful that UNCTAD has any considerable contribution to make as a continuing organization with a large secretariat, since every area of concern is already covered by some other organization, and its members already meet together in many other forums. There is clearly a great deal of duplication in the world of debate and discussion. Nevertheless, an infrequent UNCTAD conference in the future can be justified if it is thought of as a place to take stock of all the scattered efforts now made in the name of development and to suggest new directions to the various functional agencies. The experience of its Trade and Development Board in trying to prepare proposals concerning UNCTAD's contribution to the Second Development Decade are indicative of the more general problem of achieving agreement on the broad concepts which might constitute an international strategy for development. At the adjournment of its summer meeting in 1969, the President, K. B. Asante of Ghana, summarized the situation by saying that "once again, at considerable national and international expense, we have agreed that we cannot agree, and we conclude our session having achieved very little."

* * *

The establishment of present-day multilateral operating agencies, as distinct from policy discussion centers, started before the end of World War II with the creation of the International Bank for

Reconstruction and Development and the International Monetary Fund in recognition that the international financial machinery had not functioned adequately for more than a decade. There followed the establishment of various U.N. specialized agencies, important sources of technical assistance in their particular fields—agriculture, health, education, etc. The International Labor Office (ILO), established in 1919, was also included in the U.N. System.

More recently, the field of financing has seen the formation of regional banks, while the functional organizations have also expanded in number. The central U.N. structure has been supplemented with regional commissions. Other multilateral organizations outside the U.N. framework dealing with assistance matters are the OECD, the European Economic Community, and the Alliance for Progress in conjunction with the Organization of American States. Nor is the agency population stabilized yet, recent additions being the United Nations Industrial Development Organization and the still inoperative U.N. Capital Development Fund. The latest trend is the establishment of multilateral banking institutions by governments in smaller regions—the Andean Development Corporation, the East Africa Development Bank, and the Caribbean Development Bank, which opened in February 1970 with initial capital of $50 million.

Thus far, the record shows a high agency birth rate with no deaths. In 1950, the executive branch of the United States government unsuccessfully attempted to have the functions of the U.N. Children's Fund (UNICEF) transferred to the appropriate functional specialized agencies; but was unable to convince the Congress. The continuing American support for UNICEF was demonstrated in 1968 when, despite other cut-backs, UNICEF was assured of an additional $1 million. The only instance of population decrease has been the merger of the U.N. Expanded Program for Technical Assistance and the U.N. Special Fund. The result of the proliferation of international organizations is a bewildering array of agencies to which a less-developed country may turn for assistance, a confusion of advice concerning appropriate priorities which it might adopt, and a difficult problem of choice for the rich countries in deciding how to allocate their assistance among them. Clearly, the time has come when effective birth control measures are called for.

The older agencies, intended to be global in character, have concerned themselves more and more with the problems of the less-developed countries. In the period immediately after World War II, the loans of the IBRD were made largely to European borrowers. While it still makes an occasional loan to Europe, its basic interest for some years has been in economic development. Similarly, the International Labor Organization dealt originally with the problems of industrial societies, but now is deeply involved in problems of training, labor market organization, and social security measures in the less-developed countries.

The need for any further expansion of the multilateral structure is difficult to visualize, except perhaps on environmental issues. The United Nations Industrial Development Organization (UNIDO), the most recent multilateral organization to have been formed, already has many experts active in technical assistance. If new activities are to be undertaken, such as the UNCTAD-proposed compensatory financing that would provide assistance to a country whose export earnings had fallen below reasonable expectations, there is everything to be said for having them carried out by one or another of the existing agencies. Both the IMF and the World Bank are already deeply involved in such situations. The U.N. Capital Fund has no unique function to perform, nor is a special agricultural fund necessary. Proposals for new agencies, one suspects, are based on the hope that the flow of funds will increase if there are more spigots. What will certainly increase is complication and cost of administration in both the rich and the poor countries and a greater dispersion of competent personnel.

In order to avoid some of the implications of membership, meetings, and separate budgets, both UNIDO and UNCTAD were set up by the General Assembly rather than a separate intergovernmental conference. Their operations are included in the regular budgetary requirements for the United Nations submitted to the General Assembly by the Secretary General.

The United Nations development system for technical assistance was examined in detail in 1968–69 by Sir Robert Jackson of Australia, who reached the conclusion that, if it were to carry any greater load, the system would need to be drastically overhauled.[1] He described the system, which he found to be under the control of no less than 30 separate governing bodies, as "becoming slower and more unwieldy, like some prehistoric monster." He noted the fragmented, sectoral approach of the various agencies in complete disregard of a comprehensive development policy. Believing that coordination must be essentially at the country level, he advocated the strengthening of the UNDP to be "the recognized central body for consolidating and expanding co-operation with all the developing Member States," with a greatly strengthened role for the resident representatives. In addition, he urged a career development service, including a staff college, the contracting out of more projects to non-United Nations agencies, and a shift in UNDP headquarters to Geneva.

*   *   *

In general, multilateral organizations depend upon government support and the final authority over them rests in governments. To be sure, agencies may raise funds directly from the public, as with IBRD bond issues and UNICEF Christmas cards, but in the last analysis they are channels for national funds, public or private, which come largely from the rich countries. Bond sales to the public are possible because they are backed not only by the banks' portfolios but also by capital not yet called up from the rich countries. And the agencies have to find their personnel in their member countries. Nevertheless, to a considerable degree, they have developed an existence of their own, relatively free of interference or control by their members.

Although they occasionally have some second-stage organized public support, such as the United States Commission for UNESCO or UNICEF's national groups, their general public support appears to be uneven among DAC members. The Scandinavian countries have usually contributed heavily, often more than half their aid effort. Some other governments argue that their citizens will only support assistance which is identified as theirs and are thus unwilling or slow to contribute through multilateral channels where the identification of the original source is lost. Official support from DAC members for the multilateral agencies has not been outstandingly generous, only 10.3 per cent of official net disbursements in 1967 and 9.1 per cent in 1968. In those cases where financing is done by pledging rather than by assessment as, for example, the U.N. Development Program, the World Food program, and the two refugee organizations, official commitments have often fallen far below the targets set and the amounts sought by their officials.

Popular support for international institutions stems from the general notion that they contribute to the process of building an international community. Those who prefer them to bilateral programs argue that they are "nonpolitical" in character, although they do have the political necessity of satisfying their members. They can concentrate on development objectives rather than having various national interests in mind. They have a wide choice of sources for supplies and personnel, and larger staffs than most of the bilateral donors. They are in a favored position to advise less-developed countries on sensitive matters of policy, since they are not suspect of representing special interests. They can be particularly useful to the smaller suppliers who often find it difficult to develop a bilateral aid program and feel more assured when they can rely on the greater expertness of the multilateral agencies.

Legitimate complaints can also be made. The agencies are so fragmented geographically and functionally without an adequate central policy structure that they are slow to react to new situations and opportunities (for example, FAO to the food-shortage problem, WHO to the interest in family planning). They are financially dependent on the rich countries and the requirements of hiring personnel according to national quotas interferes with the selection of manpower on the basis of competence. Further, in spite of the efforts of UNDP to coordinate the activities of multilateral agencies through resident representatives in the less-developed countries, they are often competitive in their dealings with those governments. In many agencies the distribution of votes does not reflect the distribution of financial responsibility, and the status of being multilateral does not relieve them of internal and external pressures.

It is not entirely clear how the less-developed countries feel about the multilateral agencies. In the broadest sense they may feel that international agencies are their organizations, somehow not a threat to their sovereignty, neither expecting gratitude nor demanding some sort of reciprocal obligation from them. As for intervention, although sometimes the international agencies have taken strong policy positions (the IBRD would not extend credit to a country which was in default on privately held bonds), more often they have merely evaluated specific projects and not concerned themselves with the implications of broad policy.

The Pearson Commission argued strongly for a greater role for the multilateral agencies on the grounds that they can concentrate their attention on economic development without political distractions. It proposed that the developed countries raise their contributions to the multilateral agencies from about 10 per cent to 20 per cent of their official programs by 1975. Coupled with the recommendation to bring total aid up to 0.70 per cent of gross national product, this would more than quadruple the level of the 1966–68 flow. Nor does this include funds raised in private capital markets.

In the consensus reached by the Latin American countries at Viña del Mar in May 1969, there were many criticisms of both bilateral and multilateral procedures, but the general weight of the argument was that all aid systems should be reviewed with the intention of considerably expanding multilateral activity. At UNCTAD I, a resolution was adopted with an escape clause as big as a barn-door urging "the channeling of external resources, wherever possible and appropriate, through multilateral institutions." The strong support of the new U.N. Capital Development Fund suggests a further preference for an agency with a "one country, one vote" rule where less-developed countries are in the majority, as against structures such as the World Bank Group and the IMF with their weighted voting procedures. In part, no doubt, new international agencies were created because the existing ones could not promise enough.

Bilateral programs, it is frequently said, are objectionable because they are apt to exert undue political influence on the recipient. Actually, the political element is strongest when the decision is made whether or not to start or end a program. The technical assistance operator or the project manager is seldom in a position to exercise improper political or commercial influence, nor can activities be easily terminated in midstream. To be sure, it is hard to think of any national action in international affairs that is not political. This condition, seen in long-term perspective, is more likely to be beneficent than harmful since, by their very nature, political criteria tend to take into account the reaction of the other party. So far as the special political influence of individual experts is concerned, there is little difference to be noted since the expert sent by an international agency is also the national of some country and brings predilections to his work however nonpolitical the project may be.

The political problems faced by a multilateral agency arise from the need to satisfy all its members, as illustrated in President Watanabe's remarks to the second annual meeting of the Asian Development Bank. In view of the fact that to the end of 1968, nine of the sixteen less-developed Bank members had received no loans, and four received neither loans nor technical assistance, the Bank "therefore" sent out missions to identify projects and even to help prepare applications where needed.

It is impossible to make a judgment on the relative efficiency and effectiveness of bilateral and multilateral programs, particularly since there is no review and auditing system for multilateral activities comparable to that of many governments. Furthermore, multilateral organizations vary in their competence and quality just as the various national assistance agencies vary. Comparisons are hard to make in any event, since there are few instances of similar programs in similar countries at the same time. That there are so many multilateral agencies in operation destroys the obvious advantage in allocation and experience that might come from more administrative centralization.

Prevailing attitudes for and against one channel or the other depend largely on two judgments: first, whether or not a country believes in trying to transfer as many national activities as possible to supranational bodies in order to weaken nationalism and strengthen the sense of world community. Even here, however, one cannot be certain whether or not countries achieve a greater sense of cooperation from belonging to the same organization or from directly working together. The second uncertainty is the extent to which bilateral programs are based on benefits to the suppliers rather than the development of the recipient.

It is to be hoped that the multilateral agencies will take a particularly strong lead in areas where regional and subregional programs are possible, and where various sources of support are required. With increasing joint activity, the distinctions between the two channels will be reduced and some moderate allocations of function will tend to develop. Rather than the sterile debate over relative performance, efforts to improve each system would be more productive, trying to increase cooperative action whereever possible.

* * *

Flows through the multilateral agencies, including those of the lending institutions, are given in Table 23. Disbursements have increased steadily, not only because of the expansion of the older agencies, but also because of the addition of others, notably, the International Development Association, Inter-American Development Bank, the European Development Fund of the EEC, and more recently, the Asian and African Development Banks. The one sharp break with the trend is the drop in the new commitments figure in 1967 when, after approaching the $2 billion mark in 1966, it fell back to $1.6 billion. This was almost entirely the result of the exhaustion of IDA resources without timely replenishment by its Class I members, the rich countries. The continued growth of the World Bank is indicated by the fact that its loan volume for 1969–70 was $1.6 billion, up from $1.4 the previous year and $0.8 billion for 1967–68. Lending by IDA expanded even more rapidly, rising to $606 million, compared with $385 million in 1968–69.

As the volume of loans outstanding has increased and as grace periods have expired, the return flow of amortization (largely to the IBRD) has expanded to more than $500 million per year. Offsetting this are the increasing payments which must be made by the banks to those who have lent funds rather than made contributions. The item "net disbursements" is an effort to estimate the flow to the less-developed countries after allowing for their various capital subscriptions and amortization payments.

The statistical record makes it clear that there has been little correlation between general disbursements and contributions by governments. Because of the size of initial capital contributions, there was a large accumulation of undisbursed funds in the years prior to 1963. Beginning in that year, disbursements exceeded the further inflow of funds each year until 1967. The even higher level of commitments, representing prospective disbursements in the future, exhausted the funds available for new projects in some cases since funds were earmarked, and the European Development Fund, the IDB, and the IDA all had to seek replenishment from governments. Substantial government support appeared again in 1967 along with a revival in private borrowing. In 1968 official contributions declined, due primarily to a fall in payments to IDA as the plans for replenishment were delayed. However, the inflow of new funds was kept at a relatively high level by greatly increased sales of bonds in the private capital markets. The record figure of private inflow for 1968 was cut nearly in half in 1969, when the World Bank increased its direct placements of

TABLE 23

Flows of Economic Assistance to and from the Multilateral Agencies,[a] 1960–68
($ Million)

	1960	1961	1962	1963	1964	1965	1966	1967	1968
Multilateral Agencies to Less-developed Countries:									
New commitments	739	1,236	1,198	1,348	1,565	1,880	1,976	1,595	2,146
Gross disbursements	438	548	725	950	1,112	1,248	1,421	1,551	1,534
Net disbursements	284	252	412	654	790	899	893	1,041	814
DAC Countries to Multilateral Agencies:									
Official, net	601	751	526	365	380	448	530	736	659
Private, net	204	90	239	−33	141	248	15	306	604
Total	805	842	765	332	521	696	545	1,042	1,263

[a] IBRD, IDA, IFC, IDB, Asian Development Bank, African Development Bank, EEC-EDF, EEC-EIB, and certain United Nations Agencies concerned with development.
Source: Development Assistance Committee, OECD.

relatively short-term borrowings with national monetary authorities.

During this period, the multilateral lending agencies have been paying greater amortization on their own bonds than they are collecting on loans made to the less-developed countries, mainly because of differences in grace periods. Presumably, in the longer run these will tend to offset each other and new commitments will have to be financed largely by new cash, except for amortization and interest earned on the lending of government contributions which require no debt servicing. The new funds will have to come from added government contributions or from private sources. While the net inflow of private funds has seldom been as high as $300 million in any one year, it did exceed $600 million in 1968. However, private funds are likely to involve heavy service charges. If one assumes merely the maintenance of commitments at the recent level, say $2 billion per year, the new funds from governments would have to increase substantially. The Pearson Commission recommended an ambitious target, that generous government contributions to IDA should reach $1.5 billion by 1975 and that the total official flow to multilateral institutions should be $3.2 billion.

The record of the United States in the past shows a relatively low level of official contributions to international agencies, though commitments have been substantially higher than disbursements. The disbursement record, 1961–68, is given in Table 24.

TABLE 24

U.S. Disbursements to Multilateral Agencies,
1961–68
($ Million)

Year	Official	Private
1961	202	−2
1962	138	160
1963	142	5
1964	204	131
1965	164	152
1966	112	1
1967	310	256
1968	251	255

Source: Development Assistance Committee, OECD.

In order to help its balance of payments, the United States has delayed the encashment of its much larger commitments so far as was practical since 1966. Although U.S. bilateral disbursements were expected to decline in 1969, multilateral contributions should be substantially higher due to the accumulated commitments, the activation of IDA replenishment, and additional flows to the Inter-American Development Bank.

Beyond the level of commitment already established, there appears to be growing support for multilateral channels of assistance. The report of the Peterson Task Force to President Nixon (March, 1970) stated that "the United States should redesign its policies so that . . . the international lending institutions become the major channel for development assistance." With that objective in mind, it recommended an increase in the annual U.S. contribution to international financial institutions to $1 billion by 1972 and that "thereafter U.S. development assistance for international financial institutions should be increased as rapidly as is consistent with its effective use and with the willingness of other industrial countries to increase their contributions to such institutions."

The present levels of activity, while expanding very rapidly in some cases, by no means meet the needs envisaged by these organizations. UNICEF has set a target of $50 million annually to be reached by the end of 1969, an increase of $10 million. The UNDP reached $197.5 million in 1969 and U Thant has stated that, on the basis of assessed needs and the potential for concerted technical and pre-investment assistance by the U.N. family of agencies, the target for 1970 should be $350 million. Paul Hoffman, administrator of the fund, set a figure of $425 million. Contributions to the World Food Program have grown to $288 million for the biennium, 1969–70. The Asian Development Bank, which made its first loan in January 1968, approved loans of $41.6 million in 1968, $98.1 million in 1969, and hoped to reach $250 million in 1970.

These are all small programs compared with the hopes of the larger institutions. Mr. McNamara, President of the World Bank, proposed that the bank group should lend about $2 billion a year between 1969 and 1973, making this possible by securing a substantial increase in its funds through private borrowing. The IDA, being a soft-loan institution, does not raise money in the private capital markets. Its initial subscription from its 18 Class I Members and the first replenishment were each about $750 million for three-year periods. After prolonged negotiations to set a figure somewhere between proposals of $750 million and $3,000 million, and also to find an acceptable way to minimize the impact on the U.S. balance of payments, the second IDA replenishment was set at $1,200 million for three years. This sum is appreciably above the level of disbursements reached in the past, although IDA commitments in both 1964 and 1966 exceeded $400 million. In addition to these more familiar financing problems, there are new activities which will require support, such as the U.N. Secretary-General's Trust Fund for Population Problems, or those conceived but not yet alive like the U.N. Capital Development Fund and the UNCTAD scheme (drafted by the IBRD staff) for compensatory financing.

Special note should be taken of the several regional financial operations. The Inter-American Development Bank has grown steadily since its first commitment in 1961, becoming a major factor in the flow of economic assistance to Latin America. By 1969, it sold about $250 million in securities outside the Western Hemisphere, and its President predicted that its lending rate would reach $600 million per year by 1972. It finances not only economic projects but social development, such as land settlement and housing with both hard and soft loans. In April 1970, the IADB Board of Governors proposed an increase in the Bank's resources of $2 billion for normal loans and $1.5 billion for soft-loan financing. About $1.6 of the hard-loan support would be callable from governments, and would, in effect, serve as a guaranteee fund for borrowings in private capital markets. The Board forecast that its lending rate would be approximately $900 million a year by 1973. Of particular interest are the arrangements made with Canada, Germany, the Netherlands, Sweden, the United Kingdom, the Vatican, and the United States whereby it administers specific resources provided for project financing in Latin America. Although the Asian Development Bank and the African Development Bank are much younger, they are both growing rapidly.

The European Development Fund (EDF) was set up originally to deal with the problems of former overseas territories of members of the European Economic Community, particularly the French practice of market support for certain tropical products from its colonies. A new economic assistance fund was to act as a substitute for such bilateral arrangements. The third five-year agreement (in June 1969) continued the trade preferences for the 17 African countries and Madagascar, and provided $1 billion for aid rather than the $800 million which had been distributed in the previous five-year period. The former colonies associated with the Common Market had asked for $1,500 million. The new agreement called for $750 million in grants, $150 million in special loans, and $100 million in loans from the European Investment Bank. Most of the EDF's funds go for infrastructure and agriculture.

In looking at the total picture, it is clear that added funds can be easily utilized by the multilateral agencies, especially by the IDA, the UNDP, and the regional development banks. In fact, added funds will be required if the present level of commitments is to be maintained. Without reducing bilateral flows, it would probably be wise, as strongly recommended by the Pearson Commission, to provide a greater share of the growing total to these organizations in the future.

* * *

Within this complicated structure, each of the rich governments has limited freedom in deciding how much total support to give the multilateral institutions and less in allocating its support among them. The entire picture has seldom been examined so that the total can be viewed in terms of its parts. So far as the individual donor countries are concerned, their contributions to the international agencies are in large part the result of assessments, which are determined by the application of established percentages (different for each agency) to the annual budget. To be sure, as members of the organizations they participate with other members in making the basic decisions on programs and the total budget, but, that having been decided, the contribution of each country is determined automatically. However, not all DAC members belong to the same organizations: six contribute to the European Development Fund and membership varies in the regional banks. Furthermore, some make extra contributions to activities such as the United Nations Development Program or purchase World Bank bonds through their central banks. For a number of countries, arrangements concerning these funds are the responsibility of the finance officials rather than those involved in development assistance.

While the largest sums are fixed by the allocation process, there are a number of U.N. activities which are based upon annual voluntary contributions. The largest of these include the U.N. Development Program, the Children's Fund, the refugee agencies, and the World Food Program. Thus, in total, there are certain fixed amounts which governments are obligated to pay, and a wide spectrum of possible voluntary contributions which can be made.

Although there are wide differences in the contributions of individual governments, there is some relationship between the size of a country and the distribution of its development assistance between bilateral and multilateral channels. In terms of their national product, the greatest official support for the multilateral agencies in 1968 came from Austria, Norway, Sweden, Netherlands, and Denmark. Among the lowest contributors relative to gross national product were Portugal, Japan, Switzerland, the United States, and France. Since the smaller countries have much more difficulty in mounting their own bilateral programs, they make greater use of the multilateral agencies. It is also worthy of note that four of the five countries which rank the highest in support of the multilateral agencies rank relatively low in their total official assistance program. The low percentage for the United States reflects the fact that the rate at which it has agreed to contribute to multilateral agencies is considerably below its share of total gross product, a condition defended by the dubious argument that any higher percentage would give it an undue influence over the agencies, thus reducing their international character. For some years, the Senate regularly authorized the administration to transfer part of the AID funds to the IDA, but the House never agreed.

The recent economy drive in the United States has introduced a new uncertainty into existing procedures for providing funds to the multilateral agencies. The problem arises because of the several steps involved: executive negotiation, congressional authorization, and finally congressional appropriation. For example, the President's foreign aid message for 1968–69 requested $625 million to fund Alliance for Progress operations on a regionally agreed basis. The request was cut to $336.5 million in the final appropriation. Because the request for legislative action to replenish the resources of the IDA was not reported out by the appropriate committees in the 1968 session of Congress, final enactment came only in April 1969.

In another section of the 1968–69 appropriation, the regular requests for voluntary contributions to international organizations and programs were also cut in an unprecedented fashion. Under the Act, which provides for cases where there is no formal obligation to contribute, the President proposed contributions for twelve organizations and programs, principally for the U.N. Development Program, the Children's Fund, and the World Food Program, but including smaller amounts for migration, refugees, and other agencies. When the total amount requested was reduced by Congress from $141 million to $119 million, the executive branch had to allocate the cut among the programs, each of which already considered itself inadequately financed. The U.S. government did not even make a pledge to the UNDP at the pledging conference although it later pledged $70.3 million, a reduction of $5 million from the original allotment. Fortunately, 50 of the 97 supporting nations increased their contributions. As these are all continuing organizations, they must be able to make advance commitments to governments and to personnel; and since the United States is the largest contributor in most cases, any uncertainty about its contribution creates a serious problem for them.

Actual expenditures by AID under the heading of international organizations and programs for 1968–69 were as follows:

	$ Million
U.N. Development Program	71.0
U.N. Relief and Works Agency	13.3
U.N. Children's Fund	13.0
U.N. Peace-keeping in Cyprus	6.0
U.N. Population Program	2.5
U.N./FAO WORLD Food Program	1.3
U.N./WHO Cancer Research	.15
U.N. Technical Assistance for Congo	.5
U.N. Institute for Train and Research	.4
World Meteorological Organization	1.5
International Atomic Energy Agency	1.0
Special Contributions to Vietnam	.4
International Secretariat for Voluntary Relief	.05
Administrative Expenses—State Department	3.6
Dependent Education Program	2.2
Inspector General, Foreign Assistance	.6
Indus Basin loan and grant	36.1

By reducing the Indus Basin item to $7.5 in 1969–70, it was possible to reduce the total while increasing the UNDP amount to $86.2 million and the population program to $4 million. The proposed 1970–71 program further steps up these two items to $100 million and $7.5 million, and increases the Indus Basin item to $13.8.

In the past, where pledging has been involved the United States has tried to encourage other countries to increase their support, using as one inducement the so-called matching principle. Under this technique, the United States has said that its contribution might be as much as x dollars but in no case would it be more than 40 per cent of the total, thus making the U.S. amount dependent upon the contributions by other countries. The "matching principle" has come under vigorous criticism by other donors. Meaningful national comparisons of burden-sharing usually recognize differences in national income. Even without taking into account the principle of progressivity, a fair share for the United States on an income basis would be about one-half of the total, so that limiting the contribution to 40 per cent is itself subject to criticism. Some other donors, who may give considerably more than the United States through other forms of assistance, have objected to the matching principle because it puts pressure on them for a particular form of aid and might require them to change their preferred allocation. If the purpose is to hold the U.S. share to some relatively small proportion as a basis for limiting its influence, then no ceiling as to amount need be set. If the purpose is to limit the absolute amount of the U.S. contribution, there is no need to relate it to the contributions of other donors. If the matching principle must be maintained for some mysterious reason, consultation with other donors before announcing the U.S. contribution would be desirable.

This is not to say that the contributions of the United States are not of considerable importance in influencing other governments to support various agencies and activities. As Takeshi Watanabe, President of the Asian Development Bank, has said, "If the U.S. makes its $200 million contribution, this would make it much easier to get other creditor member nations to contribute, too." In this case also, a commitment was made by the executive after consultation with the Congress but actual appropriation was slow in coming. It is unfortunate that there should have appeared to have been any question about meeting a commitment openly made after much public discussion and clearly understood when the United States joined the Bank.

* * *

With the financial backing of callable capital provided by their member governments, the World Bank and the Inter-American Development Bank have been able to borrow substantial sums in various national markets. From 1960 to 1968, about one-fourth of the resources of multilateral agencies have come from private sources. The amounts have varied substantially from year to year, the levels in 1967 and 1968 having been well above any previous years despite the tight money markets. For the IBRD, 55 per cent of its total debt is held by investors outside the United States, even including such unexpected sources as the $15 million, 6.5 per cent, 26-year U.S. dollar bonds sold to the Saudi Arabian Monetary Agency. IADB borrowings have been made in a number of non-member countries.

The picture changed drastically in 1968. The President of the World Bank, Robert S. McNamara, announced an ambitious program for greatly expanding the Bank's borrowing, in order to double its annual lending to around $1.6 billion inside five years. Amazing progress towards the goal was made in the Bank's 1968–69 fiscal year when it borrowed about $1,225 million, 55 per cent more than in the previous year, of which it used $525 million in payment of its own outstanding debt. Added funds from loan repayments to it and other financial transactions added about another $600 million to its available cash. Actual disbursements to less-developed countries showed very little increase, but new commitments by IBRD and IDA increased from $953 million in 1967–68 to a record $1,784 million in 1968–69.

The long-term growth pattern is difficult to forecast. As it borrows more and more funds, the Bank will have larger repayments each year. One can imagine a future, if still distant, when the Bank will primarily be operating a revolving fund, whereby it will have to pay back to lenders in developed countries as much as it borrows from them, and similarly will be repaid by less-developed countries as much as its new loans to them. Even in that case, it will still be performing an important service by transferring funds to places where they are specially needed.

It should be kept in mind that the borrowings of the international banks are made at competitive rates in the various markets, though at rates substantially below those which the poor countries would have to pay if they could borrow at all. The result is that the banks can relend such funds only to countries which can meet relatively hard terms, and President McNamara has said that "we lend only where there is a firm basis of repayment." The average rate for the World Bank's borrowing in 1968–69 was 6.46 per cent. The interest rates on loans made to less-developed countries at the end of 1968 were as high at 7.75 per cent, including commissions. On occasion, lower rates are achieved by combining funds from IBRD and IDA in a single package.

Since there clearly are many situations where such service charges are bearable, it is important that private capital markets be fully utilized. And since such securities are backed not only by the commitments of the borrowing governments but also by capital not yet called up from the rich countries, they ought to sell at levels very close to government credit. Furthermore, central banks wishing to invest their reserve funds in interest-bearing securities can use the opportunity not only to earn interest but also to provide added assistance. However, if they are to service all nations, the IDA and the regional banks must be continually supported by government contributions so that they can finance projects in countries where high interest rates and repayment are not justifiable.

It is of course possible that hard loans by the IBRD could be made secure if they were given priority over all other claims on a poor country's ability to service external loans. In that case, however, the hard lending by the Bank results either in requiring other suppliers to give assistance on a softer basis or in pre-empting possible payment for a larger amount of soft loans, resulting in an actual reduction in the total flow of assistance.

* * *

The International Monetary Fund (IMF), usually thought of as advising the less-developed countries on balance-of-payment matters, should also be specially noted for the short-run assistance which it provides. To be sure, the main transactions between the Fund and its members are not borrowings in the normal sense but the drawing or purchase of one's own currencies back from the Fund. The main technique used by the IMF is the stand-by arrangement, under which the Fund gives advance assurance that a stated amount of resources will be available in case of need to support a program of action presented by the member. While these arrangements are usually based on a twelve-month period and the conditions which they are intended to forestall may be relatively temporary, the stand-by arrangement may involve longer-term efforts to deal with balance-of-payments difficulties of a more serious nature. The IMF also permits the use of Fund resources for compensatory financing of export fluctuations. Although monetary and fiscal problems may not appear to be immediate matters of development, inflation or default can interfere and even disrupt the flow of resources required by the development plan, as well as distort the intended pattern of investment within the country. Financial programming is therefore intimately interrelated with economic growth.

* * *

The operations of the international agencies in the financial field have changed in many ways since their doors first opened. They are breaking away from concentration on economic infrastructure projects (as has already been noted in Chapter 7). They have also tried to meet the varied requirements of suppliers and borrowers by setting up various types of funds. This effort is well-illustrated by the record of the Inter-American Development Bank and its four different windows. Its record to December 31, 1969, is shown in Table 25.

TABLE 25
LOAN ACTIVITIES OF THE INTER-AMERICAN DEVELOPMENT BANK
TO DECEMBER 31, 1969

Source	Loan Authorizations (Number)	Amount ($ Million)
Ordinary capital resources	187	1,294.1
Fund for Special Operations (soft loans)	243	1,581.6
Special Progress Trust Fund (U.S.A.)	116	496.2
Special funds from Canada, Sweden, and the U.K.	19	57.8
	565	3,429.7

Source: IDB Newsletter, Washington, Jan. 1970.

Another unusual development is demonstrated by a recent loan the IADB made to *Nacional Financiera* of Mexico to finance a Mexican export of nearly $7 million of railroad freight car components to Colombia, a third country arrangement reminiscent of the Marshall Plan.

Similarly, not only are the international financial agencies encouraging private banks to participate in certain maturities, but they are increasingly using a joint financing technique. For example, twelve countries are underwriting $42 million and the IBRD $32 million for projects to increase the supply of both water and electric power to Bogotá, Colombia. In Mexico, a World Bank loan of $90 million plus $22 million from eleven supplier countries will help to finance electric power expansion. As described by the Bank, "the joint financing technique provides a mechanism through which bilateral export credits are used to finance goods procured under unrestricted international competition for projects prepared and executed under the supervision of the Bank."

Another complex case involves the International Finance Corporation. The *Societé Minière de Mauritanie* (Somima) is a $60 million copper-mining venture in the Sahara Desert, made possible by a new process for handling copper oxide that was recently developed in Zambia. Sponsored by a British company with extensive mining interests and by four French mining and banking institutions, the investment group includes the government of Mauritania, the European Investment Bank, and investors in Italy, Germany, and the Middle East. The International Finance Corporation itself has committed $20 million to the project. This can surely be regarded as a form of multilateralization.

Developments such as these are indeed promising for increasing the effectiveness of economic assistance. However, the multilateral organizations are exerting a strong influence on the assistance pattern in another way. About 40 per cent of all official contributions are made to countries where either consortia or consultative groups exist. (These arrangements are discussed in detail in Chapter 13.) With one exception, noted below, they relate to a single less-developed country and include the main suppliers of capital assistance. In their operation the multilateral agencies play a most important role not only as the catalytic agent but as the source of expert analysis. The World Bank has announced that it is plan-

ning to review the economic and social progress of thirty countries every year, of another thirty every two years, and a final
thirty every three years. These investigations will cover all sectors
of the economy with a view to determining priorities for both investment and pre-investment activity.

The international agencies also frequently take the lead in seeking agreement between suppliers and recipient as to the appropriate and feasible mix of foreign and domestic policies. An interesting variant is the new Consultative Group of East Africa,
which includes Kenya, Tanzania, Uganda, and the East African
Community—the first instance including more than one recipient.

Beyond these formal groups, the studies of the IBRD, the annual reviews by the IMF, and the country reviews by CIAP and
by the regional commissions, all help to establish policy lines for
coordinated action. The UNDP resident representatives in each
country often are a focal point for coordinating technical assistance locally.

Bilateral and multilateral suppliers and several recipients also
work closely together in multinational projects. It may be the development of a river basin such as the Indus, the Mekong, or La
Plata; it may be a communications system, such as is being studied for Latin America; or it may be a multinational highway system. For example, the Tarbela Development Fund for the Tarbela Dam project on the Indus River in West Pakistan involves
six countries as contributors, plus local currency from Pakistan,
with the World Bank as administrator. In these cases, collaboration is a necessary condition, and the contacts developed contribute to the possibility of still wider cooperation.

All these steps are of great importance in a cobweb world
where so many separate governments and agencies are active in so
many areas. The multilateral agency makes it possible to harmonize domestic and assistance policies without charges of national intervention. To be sure, some less-developed countries are
so small as to make much coordinating machinery absurd, and
there are others which have only one main supplier and coordination is therefore irrelevant.

It may be fortunate that so many situations exist where little
coordination is required because each formal group places a heavy
burden on the agency's experts. So far as total effort by all participants is concerned, the burden is undoubtedly more than offset

by the reduction in the work of the experts of donor nations and especially of the officials in the less-developed country. The value of continuous close contact has recently been demonstrated in the IBRD's announcement that at the request of the government of Indonesia, it is establishing a resident mission to advise and assist Indonesia in formulating and executing its development plans and to help in drawing together all forms of external aid in connection with an international consultative group.

These various common undertakings can only be effective if the supplying countries are prepared to accept more responsibility than they have in the past. Many of them have feared that discussing requirements implied a commitment to meet them. Although this ought to be the outcome, it depends upon the suppliers having resources available on a longer-term basis than most of them have at present, though various governments are setting up organizations with longer-term funding, as proposed by the Peterson Task Force.

While the work of the IMF has also helped to provide policy guidance for the less-developed countries, it probably has not had as much support as it should from the rich countries. It devises an appropriate program together with a country in payments difficulties. However, other countries can greatly assist in carrying out this program by the amount of credit, especially short-term, which is extended and by the character of the terms on which official assistance is provided. The annual review made by the IMF should have policy significance for more countries than the one examined.

*   *   *

One quite different multilateral problem must be noted—the expansion of secretariats. The United Nations and specialized agencies employ more than 30,000 persons. It is regarded as a matter of status by most nations that they be represented in each secretariat. In addition, salary levels must be set to attract employees from the rich countries. The unfortunate result of these two forces is that the secretariats, operating on the basis of a quota of employees from each member nation, sometimes must employ persons of lesser competence in order to achieve a personnel roster balanced according to nationality. At the same time, the loss to the less-developed countries of needed skilled personnel is a high cost for preserving national pride. Thus the result of the system of job allocation is to lower the level of competence both in the less-developed countries and in the secretariats. Furthermore, the high salary-scale and fringe benefits are so far above those in most less-developed countries that they act as strong barriers to the return of personnel to their homelands.

The same idea of representativeness is carried over whenever teams are required for agency projects. It would somehow be contrary to the spirit of internationalism to send too many French, English, or Americans on a particular mission. The result is not always felicitous since national differences reach into methodology as well as substance. That Danes, Americans, and New Zealanders all have agricultural experiment stations operating on somewhat different principles does not mean that the best way to plan one for Somalia is to select one man from each country.

Another aspect of the manpower problem is the personnel drain involved in meetings, seminars, etc., not to mention the costs in time and energy as well as budgets. The United States belongs to more than fifty international organizations and is represented at more than 600 international conferences per year. Moreover, an organization like the OECD or the OAS may cover many fields and operate many committees and working parties or be concentrated on limited subjects such as how to have more trade in books or less trade in opium.

The General Assembly of the United Nations is but one of the many international meetings that ties up thousands of government representatives for many weeks each year. UNCTAD II, in New Delhi, was attended by more than 2,000 people, most of whom were there for the entire period. It may be that the balance of payments of India benefited substantially, although one should not underestimate the burdens of playing host. For every meeting, there is back-stopping time in capitals to be added. In addition to large-scale meetings, there are innumerable seminars and committee and subcommittee meetings usually sponsored by one or another international agency. One cannot say that these meetings are wasteful, but it is a question of comparative advantage in the use of the time of a handful of persons. For all countries, developed as well as less-developed, policy competence and administrative talent are scarce commodities. The temptation, however, is great to accept an invitation to a meeting at an attractive spot, especially if it is far from one's immediate worries. In addition to the regular sessions of the multilateral agencies, there are innumerable *ad hoc* meetings, as in the case when some country gets into payments difficulty. And there are the bilateral discussions when high officials visit each other's country.

One should not be entirely critical about this situation. The transfer of ideas is essential, and some people learn better through their ears than through their eyes. The cost-benefit calculation is not clear. However, the complexity and disorder in the present international structure has built into it the probability of excessive international meetings, and the burden needs to be examined in depth. The present responsibilities on officials, particularly in the less-developed countries, are so heavy that every effort should be made to ease the international demands on their time and energy.

All these considerations suggest that it is a misconception to feel that the administration of assistance today consists of a multitude of narrow bilateral arrangements. The multilateral dimension is everywhere apparent. To be sure, there is no single point of central authority and no agreed grand design, if one were possible. During the last two decades when the idea of foreign assistance was so novel, it probably has been fortunate that activities were so decentralized, making it possible to test various approaches. However, during the last decade coordinating activities have greatly increased, notably in the DAC, the resident representatives of UNDP, and the consortia and consultative groups. The greater competence of the governments of the less-developed countries has produced much greater coordination on the country level.

The Pearson Commission suggests that present review systems are not adequate, that there is unnecessary duplication of effort, that the division into specialities prevents the proper coordination of different policy areas, and that the multiplicity of reports and assessments confuses rather than rallies popular support. Its suggestion is that a conference to review this situation be held in 1970 with heads of appropriate international agencies and representatives of at least the major bilateral supplying and receiving governments. Such a conference may well be a first step to determine whether or not the alleged weaknesses exist and whether they really matter. Given the sensitive sovereignties of the various entities in the picture, however, it may be wiser not to push the idea of coordination too hard in a formal way. Substantial progress has already been made, and the desire to make assistance more effective should continue the pressure toward more and better coordination without raising the issue in a provocative way.

10 · More Private Enterprise?

Virtually the entire increase in economic assistance in 1968, as recorded by DAC, was in the flow of private capital. If the preliminary figures prove to be correct, growth in all categories of private capital flow brought the 1968 level to more than double the low period of 1962–63. This increase is a matter of great importance to the less-developed countries not merely because it often introduces technical and management skills as well as capital. The resultant enterprise often increases export earnings, tax revenues and government profit-sharing receipts, and employment; and it may bring foreign-exchange savings if it involves import substitution.

There is a curious illusion created by the statistical division of assistance into official and private. The distinction is based on the source of payment and the ownership arrangement, but in many ways official assistance turns out in actual operation to be private. In very few cases when plant, equipment, or commodities are transferred on government account has the item been actually produced or manufactured by the supplying government. Thus, for example, economic assistance financed by U.S. official funds in a very short period, January 1–May 15, 1968, included shipments made by: [1]

	$ Million
Caterpillar Tractor Company	5.4
International Harvester Company	3.2
United States Steel Corporation	3.2
Rohm & Haas Company	2.4
Allied Chemical Corporation	2.3

176

Similarly, while probably the larger proportion of technical assistance is carried out by government employees, even there the trend has been to put the operational responsibility on universities and consulting firms. On the receiving end, most less-developed countries have substantial public sectors of economic activity, but parts of the infrastructure, such as road-building, may be handled by the central government, the local government, or by private contract.

In addition to the private activity in carrying out official commitments, a substantial flow is generated in the private sector with private funds. There are those who argue that only official flows should be included in any statistical estimate of "foreign aid," as did the Latin American countries at Viña del Mar when they asked for agreement "that private foreign investment should not be considered as aid or calculated as part of financial cooperation for development purposes." Regardless of how it is classified, there can be no question that private flows make a substantial contribution to economic development. To be sure, the greater part of this flow represents foreign investment inspired by the prospect of profit. But the less-developed countries also profit from it.

In the development of an oil or mineral deposit by a foreign company, the greatest contribution may be the expansion of the tax base, a source from which a number of less-developed countries obtain a large part of their revenues. In a sense, the enterprise turns a frozen asset into one that contributes actively to the country's economy. However, an increasing share of foreign private capital is used to develop industry and trade, thus increasing employment and national productivity and acting as a demonstration center for modern technical and managerial methodology. Frequently a foreign company must train its own labor supply and management personnel. Although there are those who argue that it discourages local entrepreneurs and domestic savings, and this certainly can be the case, it is more likely to open up opportunities for the investment of local capital and encourage it both by demonstration and often by offering participation. Foreign private investment makes secondary contributions to development in such forms as hospitals, vocational training, or housing, while the inevitable personal contacts may yield important cultural intangibles.

To a large extent, official bilateral and multilateral capital has gone into basic development requirements such as roads, electric power, irrigation, education and health facilities, and other investments not directly profitable in themselves but essential for further growth. As it unfolds, development inevitably involves a growing demand for a wider and wider variety of goods and services and a greater possibility of their production within the country. It is in this later stage with its marked differences in products, processes, and markets that official foreign assistance becomes more a facilitator, while private operation provides the initiative and many types of special skill and capital needed. Private investment is likely to be far more imaginative and flexible than the aid activities of a foreign government, being freer to move with less red tape and to adjust to the commercial practices of the host country. To be sure, certain of the newer activities are regarded in many less-developed countries as so strategic to national life that even if privately owned they are reserved for domestic ownership. Banking, shipping, newspaper publishing, and broadcasting are common examples.

*   *   *

Unfortunately, there are no adequate statistics concerning the flow of private assistance through voluntary agencies like churches, cooperatives, trade unions, foundations, and special philanthropic agencies. Many of them carry on activities, primarily technical assistance, reaching far back into the past. The early efforts of missionary groups often involved educational and health activities as well. Agencies such as the Ford Foundation and the Rockefeller Foundation are well known for the extraordinary contributions which have resulted from their sponsorship. There are many other similar but less well-known organizations, such as the Pan American Development Foundation, which sponsors the establishment of national development foundations as well as the Tools for Freedom program. The Norway-India fisheries project has been financed officially and by a house-to-house collection. Switzerland collected dividends of cooperatives as contributions to cooperative schemes in Dahomey. In the United Kingdom, the Oxford Famine Relief Committee (OXFAM) raises money not only for relief but also supports various technical assistance experts abroad. And in the United States, CARE's activities are not restricted to food parcels.

The limited figures compiled by the DAC for the flow of private capital assistance include three somewhat different types of transfer: direct investment, including reinvested earnings; portfolio investment and bank lending, including the purchase of securities issued by the multilateral institutions; and private export credits with a maturity exceeding one year. It should be noted that even the best statistics which governments have in this field are based on samples, and are therefore merely indicative of types and trends and are subject to considerable revision as additional data become available.

The record of private capital assistance for the twelve years from 1956 to 1968 is given in Table 11 (page 62, above). The total for all DAC members reached its first high point of $3.8 billion in 1957, reflecting the Suez crisis, and a low point of $2.5 billion in 1962. For the three years, 1965–67, it stayed on a new plateau of about $4.1 billion per year but then moved sharply upward to an estimated $5.7 billion in 1968, a jump of 36 per cent over the previous year, until then the highest on record. Particularly notable in this increase are a doubling of sales of bonds to the public by the IBRD and IADB, and investment related to a rapid expansion in fertilizer plants.

Advances in private foreign investment were particularly impressive for the countries in general balance-of-payments surplus, notably West Germany, Italy, and Japan. Ambassador Martin, Chairman of DAC, attributed the increase in private investment to booming economic conditions in the developed countries as well as favorable conditions in the less-developed countries. While the tightening of the money markets may have deterred new commitments leading to future disbursements, it obviously did not act as an important restriction on disbursement in 1968, especially because much of the investment was in projects started some time before.

In 1957, the private flow was 49 per cent of total assistance in that year. In 1967, it had fallen to 37 per cent, but the upsurge in 1968 and the failure of official flows to increase brought the private contribution up to 44 per cent. In all the figures here given, "net" means minus amortization and repatriation of capital but does not adjust for any investment flows from less-developed countries to the DAC members. (For other complications in the statistics, see the Appendix.)

One is struck by the wide variations in the private flow from year to year. In large part, the irregular performance is a reflection of wide swings in net investment in petroleum and of rapid changes in the volume of portfolio investment. Other forms of direct investment are rather more stable, and private export credits show a steady and considerable upward trend.

A further indicator of the behavior of foreign private investment, available only for American corporations, is the series of reports by the U.S. Department of Commerce for plant and equipment outlays by foreign affiliates of U.S. corporations. For recent years, these reports show a gradual shift from emphasis on Canada and Western Europe to the less-developed world. With the increase in total investment, there has been a concomitant increase in plant and equipment expenditures. From an estimate of about $2.5 billion in 1965, the figure for 1969 is $3.9 billion and the forecast for 1970 suggests an increase to $4.5 billion. Latin America is the area with the highest rate of expansion in recent years, reflecting increased investment in extractive industries. However, for all less-developed areas, investment by foreign affiliates in petroleum is the leading category with manufacturing in second place.[2]

The assistance given by the private sector is not only a capital flow but also involves the services of many individuals from the supplier countries. There are no figures for the number of "foreigners" in less-developed countries. Such an estimate would have to take into account the overseas Chinese in East Asia, the Indians in East Africa, and the Lebanese and Syrians in many areas. Many of these individuals are not newcomers and have thought of themselves as permanent residents. As stated in Chapter 5, some 260,000 persons are estimated to be directly engaged in technical assistance—perhaps 110,000 under official aegis and 150,000 nonofficial, most of the latter representing commercial, engineering, and industrial staff.

In general, these persons are performing services for which no national is as yet prepared and which were formerly carried out by the metropolitan power, if the services existed at all. Such private groups as the International Executive Service Corporation and Rotary Volunteers Abroad are specially helpful in providing technical assistance to private industry. Eventually there may be a more complete record of the thousands of persons with private backing, where they came from, and what they are doing; but already there are many reports of cases where a person or an enterprise has had a great impact on a community or area.

* * *

The statistics with the long label of "the net flow of private capital from DAC members to less-developed countries and multilateral agencies" are, as has been mentioned, composites of three different elements—direct investment, portfolio investment, and private export credits. Their relative importance and trends are shown in Table 26. Because the triennium 1962–64 includes the two lowest years since the earliest data, the recent increase cannot be taken as indicating quite so steep an upward trend. In fact, the three-year period, 1965–67, was surprisingly steady. The unexpected result shown in the table, already pointed out, is the large increase in 1968, about 44 per cent above the level of the previous three years, and higher in all categories.

Probably the most significant figure for development purposes is the one representing new direct investment because this is a flow of capital which carries management and technical assistance with it. The main recipients of the increased flow have been the richer countries of Latin America, the less-developed countries of Europe, and the oil-producers. About one-third of the total direct investment over the period has been in the petroleum industry, which might not seem to have much of a multiplier effect. However, the growth records of Venezuela, Kuwait, and Libya

TABLE 26

NET PRIVATE CAPITAL FLOWS FROM DAC MEMBERS TO
LESS-DEVELOPED COUNTRIES AND MULTILATERAL AGENCIES,
ANNUAL AVERAGES, BY CATEGORIES, 1956–68
(*$ Million*)

Category	1956–58 [a]	1962–64 [a]	1965–67	1968
Direct investment, net	2,194	1,630	2,259	2,918
New investment [b]	1,664	964	1,368	1,889
Reinvested earnings [b]	529	666	891	1,029
Portfolio and other lending, net	637	421	856	1,329
Bilateral and other	412	302	666	724
Multilateral portfolio	225	119	190	605
Private export credits, net	381	754	971	1,620
Total	3,211	2,805	4,086	5,867

[a] Data later revised, but revised breakdowns not available.
[b] Partly estimated by author.
Source: Development Assistance Committee, OECD.

belie any such generalization. In these cases, the petroleum development has provided export earnings and tax revenues which have been reflected in a high rate of increase in national income.

The direct investment figure is net of any amortization or repatriation of capital. It includes not only new investment but reinvested earnings as well, which are included because they belong to the foreign investors and could be withdrawn as dividends if the ownership so desired. Actually a choice was made to reinvest them in the enterprises, thus increasing the equity. Since the reinvested earnings figure is based on total capital in place, almost automatic growth in it can be expected as capital grows, except when unusual pressure for repatriation of earnings occurs, as under the U.S. balance-of-payments program. Even if the new foreign capital should be an identical amount year after year, the accumulated total would increase unless there were offsets like the American investment losses in Cuba.

Direct investment in 1968 was by far the highest in the records of the DAC, being nearly 40 per cent above the 1967 level and 17 per cent above the previous high in 1965. It was also a year of high internal investment in most of the developed countries. In many countries, the boom period led to restrictions on the availability of funds, either indirectly through high interest rates or directly through credit controls. It seems probable that such conditions will be reflected in due course in the level of investment. Old projects will undoubtedly be completed, but new ones may be more difficult to start. The impact of the controls depends upon their character, but it is to be expected that foreign investment will be curtailed rather more than domestic. The continuing search for centers of lower costs may be an offsetting factor.

The second category of private capital, portfolio investment and other lending, includes a wide range of different flows, though the largest items are bank lending for more than one year and the purchase of securities. As Table 26 shows, the sale of securities to private holders by the multilateral agencies, chiefly the IBRD and IADB, was not large during most of the 1960s, but increased greatly in 1968. In the three years 1965–67, the United States capital markets accounted for 62 per cent of the bilateral portfolio and other lending, and 72 per cent of the private multilateral flotations.

The volume of private purchases of foreign securities from less-developed countries is still far below the level reached in the 1920s. In 1968 the bilateral flow declined somewhat from the 1967 high, but it was more than offset by increased flotations by multilateral agencies. If one uses a gross rather than a net figure and omits bank transfers, the total value of new issues placed in 1968 was $1.6 billion, of which $1.1 billion was borrowed by the multilateral institutions, chiefly IBRD and IADB, and $0.5 billion by a few of the richer less-developed countries (Israel, $162 million; Mexico, $113 million; and Argentina, $75 million). The high level of interest rates probably explains the failure of country borrowing to expand in 1968, and the probable decline in both types of flotations in 1969.

The most rapid increase in recent years in the private field is that of export credits of more than 5 years maturity. The figures are based chiefly on the record of export credits guaranteed by various national government agencies, which is the way most European trade with less-developed countries is carried on. It is a relatively new practice in the United States. A complete export credit figure, which would include credits given by the seller on his own account, would probably be somewhat larger than that recorded. Being net, the figure depicts the extent by which new credits exceeded those which were paid off.

Since trade is expanding, one would expect export credits to grow accordingly. Credits of less than five years maturity have not grown as fast as the value of the imports of the developing countries in recent years, but credits over five years have grown more rapidly, especially since 1966. Most countries participated in the increase in 1968; only Germany recorded a substantial reduction. The American and Canadian figures in this category have never been very large, whereas for Austria, Belgium, Italy, and Norway, it represented about half of their total public and private assistance.

Export credits have come to be used more and more to finance capital goods that are not covered in other assistance programs. Sometimes public and private financing are combined in the same project. Since private export credits are relatively short-lived, an increase in them leads subsequently to a corresponding increase in amortization, so that substantial net increases year after year would seem to be difficult to sustain. The implications of the relatively short-term, high-cost credits on the balance-of-payments problem are discussed in Chapter 11.

* * *

As one might expect, there is wide variation among the DAC members in the private capital they provide to less-developed countries (see Table 27). The increase in 1968 was shared by nearly all DAC members. While the tendency for differences in official flows to narrow has been noted, the national records

TABLE 27

NET PRIVATE CAPITAL FLOWS TO LESS-DEVELOPED COUNTRIES AND
MULTILATERAL AGENCIES FROM DAC MEMBERS,
ANNUAL AVERAGE, 1965–68

| Country | Total Private Flow | | | | Direct Investment [a] | |
| | ($ Million) | | (Per Cent of GNP) | | ($ Million) | |
	1965–67	1968	1965–67	1968	1965–67	1968
Australia	20	30	0.09	0.11	18	27
Austria	18	46	0.18	0.40	2	0
Belgium	94	150	0.52	0.72	47	7
Canada	53	94	0.10	0.15	34	46
Denmark	−2	45	−0.02	0.36	—	—
France	546	628	0.51	0.50	370	372
Germany	381	1,068	0.32	0.81	147	192
Italy	273	401	0.43	0.53	59	118
Japan	169	390	0.16	0.28	80	110
Netherlands	148	142	0.72	0.56	90	90
Norway	15	35	0.20	0.38	2	4
Portugal	19	13	0.44	0.26	5	6
Sweden	49	57	0.22	0.22	27	26
Switzerland	142	223	0.96	1.30	39	79
United Kingdom	434	341	0.42	0.33	200	216
United States	1,727	2,204	0.23	0.25	1,136	1,624
Total, DAC	4,086	5,867	0.28	0.36	2,259	2,918

[a] Including reinvested earnings.
Source: Development Assistance Committee, OECD.

for private flows continue to be much more varied. In terms of
the total private flow measured against gross national product,
all the countries that once had colonial empires are close to or
above one-half of 1 per cent of gross national product, although
Switzerland as a financial center turns out to be relatively the
largest exporter of capital. While the private flow from the
United States is the largest in actual volume, when measured
against GNP it ranked only twelfth among the sixteen members
of the DAC in 1968.

The variations are even greater if one disregards portfolio purchases and export credits and looks only at direct investment.
Here although the statistics themselves are rough estimates, the
United States is clearly in a much stronger position, accounting
for more than half the total. Furthermore, annual estimates by
McGraw-Hill suggest that capital spending in the less-developed
countries by U.S. industrial companies will maintain a level
during 1969–71 which is 15-20 per cent above that reached in
1968.[3] Countries which are themselves in need of more capital
than they can supply domestically (such as Australia, Canada,
Japan, and the Scandinavian countries) do very little private long-
term investing in less-developed countries, though they may extend substantial export credits. This situation was recognized by
UNCTAD, which, in setting the 1 per cent of gross national
product as the target for assistance to be provided, accepted the
arguments of several of the developed countries and agreed that
there should be "regard to the special position of certain countries
which are net importers of capital." If such an allowance is to
be made, any item in the payments account might as well be
chosen as a reason for not giving assistance. Why not excuse a
net importer of food from giving assistance?

* * *

There are wide differences in the size of the private flow to the
various less-developed countries. In part, this is a matter of
chance. Oil and minerals may be discovered anywhere: the
wealth of Kuwait and the rapid growth rate of Libya are the
result of rich natural resources located within their borders.
Likewise, improved technology may put new value in old veins,
and cheaper methods of transportation may make new locations
competitive.

Beyond the exploitation of natural resources, the flows of

private resources for development are related to the stage reached by the country. It is not unexpected that the largest flows of private capital from the United States go to Canada and Europe, then to Latin America, and the smallest to Asia and Africa. The basic requirement is an investment opportunity, which in turn rests upon the existence of a prospective market, the availability of appropriate manpower and other necessary resources, and an operating situation which permits production efficient enough to compete and obtain a market of sufficient size.

Because private investment depends upon a multitude of private decisions, which usually are not publicly explained or recorded, it is not easy to interpret the behavior of private foreign investment. It is easier to list conditions which discourage investment than those which might encourage it. For the United States, one cannot determine the relative depressing effect of balance-of-payments concerns as against the frightening seizure of properties in Cuba and Indonesia. On the other hand, opportunities are created by the process of development itself as well as by discoveries of oil or mineral resources, or by the "green revolution" with its greatly increased demand for fertilizer and other products.

Even if there is an investment opportunity and a good production potential, the decision to invest will seldom be made if the investor feels that the policies and actions of the host government are likely to be unfriendly. After all, capital is well rewarded within the more advanced countries themselves. Why should an enterprise take substantial risks in some less-developed country for an uncertain return?

Governments in the supplier countries have an interest in the expansion of the flow of private capital not only because of the values which it carries with it, but also because it adds to the flow of resources devoted to development. Even those recipient countries which are unhappy over their dependence upon foreign aid are nevertheless interested in a greater flow. But here one reaches the nub of the problem. How much private investment there will be depends upon the private decisions of many potential investors. A government can curtail or even stop foreign investment by its citizens, but it cannot make them invest—otherwise the investment is no longer "private."

Having said this, one must note that the act of investment can be made more or less attractive by governments on both sides. Without question, most less-developed countries start with a bias against private foreign investment. In part, it is a carry-over from the past when they believed that their poverty was the result of exploitation by foreign enterprises. In part, it is based on the fear that foreign penetration will somehow infringe upon their independence. In more sophisticated circles, there is apprehension of a balance-of-payments drain, and the emerging business community in some less-developed countries may fear the competition of foreign enterprise both in the product and the employment markets. Finally there is an emotional suspicion of the rich and the capitalist.

Quite apart from these hostile states of mind, there are many special difficulties inherent in the very fact of investing in a foreign country. Often there are barriers to entry which must be surmounted and, once in, there are innumerable problems resulting from local rules, regulations, and business practices, which may be different from those in the home country. There may be problems of location; of importing and exporting, activities often highly controlled; of bringing in necessary management and technicians; of governmentally regulated labor conditions; of special taxes; and of converting local currency into a medium for foreign payments. In all such areas, the less-developed country can make the situation more or less attractive by the nature of its legislation and the behavior of its bureaucracy.

Several less-developed countries have made substantial efforts to attract foreign capital. Iran, for example, offers not only tariff protection and free entry for machinery and supplies, but a 50 per cent net profits exemption for foreign investors, a five-year tax holiday for productive enterprises established at least 60 kilometers from Teheran, and a five-year exemption from income tax for producers of manufactured goods for export.

Unfortunately, a situation in which a stable government is lacking can be one in which a political change may jeopardize the investment climate. Perhaps the greatest fear of private foreign investors has been that their property, when fully developed, would be expropriated without adequate compensation. There can be no denial of the right of any government to expropriate, but fair and prompt compensation can be demanded. The usual formula for settlement is not very satisfactory, since most enterprises are planned with future growth in mind, and only the past investment is recovered without any allowance for the future prospects, or the time, energy, and risk that went into the venture along with the capital outlay. Since less-developed countries seldom have cash on hand to pay for the take-over, they frequently "negotiate" a settlement in securities. Thus the former owner may be given less than 50 per cent of an issue of new common stock, some government entity keeping the rest, and the balance in bonds which may be related to the enterprise or which may be general unsecured government securities.

The problem is made difficult by the existence of many petroleum and mining concessions granted to foreigners at some time in the past on terms that were arrived at through methods now regarded as questionable and with local governments that were highly autocratic. Even though the concessions usually were still technically valid, nearly all of these arrangements have been renegotiated, often several times, with the result that the shares of the local governments have been increased.

In Latin America particularly, there is strong and long-held opposition to foreign ownership of subsoil rights. This attitude reflects the centuries-old Spanish legal principle that private ownership of land includes only surface rights, and that everything below the surface belongs to the King, or whatever government authority is his successor. Provisions in recent constitutions reestablish this principle and often deal roughly with concessions given foreigners in the past.

"Throw out the imperialists" is a popular political slogan, an economic rendition of "Yankee go home." The Mexican expropriation of American petroleum property in 1938 after a prolonged labor dispute was a *cause célèbre*. More recently, a Peruvian incident has had special publicity because of the Hickenlooper Amendment, which requires that economic assistance be terminated if expropriation is not followed by efforts to work out compensation within six months (see Chapter 13). A threatened crisis between Chile and the Anaconda Copper Company was settled through a negotiated agreement whereby Chile is to purchase 51 per cent control of all but one of Anaconda's mines for nearly $200 million, and Anaconda will continue to manage the mines for a fee. At present values for copper, the payment can hardly be called generous, but the original arrangement would never have been made today.

The excitement over national ownership of subsoil rights seems to be a special Latin American idea. In other areas, the pressure is on turning the resources into current assets as quickly as possible with an agreed, and often renegotiated sharing of the results. Foreign extracting companies are recognized as having the necessary capital and experience and being willing to take the risks involved in prospecting and development. The issue concerns the division of the return. The nationalization of Roan Selection Trust by the Zambian government is an interesting case, since the company operated in several countries and its stock was widely held. This necessitated the separation of the Zambian properties from the others and the concentration of private holdings largely in the hands of the largest investor, American Metal Climax, Inc.

Expropriation is most often raised with extractive industries, but there are many cases in other fields to remind businessmen of the risks involved. All foreign property in Cuba was taken over. Indonesia expropriated widely, though many properties have been returned. Ceylon took over petroleum distribution, and Peru has claimed some foreign-owned sugar plantations as part of a land reform scheme.

Galo Plaza, Secretary General of the Organization of American States, has stated that "Latin American governments are deeply aware of the need for foreign investment" and that "under appropriate controls and with the proper mix between local and external capital, they are quite happy to see the foreign investor step off the plane." But he also noted that foreign investment is an expensive method of financing, that it may not fit national priority needs, and that "only the foreign firm that is able to contribute to economic progress and help promote healthy social change is wanted." [4] Much the same attitude was expressed in the Consensus of Viña del Mar, but there is no clear formula which the potential investor can apply with certainty.

* * *

Many supplying governments have become increasingly active in encouraging private foreign investment. They and the multilateral agencies assist foreign investors by providing pre-investment information and appropriate infrastructure. An interesting example of how far such assistance can go is a series of AID contracts with American food companies to test the market for high-protein foods developed from locally available raw materials.

Governments can reduce certain hazards by means of intergovernmental agreements involving investment protection and by investment insurance and guaranty schemes covering such risks as nonconvertibility, expropriation, and war damage. Even though the businessman may be prepared to accept these risks himself, insurance protection can help him raise capital. Difficulty with the transmittal of funds is illustrated by restrictions in Ghana where, because of financial difficulties, remittances of the profits and dividends of foreign companies were withheld beginning in 1961. Not until January 1968 was it announced that profits and dividends earned in the last half of 1967 might be transferred. In February 1969, the unfreezing of arrearages was begun. This is the sort of contingency against which a businessman making a new investment can be insured.

The mildly supportive attitude of the U.S. Congress toward the investment guaranty program is indicated by the fact that in 1968, the disastrous year for foreign aid appropriations, the House increased the ceilings for all categories of insurance by about 15 per cent. Although the Senate did not provide for an increase, the Conference Committee split the difference. In addition, the termination date of the authority was, as usual, extended for another year.

Governments also can enhance realized profits by special tax treatment. Subsidies to encourage capital expenditures, a form of attraction often used by local governments in the United States, have been adopted by some less-developed countries, usually in the form of some type of tax exemption for new investment. In a report prepared for UNCTAD II, Dirk Stikker has suggested that the less-developed countries consider the further use of incentive tax allowances, like those of Australia, which permits a double deduction for expenditure on export promotion, or of Canada, which has authorized a 150 per cent deduction for increased current expenditure on research.

The present U.S. tax provisions for investment abroad tend to nullify some forms of foreign tax benefits by establishing a total tax figure whereby reductions in foreign taxes are offset by increases in U.S. taxes. A continuing and annoying problem is the tax treatment of foreigners who are temporarily employed in a less-developed country and whose salaries are in line with those of their home country rather than those of the host country and may also include special benefits related to overseas employment.

Governments sometimes ease operating problems by various

forms of financial and technical assistance from public agencies. Thus the United States often gives assistance to American foreign investors in the form of loans to provide American equipment, or of local-currency financing using counterpart funds, the so-called Cooley loans. In Latin America, the proceeds of program loans can be re-lent to U.S. companies, and dollar loans may be obtained from local industrial development banks financed by AID and the international banks. Germany also uses counterpart funds to assist foreign investment by small- and medium-sized firms. French procedures include mixed credits whereby both public and private sources are combined in a package deal. An interesting illustration of an international mixture of public and private finance is the case of Freeport Indonesia Incorporated, an American copper-producing company in Indonesia which is planning to develop copper deposits in West Irian with capital provided by the Federal Republic of Germany and four private Japanese firms.

In addition, there are government-sponsored organizations which help establish new private ventures by taking equity positions that they expect to sell later to private investors. The British Commonwealth Development Corporation, established in 1948 largely with government funds, operates on its own or in partnership with governments or private concerns. It reported that in 1968 it had an investment of about $300 million in some 160 projects in 31 countries, and that it proposed to extend its operations beyond the limits of the Commonwealth. The *Deutsche Entwicklungsgesellschaft* was set up in 1962 and at first was active mainly in East Africa but has since broadened its coverage. The *Caisse Centrale pour la Coopération Economique* is engaged chiefly in lending to private enterprises and development banks in the French Franc Area.

In the World Bank family, the International Finance Corporation (IFC) is active in stimulating private investment. It can invest directly in an enterprise as well as make loans. For example, in a project involving the expansion of the Siam Cement Group of five companies, it not only took both an equity and a loan position, but it arranged for credit from ten private financial institutions in the United States and Europe. After a number of years of quite limited activity, the IFC began to expand its operations in 1966 and reached a record high in fiscal 1968–69 of $93 million in new commitments. This figure understates its influence, since IFC reports that its financing served as a catalyst in completing financing operations aggregating some $500 million in 16 countries.

At the present time, individual supplier countries vary widely in the aid and comfort they give to private foreign investment. The United States, Germany, and Japan have made the greatest efforts to encourage the private flow. Some countries take the position that any public action is inappropriate by definition if one is talking of private investment. Others have difficulty in mobilizing assistance to offer to potential private investors. Thus, the scale of their aid activity does not permit the relatively small countries to operate an insurance scheme. There should be a fresh effort to multilateralize these activities along the lines of the proposal passed on to the IBRD by the OECD in 1965 for a Multilateral Investment Guarantee Corporation. The proposal was programmed so as to permit a close relationship with existing national schemes through re-insurance. One obstacle seems to be that some private investors prefer national schemes for fear of early disclosure of their plans by a multilateral agency. There are of course many risks against which one cannot insure, ranging from inadequate auxiliary services in power and transport to the uncertain behavior of an inexperienced labor force, or from red-tape and delay in official actions to failures of government fully to respect agreements made by a previous regime.

* * *

The balance-of-payments position of a country may influence its general policy toward foreign investment: a supplier country may be concerned about the outflow of capital, while a recipient country may be worried about the transfer of interest or dividends. A voluntary balance-of-payments program in the United States was succeeded by specific regulations at the beginning of 1968. Under the regulations, however, the investment ceilings for most less-developed countries were much less severe than for the more developed, being set at 110 per cent of each company's average investment and re-investment figure for 1965 and 1966. Borrowers in less-developed countries continued to be exempt from the Interest Equalization Tax imposed earlier. In November 1968, the Department of Commerce announced that "special consideration will be given to applications from companies which are considering developmental projects in less-developed countries, but which have insufficient investment quotas and cannot arrange foreign financing in compliance with the Regulations." In April 1969, there was a slight relaxation by exempting a firm's overseas investments if they totaled less than $1 million in the year. There was a further easing of controls in 1970 when each direct investor was to be allowed a minimum outflow of $5 million, provided $4 million is to be used for projects in developing countries.

The imposition of these controls is not clearly reflected in a reduction in the flow of private investment to the less-developed countries. Since U.S. companies were permitted to borrow abroad, and did, it appears that foreign borrowings were used by them for investment abroad, a procedure which had no immediate effect on the American balance of payments. The more restrictive ceilings on financial institutions extending foreign credit also operated differentially in favor of the less-developed countries. Probably more important in the long run is the impact of tight money and high interest rates throughout the world. Individual companies may face something of a liquidity problem and find it necessary to curtail their programs of both domestic and foreign expansion.

Another aspect of American balance-of-payments control which may be more serious is a requirement that the government program will only be available for capital investments which are tied to American products. But businessmen are accustomed to buy from the cheapest or most suitable supplier, and their factories in America may well have some foreign equipment. The real effect of such a tying requirement on the balance of payments may be the export of more American goods, but as an offset it will discourage foreign investment.

One of the curious arguments gaining currency is that foreign private investment takes more out of a country than it puts in. Assume that a foreign investment of $1 million is made in a less-developed country and earns a profit of $200,000 per year, of which $100,000 per year is sent back as dividends. If one looks only at the balance-of-payments record, there is one year when $1 million came in, and after that a pay-out of $100,000 each year—seemingly a burden on the less-developed country over subsequent years. But the point is that the foreign investment in the country was busy during the year, perhaps making possible a payroll of $600,000, paying taxes of $200,000, and contributing

$1.2 million to the gross national product. This is the contribution for which the payments are made. Over time, more and more capital is put to work, some as a new flow and some as reinvested earnings. The balance-of-payments entry for dividends and interest is likely to increase as the investment grows, but so also does the gross national product which is created within the country. There is no "exploitation" here, although there may be a transfer problem if the growth in gross national product is not accompanied by a growth in exports. For example it is reported to be "a matter of genuine concern in New Delhi that India already pays in dividends and capital repayment several times the new net inflow of foreign capital." [5] Whether this is a good or bad thing depends on the structure of the economy with particular respect to payments. The problem is one of developing products suitable for export and of meeting world competition for markets. It would not be a very sensible solution to discourage the foreign investment and thus remain that much less developed so far as production, employment, and the revenue base are concerned, but the payments problem cannot be ignored. However, it has many more elements than those relating to capital flow and service, and the problem should be considered in terms of all of them.

* * *

In reviewing the general picture of private investment, it is important to keep in mind that changes have taken place in the business world. There has been a major shift in economic attitude in recent years away from the concepts of *laissez-faire* and rugged individualism to a new emphasis on social objectives and insistence upon the increased responsibility of the state, as discussed in Chapter 2. There is also a shift in the behavior of private enterprise, with less emphasis on narrow profit-making and more on growth and on broader social and economic achievement.

To an increasing degree, foreign private investment is taking place with local participation. It is no longer unusual for the foreign interest to operate through a subsidiary incorporated in the host country, with part of the common stock locally owned and local citizens playing a large part in the management. To be sure, the expectation of reasonable profits over the long run is clearly an essential requirement and has an important bearing when choosing among alternative projects in different countries. But once in the country, fringe activities and fringe benefits begin to assert themselves. What appears to be a growing cordiality and welcome being extended to foreign private investment may be based on the practical recognition by the recipient countries that the flow of official capital will not be adequate. But it also may be related to the discovery that there are real benefits for all and that in the last analysis the less-developed country can control the situation through its own rules and regulations.

* * *

In order to provide some greater assurance in the treatment of foreigners, and since there is no supranational authority to regulate the actions of individual countries, the traditional device of bilateral treaties has been extended beyond the treatment of persons, navigation, and commerce to include the general principle of nondiscriminatory treatment with occasional exceptions, and even to provide for compensation in the event of expropriation. Since 1959, many bilateral treaties dealing specifically with the promotion and protection of investments have been negotiated.[6]

In addition to the general protections provided by these treaties, the IBRD has created the International Center for the Settlement of Investment Disputes, acting under an international convention that establishes agreed arbitration procedures. While more than fifty countries have ratified the convention, the Latin American states have not joined as yet. Without question, the efforts to establish agreed principles and to institutionalize the settlement of international disputes will introduce an element of order into an area of uncertainty.

After working on it for many years, the members of the OECD approved in late 1967 a Code of Fair Treatment for private investors in the form of a draft international convention intended to establish substantive international law in the field. The OECD, not having been able to elicit the reactions of developing countries to this effort, forwarded the code to the World Bank in the hope that it would pursue the matter further. Apart from some disagreements on principle, the practical difficulty seems to be that a number of less-developed countries find it easier to approve foreign investment case by case than to take a position approving foreign private investment in general.

* * *

Direct foreign investment is so surrounded with complications that small companies are likely to be readily discouraged. The large and growing multinational corporations, however, are specially qualified for it because of their wide experience of operations in many countries. It is reported, for example, that of the ten largest industrial corporations in the United States and the ten biggest non-American companies in the rest of the world, only three are without investment or similar tie-ups in India (one of the three is the British National Coal Board).[7] Large enterprises have access to capital, manpower, and technology, and, tending to think in global terms, they wipe out nationalistic distinctions between place of production or ultimate markets.

Private groups have made efforts to enlarge the flow abroad of private investment. Not only are various business organizations active such as the International Chamber of Commerce, but special enterprises are appearing, such as the Atlantic Committee Development Group for Latin America (ADELA). With capital made available by a number of large corporations, it is investing some $30 million per year in Latin America in association with local and foreign interests. Along the same lines, 112 leading firms have agreed to form the Private Investment Company for Asia. Its initial capital of $16.8 million is one-third from Japan, one-third from the United States, and one-third from firms in Australia, Canada, and Europe. The new company will provide equity capital, make and guarantee loans, and provide technical assistance to private enterprises in Far Eastern countries other than Japan.

*   *   *

The problem of how a government should organize itself to encourage private foreign investment has been approached in various ways and is still subject to rather frequent reappraisal and reorganization. For the United States, a report in December 1968 by the International Private Investment Advisory Council,[8] picking up an idea which had appeared in several bills introduced in Congress, recommended the organization of "an overseas private enterprise development corporation" to stimulate U.S. private investment in the developing countries. It would take over certain of the activities of AID, such as providing pre-investment help and insurance against the special risks associated with investment in the less-developed countries. It would assist in

arranging for appropriate financing of worthy projects, including
direct loans and minority equity participations, and it would support privately managed technical assistance programs. It would
be financed by allocating to it the principal and interest payments of outstanding loans made by AID and its predecessor to
private borrowers, plus local currency loans. In addition, it would
be authorized to borrow from the U.S. Treasury and sell its own
securities with U.S. government guarantee.

After receiving this recommendation, President Nixon, in his
Foreign Aid message on May 28, 1969, proposed the establishment of the Overseas Private Investment Corporation with an
initial life of five years. Its scope is more limited than that
proposed by the Council, its purpose being "to provide business-
like management of investment incentives" in the insurance and
guaranty program and to operate "a small direct lending program
for private development projects." The Council's proposal for
authority to borrow from the Treasury or to enter into equity
investment was unfortunately not mentioned in the message, but
the message did state that the budget included $75 million to
augment existing reserves for guarantees to be issued.

Congress approved the creation of the Overseas Private Investment Corporation (OPIC) in December 1969. It increased
to $7.5 billion the ceiling on the amount of insurance and guaran-
tees which it might provide on private investment abroad, including that already extended by AID. In the final appropriation,
Congress cut the President's request for $75 million to $37.5
million and the number of personnel permitted in the highest
grades from 35 to 20. It did authorize the use of some of the debt
service on AID loans.

All of the functions in the President's proposal are presently
performed either within AID and the Export-Import Bank, the
U.N. Special Fund, or the IFC. The argument for bringing the
support of U.S. private participation in the development process
together in one place is that this will centralize responsibility
while giving greater freedom from the restrictions of annual appropriations, civil service personnel procedures, and expenditure
limitations, though such a separate operation would not mean an
escape from congressional review. The Council believes that
better staffing and improved programs should, over time, mobilize
significantly increased new investment each year. This position
was strongly supported by Secretary of State Rogers in testimony

before the House Committee on Foreign Affairs (July 17, 1969).
He outlined four lines of action which were to receive immediate
emphasis, the first of which was "the mobilization of private
enterprise . . . by a specialized business-type organization . . .
which would permit the handling of business questions in a
business environment."

One can agree that such a single-purpose and more flexible
agency would probably be more effective than the present scattered efforts, and yet remain somewhat skeptical about how
much a mere governmental rearrangement of functions can be
expected to increase the flow of private capital to the less-
developed countries. Most of the present flow is by large multinational corporations which are already experienced foreign investors. The existing guaranty program appears to have worked
rather well, and the Export-Import Bank has often contributed
capital for private ventures. It is unfortunate that in its establishment the new agency was not given the wider powers for making
equity investments outlined in the Council's report summarized
above.

The United States is not the only government which is trying
to encourage the flow of private capital to less-developed countries. Australia, Canada, Germany, Japan, the Netherlands, and
the Scandinavian countries provide investment guarantee schemes.
A growing number of government-sponsored development corporations help establish private ventures in less-developed countries. A few DAC countries exempt foreign income from taxation
or at least allow tax credits for foreign tax payments. And in
nearly all cases, the effort to expand exports has a bearing on
the flow of goods to less-developed countries.

A new organizational arrangement creates certain dangers. It
may lead to over-optimism, which could be used as an argument
for reducing the emphasis on official aid. Despite their best
efforts, governments in the capital-exporting countries are greatly
limited in the extent to which they can make private foreign investment move. It is the recipient countries which establish the
investment climate and the conditions under which the foreign
investor must operate.

There is also the danger that there will be a wider gap between official and private efforts. The two ought to be complementary—government investment in infrastructure may well
open up opportunities for private investment, and private invest-

ment in turn may point up some bottleneck otherwise not fully appreciated. The U.S. program is already too decentralized, and if a new agency is to be established, it is important that there be procedures which will assure consistency and intimacy with the other parts of the aid program.

Whatever the organizational arrangement, there is little question that private flows can be extremely helpful and should have vigorous government support. The essential problem is how to encourage the private investor to decide to leave his familiar domicile. Much can be done to attract him by the prospective host and much by his own country to reduce the special risks involved. As infrastructure is established and more stability is achieved, private foreign investment should make a much larger contribution to economic development.

11 · How Much for How Long?

In most rich countries, the problems of giving economic assistance to the less-developed countries come into focus in the central policy issue of how much assistance to provide. This issue brings together in a single decision the whole collection of policies concerning what kind of assistance to give, through which channels, for what purposes, to which countries, under what conditions. The global summary in Table 13 of what the answers have added 'up to, in terms of the flow to the less-developed countries, showed an increase from about $7.8 billion in 1960 to $12.9 billion in 1968. The direct flow to less-developed countries from the private sector constituted 37.7 per cent of the total in 1960 and 39.8 per cent in 1968; the multilateral flow increased over the same period from 3.6 per cent to 6.3 per cent; and the bilateral flow from all governments declined from 58.7 per cent to 53.9 per cent. The forecast for 1969 and 1970 of the Chairman of the Development Assistance Committee is that increases in official bilateral flows from nearly all DAC members will be offset by decreases from the United States although multilateral disbursements will continue to increase. Private flows are particularly difficult to predict, but most indications suggest that they will be appreciably lower in 1969 and 1970. In short, unless there are unforeseen developments, it seems unlikely that when the final statistics are in, 1969 and 1970 will record any further increases in the total figure for the flow of aid. Probably the increases by most countries giving aid will not offset the reductions on U.S. aid and in private flows.

Questions can be raised about any set of figures relating to economic assistance, which the Appendix, "The Foreign Aid Numbers Game," discusses. Nevertheless, the definitions and coverage used above have remained relatively constant, so that one can feel somewhat secure about the trend if not the absolute level. Part of the flow is omitted, however, since the figures do not include assistance from private nonprofit groups, which might add as much as another billion dollars to the total. One also might argue that gross disbursements, being the form in which appropriations are made, would be a better measure of the intention to assist, and there always is a choice as to whether or not to keep a revolving fund revolving. Amortization already deducted from the official and multilateral flows exceeds $1.2 billion and will increase rapidly because of the expiration of grace periods on loans already made.

On the other hand, the figures overstate the increase in real flow because they are in current prices. Correction for price changes is difficult due to the variety in source and character of the specific goods and services included. Prices of capital goods and technical services are among the most difficult items to assess in any price comparison. An examination by the OECD secretariat concluded that the price increase from 1960 to 1968 applicable to officially financed goods and services was about 14 per cent, having been held down by the proportion of foodstuffs in official aid and the limited rise in the prices of chemicals, machinery, and other manufactures exported to less-developed countries. However, even a 14 per cent price increase, if applied to all aid flows, would mean that the current-dollar increase in net flows reaching less-developed countries of 65 per cent from 1960 to 1968 would be reduced to an increase of 45 per cent if stated in terms of constant prices.

Finally, it should be noted that the data are for disbursements, which is the final stage in the provision of aid. Deliveries of food and fertilizer can be completed without much delay but to complete a hydroelectric plant may take ten years. Because of the time required for contracting, procurement, and other preparatory steps, only 3 to 5 per cent of the committed funds are likely to be disbursed in the first year of a loan. Thus there are large sums in the "pipeline," committed but not yet disbursed, and a decision to reduce or increase assistance may not be reflected to any considerable degree in disbursement figures for several years.

Knowing what the present level is does not answer the question of what the level ought to be. In order to answer the question for any supplier country, if it can be answered at all, the logical approach would seem to be to establish the global requirement for the less-developed countries from all sources and thus apply some formula for equitable burden-sharing among the potential suppliers. To be sure, there are areas such as dependent overseas territories, where a single supplier works out a bilateral requirement-supply equation. However, this frees other suppliers from responsibility for those areas and does not necessarily destroy the basic concept of a global requirement for assistance.

With such a range of needs and so many gaps in the available information, any estimate of requirements is difficult, though the demand for it is not new. Estimating the requirements for assistance was the first step in the Marshall Plan. Congress was presented with a detailed four-year program to put Europe back on its feet. Unusually bad weather in the first winter made the food requirement more than had been estimated, and machinery shipments that year had to be postponed. Surprisingly, the four-year total turned out to be $14 billion instead of the $17 billion which had been forecast.

The problem of estimating requirements for the less-developed countries is much more difficult. It is not the foreign supply of goods required for the reconstruction of a previously existing establishment but the building of a wide variety of new economic and social structures—not a four-year task but one involving decades. Furthermore, much depends on factors other than economic assistance, many of which are unpredictable. Nevertheless, foreign aid is an important contributing factor and it should be possible to get some notion of the relationship between the amounts being provided and the requirements for effective assistance.

* * *

Any estimate of requirements must be related to some objective —a rate of income growth or an employment goal, for example. It must make assumptions concerning rates of domestic savings and investment as well as probable foreign-exchange earnings. It cannot be merely a projection of the past since the purpose is to change the past.

Human and electronic computers have tried for at least twenty years to set up some measure of over-all requirements for foreign aid. The first estimates were very simple—merely the use of capital-output ratios indicating the amount of added output which might be expected to result from an added amount of capital. Estimates made in the early 1950s using this approach gave figures varying from $3.5 billion to $14 billion per year. The approach was soon discarded because there was no such simple coefficient, the ratio of output to capital differing greatly for agriculture, electric power, industry, or education, and even then varying with the environment in which the capital is applied and the quality and quantity of the other factors available for production. A slightly more sophisticated way of using much the same approach is to estimate what investment is needed to maintain a rate of growth, say 5 per cent annually, deducting that which can be provided from local savings, and establishing a so-called investment gap.

Additional factors were introduced by Chenery and Strout in a study made for AID based upon data for 50 less-developed countries.[1] Their analysis took into account measures of domestic performance reflecting absorptive capacity, capital productivity, import substitution, and savings rates. It also included rates of growth of exports as an independent variable. Arbitrarily setting an annual rate of growth in GNP at 5.1 per cent as a target, they concluded that under the best conditions of domestic performance and a high rate of increase in exports the target could be achieved in 1970, if there were foreign assistance of $7.1 billion a year. If the continuation of historical domestic performance and low export growth were assumed, reaching the same growth target would require $12.8 billion of assistance annually. To raise the target to 5.9 per cent would increase the comparable capital figures to $9.2 billion and $17.7 billion. Like many of the estimates, these figures probably need to be raised to include technical assistance.

Another approach has been to examine the elements in the balance of payments and determine the amount of needed imports which the less-developed countries cannot finance by foreign earnings. Estimates presented by the secretariat to the first UNCTAD, using a 5 per cent growth-rate target, set the foreign-exchange gap at $20 billion for 1960 and $32 billion for 1975. This requirement could be met, of course, by increased exports, reduced imports, improvement in the balance of invisible items, or by foreign aid. A review of the calculation made for UNCTAD II, taking into account changing trends in trade, suggested that the foreign-exchange gap to be met by less-developed countries in 1975 would be between $17 billion and $26 billion, not allowing for any price increases.

These mathematical models suggest what the requirements would be under the assumptions made. Necessarily, they simplify greatly the factors which will finally determine the results. As improved data become available, the importance of various independent variables will be more calculable. But the elements of institutional resistance, political instability and uncertainty, internal unrest, military diversion, natural disasters, and technological displacement all enter into the determination of the rate of development and may even affect the productivity of foreign assistance. The mathematical approach is necessarily abstract and rigid and can only be indicative in our complex world.

Other efforts at estimating requirements have relied heavily on an examination of the requirements of individual countries, an approach which is more closely related to operations. The country experts in the IBRD produced an estimate in 1965 that "the developing countries could effectively use, on the average over the next four years, some $3 billion to $4 billion more of external capital per year than has been provided in the recent past." [2] This is not an estimate of specific projects and programs standing ready to go, but rather of what could be utilized if it were available. Since the reputation of the Bank's experts is that their requirements are relatively tough, and since expenditures for technical assistance are probably understated, this figure is more likely to be a low rather than a high estimate. A similar judgment that opportunities for high-yield profits exceed presently available funds is also the opinion of the various operators of bilateral programs.

Based on CIAP's annual review of Latin American programs in development, its Chairman, Sanz de Santamaria, said in May 1969 that "Latin America needs about $2 billion a year more in external financing than is coming into the region." He commented further that the region's ability to make productive use of external financing is rising much faster than is its export earning potential.[3] His statement of the requirements, being limited to Latin America, would imply that the IBRD global total is exceedingly conservative.

Referring to various estimates, Mr. Herrera, President of the Inter-American Bank, suggested that "the developing countries can use between $15 and $20 billion a year of development assistance in the early 1970s—a level which compares with a net transfer of $11 billion achieved in 1967." [4]

National plans, it would seem, could be used as a basis for estimating aid requirements, but many of them are still in a very rudimentary stage. President Senghor of Senegal was in no way embarrassed in reporting late in 1969 that the first two Senegalese development plans were only 71 per cent and 75 per cent realized. Furthermore, national plans are usually built upon some estimate of prospective foreign aid and thus can hardly be taken as an indicator of assistance requirements. At any rate, the application of planning is relatively new, and for many countries it is still highly imaginative. However, this approach is now in practice in CIAP, where each Latin American country annually presents and defends its economic program, leading to a summary analysis of the needs of the area (see Chapter 12). At least it may be possible for the consortia, consultative groups, and other reviewing organizations to evaluate the opportunities and difficulties in the short-run ahead, so that the relation of requirements to achievement for a number of major aid recipients can be more clearly seen. Such a procedure will also act to bring the planning process more closely into the realm of the practicable, and to clarify greatly the measure of requirements.

Some notion of the gap between the amount of assistance and plan requirements is suggested by the data for four East Asian countries, given in Table 28.

TABLE 28

AID REQUIREMENTS IN NATIONAL PLANS AND AID RECEIPTS,
FOUR COUNTRIES

		Plan		Official
		Projected Increase in GNP	Projected Annual Foreign Capital Requirements	Bilateral and Multilateral Receipts, 1964–66
Country	Period	(Per Cent)	($ Million)	($ Million)
Malaysia	1965–70	4.9	425	33
Philippines	1967–70	5.4	282	88
South Korea	1967–71	7.0	550	201
Thailand	1967–71	8.5	140	45

Source: Chase Bank, *World Business*, April, 1968, and OECD *Press Release*, Press/A(68)34, July 4, 1968.

The record given in Table 28 for receipts in 1964–66 does not include any private capital flow; but even in making a generous allowance for this, the large size of the gap to be filled between the national plans and the actual level of aid is clearly evident.

Although a few less-developed countries may not be able to make effective use of more capital than is already available to them, it is doubtful whether this is true in very many cases. For some, like Pakistan and India, there are no observable limits in terms of their absorptive capacity. Furthermore, such limits as there are at any given moment are steadily being extended as infrastructure is created, as manpower is trained, and as underlying institutions are strengthened.

In summary, all estimators agree that considerably more assistance can be effectively used. It is probably a waste of time to seek any single figure for the requirements of the less-developed countries. In each country there is a long list of possible uses for aid, with a descending scale of utility, which suggests that there is no one place to draw the line, and no such thing as a single figure for aid requirements. With a certain amount of aid, a given program can be carried out. With more aid, the program can be broader, more ambitious, etc.

These circumstances have led in recent years to a recurring dialogue between the United States administration and Congress, running as follows: A: "The proposed expenditures for foreign aid represent rock-bottom estimates from which all water has been ruthlessly squeezed." C: "We don't believe that this is a rock-bottom figure. We will provide only 80 per cent of your request." And then a year later, C: "Didn't you get along all right after the cut? What specific harm was done as compared with the budgetary savings?" The exchange suggests that the ideal procedure would be for the planners in a less-developed country to work out what would be the results of varying amounts of aid so that, all other things being equal, the suppliers could consider the consequences of alternative sums. This does not happen for two reasons: no recipient wants even to suggest that it could get along on a low figure, and providing alternatives seems to put the final control over a national plan in the hands of the suppliers. These difficulties can largely be removed when the recipient and its suppliers have effective working relationships.

*   *   *

Another way of dealing with the problem, hallowed by United Nations practice, is to rely on the simple proposition that public and private assistance flows, taken together, should reach a target of 1 per cent of the national income of the donor countries. The "one per cent" is an arbitrary figure with no calculated relevance either to requirements or to the increase in growth rates that might be achieved if the target were met. It was probably chosen because the same figure was accepted and used as the basis for contributions to UNRRA for postwar relief and rehabilitation where no estimates of need were possible, and because it was higher than the amounts then being supplied by most of the developed countries.

The moment one begins to set up an exact formula, terms must be defined more precisely.[5] There are questions as to which countries to include among the less-developed and what to include as assistance flows. The estimates made by the OECD Development Assistance Committee include aid to European less-developed countries and private export credits of more than one-year duration, while those of the U.N. and UNCTAD secretariats do not. Neither set of estimates includes any allowance for assistance given privately by nonprofit organizations, nor does it make any adjustment for qualitative differences—grants as against loans, tied vs. untied aid, and so on.

Even with agreement on what to include as assistance, the problem remains of selecting the appropriate denominator to represent national capacity to assist. While the decision to use gross national product, as distinct from national income, was one of the few decisions made at UNCTAD II, it is not entirely satisfactory since it makes no allowance for capital depreciation, which is a real burden on an economy.

The 1 per cent figure as a target for assistance has the great advantage of apparent simplicity and makes it clear that the volume of assistance is slipping if it does not keep up at least with growth in the rich countries. One per cent of GNP for DAC members in 1968 was $16.6 billion. Actually, the total net flow of aid from all DAC members was 0.78 per cent of the target.

Not only has the 1 per cent target been formally approved by governments (though not the date when it is to be achieved) but five countries were above the level in 1968—Belgium, France, Germany, Netherlands, and Switzerland. Canada, Denmark, Norway, and Sweden have made plans to reach the goal by 1975 or earlier. However, the present level for DAC members in total is below the target level, and the target itself keeps rising in terms of the actual amount of assistance as the economies of the DAC members grow. If the OECD goal—set at 50 per cent real growth for the 1960s—is extended, GNP for the DAC members would rise to $2,500 billion by 1978. One per cent of this, $25 billion, is slightly less than double the present level of public and private economic assistance.

Interestingly enough, this figure falls within the range of most estimates recently made, if those of the IBRD, the UNCTAD secretariat, and the AID staff are projected to 1978. It is above the level of $15.6 billion in 1973, or about $18.5 billion by 1977, recommended by the President's General Advisory Committee on Foreign Assistance Programs, but that figure was presented as meeting the lower end of the range of estimated needs.

These are figures of real growth, but no one expects price levels to remain unchanged during the decade. Even if prices should advance by only 2 per cent per year, this would raise the target by another 25 per cent by the end of a decade, which would give a figure in current prices of about $31 billion as the amount of aid required. The price increases would, of course, cause a corresponding increase in current figures of gross national product and, in countries with progressive tax rates, presumably a more than proportional increase in government revenues.

Since the national income of the United States is about equal to that of all other DAC countries, its performance will be of critical importance—and the recent setback is hardly a cheering augury either to the less-developed countries or to the other members of DAC who have been subject in the past to strong U.S. pressure to increase their "share in the common effort."

* * *

There is one disturbing element in the future which will substantially affect any estimates of requirements—the increasing indebtedness of the less-developed countries. The loan proportion of official assistance is increasing. High-interest, short-term, private export credits are expanding rapidly. The widespread use of grace periods, which averaged 5.8 years in 1968, has only temporarily postponed the full burden of service payments. Table 29 presents estimates prepared by the OECD secretariat to show the situation in 1967.

TABLE 29

Estimated Debt-Service Payments of Less-developed Countries,
1967
($ *Million*)

	Interest	Amortization	Total
DAC official bilateral loans	520	830	1,350
Multilateral loans	250	270	520
Private export credits			2,100
Other private long-term	830	1,960	
and unallocated			700
Total	1,600	3,060	4,660 [a]

a Because of different bases for estimating, total does not cross-check.
Source: Development Assistance Committee, OECD.

The figure usually given in describing assistance flows is net of repayments, i.e., amortization. Interest is not deducted—if it were, one would have to assume that the capital was still owned by the lender and include the project of the investment as assistance. By not making this adjustment, one is assuming that the interest payment corresponds to the contribution made and thus they offset each other. If amortization increases, as it is sure to do, this will require a larger gross assistance figure in order to maintain the same net, and an even higher gross if one is concerned with the net transfer. In 1960, the $450-million amortization on official DAC loans absorbed 8.4 per cent of the gross official aid flow; in 1968, amortization of $951 million was 15.9 per cent of the larger total flow. The figure for interest payments is considerably smaller than that for amortization, suggesting that the extension of maturity dates is quite as important as lowering the rate of interest.

It is important to keep in mind that most loans have an appreciable grace period, so that debt payments lag considerably behind increases in debt. Based upon estimates by the OECD secretariat (on the assumption that present terms and composition of members' programs are maintained), the total debt service payable to DAC members is likely to increase by as much as fourfold over the next decade. Thus, to achieve the net aid target discussed above, the gross volume would have to be increased even more unless there were an extraordinary increase in export earn-

ings, since the target itself makes no allowance for the large increases in interest payments.

A similar increase in debt service is found with the loans of the
multilateral agencies. The IBRD lending rates reflect the cost to
it of raising funds in the money market. In 1950, it made a few
loans at interest rates of less than 4 per cent. In 1969, its rates
were around 6.5 and 7 per cent with maturities of up to 25 years
and 3- to 5-year grace periods. On the other hand, the IDA makes
50-year interest-free loans with 10-year grace and only a service
charge of ¾ of 1 per cent. In 1969, typical loans by the IADB
from ordinary capital resources were 18-year maturity, 3.5-year
grace period, and 8 per cent interest rate. Loans from the Fund
for Special Operations were at 4 per cent.

In view of this situation, total assistance will have to grow
higher and higher to make possible increased repayments to the
suppliers of assistance. If not, the real amount of assistance, while
it may appear to increase, will decline in fact. Although legislatures may think they are increasing the aid flow, they seem unwilling to allow for the fact that there is an offsetting back flow.

The problem has come into prominence as certain less-developed countries have had more and more trouble in meeting their
debt-service payments. While there are infrequent cases of default, it is more often true that the debt-service outflow is managed but nevertheless remains a great burden. Thus debt servicing
costs India about $500 million a year, or nearly one-third of its
total receipts from exports. Under these circumstances, any postponement of payments due is as good as new aid—perhaps better
since it frees India's own untied foreign exchange. The Indian
Consortium has set the postponement of payments of $100 mil-
lion per year as a tentative target. As for Indonesia, its Five Year
Plan for 1969–74 includes a program for the repayment of back
debts that is to use nearly one-fourth of export receipts for the purpose. Pakistan's debt service exceeds $200 million a year and ab-
sorbs more than 19 per cent of its foreign-exchange earnings; repayments to some suppliers are now in excess of the new aid
which they are extending.

The situation becomes critical when a less-developed country
finds that it does not have the foreign exchange required to meet
its current debts. Often, it does not know the total of its own obligations, many of which may be private in the form of trade credits. Usually, a number of meetings are held with the various cred-

itors and some solution is worked out, involving the rescheduling of debt payments and commitments by the debtor with future limits on borrowing. The procedure not only shakes the whole credit structure, but also disturbs normal trade activities. Under these circumstances, the World Bank and the OECD have undertaken to improve statistics concerning debt. Even more valuable is the suggestion that the IMF examine the capacity-to-pay position of each country as part of its annual country review. An early warning system might prevent the final stages of financial collapse.

A cooperative effort among the lending countries is necessary to face the debt-burden problem, for if one country lowers its debt-service requirements, the relief can be offset by another increasing its charges. On the other hand, the country with the harder rates may charge the softer lender with "unfair competition." It is rather bewildering to a less-developed country to receive assistance from different sources with different terms, and there is strong justification for the effort to harmonize the terms offered to each less-developed country. Harmonization is not an easy task since there is no simple formula for deciding which countries need soft terms—and how soft. A healthy situation requires proper action both as to quantity of debt and appropriate terms. Presumably, the test is future capacity to pay debt service, which is related to how much debt there is already and the prospects for growth in the country's exports. But it is difficult to translate future prospects into specific interest rates and maturity dates. This is one useful function which the consortia and consultative groups might fill.

In 1965, the DAC adopted a Recommendation on Financial Terms and Conditions. Under it, a member was expected either to provide 70 per cent of its assistance as grants, or to provide terms for a minimum of 80 per cent of its lendings at least as soft as 25 years maturity, 7 years grace, and 3 per cent interest. Since then, most countries have softened their rates. The United States, which earlier provided the softest bilateral development loan terms, has hardened its terms in recent years until it was about the DAC average in 1968. On the other hand, Canada, Denmark, Sweden, and the United Kingdom now give interest-free loans in appropriate cases. Austria, Italy, and Portugal, however, still give few grants and employ relatively hard loan terms.

In February 1969, the DAC adopted a Supplementary Recommendation on Terms relating to official development assistance, newly defined as "flows which are intended primarily to promote the economic development and welfare of developing countries, and which are intended to be concessional in character." This definition will improve the record of Canada (already above the requirements), Germany, and the United States. The new formula maintains the 70 per cent grant test but, for those not meeting it, requires softer terms than before for at least 85 per cent of transactions. Technically, the requirement is that at least 85 per cent of the commitments in an official development assistance program should contain a concessional element of 61 per cent.[6]

While the trend toward softer terms for official loans has been evident for most countries except the United States, the general debt-service burden has not been eased because of the smaller proportion of grants and the substantial increase in export credits. One wishes that this increase in debt represented the reaction to an improvement in the credit standing of the borrowers, and to some extent this may be so. But most recent cases of payments difficulty have come from excessive short-term borrowings and the heavy burden of repayment. (See Chapter 6 for a discussion of forms of capital flow.) Debt service is only one of the external costs which may be created by development and the general subject will be discussed further in Chapter 14, along with various trade problems. At this point, it is important merely to note that substantial increases in debt service put an added claim on the foreign exchange available to the less-developed country, which in turn makes necessary increased assistance to maintain a fixed net flow of development aid and a given contribution to the rate of growth.

* * *

Since development assistance involves a flow of resources from the supplier country, it is not surprising that such operations come under special questioning if and when the country finds itself in balance-of-payments difficulties. In the late 1960s, both the British and American programs have faced this situation.

In the British case, a ceiling was put on gross aid, which, in dollar terms, was set at 3 per cent below the average level of 1965–67. Certain supplementary items were added to this, such as the Kennedy Round food aid, part of the new subscription to IDA, and special assistance to Zambia and to Malaysia and Singapore. Since the DAC figures are given in dollar terms and devaluation has intervened, there could be an apparent reduction even though the actual amount of aid in real terms might even be higher. Nevertheless, the dollar level of Britain's official aid, when placed under a ceiling limitation in 1966, fell in 1967 to $498 million from $526 million in 1966, and dropped in 1968 to $428 million because of the devaluation from the 1967 level. As for private capital, no official restraints have been placed on flows to less-developed countries in the Sterling Area. The British private flow had peaked in 1965 at $547 million; by 1967, it had dropped to $343 million, and the flow was virtually unchanged in 1968. As a result, the United Kingdom is the only country whose flow of assistance to less-developed countries has declined each year since 1965, though apparently not entirely as the result of deliberate government policy. Of the reduction in the total of 25 per cent, 14.3 per cent can be attributed to the devaluation. The official flow is expected to increase in 1969 and again in 1970, largely as the result of increased activity in the commitments to Singapore and Malaysia.

The balance-of-payments problem in the United States corresponded with the budgetary deficit created by the Vietnam War. Official assistance declined slightly in 1968 and promised to do the same in 1969 and 1970. Disbursements have been sustained despite a drop in new commitments because of the large amount already in the pipeline. However, the total flow reached new highs in 1967 and again in 1968 as a result of increases in the private flow.

Perhaps of greater importance to the total common effort has been the fact that because of balance-of-payments pressure, the United States has increasingly emphasized the use of American goods and services as much as possible, thus keeping purchases abroad with U.S. dollars to a minimum. Until 1959, the United States assistance program permitted world-wide procurement although it has always been a requirement that one-half of the assistance be carried in American ships. In that peak year, commodities valued at $514 million were purchased in other developed countries and $104 million in less-developed countries. Since then, aid has been more and more tied to procurement in the United States. The only offshore expenditures permitted under the Foreign Assistance Act (other than those still being made under old commitments) are salaries and payments to overseas personnel and contractors, procurement for Vietnam in certain countries which must in turn buy from the United States, contributions to international organizations, administrative and technical assistance procurement in less-developed countries if U.S. costs would be at least 50 per cent higher, and limited purchase abroad of locally available parts and accessories of U.S. origin. Something like 92 per cent of total AID expenditures for 1967–68 would be in the United States. The assistance given under the Food for Peace Act as well as the bulk of Export-Import Bank loans involve only U.S. commodities.

As U.S. controls tying aid became more and more restrictive, other donors began to follow suit and it has now become the usual practice in bilateral assistance, although the IBRD still employs international competitive bidding. Part of the enthusiasm for tying, one suspects, is that it is clearly a form of export promotion, an objective sought by developed and less-developed countries alike. In addition, some countries insist that they can get popular support for development assistance programs only if they can say that it is a source of domestic employment.

Even without any formal restrictions, many of the goods and services are bound to come from the country providing the assistance. All grants, including technical assistance and food aid, are almost certain to come directly from the grantor. And suppliers are most likely to provide assistance in the areas of their special competence. Nevertheless, aid-tying does restrict the recipient and may force purchases at higher prices, though not necessarily. An UNCTAD secretariat paper set the higher costs at an average of at least 10–20 per cent, though this assumes that the purchase would have been made at the lowest price and that all other elements in the transactions would be equal. At any rate, the suppliers feel that they must tie their aid as a protection against each other, while the less-developed countries feel that it is highly damaging to them. If and when the day comes when tying will no longer be required, the amount of assistance received per dollar spent will be increased.

Since aid-tying is really a protective device among competing suppliers, any reduction in the practice will have to come from mutual action. Presumably, if a country providing aid opens up the possibility of its aid being spent in a third country, it must also be able to compete for its share in the provision of goods and services which are to be financed by other countries. Because the distribution of aid by country is not identical with the share of each in world trade, it is obvious that the result of untying could help some and hurt others. However, this is no different from the argument against trade barriers—that they must not be allowed to encourage inefficient, high-cost use of resources.

One can argue that the use of tying ignores the basic idea that currencies, except for key currencies (those held by other countries in their official reserves), have a homing instinct. If country A gives aid in the form of goods purchased and paid for in country B, the latter will use the cash in payment for some foreign purchase, and it will finally find its way back to country A again in the form of a demand for its goods. But the key-currency exception is all-important. In the case of the dollar, this out-payment may not be offset by purchases from the United States; instead the dollars may enter into some country's reserves, representing an unrequited outflow. Thus, the United States tied its aid to reduce the outflow of dollars and increase the outflow of commodities, causing other countries to take defensive steps. It is doubtful that the situation can be unwound again until the United States is willing to relax its procurement restrictions.

In the meantime, under DAC pressure, steps have been taken by various governments to try to ease the situation. Many countries provide technical advice on efficient purchasing. So far as possible the United States finances commodities which are competitive in international trade. It also has procedures for price tests aimed at getting the lowest U.S. price.

During 1967, in a further effort to help reduce the deficit in the U.S. balance of payments, AID introduced the concept of additionality. The basis of this new step was the belief that, although all U.S. assistance to a given country consisted of American goods and services, the aid flow might merely be substituting for what would have been purchased commercially, which would have resulted in a payment to the United States and a reduction in the deficit. What the recipient would have purchased from the United States in the absence of aid was estimated from past patterns of trade, and aid was expected to be an amount above the estimate for anticipated commercial purchases. Such an estimate was bound to lead to vigorous disagreement between the United States and each less-developed country. Nevertheless, the United States forced extensive "additionality measures" to be instituted in AID recipient countries. It has been estimated that these steps

may have contributed to improving the balance of payments by
about $35 million annually over a four-year period. An AID esti-
mate in early 1969 was that AID-financed commodity exports displaced no more than 2 or 3 per cent of their value in normal commercial exports.

The Latin-American countries were forthright in the Viña del
Mar Consensus in stating that "all stipulations and criteria which
tie the use of loans to the acquisition of goods and services in
given countries or from given sources should be abolished" [par.
28 (e)]. A preliminary U.S. response came five weeks later in the
immediate discontinuation of the additionality requirements, to
the relief of nearly all persons involved in their administration. In
his speech on Latin American policy on October 31, 1969, President Nixon went a small step further by allowing dollar proceeds
of loans made to Latin America to be spent for purchases anywhere in Latin America. This is not a matter of great economic
importance since there is little prospect of the Latin American
countries piling up large sums of dollar reserves, and even the dollars spent in third countries are likely to return to the United
States. More important is the break, even though small, in the
dominance which balance-of-payments considerations have had
over American foreign economic policy.

There is no doubt that balance-of-payments difficulties add to
the pressures to cut back foreign aid, even though it is clear that
most assistance, taking the form of domestic goods and services,
does not involve actual out-payments. Since economic assistance
involves a considerable lead-time, however, any adjustment is slow
in being reflected in operations but is immediately very disturbing to any long-term planning, as is needed for the development
process. Since the balance of payments is the result of many inflows and outflows, there is much to be said for making adjustments elsewhere and regarding foreign economic assistance as an
item whose effectiveness suffers drastically from irregularity, and
which therefore should follow a regular path.

* * *

Even if a set of assumptions about the many uncertainties of the
future were accepted in order to establish some figure for the requirements of the less-developed countries for foreign assistance,
the task of allocating this total among the potential suppliers
would still remain. Burden-sharing is an attractive concept, but a

troublesome one to apply specifically. Although the 1 per cent target has been accepted by both rich and poor countries, the UNCTAD recommendation decries its use as "a suitable method for comparing the appropriate quantitative or qualitative development assistance efforts as between economically advanced countries," thereby implying that the 1 per cent is an aggregate target with individual countries reaching different levels so long as the total meets the goal. Actually, the implication of the disclaimer is universally disregarded, and the 1 per cent is interpreted as a minimum to be achieved by each supplier of assistance, with some of them presumably well above the mark.

There are many important questions in defining an equitable sharing in the common effort. Should only official aid be included, since it most clearly represents explicit national policy, or should private flows be included because they also involve a flow of resources and a cost to the economy? What about reparations payments or export credits? And should some allowance be made for differences in terms, the extent of tying, the degree of support for multilateral agencies, etc.? Furthermore, should the burden for economic assistance appropriate to the United States, make any allowance for the large contributions it makes for collective security? And should the fact that some countries, such as the Netherlands, Belgium, and the United Kingdom, are structurally exporters of capital be taken into account when comparing their total flows with capital-importing countries, such as Australia, Canada, Denmark, and Norway? Since some suppliers are much better off than others, should the same percentage target be applied in all cases, or should there be a progressive rate recognizing different degrees of sacrifice? And how should contributions to the multilateral agencies be incorporated in the formula?

Not only do these questions arise, but the burden of a given amount of assistance on an economy is not easy to measure, especially in terms of analyzing real costs and the alternatives. If an economy is not operating at capacity and there already are costs resulting from unemployment, idle capital, and operations at less than the optimum scale, then the reduction in these costs are offsets to the costs of foreign aid. Thus, in the United Kingdom, it is probable that the real costs of assistance to the nation have been below Treasury cost. In fact, the British government has deliberately tried at times to structure its aid program so as to help some of its own depressed areas. The use of American farm surplus is another case where foreign assistance was of help in dealing with a domestic problem. To be sure, there are domestic uses which might serve the same purposes, but reducing foreign aid does not necessarily result in a domestic counterpart use.

In actuality, there is no formal burden-sharing exercise in the economic assistance field. In the DAC Annual Review (see Chapter 13), each member describes its program and is exposed to the opinions of others concerning its adequacy. The annual statistical record makes certain comparisons possible as to quantity and quality. The fact that the original resolution setting up the DAC spoke of a "common effort" does put some responsibility on each member to think in terms of doing its share.

In considering the matter of burden-sharing, the problem of size can be roughly eliminated by using the per cent of GNP figure, and allowance for the other structural and qualitative differences can also be made. In addition to the basic assistance record, rankings are given for four variables in Table 30, in which the countries are arranged according to per capita income.

If anything, the connection between national income per capita and the level of either total or official assistance appears to be negative. Mathematically, there is no way to arrange two sets of rankings of 16 cases so that the sum of the differences between the paired rankings would add up to more than 128. If the rankings were identical, the sum of the differences would obviously be zero. The differences between rankings for income per capita and total assistance are not far from the maximum, totalling 106. The differences when only official assistance is considered total 100. The five countries whose citizens are economically the best off—U.S., Sweden, Switzerland, Canada, and Denmark—ranked in official assistance 9, 11, 10, 16, and 14 in that order. It appears that the richest countries are doing considerably less than their proportionate share rather than more.

The relative evaluation of economic assistance is not merely a matter of quantity since various qualitative characteristics are important as well. The last three items in Table 30—grant element, multilateral contributions, and support of technical assistance—may all be regarded as ways of making assistance more effective. Norway, Belgium, and Netherlands rank highest in the three quality items while Austria, Italy, and Japan are the lowest. There are still other characteristics which might be taken into account—the percentage of aid which is tied, the division between project and

TABLE 30

INDICATORS FOR BURDEN-SHARING AND RANKING, DAC MEMBERS, 1968
(*Rank Order*)

Country	GNP Per Capita	Total Assistance, Per Cent of GNP	Official Assistance, Per Cent of GNP	Grant Element[a]	Multilateral Contributions[b]	Technical Assistance[c]
United States	1	11	9	7	14	11
Sweden	2	15	11	12	3	8
Canada	3	16	10	9–10	7	12
Switzerland	4	1	16	16	2	6
Denmark	5	14	14	13	4	4
France	6	3–4	1–2	1	15	3
Norway	7	13	12	9–10	1	1
Australia	8	10	3	2	10	10
Germany	9	2	6–7	8	11	7
Belgium	10	3–4	6–7	5	6	2
Netherlands	11	5	4	4	5	5
United Kingdom	12	7	8	6	13	9
Austria	13	12	13	15	8	14
Japan	14	8	5	11	12	13
Italy	15	9	15	14	9	15
Portugal	16	6	1–2	3	16	n.a.

[a] Grant element ranked according to gross disbursements less estimated present values (discounted at 10 per cent) of expected future receipts of amortization and interest on loans disbursed in 1967.
[b] Multilateral contributions ranked according to percentage of total net official disbursements.
[c] Technical assistance ranked according to percentage of total bilateral commitments.
Source: Development Assistance Committee, OECD.

program aid, the variation from year to year, and the level of barriers to imports from the less-developed countries.

It is often argued in the United States that any attempt at burden-sharing should take into account defense expenditures for security, and that either the other countries should carry more of that burden or the United States should be given credit in international comparisons of economic assistance to less-developed countries. This position is not accepted either by the other developed countries or by the less-developed ones. The former argue that they are already sharing in the burden of NATO costs, on which there have been endless international discussions, and that they have had nothing to say about U.S. expenditures in Vietnam, which can hardly be called an international effort except for a few countries within the region. The less-developed countries argue that the United States should not make them pay for its military expenditure by taking it out of economic assistance funds. At any rate, since the countries involved, the institutional setup, and the criteria are all different, and since still other international activities such as United Nations support involve burden-sharing also, the only practical approach is to consider each situation separately.

In matching the total supply of assistance against some measure of requirements or of economic outflow, the total flow is the more important indicator, and whether or not the flow is public or private is irrelevant. However, in measuring the conscious effort put forward by a country, the official flow is the better measure, for, by definition, the private flow is private, the result of the decisions of many individuals. In comparing national effort, then, it seems fairer to compare official flows rather than to imply that the country which is an established capital exporter need not draw as heavily on government funds. On this basis, the comparative position of the United States is raised slightly to the rank of ninth.

The Pearson Commission recognized the wide difference between official and private flows and the difficulty of controlling the latter. Accordingly, it recommended that there be a separate target for official aid and that each aid-giver increase its official commitments to a level which would bring net official disbursements to 0.70 per cent of gross national product by 1975, and in no case later than 1980. In 1968, no country had reached this target, although France and Portugal were both at 0.68 per cent, and only Australia and the Netherlands were above 0.50 per cent.

* * *

The President's General Advisory Committee on Foreign Assistance Programs has recommended that the United States should set as its goal 1 per cent of national income, a figure which was exceeded in 1961 (1.06 per cent) and nearly reached in 1965 (0.99 per cent). It used the national-income denominator, rather than the more recent GNP base. The Committee recognized that the 1967 disbursements had already fallen to 0.86 per cent of national income and therefore were $1 billion short of the target. (The 1968 figure showed a further drop to 0.81 per cent.) Its recommendation therefore involves restoring the level to 1 per cent of national income and increasing it annually as national income expands. The report states that this would meet the lower end of the range of estimated needs and is the minimum objective which can responsibly be considered.

While this formula is a great improvement over the actual trend of appropriations since 1965, it falls considerably short of the assistance that ought to be forthcoming from the United States. To be sure, the low rankings on structural qualities could be taken care of without added appropriated funds although they are largely the result of congressional dicta. But if this is a real burden-sharing exercise, and an allowance is made for the per capita income level of each contributor, the United States ought to be above rather than below the effort of the median DAC member, and it should be dissatisfied with merely meeting only the lower end of the range of estimated need. Not only does curtailed assistance mean a less effective effort to encourage orderly development in the poor countries, but smaller assistance now will prolong the length of time over which assistance will be required.

Thus the second part of the question, "How much for how long?" is closely related to the first. While the ascription of cause-and-effect sequences in human affairs are always suspect, it is reasonable to assume that foreign assistance in substantial amounts given now will accelerate the rate of growth on a sort of compound-interest principle. Other things being equal, it raises the gross national product, permitting more domestic saving, more investment, and a further gain in gross national product. In other words, the sooner the less-developed country has the benefit of the assistance, the sooner it will reach some level when assistance is no longer needed on concessionary terms.

At best, growth is sure to be slow. There are some areas which may be able to maintain a rate of growth well in excess of 5 per cent per year. But even the developed countries, with built-in growth elements of capital accumulation and technological improvements, set 50 per cent growth in ten years as their target in the OECD. The length of time required at various rates of growth to double and to multiply ten times is as follows:

| | Years required | |
Per cent increase per year	To double	To multiply ten times
2	35	116
3	23	78
4	18	59
5	14	47
6	12	40

A more meaningful long-run economic target is expressed in terms of per capita income. Given present population growth rates of around 2.5 per cent per annum and the fact that, even with a major effort, lowering the birth rate will be a slow process, one can expect very few less-developed countries to achieve a per capita increase of 5 per cent per year. At present rates of increase per capita income in the majority of the less-developed countries by the year 2000 will still be less than $700 per capita.

The problem actually takes form country by country, and the recent record makes it clear that some countries will make much faster progress than others. A number of them may no longer need special concessions, but others may be distressingly slow. There will also be dramatic setbacks in what seemed to be promising situations, for example, Nigeria and Pakistan, and dramatic recoveries as in Indonesia. It is to be hoped that these are random variations in a long trend. At any rate, an assistance program must be built on the certainty that economic development is no rapid process and that foreign assistance will be needed far into the future. Most donor countries—unfortunately the United States is not included among them—have recognized this fact and have given foreign assistance a permanent governmental and budgetary status.

12 · Internal Government Coordination

Organization and management are key elements in foreign aid operations because the flows of assistance to less-developed countries comprise such a variety of resources and services, come from different sources, and end up in so many different places. The internal structure of each supplier and each recipient affects organization and management, as does the bilateral relationship between them. Relations among the several suppliers or the recipients themselves and between the two groups raise other problems of effective arrangements and handling. Further complexity is added by the network of multilateral agencies with their own internal organizational problems and their external relations. Although inextricably interrelated, the problems of organization within individual countries are discussed in this chapter, while their external relations are dealt with in the next.

The coordination of development efforts within a less-developed country is in many ways a more difficult task than the administration of aid programs in a supplier country, for it involves not only the programming of foreign economic assistance but also the optimum allocation of domestic resources. In addition, the government cannot avoid getting deeply into operations, as much of the expenditure must be used to create infrastructure and clearly falls within the public sector. While private enterprise, including banking, is fairly well developed in some countries, many of the newer countries have a private sector limited to handicraft-type operations, and no capital markets which might select and finance larger enterprises. Recently, this lack has been partially filled by the creation of national industrial development banks with government funds, and often with support from foreign financial agencies. As already noted, both supplier governments and the World Bank have advanced funds to many of these banks. In some cases private investors have also participated, as in the Industrial Development Bank of Turkey, for example.

In Chapter 2, some of the difficulties of creating a new national government were described. Recognition that programming would be essential in coordinating the development activities of the less-developed country led, among other results, to the drawing up of national plans. In many cases, the United Nations Secretariat provided technical assistance for this purpose, as have countries experienced in planning. The IBRD has frequently organized survey missions to make general studies of needs and priorities.

The process of developing a plan ran into many difficulties, often because of a lack of essential data, and raised many hard questions. Should the target be some projected rate of growth, some level of employment, or some expansion in foreign earnings? How long a period should it cover? Should the plan assume a level of foreign assistance or should that be a dependent variable? What should be the distribution between consumption and investment, short-run and long-run benefits, social security and productivity? How much participation by local governments and private groups should there be in developing the plan? Should the plan, once adopted, be controlling or should it be merely a desirable target, what the French have called an "indicative plan"?

In earlier phases, there often were wide gaps between the exceedingly optimistic plans and the actual results of operations. There also was and still is a lack of discipline within governments so that the group supporting operation-by-plan may find itself pushed around by special interests with political ambitions and strength. However, the planning process has gone on and improved and, in cases such as India and Pakistan, has assumed tremendous importance. Nevertheless, the lack of effective organization in the less-developed countries, often reflecting shortages of skill and experience in public administration, is a complicating factor in working out and implementing foreign assistance arrangements, especially in first agreements. Once an operating relationship has been established, things go more smoothly, except for frequent and costly turnover in personnel in both the supplier and recipient governments.

While these problems seem particularly difficult in the relatively new governments, they are also evident in the older countries, as in Latin America. New functions relating to social and economic development must be superimposed upon a long-established government with an entrenched personnel and bureaucratic structure.

A further problem of coordination is the classic conflict between the central government and state or local subdivisions, which may also mark tribal, language, and religious differences. The conflict between the center and regional administrations can have an important effect on the selection of development programs, tending to encourage the choice of specific projects like building a power plant, while discouraging programs requiring local participation like family planning or agricultural improvement.

Although it is possible to transmit methods of administration and management through advisers, seminars, and group training, efficiency in government is difficult to achieve in any country. Any review of foreign assistance operations must make large allowances for lack of experience, confusion as to the location of responsibility, and uncertainty on some policy matters and excessive rigidity on others. The various activities in the United Nations and in bilateral programs to improve "public administration" deserve high priority because of the strategic importance of government decisions and actions.

* * *

There is similarly a management problem in the developed countries. In the days of empire, the metropolitan powers usually had an office which handled colonial affairs, separate from the foreign office. However, governments are organized mostly on a functional basis, and such economic assistance as there was tended to be scattered through many departments and agencies. It was natural that many of them, expert in agriculture, forestry, health, road-building, transportation, etc., should have direct and often independent relationships with the colonies on projects within their competence. Such coordination as there was, was done by the colonial office or the treasury, or both; but more often there was no coordination at all in the sense of active centralized leadership directed toward social and economic development. High-level officials became involved only in times of crisis. Until the DAC began to ask statistical questions in 1961, few of the former metropolitan countries had any record of the volume or characteristics of the assistance being given to less-developed countries.

As the colonies became foreign countries, one might have expected that the functions of the colonial office would have been easily transferred. But foreign offices are primarily concerned with political and commercial arrangements, having never been dispensers of economic assistance on any significant scale. Thus, after considerable floundering, most governments have now created separate central offices for overseas development matters, the form reflecting the nature of the governmental structure in each country.

The most general solution has been to place the responsibility in a single agency, headed by a person of cabinet or quasi-cabinet level. For example, in 1963, the Netherlands appointed a Minister Without Portfolio to be in charge of development assistance. In 1964, the United Kingdom established the Ministry of Overseas Development, and starting from 1971–72 all its economic aid will be consolidated into one official aid program. The French government regrouped its economic assistance activity in 1966 to give much more responsibility to the Minister of Foreign Affairs, although it still has many specialized agencies set up in the various technical ministries.

In some cases, a cabinet committee provides coordination. In Germany, the Inter-Ministerial Committee on Development Policy includes the Ministries of Economic Cooperation, Economics, Finance, and Foreign Affairs along with other consultative members. Austria, Belgium, Italy, and Japan have similar coordinating groups. Another solution is to establish semi-independent institutions, such as the Swedish International Development Authority (SIDA), the Canadian International Development Agency, and in less general form, the U.S. Export-Import Bank, and the Commonwealth Development Fund. It should be noted that the foreign office and the treasury are never completely displaced by any of these arrangements, and the expert capacities in other departments are usually actively utilized. In virtually all cases, export credits are handled separately.

The structure of aid agencies in the United States has gone through a series of reorganizations. The early postwar programs were administered by the State Department. For the Marshall Plan, Congress provided an independent agency, the Economic

Cooperation Administration (ECA), reporting directly to the President. A separate Technical Cooperation Administration (TCA) was established within the Department of State in 1950. With the rapid rise of military aid, the Mutual Security Agency (MSA) was created and took over in 1951. Its functions, along with those of the Technical Cooperation Administration and the Institute of Inter-American Affairs, were next transferred to the Foreign Operations Administration (FOA) in 1953, whose director was given cabinet status. The FOA operated a small central office, presiding over the various segments of the program, including military assistance, although the operation of the military aid program was moved to the Defense Department.

In 1955, the International Cooperation Administration (ICA) was established as a semi-autonomous agency within the Department of State, taking over the economic and supporting assistance functions from FOA. In 1957, the lending activity of ICA was transferred to a government corporation, the Development Loan Fund. In 1961 the Agency for International Development (AID) was established as a semi-autonomous agency within the Department of State with the functions previously performed by ICA and DLF. By statute, its director reports both to the President and the Secretary of State. During this entire period, the Export-Import Bank operated as an independent government agency. And when PL 480 (Food for Peace) was enacted in 1954, it was placed under the Department of Agriculture.

Undoubtedly this record of shifting responsibility reflects a basic American notion concerning successful bureaucratic strategy, namely, that structural reorganization is a way of reducing dissatisfaction and buying time. Throughout the entire period, however, three substantive issues were always present: Where should the handling of military assistance be located? How much should the whole operation with all its elements be centralized? And what part should the Departments of State and the Treasury play?

To what extent should economic and military assistance be handled by a single organization? Centralized operation made considerable sense in the early days when both military and economic aid were centered on Europe. It was not easy to delimit the two categories, since the recovery of Europe's economy was basic to its military strength. Furthermore, machine tools may be used for many purposes and roads are essential for both military and civilian use. Even the identification of the actual assistance may not define its ultimate contribution, for economic assistance may ease internal budgetary pressures and permit increased military spending by the recipient country from non-aid resources. And the financing of military aircraft with Export-Import Bank funds has been another source of confusion, at least for the record.

Military and economic aid activities have had much less in common in later years. In fact, they may be antithetical in the sense that military aid may have encouraged competitive military development in Latin America, putting an increasing burden on national budgets and reducing the resources available for economic development. While military and civilian assistance probably should be separate operations, they need to be considered together at some point in terms of the total utilization of the recipient's resources. In 1953, military aid exceeded $4 billion and was more than double the amount of economic aid. From that date on, the proportions gradually changed with increases in economic assistance and declines in the military subtotal. In 1961, a three-way division was established within the Foreign Assistance Act—economic assistance, supporting assistance, and military assistance. The first two were handled by AID and the third by the Department of Defense. The military assistance program provided military equipment, training, and related services, while supporting assistance involved support of internal security measures and economic aid to countries "having urgent needs for outside help in the interest of economic or political stability," primarily those threatened by Communist expansion. It usually has taken the form of financing imports; the proceeds of their sale are used by the local government to help finance defense.

Supporters of economic assistance have sometimes felt that relating it closely to military aid would help its passage through Congress. Others have argued that since military aid was so anti-Communist oriented, a close relation to economic aid prejudiced the "neutral" countries against accepting any aid at all, and made it more difficult to win the support of church and other humanitarian groups within the United States.

The proposals of the Peterson Task Force urge the separation of economic development from security and political programs. All types of security assistance—military assistance grants, use of surplus military stocks, military credits, economic assistance in support of military and public safety programs, budget support for political purposes, and the contingency fund—would be grouped in one legislative act under the firm policy guidance of the State Department. This proposal carries out what has been the trend for some time, with support assistance and military assistance becoming a smaller part of the Foreign Assistance Act appropriation, and being increasingly carried by the Department of Defense. While it is not clear as to who would actually carry out the operations and what is meant by "firm policy guidance," there is much to be said for some such rearrangement.

* * *

The second issue, that of centralization, arises because AID is only one of the actors in official American economic assistance. The Export-Import Bank was established as a semi-independent corporation in 1934 to promote American exports. Its policy guidance has come chiefly from the Secretary of the Treasury. Although it has a substantial income from debt-service payments, its lending authority has been increased from time to time. In 1953, the President placed it under Treasury control but a consequent sharp drop in development loans caused Congress to re-establish its semi-independent status.

Another important aid activity began in 1954, under the Agricultural Trade Development and Assistance Act (PL 480), operated by the Department of Agriculture. Amended in 1966 and generally known as the Food for Peace or Food for Freedom Program, it was then given more permanence by being no longer based on surpluses but on availability. The Peace Corps, established in 1961, is another independent activity, though nominally within the State Department. And finally there are a number of specialized activities for which responsibility is exercised by the functional agencies.

The Peterson Task Force proposals apparently would run counter to the experience of other countries and reorganize the aid effort of the United States into even more separate activities. Action has already been taken, as described in Chapter 10, to place the programs for mobilizing private capital and business skills in the new Overseas Private Investment Corporation. The proposed new framework would also include "a United States international development bank, responsible for making capital and related technical assistance loans in selected countries and for selected programs of special interest to the United States." It would be run by a full-time chairman and a mixed public-private board of directors.

Another new agency would be "a United States development institute to seek new breakthroughs in the application of science and technology to resources and processes critical to the developing nations. The institute would concentrate on research, training, population problems and social and civic development." It is implied in the report that this agency will not be active abroad, but would work largely through private organizations endeavoring to increase the body of highly skilled American scientific and professional personnel through support of local training and research institutions, although the suggestion has also been made that it should take over all technical assistance programs.

The first new agency would not appear to have any functions not already in AID. However, it would have "assured sources of financing, including authority to borrow in the public market." Initial capital of $2 billion is suggested in the report, with a borrowing authority of an additional $2 billion. It would also be free to use payments on outstanding AID loans, expected to reach $300 million by 1975, thus moving in the direction of a revolving fund. Presumably, it would be free of the burden of the detailed annual authorization-appropriation process.

The second proposal also covers ground already occupied, although it may be intended to give new emphasis to the effort to "multiply this corps of U.S. talent and experience." Its initial authorization would be for $1 billion. The intention seems to be to bring the universities and research organizations more closely into the program.

* * *

The third problem concerning coordination and the role of the State Department first arose when the Marshall Plan was set up. The immediate postwar assistance programs had been operated by the State Department; but after much controversy, the Congress, feeling that the State Department was more a policy center than an administrative overseer of economic operations, placed the program in a separate, newly created agency, the Economic Cooperation Administration (ECA).

The various legislative acts relating to assistance have all vested the ultimate authority in the President, as the head of the executive branch and the officer constitutionally responsible for the conduct of foreign policy. He is given the authority to have the duties involved carried out through any agency or officer of the government. In the early period (1951–53), economic and military assistance operations were lumped together under the direction of the Mutual Security Agency, which was part of the White House administrative structure. The legislation since 1954 has stated that "Under the direction of the President, the Secretary of State shall be responsible for the continuous supervision and general direction of the assistance programs authorized by this Act . . . to the end that such programs are effectively integrated both at home and abroad and the foreign policy of the United States is best served thereby." (Section 523)

These problems were dealt with again when the 1961 Act created a new agency, the Agency for International Development, with responsibility for nonmilitary aid functions, to be headed by a person with the rank of an Under Secretary, with two Deputy Under Secretaries and nine having the rank of Assistant Secretary, all requiring Senate confirmation. The AID appropriation is separate from that of the State Department, and the agency has its own staff at home and abroad. Its relationship with the State Department, like most foreign relations matters where the operational authority is in another agency, is really on a case-by-case basis and handled most often through personal contact rather than some formal procedure.

The frequent reconstitution of the aid agency and the existence of other agencies concerned with overseas development indicate only the boxes on the statutory blueprint. Since the organization of the executive branch of the U.S. Government is on a functional basis, it was inevitable that many agencies not normally active in foreign assistance should be drawn into the orbit. They have been called on to help man the technical assistance programs and to provide advice on projects in their fields. In fact, in 1966, special legislation was proposed to cover the priority areas of agriculture, health, and education, authorizing the carrying out of special tasks by the appropriate functional agencies, though generally financed by AID funds.

In the conduct of foreign relations the U.S. government relies upon the functional agencies to provide representation at specialized international meetings and to back-stop the multilateral agencies. While the State Department is always included in delegations to help handle such political problems as the seating of mainland China, and on the various Washington interdepartmental committees where policy issues are discussed, the principal connection with each specialized multilateral agency is most likely to be through the related agency in the U.S. government. As a result, the U.S. delegation at an International Labor Office meeting may march off in quite a different direction from the parallel but dissimilar group at the United Nations Education, Scientific, and Cultural Organization. Except for brief periods, the responsibility for representation at the World Bank and the International Monetary Fund, as well as the several regional banks, has been in the hands of the Treasury. This situation is paralleled in other governments. The annual meetings of the Bank and Fund are gatherings primarily of central bankers and Treasury officials.

A political skeptic might explain this confusing record as either the result of government agencies competing for power and increased functions, or as the resort to reorganization as a bid for "another chance," or as a way of concealing the grand total of aid to less-developed countries. But the lack of centralization is easily explainable in a government where the activity cuts across so many agencies. Since the existing actors are all needed for the play, the problem is not how to consolidate the activity into a single agency but how to achieve coordination among the various parts. Under the 1961–70 structure, there is no agency other than AID which is involved and expert in the total problem of social and economic development. It would make sense for AID to have much more to say about the policies and allocation of aid under both the Food for Freedom program and Export-Import Bank lending. It should be responsible for back-stopping all multilateral agencies, with the advice of the State Department and the functional agency most closely involved. There is a growing realization that because resources are limited, priorities must be established among countries and among programs within countries. Cooperation and coordination are needed with other suppliers, because effectiveness in any recipient country is less the sum of a number of worthwhile projects than it is of cumulative and interrelated result of an over-all balanced effort. For many purposes both within and outside the U.S. government, authority at cabinet level would also be extremely helpful.

The Peterson Task Force has tried to solve this problem by proposing the establishment of a U.S. international development council to coordinate "trade, investment, financial, agricultural, and export-promotion policies. It also would be responsible for making sure the U.S. assistance policies are effectively directed toward long-term development purposes and are coordinated with the work of international organizations." Like the other White House coordinating agencies, it would include the Secretaries of State, Treasury, and Agriculture, the President's special trade representative, and the heads of the Export-Import Bank, the Peace Corps, and the new bank and institute. The chairman would be a full-time appointee of the President. (Curiously, the two cabinet officers concerned with education and health, and with industry, are not included.)

The proposed machinery is certainly better than no machinery at all. Undoubtedly it would set up numerous subcommittees to deal with individual countries and separate types of activity. It runs the danger of complicating operations by requiring more approvals than are really appropriate, or on the other hand of operating on such a high policy level that it gives little guidance to the particular case. In the last analysis, the organizational blueprint is much less important than the quality of the people in the various rectangles.

* * *

The foreign assistance process is not solely a matter of organization within the executive branch. In every government it must be fitted into general personnel and budgetary policies. The tripartite system of government in the United States brings the Congress directly into the area of foreign policy. Each year a substantial amount of time and energy is devoted by both branches of Congress to reviewing the past record, hearing from officials and private witnesses, debating policy, and enacting both authorization and appropriation legislation. The congressional procedures place a heavy burden on various officials in the executive branch of the government.

This procedure is unique to the United States. In other governments the executive is presumed to represent the majority in the legislature and either its proposals are approved or the government falls. There is seldom any activity comparable to the American system of report-writing and hearings where the performance of the executive agencies are publicly examined and private citizens may express their opinions.

One by-product of the situation is that many more comments about the U.S. assistance program are made, published, and circulated around the world than is the case of other supplying countries. Other countries face the same scrutiny, but within the executive branch and without much public debate. Since colorful criticisms are more likely to be considered news, and since the Congress spends most of its time in reducing and restricting the program proposed by the President, the result is a widespread impression of activity approved only reluctantly, no matter what the final outcome.

There are five elements in the Foreign Assistance Act of 1961 as amended: a general statement of objectives with a number of specific suggestions scattered throughout the act; various requirements on the procedures to be followed by AID; a limitation on the number of countries to receive aid and specific prohibition in certain cases; an indication of conditions which must be met by recipient countries if aid is to be provided; and the authorization of funds by various categories.

The general statement of policy includes a declaration of purposes—to limit aggression and subversion; to strengthen national security; to support the principles of economic cooperation and trade, freedom of the press, information, and religion, and nondiscrimination because of race, color, or religion.

To achieve these objectives, seven operating principles are stated: Self-help is essential, including the encouragement of democratic participation. The involvement and cooperation of other donors is needed, particularly in supporting multilateral activities. Emphasis should be given to regional cooperation. Priority should be given to food production and family planning within the fundamental requirements of food, health, housing, and education. American commodities and services should be used wherever practicable. In all cases, efficiency and economy are essential to bring maximum effectiveness. Activities should be coordinated as much as possible with other programs such as the furnishing of agricultural commodities, disposal of excess property, and U.S. payments to international institutions. Some of these principles are restated in later sections of the law. For example, since 1961 a specific provision has been included that any attempt by countries to make any distinction among American citizens because of race and religion is repugnant, and that this principle shall be applied as the President may determine.

As an illustration of a Congressional directive, a new Title IX was added to the Development Assistance chapter of the Foreign Assistance Act in 1966, entitled "Utilization of Democratic Institutions in Development." It stated that "emphasis shall be placed on assuring maximum participation in the task of economic development on the part of the people of the developing countries, through the encouragement of democratic private and local governmental institutions." The Senate Committee illustrated what it had in mind: local programs of self-help and mutual cooperation through loans to small farmers; encouragement of cooperatives, labor unions, and savings and loan institutions; utilization of voluntary agencies; and support of integrated programs of community development designed to promote stable and responsible governmental institutions at the local level. It asked that a report be submitted each year describing the steps which had been taken toward this objective.

* * *

The Act spells out in detail (Section 634[d]) the limited flexibility which Congress is willing to give to the executive branch in carrying out the program. The presentation must include data on a country-by-country basis of all assistance planned, including food and military assistance under other Acts, proposed contributions to multilateral financial agencies, and the previous year's record of Export-Import Bank financing. The Appropriations Act provides that no funds are to be used for projects not justified in the presentation. In a few cases, however, permission has subsequently and reluctantly been granted by the Committees after formal submission. More often, they have insisted that new projects be delayed until the regular presentation. At the end of the fiscal year, the President must report to Congress describing and explaining all actions "of a kind, for a purpose, or to an area substantially different from that included in the presentation to Congress." The Congress has been particularly critical of alterations made in technical assistance programs.

The presentation is made to Congress in writing as well as in oral testimony before the appropriate committees. After a general presentation by the Secretaries of State and Defense and the AID Administrator, testimony on geographical areas is given by the regional directors. There is usually substantial cross-examination and often supplementary information is submitted.

The procedure is certainly very burdensome on the already over-worked officials involved and also on certain members of Congress. It provides a maximum of public exposure for a mass of detail concerning other countries. In the end, it tends to freeze a program for a given year in accordance with programming done many months before the fiscal year begins.

Another way in which the hand of the Congress appears in the economic assistance program is in the form in which final appropriations are made. Thus when AID requested $3 million for 1968–69 for surveys of investment opportunities, it was denied any funds in the authorization bill. On the other hand, as described in Chapter 7, $50 million for 1968–69 and $75 million for 1969–70 were earmarked for use only in the field of family planning. None of the reduction in the amount for international organizations was to apply to the Children's Fund—in fact, it was to get an extra million dollars. Another specific appropriation is to be used for the support of American schools and hospitals abroad. And, perhaps most important of all, the assistance to be given to Latin America is provided under the separate heading "Alliance for Progress," divided into technical assistance and development loans.

*   *   *

The legislative requirements on procedures are very detailed, often originating in some situation which came to the attention of Congress. Thus, to choose some illustrations at random, any flood control, reclamation, or other water or related land resources project must meet U.S. standards. All procurement contracts must contain a cancellation clause. No assistance is permitted to a productive enterprise which will compete with U.S. enterprises unless its exports will be limited by agreement to not more than 20 per cent of annual production. The terms of contracts made by recipients and the firms providing engineering, procurement, and construction services must be approved. A complicated formula restricts the procurement of iron and steel products or components for use in Vietnam according to source and amount of foreign content. United States citizens employed overseas by AID must have security clearance. Fifty per cent of all ocean shipments must be carried in American ships, a provision which greatly irritates the recipients, since it requires an actual payment by them above that which the market requires.

Payments to suppliers of U.S. source commodities must be made to an address in the United States. No more than 20 per cent of the total appropriation can be obligated during the last month of the fiscal year. The 1968 revised version included a new provision involving advance clearance to make certain that only approved items were included in program loans. In some of the foregoing cases, however, the President has authority to waive the requirement upon a finding of national interest.

In addition to those special requirements, AID must follow the general government regulations with respect to personnel and procurement. To these, AID has added regulations to deal with its own special problems. Unfortunately, all these rules, regulations, and prohibitions add up to a very heavy burden on the agency and on the less-developed country seeking assistance. Presumably each regulation is justifiable. But it is the total impact which must be considered.

It is an illusion to believe that any set of regulations can assure perfect expenditure free of waste. The state fishing corporation in Ghana owns ten Soviet-built trawlers that have never been used. They had become so dilapidated that a consultant suggested they be filled with concrete and sunk to form breakwaters. One can get full protection from criticism by not acting at all or by devoting tremendous effort to watch-dog activities plus audit. But it seems that the efforts of Congress and of AID to establish protective procedures have gone beyond the point of careful expenditure to that of excessive and delaying regulation.

While the recipient countries are increasingly critical of procedures which affect their operation, involve them in detailed reporting, or delay the initiation of projects, many of the difficulties are the inevitable result of the gap between the rich and the poor. For example, it has been reported that Ecuadorian officials were critical of "United States aid procedures, including requirements that United States engineering consultants be hired —many of them at salaries 10 times higher than those paid Ecuadorian engineers for United States–financed highway projects." [1] One can easily understand both the concern of the U.S. government to make certain that proper standards are being met, and the feeling of the Ecuadorians that they are able to do the job of road-building at much less cost.

Many of the qualifying provisions are intended to assure honesty and efficiency, because from time to time, the charge of fraud and corruption is raised against the assistance program. However, it must be kept in mind that assistance consists of goods and services rather than a hand-out of cash—that payments are made by the U.S. Treasury through U.S. banks to U.S. business firms. When the items reach the recipient country, they are observed, audited, and investigated by U.S. government employees. In addition to a controller's office and a Management Inspection Staff in AID, Congress has established an Inspector General for Foreign Assistance in the Department of State with unlimited powers of inspection and even of suspension of projects, although the latter has never been invoked. Most of the recorded violations relate to technical requirements with respect to prices, shipping, or commodity eligibility. If improprieties are uncovered, action is taken to obtain reimbursement from the recipient.

Considering the widespread distribution of economic assistance so much of which has gone to countries with business practices differing from those in the United States, it is surprising that outside observers and disgruntled employees have produced so few charges of mismanagement. The most serious criticisms had to do with aid to Vietnam, which expanded rapidly at a time when harbor, dock, and inland transportation were all so chaotic that disappearance of goods in transit was not unusual, and it took some time to bring order into the situation. However, the purpose of the imports at that time was not so much to facilitate economic development as to increase the supply of goods in order to restrict inflation. For this purpose, even those goods that were finally sold on the black market were useful, for they reduced the demand and the local criticism of the Vietnamese government. This particular case can hardly be taken as indicative of the normal flow of economic assistance. Mr. William Gaud, then the administrator of AID, commented more generally, "This is the most inspected program that anyone could imagine. Still, we do make mistakes, and there is a constant effort to tighten up. But these cases are a minor factor of our total operations; they are the exception." [2]

In the widely publicized case of a U.S. contract in Belgium for reconditioning surplus army equipment, there was no evidence of any improper payments but rather of poor business judgment in selecting the contractor and in personal misconduct by officials immediately involved, a situation which is not unfamiliar in domestic programs. Some highly publicized charges are clearly unfounded: cocktail glasses for the Dominican Republic were, in fact, provided to equip a tourist hotel; no aid was given to Kenya to buy additional wives for government officials; nor did AID contribute any assistance to the building of the municipal center in Addis Ababa.

Only occasionally is evidence uncovered in any country of the use of American assistance which might be described as corruption. The requirements placed on official transfers are much more stringent than those in the private sector, where there is much more pressure on the foreign enterprise to conform to local practices. General Ankrah, chief of state for Ghana following Nkrumah, resigned after three years in office, admitting that he had received money for political purposes from various foreign countries. President Nkrumah had himself been overthrown by the military on charges of misuse of power and improper use of government funds.[3] Without doubt, many governments in the less-developed countries have not yet established the same standards of conduct as those presumably observed in the developed countries. The extended family system leads easily to nepotism, and the allocation of benefits may be subject to inducement.

While the developed countries cannot force their standards of official morality (which even they have difficulty in realizing) on the recipients of assistance, they can see that the assistance provided does reach its goal, and that their own performance is as correct as is humanly and institutionally possible. One must balance the effort to increase protection from fraud and inadequate review against the certainty of delay as well as the distortion created by the effort to program in a way that will avoid complicated procedures or the possibility of being charged with an error in judgment. Given the number, variety, and scattered location of assistance projects and the amount of inspection and audit, the record is surprisingly free of evidence of personal misbehavior. This should not, of course, be confused with those occasional cases where, for one reason or another, a project has not made the expected contribution to development.

* * *

Legislation which establishes conditions for *not* giving assistance often raises the greatest difficulties. That supplier countries, in deciding how to allocate their assistance, take into consideration the behavior of the recipient should come as no surprise. For most countries, however, there are no publicly stated indicators of the conditions under which assistance will or will not be provided, though they undoubtedly exist.

Congressional designation of certain countries which for political reasons are not to receive aid has been discussed in Chapter 8. Moreover, the prohibition has been extended to include other countries indirectly involved. Thus, aid is not only prohibited to Cuba but also, since 1962, to whichever country may furnish assistance to Cuba and since 1963 to countries whose ships or aircraft are carrying goods to or from Cuba. Similar prohibitions applying to countries trading with North Vietnam were added in 1964 and 1965. To enforce the embargo on Cuba, Congress requested the President to try to make certain that no U.S. contribution to the United Nations Development Program should be used for projects providing economic or technical assistance to the government of Cuba so long as Cuba is governed by the Castro regime. Any such restriction on the use of the U.S. contribution is meaningless, however, since the UNDP has contributions from other countries which are not thus limited.

Other provisions deal with financial obligations. In the act passed in 1961, assistance was to be denied to any country whose government is indebted to any U.S. citizen for goods and services rendered and, the legal remedies having been exhausted, the debt is not denied or contested. In 1962 this provision was extended to include loans with a direct or indirect government guaranty; in 1966 it was extended to include defaults of more than six months in payments to the U.S. government, unless the President finds that such action would be contrary to the national interest.

The Hickenlooper amendment was enacted in 1962, directing the President to suspend assistance to the government of any country which had nationalized, expropriated, or seized ownership or control of property owned by any U.S. citizen or business, or had imposed taxes or operational conditions which have the same effect, and which had failed to take appropriate steps within six months to discharge its obligations, including equitable and speedy compensation. It also stipulated that no aid may be extended to finance such compensation. This provision first came into operation in 1963 when U.S. assistance to Ceylon was terminated because of the nationalization of certain petroleum distribution properties. The matter was finally settled in July 1965, and assistance was resumed. More recently, the question has come up with the nationalization of certain petroleum properties by the Peruvian government. Unwillingness to let this affair dominate American relations with Peru would appear to have led to a rather liberal interpretation of what is meant by "appropriate steps."

Another provision, intended in a backhanded way to encourage foreign investment, was enacted in 1963 whereby no assistance was to be given to a country which has not agreed to institute the investment guaranty program as of December 31, 1965. (The date was regularly moved forward thereafter.)

An area of increasing Congressional concern has been the extent to which a less-developed country diverts its resources into military expenditures. A provision in 1967 stated that, upon taking into account the burden of military expenditures on the recipient's budget and the availability of foreign exchange, the President should terminate assistance if it is being diverted, or if the country's own resources are devoted, to unnecessary military expenditures. This restriction was made more specific in 1968 with the statement that none of the appropriated funds are to be used to furnish sophisticated weapons systems, such as missile systems and military jet aircraft, unless the President makes a national security finding. Furthermore, if such weapons are purchased elsewhere, an equivalent amount of economic assistance is to be withheld. In the Appropriation Act for Fiscal Year 1968, Greece, Turkey, Iran, Israel, the Republic of China, the Philippines, and Korea were exempted from these provisions.

In addition, certain provisions are clearly the result of congressional reaction to unpleasant incidents. Attacks on the USIS libraries and embassies led to a provision in 1965 whereby "assistance should be terminated to any foreign country which hereafter permits, or fails to take adequate measures to prevent, the damage or destruction by mob action of U.S. property within such country unless the President determines that appropriate measures have been taken by such country to prevent a recurrence." A similar explanation accounts for the 1965 provision that "consideration should be given to excluding from assistance any country which hereafter seizes, or imposes any penalty or sanction against, any U.S. fishing vessel on account of its fishing

activities in international waters." In 1966, assistance was prohibited to countries officially represented at any international
conference planning activities involving insurrection or subversion,
directed against the United States or recipients of American
assistance or agricultural sales.

It is not unusual for a quite unrelated amendment to be added
to legislation. In some cases, it provides an opportunity for the
Congress to express itself on a current foreign policy problem; in
others, it may protect a provision which might otherwise be
vetoed by the President. For many years, the appropriating
legislation for AID has reiterated that Congress opposes the
seating of the Communist Chinese regime in the United Nations.
A provision reaching far beyond the subject of foreign aid was
first included in 1963, prohibiting the granting of a sugar quota
"or any other benefit under law" to Cuba until it made restitution or compensation for nationalized property of U.S. citizens.

In 1967, Congress advised that in the allocation of assistance,
the status of the recipient with respect to dues, assessments, and
other obligations to the United Nations should be taken into
account. Also in that year, it was stated that "it is the sense of
the Congress that every effort must be made to obtain a permanent peace in the Middle East." Congress called for direct talks
among the parties concerned, and for the President to undertake
a review of the area's needs and a re-evaluation of U.S. policies
aimed at helping meet those needs and securing a permanent
peace in the area.

An amendment in 1968 informed the President that it was
the sense of Congress that he "should take such steps as may
be necessary . . . to negotiate an agreement with the government
of Israel providing for the sale by the United States of such
number of supersonic planes as may be necessary to provide
Israel with an adequate deterrent force." This was a reaction to
the decision of the French government to cancel Israel's outstanding order for French planes. There was no mention in the
debate of the more general provision in the act aimed at discouraging less-developed countries from acquiring jet aircraft for
military purposes!

Another such provision, incorporated in 1968 at the insistence
of Senator Morse, restricted for 1969–71 the amount of un-
processed timber to be sold for export from federal lands located

west of the 100th meridian (a line passing through the center of the Dakotas and Texas).

Having described some provisions which were incorporated in legislation, it is only fair to say that individual congressmen have proposed many more which were either not passed on the floor or finally dropped in the Conference Committee. Thus, the Senate included a provision relating to the *Pueblo* incident in the 1968 legislation, but it was dropped in conference, as was a requirement for school assistance in federally-affected areas. In 1969, proposals were rejected to deal with hijacking, to remove all sanctions against Rhodesia, to require the President to consult with Congress concerning Okinawa, and to prohibit military aid to Greece.

Nearly all the various provisions that have accumulated in the foreign assistance acts represent matters which seem reasonable on their face. Their purpose, like that of criminal penalties at law, is to be a deterrent to undesirable actions. Nevertheless, the central problem is that the relationship of the United States to any one country is a complicated matter with a number of pluses and minuses at any moment of time. If legislation raises some one consideration to such major importance as to lead to automatic action by the President or the AID authorities, a chain reaction of much greater dimensions may be started. The particular set of circumstances leading to the specific difficulty may have a history not entirely favorable to the American interest. Furthermore, some of these legislative provisions are stated in such general terms or use judgmental words, such as "necessary," so that the application to a nonstandard case is not clear. Finally, a satisfactory solution may be much more difficult to achieve through public pressure than through quiet negotiations. Not only is national pride aroused, but those individuals who favor the U.S. position are likely to be undercut by charges of being excessively pro-American.

The leverage of withholding aid depends upon its importance to the economy of the recipient country. In some cases, such as Laos, Vietnam, and Jordan, aid makes a major contribution to the government's budget. In others, such as South Korea, Turkey, India, and Pakistan, the imports are essential to the operation of the economy. However, in many cases the refusal of assistance may mean a slackening of the rate of economic growth rather than pressure on the economy that leads to explicit action contrary to some line which is politically popular in the country. One must also remember that the United States is not the only source of assistance. After the termination of Western aid to Indonesia in 1963, assistance was supplied for a considerable period by Communist countries.

The resistance of the Congress to many of the proposals for amending the Act is to be commended. However, it is highly desirable that absolute instructions be avoided in legislation and that the President be given some flexibility in dealing with foreign countries. There can be no question about the propriety of Congress declaring its general position through "It-is-the-sense-of-Congress" provisions, which can in fact strengthen the hand of the President when such problems arise. Rather, it is the flat prohibition which can be troublesome all around. Asking the President to explain his actions to Congress is also questionable, since it may be undesirable to put on the public record the details of a particular case that may then be claimed to be a precedent in a somewhat different situation. It would be more appropriate to examine the unusual situations at the time of the Committees' annual review rather than to require frequent declarations by the President of his judgment concerning the national interest.

* * *

One further difficulty about the operation of present Executive-Congressional procedure is the way the timing works out. AID must develop its programs by the autumn of a year for the fiscal year which begins on the following July 1. It then must discuss them with the Budget Bureau in the last part of the calendar year so that an agreed figure be included in the Presidential budget, usually forwarded to Congress in January. This is soon followed by a specific message concerning foreign aid, presenting the proposed program in much more detail.

The complicated process of reaching agreement between both Houses on the authorization involves public hearings and congressional action and negotiation. Only after this, do the Appropriation Committees report. The actual timing of final Congressional action for the last eight fiscal years has been as follows:

Completed Congressional Action

For Fiscal Year	Authorization	Appropriation
1961–62	Sept. 4, 1961	Sept. 30, 1961
62–63	Aug. 1, 1962	Oct. 23, 1962
63–64	Dec. 16, 1963	Jan. 6, 1964
64–65	Oct. 7, 1964	Oct. 7, 1964
65–66	Sept. 6, 1965	Oct. 20, 1965
66–67	Sept. 19, 1966	Oct. 15, 1966
67–68	Nov. 14, 1967	Jan. 2, 1968
68–69	Oct. 8, 1968	Oct. 11, 1968
69–70	Dec. 19, 1969	Feb. 9, 1970

During this period, the authorization legislation has never been completed before one month of the fiscal year starting on July 1 had already passed, and in half the cases not before the second quarter. Although the gap between authorization and appropriation has been three days or less in two cases, it has averaged about thirty days. Only once has all Congressional action been completed by September, in five cases in October, and in three cases not until January, the seventh month of the fiscal year. Operating an agency for a considerable part of the fiscal year without either Congressional decisions on policy directives or any assurance on the extent to which new funds will be available seriously affects its performance. It is disturbing to all personnel, and it creates embarrassments with respect to various international bodies where the United States cannot make a timely declaration of its contribution.

* * *

The annual legislative examination is no simple affair. The amount of information provided is very detailed and voluminous, including not only the record of the past, but a description of the next year's program. Nongovernmental witnesses are heard, often the same organizations appearing year after year—condemnation by the Liberty Lobby and the Citizens Foreign Aid Committee, and support, though not without suggested improvements, by the AFL-CIO, various church groups, the League of Women Voters, and the Chamber of Commerce. The four committees directly involved spend many hours in preparing legislation, and the resulting bills are seldom passed without prolonged debate and amendment on the floor.

It is absurd that after twenty years the Foreign Assistance Act should still have a life of only one year, with the inevitable emphasis on short-run considerations. Because economic development is a slow and long-term process, assistance to that end should not be regarded as a temporary activity. There should be a basic authorization with no specified expiration date, subject of course to periodic amendment. It should not include any ceiling on appropriation but follow the usual form of other authorizing legislation by permitting the appropriation of such sums as may be decided through the appropriation process.

Similarly, appropriation should be on as long-term a basis as possible. Individual projects may require several years to be accomplished, and certain programs may need support for a considerable period before assistance can be phased out. Many of the less-developed countries, with the encouragement of the West, have five-year (more or less) plans, and it should be possible to indicate to them whether or not the general structure will be supported. To be sure, no Congress likes to set aside funds for the future, since it may appear on its own records as contrary to the objective of current budget-balancing. However, the effective handling of aid funds requires the agency to be able to make long-term commitments.[4] The two-year authorization enacted in 1969, for 1969–70 and 1970–71, was not in recognition of this need, but to give the new administration time to work out and present revised aid legislation and the Congress time to consider it without the special time pressures of an election year.

The problem of carrying out a foreign aid program is rather different from any governmental function prior to World War II because it involves government expenditure in collaboration with another government on a continuing basis. One exception to usual practice was the international character of tariff-making, where the Congress gave the executive branch authority to negotiate and sign agreements within certain specified limits. However, foreign aid involves an appropriation, and not only is the legislation rather detailed, but the appropriations process is exhaustive. Some way must be found—perhaps through the new proposals of a public corporation or bank—to create a situation which will permit effective operation, while still recognizing that the executive and the Congress have a joint responsibility for national policy.

13 · Relations with Other Governments

In the days of empires, when there was a tight link between the metropolitan power and its colonies, the imperial powers had no particular reason to discuss development problems with each other; and the colonies, having no "foreign relations," talked to no one else. The multiplication of independent countries and the emphasis on development created an entirely new situation. Not only have the last ten years seen significant progress toward more effective organization within governments, as discussed in the preceding chapter, but there also have been notable advances in their working relations with each other. This is apparent in the number of new arrangements, often new organizations, which endeavor to "harmonize" or "coordinate" policy positions and operational procedures and to promote the concept of a common aid effort. These involve groupings among the richer countries supplying assistance, among the less-developed countries receiving it, and arrangements involving both.

* * *

Supplier countries have had reservations concerning any commitments likely to interfere with their individual freedom of action. They are reluctant not only to reach agreements among themselves but even more to make long-run commitments of specific amounts to specific less-developed countries. In addition, suppliers have assumed, although less so now than in earlier days, that the less-developed countries would regard any formal grouping as "ganging up" against them for some devious purpose or other. The less-developed countries have sometimes suggested that they also

preferred a less-ordered situation as giving them more freedom
to shop around among potential suppliers. Despite the evident
benefits from more collaboration, it has not been easy to develop
forms of coordination that are effective in their economic and
social impact as well as politically acceptable.

It was a surprisingly long time before the countries providing
assistance recognized in a formal way that they might usefully
consult together about their programs. In early 1960, there began
a series of occasional meetings in national capitals by a small
group called the Development Assistance Group (DAG). The
initiative had been taken by the United States, primarily for the
purpose of encouraging other countries to do more about foreign
aid. At the time there were no statistics for the various national
programs, and the American impression, which proved to be in-
correct, was that little was being done by anyone else.

The possibility of putting the activity on a more permanent
basis appeared in connection with the transformation of the
Organization for European Economic Cooperation (OEEC) into
the Organization for Economic Cooperation and Development
(OECD) and the inclusion of Canada and the United States as
full members. The DAG was incorporated in the new organization as its Development Assistance Committee (DAC). Its
membership was not limited to OECD members, for Japan and
the European Community were members from the start. The addition of Switzerland in 1968 increased the membership to sixteen countries plus the Commission of the European Economic
Communities. The DAC has never had any funds of its own for
aiding development; it is instead a center where new policies,
problems, and practices are discussed and old ones reviewed. It's
activities derive from the Resolution on the Common Aid Effort
adopted in March 1961, establishing as objectives the expansion
of the flow of resources to the less-developed countries, the improvement in the effectiveness of development assistance, and the
provision of assistance either as grants or as loans on favorable
terms.

. The DAC members are represented at an annual meeting by
high-ranking officials who are involved in their country's assistance
programs. At the other more frequent meetings, the representatives are either persons regularly assigned to the OECD delegations or individuals sent by governments because of their interest
in particular agenda items. The latter form of representation is

common in the specialized working parties dealing with such subjects as assistance requirements, financial aspects of assistance, or the advance consideration of issues on the UNCTAD agenda. The DAC is the only OECD Committee with a permanent, independent chairman, and its secretariat is part of the staff of the OECD.

DAC's initial activity was to develop a statistical exercise which produced for the first time fairly comparable national records of assistance to less-developed countries and of contributions to the multilateral agencies. These could then be added together to give a figure for the total flow of assistance. Since then, the statistics have been improved in reliability and published in more and more detail. Whether or not one agrees with the definitions established (see Appendix), there is now a quantitative sense of general trends and changes in structure. And because of the detail in which the data are published, they can be adjusted to any other definition desired.

In operational terms, the most important activity of the DAC in its corporate form is the Annual Aid Review. In the spring of each year each member submits a statistical and substantive report on its past year's performance. For example, the submission made by the United States in 1968 was 107 pages long with a 90-page statistical annex. The Secretariat prepares an analysis of each submission and a series of questions to be discussed. Then each country appears before the entire Committee to explain and defend its performance. In each case, two or three members are assigned to provide special inquisitors. These sessions are completely off-the-record and range from one-half day to two days, depending on the size and complexity of the program. At first, the questioning was relatively limited, except by the independent Chairman; more recently, however, it has become much more penetrating and critical.

At the end of each Annual Aid Review, there is no formal finding by the DAC as such, but the Chairman summarizes the discussion and sends a report to each country noting particularly whatever critical comments were made. This is then followed up by the Chairman in his visits to capitals when he again emphasizes those aspects of the country's program which appeared from the Annual Review to be in need of strengthening or reconsideration. Finally, the Chairman's annual report, so constituted in order to avoid the necessity of its formal approval by all members, is built largely on the Annual Review material. It makes public a general summary and analysis of the year's record.

The suppliers of economic assistance have two basic reasons for needing a point of meeting. The first is to exchange information, especially with respect to emerging problems and accumulated experience. Why do some demonstration farms work and others not? In what fields are there serious shortages of technical experts compared with the demand for technical assistance? What are the priority needs for agricultural research? What can be done if the promised permanent support by the recipient for hospitals, technical training centers, and the like is not forthcoming?

The second purpose relates to situations where there are advantages in having a common program or position—or at least in understanding why there may be differences. As to the quantity of aid, a country is stimulated to increase its assistance if it is clear that other countries are closer to an agreed target, that assistance to the less-developed countries is a common task in which all richer countries should carry their share. There is an even clearer case for concerted action with respect to terms. Easier terms by one country will have a diminished utility if offset by increased loans or harder terms by another supplier. The soft lenders see themselves as financing the harder terms of harder lenders; the hard lenders, who must listen to the complaints of their exporters, regard the soft as guilty of unfair competition. Examples of other subjects where common positions have been discussed are aid-tying, the coordination of technical assistance in the less-developed country, the requirements for accelerated agricultural development, the treatment of countries in default, the development of education, and methods of assuring a more adequate supply of experts.

It is not difficult to hold discussions on subjects such as these and even to arrive at a "sense of the meeting." In most cases, this is as far as the DAC goes—often somewhere near the lowest conceptual denominator and usually expressed in fairly general terms —thus avoiding the tedious process of agreeing on a specific set of words. Since the OECD and the DAC require a unanimous vote on all matters, it is not surprising that the number of formal resolutions enacted by the DAC have been few. The more important actions have been recommendations to governments relating to the volume of aid, terms and conditions of aid, and aid to agriculture. The specific definitions and targets in these resolutions put the general policy agreement into terms which can be the basis for evaluating the effort made.

Resolutions by international bodies are likely to be ineffective unless they represent a real meeting of minds to make a common effort in some direction, in which case each member presumably does not need a resolution. There is no international enforcement procedure, but the record is clear that the policy recommendations by the DAC and the publicity relating thereto have been helpful to governments in carrying out the actions which are indicated, though some are more sensitive to international opinion than others.

The DAC has served as a center for discussion of policy positions to be taken in conferences such as the UNCTAD and on subjects such as the consideration of a blueprint for the Second Development Decade. The larger international conferences cannot get anywhere on the basis of independent participation by each member. There must be some system of representation or of groupings. At the first UNCTAD the less-developed countries complained that the developed ones were not sufficiently organized to make possible the negotiations necessary to find agreed compromises. DAC activity provides such background material and understanding as may be needed by the members, while the discussion in the DAC tends to develop common ground and reduce, though not necessarily eliminate, such differences as may exist. It should be noted that for such subjects as trade preferences, limitation on export credits, and the development of local insurance and shipping enterprises, there are other expert committees within the OECD to which these subjects are referred.

At the beginning, the United States was the prime mover in the DAC. It made most of the proposals for agenda items and was much more active than any other member in submitting material and sending experts to meetings. The growth in programs of other developed countries, the strengthening of the position of aid administrators in governments, and the impact of the Annual Aid Review have led to a much greater interest and participation by other member governments. To the extent that this was the result of outside influence, it came in part from the DAC and in part from direct urging by representatives of the United States. With the relative deterioration in the enthusiasm for foreign aid in the United States and the accompanying pressure on AID's

administrative budget, U.S. participation in the DAC has become
much less vigorous. It has taken a less active part in originating
proposals for consideration and in discussing the matters on the
agenda. There is no real excuse for this, since the American program is still by far the largest and should have both the greatest
variety of problems to inquire about and the widest experience to
contribute. Though it cannot provide an example of an expanding program at present, this should increase its interest in effectiveness. It can make its contribution more effective and increase
the benefits received by sending its Washington experts to meetings more frequently. Above all, the DAC must have strong and
intimate back-stopping in Washington.

Testifying before the Senate Committee on Foreign Relations
on July 14, 1969, Secretary Rogers stated that "We will increase
. . . our efforts to coordinate our aid with other donors." [1] The
DAC should be a useful vehicle for approaching this objective.
Greater coordination also implies more American acceptance of
common policies and practices. To a considerable extent, the
AID administrator is able to work closely with other suppliers if
he wishes to do so, but the greatest concern of the DAC is with
volume and terms, both of which are established by Congress.
Most congressmen, however, seem to feel that more should be
done by other countries without appreciating that, if one sets up
some measure of international participation, the United States
should apply it to itself as well.

One must also note the increasing number of cases where donors, in addition to their collaboration in the DAC, combine their
efforts in specific projects. The growing practice of multiple participation in financing has been noted in Chapter 9. But even
closer relations have been established in some projects, notably
by the Scandinavian countries. The Nordek Treaty of February
1970 (Denmark, Finland, Norway, and Sweden) includes a provision for greater cooperation on aid to developing countries.

*   *   *

There is no organization among the less-developed countries comparable to the DAC, but nevertheless they do have many opportunities to consider their common problems together. Although
some of the assistance-suppliers are members, the regional United
Nations organizations for Latin America, Asia and the Far East,
and Africa (ECLA, ECAFE, and ECA) concentrate their efforts

on development problems in their areas. Furthermore, there are various smaller groups of neighboring countries that endeavor to reduce the degree by which boundaries are barriers; usually their particular interest is in freer trade. As yet none of the groupings of less-developed countries has developed the political and economic coherence of the European Economic Community, but in Central America and in Africa there are significant experiments toward regional association.

The assistance process makes general-purpose organization more likely for providers of assistance than for recipients. While aid receivers can undoubtedly learn from each other, the typical situation is that each is receiving aid from several sources. It has few problems of coordination with other recipients except in regional projects or international meetings. As a result, there are innumerable *ad hoc* meetings, ranging from the major attempt to prepare agreed positions and proposals for UNCTAD II, which became known as the "Algiers Charter," to limited seminars on specific subjects organized by the specialized agencies or by private nonprofit organizations. Bloc activity among the less-developed countries, though often on a continental basis, has long been common at United Nations meetings.

One of the most interesting developments is the Special Commission for Latin American Coordination, formed in 1964 in preparation for UNCTAD II. At a subsequent meeting in Chile in May 1969, high-level representatives of twenty Latin-American nations approved a document subsequently presented to President Nixon expressing dissatisfaction with their economic and political relations with the United States and calling for more trade and more aid with fewer conditions. The group further stated that it intended to set up a number of technical subcommittees and to represent a common viewpoint in behalf of Latin America in negotiation with the United States. Undoubtedly, something of the same sort takes place at meetings of representatives of the members of the British Commonwealth and of countries in the Franc Zone.

*　*　*

Contacts between suppliers and recipients take place at many points. Bilateral diplomatic relationships are carried on by ambassadors, presumably covering all matters of common interest. In addition, many countries maintain representatives at multilateral centers, and various meetings are attended by representatives from capitals. Special emissaries from less-developed countries, including heads of governments, visit potential suppliers, which in turn may send their representatives to keep in touch with situations of interest.

But such occasional and irregular contacts are not adequate for the development assistance relationship. The flow of assistance requires initial collaboration in working out a project or program, and the supplying government is inevitably concerned later in how the operation of the project or program is proceeding. Even when it has been subcontracted to an engineering firm or a university, it is necessary to check on performance from time to time. Development assistance requires a new sort of working relationship between governments.

The United States is the only country that maintains in a large number of countries special staffs which concentrate on assistance matters. In the Franc Area, the French government has supplied personnel for many posts in the government of a newly independent country, and through them there is a continuing liaison between supplier and recipient. The Federal Republic of Germany has relied largely on sending special representatives for short visits. The United Kingdom has, for the most part, used its regular diplomatic establishment.

In general, reliance on diplomatic missions often proves unsatisfactory because of the priority inevitably given to regular political duties and reporting functions, as well as the absence of training and even information about the process of economic development. The problem of special field representation is especially difficult for the smaller supplier countries, which have a limited number of diplomatic missions and which tend to provide aid in the form of technical assistance in relatively small and often scattered projects. As a result, they find it more satisfactory to give more of their assistance through multilateral channels than do the larger countries, and to concentrate their bilateral assistance in a relatively small number of countries.

Representation in the less-developed country was essential in earlier years when the local government had few experts and an inexperienced administration, and the supplier helped in the development of well-defined project proposals—itself a kind of technical assistance. As the governments of the less-developed countries build up stronger civil services with the help of the training centers of the United Nations, the World Bank, the IMF, and of special seminars, the need for suppliers to maintain large supporting local staffs is being reduced. A recent trend has been to establish regional centers for a supplier's representatives. The British government has had a center in the Middle East for some time. Given the number of African states, the United States has consolidated much of its African business in Washington, although there are regional offices in Dakar and Nairobi. The IBRD also has established several regional offices.

* * *

No aspect of development aid has been as confused and disorderly as technical assistance. Its fragmentation into a multitude of small, scattered projects with a large number of potential suppliers of experts makes for complexity in administration and uncertainty as to the best use of the limited resources available. Although the situation is vastly improved over earlier years and although some of the less-developed countries organize their requests for outside assistance reasonably well, in too many cases different individuals or departments make duplicate requests of potential suppliers, asking for experts to cover subjects vaguely defined. Likewise, requests are duplicated over time. One case is on record where over a span of years more than a dozen different experts were requested to submit proposals concerning the development of tourism in a particular country. Confusion may be further compounded by representatives of the suppliers whose enthusiasm about their various special abilities and interests resembles that of the traveling salesman. In addition to a disorderly demand, the supply of individuals available at any moment in time who can meet the needs of the less-developed countries— given the gaps and discontinuities in language, culture, the level of technology, and the skills at hand—is not only limited in total but scattered in location.

The need to reduce the number of separate agencies dealing with the less-developed countries was first recognized by the United Nations Development Program. It has gradually built up a staff of Resident Representatives stationed in the less-developed countries to represent the specialized agencies providing technical assistance other than the IBRD and IMF.

The problem of coordinating technical assistance among the bilateral donors has been frequently discussed at the DAC at the Annual Aid Review. The DAC suggested in 1963 that the representatives of its members should meet regularly with representatives of the Thai government to discuss improvements in handling technical assistance, and the group is still active. A complete record was made of all technical assistance projects in Thailand, which provides information about current projects—a "memory bank"—so that experts newly arrived can review what has gone before. Perhaps the most important result of the experiment has been the upgrading and coordination of technical assistance within the Thai government itself.

The need for some sort of coordination became so serious that in February 1966 the DAC adopted a set of guidelines for coordination of technical assistance on the spot, intended primarily to reduce the amount of duplicating effort in programming by both suppliers and recipients. Based upon the Thai experience and that of OECD with Greece and Turkey, the main emphasis was put on the necessity for the beneficiary country to create some central office with programming authority through which all requests for assistance would be channelled. The guidelines were sent by the DAC members to their field missions and embassies with the suggestion that they consult together concerning the present state of program coordination in the country and follow up with such action as might be appropriate.

Even this suggestion has not proven fully effective. The need for more coordination in the field runs into the obvious difficulty that it is impractical for every prospective or even actual supplier to have a representative properly qualified in assistance matters in every less-developed country. This gives another reason for emphasizing the importance of a strong central office within each less-developed country's administration to handle technical assistance requests and arrangements. Whatever the arrangements are, it is desirable that suppliers be informed as to what each is doing or proposes to do, in order to avoid duplication and to achieve the benefits of the cumulative effect of change described in Chapter 5. Informal arrangements may be adequate in some cases; in others, where the activities are more complex, there may be need for regular consultations concerning both procedures and priorities for technical assistance programs.

* * *

The problem of coordination with respect to capital flows becomes more urgent as the number of suppliers increases. The size of capital projects and their relationship to long-run priority requirements and to other related investments make it important that domestic and foreign funds for development be fitted within some over-all blueprint. This does not necessarily mean the elimination of separate programs. Since the most effective ways to provide assistance are still insufficiently clear, multiple programs and the opportunity for a variety of expressions of inventiveness and judgment are necessary. Furthermore, too centralized an operation might reduce the sense of national participation by suppliers.

It is possible to overstress the need for coordination. Many less-developed countries are so small that there cannot be great confusion among suppliers. In other cases, most of the assistance may still come from a single bilateral source. Thus, U.S. flows to Latin America and French and British flows to Africa often are the major source of bilateral assistance for individual countries. To be sure, in such cases the domination of a single supplier is being lessened with the expanding programs of other countries like Canada, Germany, and Japan. Since the World Bank's projects are usually sizable and are announced for public bidding, they raise less important problems of formal coordination. Other suppliers take these projects into account in designing their own bilateral programs. The kind of planning most needed is to make use of the newly created opportunities within some set of priorities.

Coordination among suppliers of capital can be adequately handled on an informal basis most of the time in most countries. However, there should be ways of bringing all the interested parties together if some special need for consultation arises. The special machinery which is called into play when some less-developed country has balance-of-payments trouble has already been noted, but all too often this happens only when the crisis is reached. The DAC, the IBRD, or the Resident Representative might be given responsibility for initiating discussions whenever a problem of concern to several suppliers develops in cases where neither a consortium nor a consultative group exists.

*　*　*

The need for much more formal and regular coordination is crucial for the larger less-developed countries that receive outside capital assistance from a number of sources. Thus, at the end of

1968, special coordinating arrangements were in existence for the 18 countries which receive about 50 per cent of the net total official bilateral assistance. Over 90 per cent of AID's development loans in 1968 were committed in countries covered by consortia, consultative groups, and CIAP.

The consortium technique was started by the IBRD for India in 1958 and Pakistan in 1960. The OECD formed consortia for Greece and Turkey in 1962. However, the capital-supplying countries felt that the pressures of the pledging procedure used in those cases interfered with their freedom of action in allocating their available funds. At any rate, no more consortia have been organized, but since 1962 ten consultative groups have been established under the aegis of the IBRD for Colombia, East Africa, Korea, Malaysia, Morocco, Nigeria, Peru, Sudan, Thailand, and Tunisia, and in 1969 it took over from the IMF the coordination of aid for Ghana. There is also a less active group for Ceylon. The Dutch have sponsored a group for Indonesia, and Guyana has its own group to which the IBRD belongs. The countries which are members are expected to provide some assistance to the subject country. Most groups have about a dozen country members, though those for Nigeria, Ceylon, and Indonesia have only nine; the groups for Tunisia with sixteen and Turkey with fourteen are the largest. In addition, the IMF and UNDP are members of most of the groups.

Each group generally includes nearly all the important suppliers of capital to the less-developed country. The country itself is not a member of the group, but is usually invited to all formal meetings to present its program and aid requirements and to participate in the related discussion. An international agency, most often the IBRD, usually itself a supplier of capital, provides the leadership and such secretarial services as may be required. In the case of Indonesia, the Bank has established a resident mission to work closely with the government as well as to service the group.

Studies in depth concerning the performance and policies of the recipient are made, and are then discussed by all interested parties. In the case of consortia, this is followed by a pledging session, or perhaps a series of meetings if the gap is wide between the recognized requirements and the prospective amount of assistance. The actual flow and form of assistance is then arranged bilaterally by each supplier. Formal meetings of the consortia are held at least once a year, though they can be held more often.

The consultative groups have no regular schedule, meeting whenever a general review of the situation seems appropriate, though World Bank policy is to have such a meeting at least once every two years. In addition to meetings, the Bank staff circulates reports and its experts visit the various member capitals from time to time.

The servicing of these various groups is no simple matter. The executive agency is responsible for making basic studies of each less-developed country's requirements, policies, and performance. If a new five-year plan is presented, the agency must examine it with great care, which in a large country may mean providing a considerable number of specialists for some months. Moreover, all members must be kept informed of any new developments. Thus the burden, while far less in total than if each member tried individually to cover the same ground, is exceedingly heavy, particularly on the staff of the World Bank.

The consortia not only review the policies and plans of the recipient country but also discuss together the target to be met and engage in a pledging session to commit specific amounts by individual suppliers. Distribution of the aid between project and nonproject assistance may also be discussed, and, as in the Turkish and Indian cases, schedules worked out for the postponement of debt service. To illustrate the operation of a consortium: the Indian Consortium met in Paris May 22-23, 1969, attended by representatives of twelve supplier governments, the IMF, and the OECD, and with the World Bank as chairman. It reviewed and commended the considerable improvements in India's economic situation and its program in family planning, and emphasized particularly its strong export performance. It was agreed that for the year beginning April 1, 1969, India required nonproject assistance of about $700 million, including $100 million in the form of debt relief, and most members indicated the contributions they would be able to make. It was agreed that the request for $400 million of project aid was reasonable, and that efforts would be made to meet it. There was also agreement to further improve the terms of aid.[2]

The consultative groups do not have formal pledging of assistance. These groups economize effort in that one expert review is done in behalf of all, the recipient does not need to defend his program with each separate supplier, and there is a general discussion in which the recipient and all potential suppliers participate. The absence of any assurance of financing tends to make the procedure appear to be a one-sided exercise to the recipient, which receives advice from the potential suppliers without any indication of what benefits may come from its acceptance. However, it does have an unusual opportunity to present its case.

* * *

It is not enough for the experts, the recipient, and the various contributors to work out a balance between the domestic policies of the country concerned, the assistance requirements, and the total amount of assistance which they should supply. There still remains the problem of dividing the responsibility. In financing multilateral agencies, there are fixed percentages according to which the established total is allocated and collected. But there is no such principle for allocation to meet the requirements of individual less-developed countries. In fact, there can be no general formula since membership in the groups and interest in specific less-developed countries are not identical. Germany, the United Kingdom, and the United States are the only countries belonging to all groups, though Italy and the Netherlands are in all but Guyana, and France in all but Nigeria and Guyana. Canada has an observer status in the groups for Sudan and Indonesia.

There are several further difficulties. The first is that the amount of the funds available to the individual provider of assistance is not always clear in advance. The final sum emerging from its budgetary and legislative process does not necessarily match the intentions of the supplier as indicated in its various bilateral commitments, plus its appropriate share in the various countries where group action exists. Thus the Congressional reduction in U.S. aid funds substantially reduces the amount which AID can contribute to many programs, including that approved by the Indian Consortium.

In addition, it should be noted that no country has much short-run flexibility in its aid program. Governments cannot reallocate all their assistance freshly each year, since there are many continuing commitments implicit in past flows and in current foreign policy. In fact, only when its volume of assistance is growing, as in the case of Canada for example, or when assistance to a recipient can be terminated, can substantial shifts take place in the geographical or functional structure of a donor's program. Since one purpose of the coordination exercise is to improve the distri-

bution and effectiveness of assistance, the inability or unwillingness to make adjustments by suppliers reduces the effectiveness of
the operation to the recipient.

The next step in the development of consultative groups must
be for them to face the necessity of giving at least tentative indications of levels of support, based on certain assumptions of
domestic performance by the less-developed country. Commitments obviously cannot be unalterable; but a responsible relationship between domestic performance and foreign assistance requires that both sides enter into a "best efforts" understanding.
This in turn makes it necessary for the legislative basis of aid to
permit long-term programming.

A third source of difficulty has been the existence of long delays
between commitment and the actual utilization of assistance already pledged. Delay may stem from the recipient country's difficulty in translating its general program into individual projects
with detailed specifications. It also may arise because the terms
and conditions of the proffered assistance, particularly when tied
and with relatively hard terms, may make the recipient less willing to use it or make it more difficult to work out an agreed program. Long delays can upset the contemplated relationship between foreign aid and domestic programs.

In spite of the difficulties, the consultative procedures achieves
a number of useful purposes when working well. It enables the recipient country and interested governments and institutions to
consider jointly the development needs and program on the basis
of expert analyses; it facilitates the exchange of information and
the consideration by capital-suppliers of their several programs
and the appropriate character, terms, and priorities of assistance;
it reduces duplication of effort in the presentation and review of
programs and projects; it encourages harmonization by putting
on the table the differences in terms and types of assistance
among the supplying countries; and it permits a review of the
country's economic performance with a view to making as effective as possible the contribution to be made by outside assistance.

As might be expected, the groups are not identical in character
or interest, depending on such variables as the personality of the
chairman, the quality of the national representatives, and above
all the nature and severity of the problems to be dealt with. Crises
may arise because of debt payments (Turkey and Indonesia) or
famine conditions (India) or restrictive trade policy (Pakistan).

Very little is ruled out of these country discussions except the lending policy of the World Bank and general aid policy under review in the DAC. A further development has been for certain groups to have special meetings focussed on specific sectors. The Indian consortium meeting in Stockholm in November 1969 centered on India's family planning program and the contribution which external support can make. There have been informal meetings of the East African group to discuss agriculture, education, and transport. The Tunisian group has a special working party on agriculture.

The operation of groups active in coordination gives some assurance that a vigorous effort will be made in each case to program the assistance as effectively as possible by developing a coherent relationship between national objectives and policies and the quantity and quality of aid provided by the various suppliers. An obvious flaw in the present structure is the lack of coordination between financial and technical assistance unless it is done by the recipient country. To be sure, the individual project may itself be a source of coordination; the building of a factory with foreign assistance is likely to include the necessary training of the operatives as part of the undertaking. As far as more general coordination is concerned, the countries or agencies supplying technical assistance often differ from those supplying financial aid. This is particularly evident in the United Nations system, but the two types of assistance also may be handled by two unrelated agencies in the supplier country. Similarly, in the case of the recipient, the two aspects of development assistance may come under several different agencies. Recently, there has been some effort to consider the coordination of technical assistance programs in the consortia and consultative groups, but their members are the capital suppliers and the coordination of technical assistance must include a number of other countries.

Another weakness in the present structure is that it leaves the broader problem of allocation among the recipient countries unsolved (see Chapter 8). Although analytical work on each case is done by the IBRD's staff, even here different individuals and different departments are responsible, and apparently no attempt is made at comparisons among the cases. Similarly, since the assistance ogranization in most supplier countries is organized on a geographical basis, different individuals may appear at different group meetings and thus not develop the necessary background to make inter-country comparisons. Existing coordination techniques, while presenting each national situation in a more orderly and thorough form, still leave unsolved the country allocation problem.

The question has been raised whether or not the less-developed countries with groups receive more than their share of the assistance available because of the pressure generated on suppliers by the group itself. It is impossible to say how these countries would have fared without the groups. From the record of 1960–66, it would appear that official aid receipts increased to India, Pakistan, Ceylon, Malaysia, and Nigeria after the establishment of the coordinating organization. No favorable change in the share of the total is evident in the seven other cases, and Turkey, Greece, Colombia, and Tunisia appear to have received a decreased amount. This may, of course, have been an appropriate redistribution of the assistance available.

* * *

In addition to the United Nations regional commissions, there are other regional groupings where common problems can be discussed. The United States has taken a leading part in trying to encourage a variety of policies in Latin America for economic growth and stability, social progress, and improved government administration. In Brazil and Chile, it has even worked out specific programs of domestic action tied in closely to the flow of assistance.

Taking a leaf from the notebook of European experience, and in order to involve the recipients more clearly in a joint effort, the Alliance for Progress was established in 1961. Probably the most ambitious regional group directed at economic and social development, it represents primarily an agreement on objectives and a commitment to a common effort. The animation has been provided by two regional institutions. The first is the Inter-American Development Bank (IADB), which not only has been the means for raising and dispensing a substantial amount of financial assistance but has also been active in encouraging various nonfinancial objectives such as greater integration within the area. At its annual meeting in April 1970, it reviewed its first decade of existence and considered ways of improving Latin American institutions concerned with development and of supporting more rapid progress in the educational, scientific, and technological sectors.

The other regional institution is the Inter-American Committee of the Alliance for Progress (CIAP). Each year it examines the progress of each member, subjecting economic policies and programs to criticism both by other members and representatives of international agencies and by a special panel of development experts. It has pushed hard for limiting inflation (a prevalent disease in Latin America), better tax systems and tax collection, land reform, improved credit institutions to encourage savings, better water systems and housing, and other agreed economic and social objectives. There is no way of measuring the impact of the CIAP review on the subject governments, but it cannot help but strengthen the hand of those in agreement with CIAP's judgments. Nevertheless, its influence is limited because it can only recommend and it has no funds of its own to dispense.

In his address to the Inter-American Press Association on October 31, 1969, concerning Latin-American relations, President Nixon may have been pointing at these weaknesses when he said that what was needed was "an effective multilateral framework for bilateral assistance" and "over time, to give it major operational and decision-making responsibilities." Although a new agency might be created, he noted that CIAP might be given the new function. "The other American nations themselves would thus jointly assume a primary role in setting priorities within the hemisphere, in developing realistic programs and in keeping their own performance under critical review." He extended the process of consultation to include a periodic review by the CIAP of U.S. economic policies that affect the other nations of the hemisphere.

While there is no reference to the Marshall Plan, this is clearly an effort to build a central policy and consultative point like the OEEC, although the suppliers, the United States and Canada, were not members of the European organization. Whether the Latin American countries have a great deal in common other than that they are in the same hemisphere with the United States, whether or not the drive for economic growth is as strong as that for resisting change, and whether nationalism may not be stronger than any hemispheric feeling are by no means clear. From the United States side, there will always be the problem of the executive branch negotiating from an uncertain Congressional position. Basically, the proposal is much like that of the Alliance for Progress. If it is possible to strengthen the concept of partnership, and the extent of consultation by new procedures, they should be adopted. But the ultimate result will depend much more on the volume, terms, and conditions of assistance to be made available.

* * *

Regardless of whether or not the structural arrangement between suppliers and recipient is a simple bilateral one or a formal group, the central consideration is the basic spirit of the relationship. Clearly, the old days of dominance by the rich country are ended. The richer country cannot order or direct, nor is it any longer as necessary as it was at first. It does have the option of whether or not to provide experts and resources. But in making that choice, how far can it concern itself with the performance of the less-developed country before it is charged with "interference" and "intervention," words which have replaced "exploitation" and "imperialism" in the vocabulary of political oratory? In a sense, the whole process of development assistance is one of intervention. It is intended to make some contribution, some change in the situation. However, since it is provided through a process involving the agreement and often some positive action by the recipient, the supplier may be intervening but not interfering.

International agreements frequently carry provisions considerably removed from the central purpose of the exchange. Thus the Lend-Lease Agreements, primarily concerned with the flow of United States supplies to Britain and a dozen other wartime allies, included commitments for the postwar reduction of tariffs and other trade barriers.

The legislation establishing the Marshall Plan required the immediate negotiation of bilateral agreements between the United States and each recipient. These agreements had to include best-efforts commitments by each European country to expand production, stabilize its currency and establish appropriate exchange rates, balance its budget, reduce obstacles to trade, eliminate monopolistic practices and restraints on competition, and coordinate its policies with the other recipients through the Organization for European Economic Cooperation. In addition, certain operating arrangements were stipulated, such as the right of the United States to establish special missions and to procure relevant information in the recipient country.

Since that time, the U.S. assistance legislation has gone through a series of revisions. At one time, the recipient was required to assert that it endorsed the United Nations Charter, even though it might already have been a member. In the last over-all rewriting of legislation, the Foreign Assistance Act of 1961, there is no explicit requirement for any policy declaration by the recipient country.

Since its establishment, AID has been concerned with the economic policies and programs of the countries to which it is providing technical assistance and capital. Its concern may be expressed in the form of a specific condition, such as the new provision for U.S. food assistance which requires the recipient to have an active agricultural development program. Or it may merely be the application of the general criterion of giving assistance more generously to countries which have a performance record of being actively engaged in self-help. At times and in a few cases, there have been very specific commitments relating to economic performance in such matters as limiting price and wage increases, reducing the deficit, or lowering tariff barriers. For example, some years ago, aid to Brazil was provided on a three-month basis with a regular check to see if Brazil had met certain agreed targets. But some of the requirements proved to be subject to forces beyond the control of the executive branch of the Brazilian government, and the arrangement, almost contractual in its detail, was soon abandoned. In cases where debt payments have been subject to renegotiation, one common result has been an agreed pattern of performance in the way the less-developed country would handle its external financial affairs in the future.

For a country with as widespread a program as that of the United States, withholding aid is itself a matter of exerting influence. To be sure, the absence of any assistance flow to the Communist countries except PL 480 wheat to Poland up to 1964, Danube Flood Assistance through the Red Cross in 1955, and aid annually to Yugoslavia, has been merely one expression of bipolarity, reinforcing the existing political alienation. The cessation of both military and economic aid to Pakistan and India in 1965 was an expression of displeasure at their resort to arms, and was a potent influence in ending the hostilities. The denial of development loans to Indonesia from 1964 to 1966 was in protest against Sukarno's foreign and domestic behavior. However, the number of cases calling for a complete stoppage have been relatively few, and should be.

The amount of assistance given by the smaller aid-providing countries and the scale of their personnel structures limit their influence to specific sectors. On the other hand, the larger countries and the multilateral financial agencies cannot help but influence the economic situation by the nature of the assistance given. The increasing activity of the multilateral agencies has shifted the charge of interference away from individual supplier countries to a considerable degree. In the financial area, for example, the IMF not only conducts an annual review of its members, but attempts to deal with inflationary tendencies by giving support under stabilization agreements (Korea, Ghana, Colombia, and elsewhere), which involve commitments by the recipient governments. The announcement by the IMF is more or less as follows: "The stand-by arrangement is in support of the government's program of fiscal and monetary measures and will provide the authorities with a secondary line of reserves to help to sustain the present liberal system of trade and payments."

The increased competence in the less-developed countries and the growth of consultative groups have reduced the role played by individual suppliers. Furthermore, the World Bank can be expected to play a much more influential part in the future in less-developed country planning and policy determination. Its expanded staff of experts, its announced program of country reviews, and its plans for increasing its resources are certain to increase greatly its influence and to reduce the visibility of the bilateral suppliers.

* * *

Neither foreign relations nor assistance programs are limited to the economic field, and one of the most sensitive areas has been that of security. While most supplier governments have attempted to separate economic assistance from military aid, the economic aspect cannot be divorced from the military when looking at the manner in which the less-developed country is using its resources.

The relationship between American military and economic aid has varied greatly. The Marshall Plan was economic in character, except for military aid to China, and its absorption of the Greek-Turkish aid program. However, beginning with the signing of the North Atlantic Treaty in April 1949, the United States was strongly urging the build-up of national defenses, and both economic and military assistance were consolidated under the Mutual Security Act. Additional military assistance was provided in the Defense Department's budget and in the procedures for disposing of military surplus.

With the withdrawal of troops from their former colonies by the metropolitan powers, the newly independent less-developed countries had to build up their own military establishments. This required technical assistance, training, and military goods. Countries long independent, like those in Latin America, also had ambitions to modernize their military establishments. With the military group often in a strong position in the government of the less-developed country, requests for military aid had a high priority.

For most of the less-developed countries, especially those in Latin America and Africa, the United States has tried to discourage extensive expenditure on the military establishment. But in a number of instances, military training and American equipment have been provided to forestall their being supplied by Communist countries.

It is important to persuade less-developed countries that extensive and modern military establishments are extremely expensive in terms of their available resources. This idea is reinforced by the provision in the legislation requiring a cut in U.S. economic assistance equal to any amount spent by the less-developed country on foreign advanced weapons. To be sure, many less-developed countries are engaging men in uniform in useful activities like road-building, or using the period of military service for vocational training. However, arms sales and training activity have a strong tendency to encourage the use of resources in nonproductive expenditure for unnecessary defense objectives, and have contributed to competitive arms races in areas where military parity would be sufficient.

* * *

It is much easier for an aid supplier to work out an agreement for a particular project or even a short-run economic policy than to make much progress in bringing about meaningful social and economic reforms in the recipient country. Economic habits, class structures, systems of land ownership, and social institutions are not easily changed. The nature and shape of the political system cannot be readily modified from outside. Quite possibly the political structure has been a major force resisting social change in the past, and foreign assistance may actually tend to reinforce the existing power complex since it must work with and through it. However, projects and programs, properly conceived, carry within themselves the seed of change. The social sedatives of ignorance and isolation become less and less effective. It is possible that the withholding of economic aid, even where there is little sympathy for social reform, may in the long run actually delay the process of change.

Under most circumstances, it seems unlikely that oppressive social and class rigidities will persist indefinitely. A donor country can at least urge and support specific ameliorating developments —tax reform, land reform, reduced military expenditure, improved education, and greater social mobility. However, the process of encouraging such internal programs from outside requires a delicate appreciation of the sensitivity bred by nationalism.

The granting or withholding of economic assistance can sometimes be of considerable influence in the social and economic field, but as to more specific objectives, there is little evidence to indicate that it is very effective in influencing unrelated matters such as voting in the United Nations, cooperating with the Communists, mistreating the political opposition, or indulging in unfriendly political oratory. A policy of limiting aid conditions to operational requirements does not mean that a supplier country cannot express itself concerning these various matters. In that case, however, it becomes the usual diplomatic problem of how best to influence the situation without doing more harm than good because of the charge of foreign interference.

Sometimes there are choices of form or substance about which there may be conflicting interests in the less-developed country, and where a decision with respect to the aid program may influence the relative positions of various political figures or groups. Because of political implications, there is an inevitable temptation to shape the assistance program to support those with whom the supplier has the greatest sympathy, rather than to focus strictly on economic and social development. The short-run political criterion is always appealing, but does not necessarily correspond to development objectives. The political game is indeed difficult because it is not always easy to judge whether a political change will result in improvement or not. Furthermore, the·cry of foreign interference carries farthest when the action being criticized can be charged with having some political objective.

In the assistance field, the relationship between supplier and recipient is usually most durable when it is focussed on the common goal of accelerating economic and social development. Even then there is bound to be difficulty because of the inevitable "difference of viewpoint between large and small sovereign countries, between countries which export capital and those which receive capital." [3] The course of true economic assistance seldom runs smooth.

14 · Trade, Aid, or What?

Both suppliers and receivers of assistance insist that foreign aid in the form of grants or concessionary loans is a temporary phenomenon. At some point in the near or distant future, each less-developed country is expected to reach a "take off" stage after which its further progress can be financed by internal savings or by market flows of foreign capital. To the extent that it is unable to obtain domestically the wide variety and increased quantities of raw materials and finished products it requires, it will need foreign purchasing power to get them abroad. Expansion in trade seems to be a part of the growth process for all countries, rich as well as poor. It is not necessarily a sure-fire "engine of growth," but it is a necessary condition and can have a high multiplier effect.

Foreign trade is necessary because every country has requirements for products which it otherwise could only produce synthetically or for which it could find substitutes only at high cost. For the United States, for example, the outside requirements run from coffee to copper and from diamonds to pepper. Less-developed countries must import machinery and equipment, without which they cannot take advantage of modern production methods. Imports are also important as a real or potential protection against domestic monopoly and as an element of resistance against increasing prices.

Trade is of the greatest importance to the countries that are very small or handicapped by inaccessibility or by poverty of resources. These areas must trade to live or at least to live decently. Although they could eliminate the circumscribing boundaries by consolidation or federation, this would be a most unusual political event. More often, they try to join in a larger economic grouping, as have the countries in Central America and various parts of Africa.

Exports are important primarily to provide the means for paying for imports; they also add to the amount which is produced for the domestic market so that production can take advantage of the economies of scale. The importance of economies of scale is illustrated in Table 31.

TABLE 31

RELATIVE COST PER UNIT BY SIZE OF PLANT, FOUR INDUSTRIES

| | | Size of Plant | | Reduction in Cost per Unit |
Industry	Units	Small	Large	(Per Cent)
Alumina	tons per day	300	1,000	16
Cement	tons per year	40,000	900,000	39.3
Rolling flat steel	tons per year	100,000	1,500,000	46.1
Hydroelectric	megawatts per year	100	300	50.0

Source: G. Nguyen Tien Hung, "Economics of Scale and Economic Integration," *Finance and Development* No. 2, 1968, p. 35.

Imports promote consumption within the country to a size which makes local production possible. The initial costs and risks of market development are taken by the importer. When the local market has become large enough, local production can begin, a process known as "import substitution." One difficulty with this approach is that it does not necessarily direct development into the pattern which best uses the available resources, since often foreign production may, for one reason or another, be much more efficient. In order to get started, import-substitution often is accompanied by infant-industry protection and increased cost to the consumer. Since protection is not easily removed, the making of wise choices for this kind of subsidization is of considerable importance.

An argument frequently offered for import substitution is simply that it frees foreign exchange for other purposes. The outstanding illustration is the expanding production of wheat in

India, replacing an enormous bill for wheat imports. Sometimes it may even be sensible to produce domestically at a higher cost. For example, according to estimates made by the OECD Development Center, fertilizer production in less-developed countries is somewhat more costly than would be the import of fertilizers. In terms of foreign-exchange requirements, local production is likely to involve investment for the needed new capacity and certain imported raw materials, which might even come from other less-developed countries. However, these foreign costs are less than the foreign exchange which would be required to purchase the finished product. Nevertheless, since domestic resources are plentiful and foreign exchange scarce, it may be a wise choice to give priority to methods of obtaining goods that require the least foreign-exchange component.

Since, in any event, the possibilities of improving a country's payments position through import substitution are limited by the amount and category of imports, greater emphasis is usually placed on the expansion of exports. Here, the general record has been rather disappointing. While total world trade has been expanding and the value of exports of the less-developed countries has also been rising, their share in the world total has dropped from around 30 per cent in 1948 to 23 per cent in 1958 and about 18 per cent in 1969. To put it another way, exports from developed countries increased 156 per cent between 1959 and 1969 while exports from the less-developed countries gained 87 per cent. Part of the difference is due to the fact that export prices of primary commodities declined from about 1954 to 1962 (much more in Latin America than elsewhere), while export prices of manufactured goods were rising. Furthermore, the volume of trade in primary products has not been expanding as rapidly as that in manufactured goods.

There are a few manufactured products in which one area or another clearly has a natural advantage. However, the common characteristic of less-developed countries is their supply of low-cost, relatively unskilled labor. Hal B. Lary's examination of labor-intensive manufacturing industries suggests that industries rank much the same on this basis from country to country. It would appear that the greatest possibility for expanding exports would lie in the industries with such a comparative advantage. Advancing labor costs in the richer countries have expanded the list of industries which can benefit from such a differential. Recently the

growth in exports from less-developed countries has been much
faster in the industrial group known as "light consumer manufactures" than in the classic groups of textiles and clothing, food
products, and processed materials.[1]

A summary of the growth of exports between 1950 and 1965
given in Table 32 shows the shifting pattern of trade. Although

TABLE 32

EXPORTS BY DEVELOPED AND LESS-DEVELOPED COUNTRIES,
1950 AND 1965

Exports	Value ($ Billion, Current Prices)		Compound Annual Rate of Growth (Per Cent)
	1950	1965	
Developed countries, total	35.9	122.5	8.5
To each other	25.0	95.5	9.4
To less-developed countries	10.9	27.0	6.2
Less-developed countries, total	17.6	33.8	4.5
To developed countries	12.4	26.2	5.2
To each other	5.2	7.6	2.5
Less-developed countries, excluding major oil producers, total	14.1	23.7	3.6
To developed countries	10.0	18.5	4.2
To each other	4.1	5.2	1.7
World total [a]	53.5	156.3	7.4

[a] Excluding U.S.S.R., Eastern Europe, and Mainland China.
Source: Hal B. Lary, *Imports of Manufactures from Less Developed Countries.* New York, 1968, p. 2.

trade data have usually been regarded as more reliable than most
national statistics, recent studies have suggested that they are
more inaccurate than has generally been assumed. A comparison
of recorded exports from one country to another with the corresponding import figure in the second country shows variations
much greater than can be explained by transportation and other
charges.[2] The discrepancies are much greater for trade among the
less-developed countries than for their trade with the developed

world. Nevertheless, the differences shown in Table 32 are too great to be explained away by statistical inaccuracies.

The table verifies the fact of much slower growth in the trade of the less-developed countries, especially with each other. As in other matters, there is a wide variation among countries. Between 1950 and 1967, Latin American exports rose 3.6 per cent per year, while those of Asia increased 4.6 per cent and Africa 6.4 per cent.

Some special opportunity for trade has resulted in greatly accelerating economic development in certain cases. The silk industry is often cited as having played a highly strategic role in Japan's development; the fortunate countries where petroleum has been discovered have benefited similarly. More recently, certain less-developed countries have found world markets for exports of ready-made clothing; the members of the OECD, not the only importers of clothing, doubled their imports in this category between 1962 and 1966, when the figure reached $2.4 billion, which is expected to expand by another $2 billion by 1971. The Far East is responsible for about one-fourth of the total.

An effort made by the UNCTAD secretariat to forecast the pattern of trade gives annual percentages of projected change for 1960–75 (see Table 33). Such projections are extremely uncertain, but they do suggest interesting conclusions. The differences in the rates of growth indicate a major shift in the export struc-

TABLE 33

PROJECTED GROWTH OF VOLUME OF EXPORTS BY
LESS-DEVELOPED COUNTRIES, 1960–75
(Per Cent per Annum, Compounded)

Product	Low	High
Food and beverages	2.8	3.5
Agricultural raw materials	1.6	2.3
Minerals other than fuels	4.3	4.8
Fuels	7.5	8.0
Manufactured goods	8.3	9.3
Total	5.0	5.6

Source: U.N. Conference on Trade and Development, *General Survey of Trade Prospects and Capital Needs for Developing Countries* (to be published). Quoted by Louis M. Goreux in *The Role of Agriculture in Economic Development.* National Bureau of Economic Research, New York, 1969, p. 54.

ture. In 1960, agricultural product exports were double that of petroleum. By 1975, they would be only one-half. This has important effects. Petroleum production has much less impact on the country of origin than does agriculture. Petroleum production involves much more in the way of foreign payments. And petroleum production is much more concentrated in location among the less-developed countries.

* * *

There appears to be a close relationship between the growth of exports and the growth of the economy in general though it is not clear whether there is a direct line of causation between them. Rapidly growing exports not only seem to be related to a growing sector of production and its servicing, but may also help finance strategic imports that permit further increases in productivity. On the other hand, a growing economy may imply diversification, yielding new items for export as well as improvements in the cost structure. At any rate, the rapid growth of the economy in general and exports in particular may reflect qualities of administration and domestic and foreign policy which are particularly conducive to expansion in both areas.

The relationship between exports and the economy is suggested in Table 34. The high-growth countries are those whose trade is also expanding most rapidly. And the low-growth countries, accounting for more than half the population, are clearly those where trade is also lagging.

* * *

For all of these reasons, the failure of exports of less-developed countries to rise faster has been a matter of concern to those interested in their development. But there has been only limited agreement on what to do about it. Discussions have centered largely on reducing trade barriers, while very little has been said about improving a country's trading position by adjusting exchange rates, although it is frequently pointed out, as in the Pearson Commission Report, "overvalued exchange rates . . . stunt the development of old and new export lines." The maintenance of fixed exchange rates is an exaggerated element in the IMF orthodoxy; and for countries whose main exports are priced in relatively inelastic world markets, exchange-rate adjustments, intended to encourage exports in general, may result in smaller

TABLE 34

GROWTH AND EXPORT PERFORMANCE OF LESS-DEVELOPED COUNTRIES, 1960–66

	Countries		Annual Percentage Increase, 1960–66		
Average Rate of Growth [a]	Number	Per Cent of Population	GDP	Exports [b]	Imports [b]
6.0 per cent or more	20	17	7.1	9.9	8.8
4.0–5.9 per cent	25	30	4.8	4.9	4.5
Under 4.0 per cent	18	53	2.3	2.6	0.9
Total	63	100	4.5	5.8	4.7

[a] Based on gross domestic product.
[b] 1959–60 to 1965–66.
Source: Committee for Economic Development, *Assisting Development in Low-Income Countries: Priorities for U.S. Government Policy.* New York, 1969, attributed to UNCTAD, "Review of Recent Trends in Trade and Development, 1968," TD/B/184, p. 31.

foreign-exchange earnings. Nevertheless, the long-run objective must be greater diversification and an overvalued exchange rate will be an obstacle to the expansion of exports.

Exchange rates are seldom matters of public discussion; much more attention has been given at international meetings to the lowering of trade barriers. At the UNCTAD I, while the less-developed countries argued for a general tariff preference in their favor and the United Kingdom supported the idea, France and Belgium favored a system of selective preferences, and Canada, Norway, Sweden, Switzerland, and the United States opposed spreading the use of preferences. By the UNCTAD II, however, there appeared to be acceptance of the general principle of tariff preferences, though little agreement as to how it should be applied.

In the meantime, the GATT paid more attention to the problem, and at its meeting in November 1968, the Chairman stated that the "trading opportunities of the less-developed countries remain the forefront of our concern, and constitute an important element of the work program." His reference was to such items in the program as advance implementation of the Kennedy Round reductions, an examination of problems such as internal charges and revenue duties affecting trade in tropical products, the early removal of import restrictions in the rich country markets on industrial products of particular interest to less-developed countries, questions of preferences by developed countries to less-developed countries, and the possibility of trade negotiations among the less-developed countries.

In various international conferences the less-developed countries have constantly pressed for action which would help to increase their foreign earnings. Many of them feel that the best hope for attaining their economic, and ultimately social goals, is to expand their exports. To be sure, their interest varies according to the present and prospective trade pattern of each country. To some, the market behavior of a single export like cocoa or tin is all important, while others hope to expand the export of manufactured and semi-manufactured goods. Although the Latin American Consensus of Viña del Mar was directed primarily at the United States, it summarizes neatly the steps in the trade field which are desired by the less-developed countries. The proposals presented on trade were as follows:

1. Establish better and more respected consultative machinery (a demand which underlies the whole document).
2. Continue to take steps to eliminate tariffs on primary commodities and nontariff obstacles such as quotas, safety and health regulations, and the like.
3. Initiate another GATT round on primary commodities.
4. Move ahead on commodity agreements (on the UNCTAD II timetable), to ensure fair and remunerative prices.
5. Abolish policies which encourage uneconomic production of primary commodities and prejudice the sale of Latin American products.
6. Eliminate discriminatory preferences against the sale of Latin American primary commodities.
7. Improve the consultative machinery for the disposal of surpluses.
8. Prevent trade distortion created by tied loans and the haphazard sale of surpluses.
9. Follow the established schedule for putting into effect a general, nonreciprocal, and nondiscriminatory system of preferences to facilitate the exportation of manufactures and semi-manufactures from the developing countries.
10. Eliminate restrictions in close connection with item 9 above, being sure the escape clauses relate to suitable criteria and consultative machinery.
11. Select industrial sectors or branches in which the United States might take measures to change its production pattern to provide an expanded U.S. market for Latin American manufactures and semi-manufactures.
12. Improve the machinery for promoting Latin American exports.

While most of the above proposals relate to improving existing machinery, two basic policy changes are proposed—the elimination of the idea of reciprocity whereby each participating country is expected to make tariff concessions equivalent to those it receives; and the modification of the nondiscrimination principle whereby each country should treat all others alike. Furthermore, one really revolutionary concept is advanced in item 11 above: that a country like the United States should deliberately plan to create opportunities for Latin American imports by changing its own production structure.

The policy of the General Agreement on Tariffs and Trade (GATT) has always rested on the concept of reciprocity. Equivalent reductions in tariffs should be made on both sides of a trade agreement negotiation, while the withdrawal of concessions justifies equivalent withdrawals by the injured party. However, a new chapter to the Agreement was adopted by the contracting parties in November 1964, in which the advanced countries indicated that they did not expect reciprocity from the less-developed countries. Specifically, the chapter recorded agreement to give priority to the reduction and essential removal of barriers on exports of interest, actually or potentially, to less-developed countries. In spite of this expression of intent, one cannot find evidence in the Kennedy Round of special relief from barriers directed at less-developed countries, even though many of their exports were affected. There is nothing in the new chapter which waives most-favored-nation treatment, so that benefits given to one less-developed country are expected to be given to all.

The second idea that there should be discrimination which favors less-developed countries runs head on into a set of ideas which economists have been demonstrating for nearly two centuries with increasingly beautiful logic—namely, that the most efficient international use of resources results from an unrestricted flow across international boundaries. The beneficence of nondiscrimination is an inevitable deduction from the simple assumptions of the wisdom and efficiency of the law of supply and demand. So far as governments are concerned, nondiscrimination became the agreed, though not fully established, position at the creation of the GATT in 1947.

One can raise questions as to the relevance of this logic in a world where the necessary assumptions are no longer so evident— where prices are often subject to government support or institutional rigidities, where demand may be related to variables other than cost, and where large capital investments and the requirements of specially trained manpower may make costly the process of structural change, and so on. Nevertheless, trade policies for nearly all countries during the last thirty years have generally reflected the effort to lower trade barriers on a nondiscriminatory basis. Through a series of negotiations in the GATT, tariffs have been greatly reduced, though more for products involved in trade among the developed countries than those of interest to the poorer nations. There have been exceptions in individual cases where, for political reasons, barriers have been raised or not lowered—for example, the special U.S. restrictions on trade with mainland China, Rhodesia, and Cuba; or the maintaining of the Smoot-Hawley tariff rates on goods from Communist countries. Correspondingly, there have been cases where advantageous positions have been given, as in the British Empire Preferences, the U.S. sugar purchases from Cuba, and, more recently, the Common Market of the European Economic Community and associated countries.

Today the demand by the less-developed countries is for a preferred position. Instead of basing trade arrangements on nondiscrimination and presumably the most efficient use of resources, trade regulation would be used to accelerate growth in the less-developed countries by encouraging their exports. For their unique products—cocoa, bananas, oil seeds, and a hundred more—they would like free access to all markets, and no excise taxes after arrival. Such a proposal for this group of products does not raise the discrimination question directly, since they are generally produced only in less-developed countries. In fact, it may reduce discrimination since some less-developed countries already have special privileges in some markets while others do not. The proposal is not as enormous as it might appear, since many of these commodities are already on the free list in important markets. In 1968, the United States imported $8,906 million from less-developed countries, and 54 per cent entered duty free. It is estimated that the figure will reach 60.9 per cent when Kennedy Round cuts are completed.

While a few raw materials (such as tropical hardwoods) and foodstuffs produced in less-developed countries may have an elastic demand, it does not seem likely that even the steps demanded could lead to a substantial expansion in trade: the real quest is for preferential treatment for their exports of manufactured and semi-manufactured goods. In view of the fact that most of these products are subject to tariff charges, placing them on the free list when they come from less-developed countries would mean an advantage for exporters from less-developed countries over exporters from more advanced countries. They would still have to face competition with the home industry and would have to overcome transportation charges and such prejudice as may exist against foreign-made products. Most difficult of all, they would have to meet the requirements of the market, not only in quality, packaging, etc., but also in the promotional and organizational activities needed to take business away from established competitors.

The figures for exports of manufactured goods from less-developed countries show rapid rates of growth, largely because of the very small base from which they start. An OECD estimate indicated that imports of manufactured goods into OECD countries from less-developed countries more than doubled between 1960 and 1965, but that more than half of the total came from five countries—Hong Kong, India, Israel, Yugoslavia, and Mexico. In the majority of less-developed countries, the manufacturing sector is still very small compared with agriculture.

The demand for trade preferences for manufactured goods was obviously going to be a major subject on the UNCTAD II agenda, and the developed countries had many meetings to consider what attitude to take. The idea of giving preferences to less-developed countries was hardly a new idea. Those which had been colonies had had full access to the markets of at least one developed country. The six members of the Common Market carried on such an arrangement with their former colonies, originally established in the Convention of Yaounde and gradually expanded to include other African countries. In July 1968, Kenya, Tanganyika, and Uganda became associated members with the understanding that all their exports except coffee, cloves, and tinned pineapple, which were to be limited to existing levels, were eligible to enter the Common Market without duty or quota restrictions. In turn, they granted tariff concessions to the Six on a list of about 60 products, a kind of reciprocity arrangement. Israel signed a four-year preferential trade agreement in February 1970, which involved various tariff reductions and other concessions on both sides.

At the UNCTAD II the industrial countries made a small gesture by indicating a willingness to speed up the Kennedy Round cuts as they applied to less-developed countries. Furthermore, an UNCTAD intergovernmental committee was established to work out the details, aiming for a preferential system which might come into operation in 1970. However, the broad formula left many operational problems to be settled, not the simplest of which are to define more exactly the coverage of the term "less-developed country," and the products to be included. The OECD countries have been unwilling to include processed and semiprocessed agricultural products in the preferential system. There is also the question of how to reconcile new preferences with existing ones, including those now given to particular industrial countries for their exports to less-developed countries, as in the Common Market case.

The suggestion made at UNCTAD in 1968 to advance the timing of the Kennedy Round cuts loses its meaning as time passes and a slower schedule is followed. Nevertheless, the resistance to the idea of preferences for less-developed countries has been weakened if not broken. The Council of the OECD, meeting in February 1969, instructed the Organization to proceed with its work on preferential tariff treatment for exports in preparation for consultations to be held with developing countries, and the United States submitted illustrative lists to OECD in July 1969. Among the key provisions in the United States proposal were the following:

(1) All duties on manufactured and semimanufactured products imported from less developed countries, except textiles, footwear, and petroleum and petroleum products would be eliminated. A selected list of agricultural and fishery products that would also benefit from the preferences is provided.

(2) There would be no quantitative limits on the additional imports eligible for preferential treatment. Injury to domestic producers would be handled by standard escape clauses and adjustment assistance.

(3) The preferences would be temporary, scheduled to last no more than 10 years, and should not obstruct further general tariff reductions.

(4) All major developed countries would adopt a common plan.

(5) The United States would not grant preferences to any country that received an exclusive trade preference from any developed country for a product covered by the plan, nor would we grant preferences to LDC's that gave exclusive trade preferences to any developed country (reverse preferences).[3]

In November, following discussion in the OECD and a go-ahead declaration by President Nixon on October 31, suggestions for eliminating a wide range of tariffs were submitted to the UNCTAD by 18 industrial countries. They were not identical. The widest disagreement was between the proposals of the Common Market and the United States. The Common Market would set quotas within which zero tariffs were to apply, along with continued preferred treatment to its 18 associated African states.

The United States would require most-favored-nation treatment
for all less-developed countries, would exempt textiles, footwear,
and oil, and would include an "escape clause" in the case of
undue hardship resulting from increased imports. Japan's proposal included quota limits on tariff reductions, while Britain
and the Scandinavian countries supported generalized preference
plans. In view of the apparent impossibility of reconciling these
several positions, the latest suggestion has been to permit each
developed country to use whatever formula it chooses, so long as
the results are concessions by each country of an equivalent
amount. The latter concept has obvious difficulties of calculation, but the measurement of concessions has always been a
difficulty with the reciprocity concept.

At the same time, the problem is being considered at GATT.
Olivier Long, the Director-General, has proposed that the next
set of GATT negotiations should deal with nontariff barriers, the
rationalization of agriculture, and the trade problems of the developing world. He suggested that by the end of 1970 exploratory
conversations between member countries in GATT could lead
to a decision to enter such negotiations and they could be completed in 1972.[4] Anyone familiar with the difficulties of such
trade negotiations would have to regard such a timetable as
clearly on the optimistic side.

The general idea of using trade arrangements to help the less-
developed countries received a great boost when President Nixon,
in his message to Congress submitting The Trade Act of 1969,
on November 18, 1969, said that he was delaying any recommendations to give improved access to the less-developed countries because international discussions were in progress, but that
"at the appropriate time, I will submit legislation to the Congress
to seek authorization for the United States to extend preferences
and to take any other steps toward improving the market access
of the less-developed countries which might appear desirable."[5]
He had earlier suggested that if it were not possible to get a
satisfactory general solution, the United States would be prepared
to work out a system of preferences for the less-developed countries in the western hemisphere.

The idea of expanding trade through giving preferences to the
less-developed countries is not as promising as it seems on the
surface. It may not amount to much, since the imports will still
have to compete with production in the industrial countries;

and on many products, tariffs have already been reduced to nominal levels. Furthermore, there are nontariff barriers—quota restrictions, technical and sanitary regulations, excise taxes and domestic subsidies, and restrictive agreements. In many ways, these barriers can be as restrictive as tariffs. Even without such obstacles, there is the problem of achieving and maintaining quality standards over the necessary quantity, since the quality required for the home market in a less-developed country is likely to be lower than that needed for export. There is also the difficulty of breaking into a market already having entrenched suppliers, including special packaging and labeling problems. If tariff reduction does encourage trade, it will stir up the familiar and easily aroused demands for protection from the industries affected. The sensitive areas of textiles and textile products, petroleum, iron and steel products, agricultural products, meat and processed foods are all involved. Sugar and petroleum are already under quota control in the United States, and imports of meat and cotton textiles are also limited by other devices. The difficulties which Japan has had, and still has, of breaking into established markets is an indication that serious obstacles exist, but also that they are not entirely insurmountable.

On the other hand, if aid is ever to be ended and if the increasing loans and equity investments in less-developed countries are to be serviced, there must be a substantial increase in the earnings of foreign exchange by these areas. It is not a new problem, and already most developed countries have programs for aiding enterprises and workers to shift out of industries which cannot meet foreign competition. It ought to be relatively easy to remove all barriers to products not produced in the recipient country—tariffs and internal taxes on products of tropical agriculture, for example. The situation also may be eased by making markets more accessible while limiting sudden disruptive influxes of foreign goods.

One other matter where considerable progress can be made is to encourage more processing of raw materials in the country of origin. In many cases, tariff rates increase sharply according to the amount of processing which has taken place, thus discouraging the country producing the raw material from carrying out intermediate processing steps and selling a more valuable product. Generally, however, there is an established industry in the developed country accustomed to performing the processing function, so that the suggestion raises all the usual demands for protection from injury.

Despite these many difficulties, progress must be made in encouraging imports from less-developed countries. Their rising debt service and growing needs for foreign goods make increased earnings essential. In 1966, Australia created a preference system, for which a waiver was obtained from GATT, providing preferential duties, sometimes zero rates, on some sixty items from less-developed countries. These rates were to be applied within quota limits above which regular duties would apply.

Hal Lary, who is quite optimistic over the possibilities of expanding the exports of less-developed countries, has suggested that each developed country "provide a quantitative analysis and projection, by main groups of manufactures, of the expected evolution of its imports from less developed countries, taking account of market trends and its own commercial policies." [6] He argues that this would focus attention on the results which policy is intended to achieve.

> Fulfillment of targets by the developed countries . . . would not be a matter of creating artificial inducements but of removing artificial impediments to the trade. Some developed countries might elect to do so by reducing import barriers over the whole range of products of interest to less-developed countries and to do so on a most-favored-nation basis. Some others might choose to proceed much more selectively with respect to both the products and the countries benefiting by the concessions.

It may be that some such target scheme would help to overcome the political obstacles to increasing imports by making the objective clearer. But to achieve the objective, assistance to the less-developed countries would itself need a higher priority than at present in the larger importing countries. The setting of the target would be a highly controversial matter, and the problem of how to meet the target would still remain a battleground.

* * *

Tariff rates are only one of the obstacles to be overcome in building up exports, and one can question how soon any reductions by the more advanced countries will have an appreciable effect. There is a growing recognition that trade among the less-developed countries themselves may offer a more practical way to expand their markets. Toward this end, India in 1967 concluded contracts for transmission equipment with Sudan, Nigeria, and Kuwait; for railway cars with Korea; and for railway coaches with Burma.

The Pearson Commission regards the expansion of trade among low-income countries as having a very great potential. A broader application of the concept of import substitution might take place if they bought things from each other which they now purchase from developed countries. Negotiations began in Geneva in 1967 to work out a multilateral exchange of mutually advantageous concessions on tariff and nontariff barriers between developing countries, but progress has been slow. Along with the removal of barriers, it is important that some attention be paid to the financial aspects of this growing trade in terms of possible clearing and credit arrangements. There is the beginning of such facilitation in Latin America, where the Inter-American Development Bank is financing purchases of one Latin American country from another.

To reinforce the possibility of increased trade among themselves, various groupings are moving toward the common market concept. The countries of Central America have operated on this basis since 1960. In 1961, the Latin America Free Trade Area was created, but it has met with delays and disagreements. It has extended the date for final achievement of the goal to 1980, and has recommended that meanwhile its members grant an annual 2.9 per cent tariff reduction, based on a weighted average of duties charged on imports from third countries. Plans are to be made for a more rapid procedure toward a common market to begin at the end of 1974. In the meantime, Bolivia, Chile, Colombia, Ecuador, and Peru—Venezuela having withdrawn—agreed in May 1969 to develop an Andean Common Market whereby tariffs between them will be abolished within eleven years, and a common external tariff adopted. In Africa, various efforts have been made to develop economic groupings, but the instability of political relationships and the lack of communication and of substantial common interests have made them rather fragile. As the European Economic Community has demonstrated, a common market requires action in many fields in addition to eliminating trade barriers. Less-developed countries would benefit greatly by common planning, as in the Turkey-Iran-Pakistan case, so that surplus capacity would not be constructed and new facilities can be based on the common market.

The possibility of greater trade with the Communist countries should also be noted. Foreign trade by the members of the Soviet bloc has always been limited, except within the group. Presumably, this was for political reasons as well as the bias of economic planners to keep as much of economic activity under their control as possible. Foreign trade is carried on through bilateral agreements, which make it clear that it consists basically of exchanging goods for goods. More recently, a slightly more sophisticated arrangement has appeared whereby Bulgaria and Czechoslovakia, both having a trade surplus with India and therefore holding rupee balances, have agreed with Hungary and East Germany, which have rupee deficits, to a triangular payments arrangement.

* * *

It is a common notion that if less-developed countries can obtain more foreign exchange by increasing their exports, their requirements for aid will be correspondingly reduced. The phrase "trade not aid" has often misled people into believing that the acceptance of more imports by industrial countries is the equivalent of an equal amount of aid. Items formerly obtained through the aid channel can now be paid for with foreign earnings.

This is a grossly oversimplified proposition. Trade can supplant aid if the larger foreign earnings have come from higher selling prices, so that earnings are increased without any offsetting drain on domestic resources and labor, as in the copper market of 1967–68. In a sense, the foreign consumer is unwittingly providing added assistance. The added earnings might also come from exports whose production has been achieved by the use of otherwise idle labor and resources, in which case their production is a net addition. But to a large degree, the expansion of exports is likely to be based on capital and labor which might otherwise be used for some domestic purpose. Such a shift into exports does not increase gross national product, but alters the production pattern by increasing exports rather than goods for domestic markets and changes the consumption pattern by reducing domestic products consumed domestically and increasing imported goods and services. This can be a highly useful rearrangement, since it may permit larger-scale, more specialized production and increase the variety of goods available to producers and consumers. These advantages are particularly important for relatively small countries which must rely on trade for sizable markets and for a wider variety of goods. However, the point is that foreign goods obtained in trade are in exchange for domestic products, whereas goods obtained through aid are costless to the recipient, insofar as they involve some concessionary element.

Furthermore, the expansion of capacity to produce and export manufactured goods must be the result either of aid or of domestic savings, plus policies which make costs in the economy such as to earn admission into foreign markets. Harry Johnson has suggested that "high sales taxes will have to accompany trade liberalization on their part [the less-developed countries] if domestic savings ratios are to be kept high enough." [7] He goes on to point out that trade and aid are complementary. Aid is needed to support liberalized trade policies. Otherwise it may operate merely to subsidize increasingly nonviable industrial structures. But if trade is the objective, then aid operates with a kind of market test.

Finally, it should be noted that assistance given to expand exports will tend to help the more advanced among the less-developed countries and may do very little for others. As in Taiwan, for example, exports might increase so much that there is no balance-of-payments problem. But for others, including a number of the sub-Sahara African countries, the possibility of substantial sales in foreign markets is so slight that trade cannot take the place of aid for many years to come.

* * *

An important development which has substantial implications for trade has already been noted in Chapter 10 on private enterprise —the growth of multinational enterprises. Too often private foreign activity is described as investment rather than production.[8] The multinational corporation often sells its product in more countries than those in which its production centers are located, thus automatically creating foreign trade activity. The remarkable development of Puerto Rico's productive capacity has been less for the Puerto Rican than for the American market, and was largely achieved by American firms. In most cases of petroleum development, increased exports have resulted. New methods of transportation—the speed of planes, the convenience of containers, the improvement in port facilities, and the larger size tankers—have all reduced one barrier to trade, namely, the added costs of moving goods from one place to another.

*   *   *

Foreign exchange can be earned through invisible exports as well as commodity trade. The expansion in foreign-exchange earnings does not come solely from visible exports. Longer vacations and higher incomes in the developed countries have greatly expanded tourist trade. The increase in the number of foreign visitors to Yugoslavia from about 3 million in 1963 to 23 million in 1967, most of whom came by bus or car, has been related not only to hotel development but also to an improved highway system, financed in part by the World Bank. Similarly, foreign-exchange earnings can be increased by forms of invisible import substitution, particularly in the shipping and insurance fields.

*   *   *

A second complaint of the less-developed countries is that the long-term trends of export and import prices have operated to their disadvantage—that the prices at which they have been able to sell their products, mostly raw materials, have not advanced as much as the prices which they have had to pay for imports, mostly manufactured goods. It can be argued that primary products, because they are subject to natural limitations on their supply, ought to become relatively more and more valuable. On the other hand, there is limited elasticity in the demand for food, and manufactured products tend to have a lower and lower percentage of their total value derived from their raw materials component. Endless arguments still continue over the statistical record of the terms of trade, and the answer seems to depend on the period taken, the composition of the goods included, the question of changing quality which is more likely in manufactured goods than in primary commodities, and the allowance made for shipping costs.

Whether or not the situation has deteriorated, those in the less-developed countries believe it to be so. Summarizing the situation in Asia and the Far East in June 1968, Mr. Takeshi Watanabe, President of the Asian Development Bank, emphasized the importance of export earnings. He noted that, owing largely to slumping commodity prices and a falling market in Western Europe, the developing ECAFE countries earned 15 per cent less foreign exchange in 1967 than in the previous year, when they added $442 million. The President of Cameroon, Mr. Ahidjo, in a speech describing his country's growth rate of 9 per cent a year and a rise in per capita income from $100 to $133 from 1959 to 1965–66, said that "the worsening in the terms of trade during the last ten years [since 1959] had deprived the country of financial resources equivalent to all the foreign aid it had received." [9]

No one has proposed any very good scheme for changing the long-term trends of subgroups of prices. Even if prices were higher, only the less-developed countries producing the item would gain, while the purchasers would lose. In the past, some metropolitan powers did support prices for certain products from their colonies. The French had such a system, and its presumed liquidation was one justification advanced for the Common Market's program of more direct assistance to the Associated States. Italy still supports the price of bananas from Somalia. When high prices are maintained through some such arrangement, there is a real transfer of assistance from the purchasing nation to the country of origin, financed unwittingly by the consumer.

Representatives of the French government frequently speak of "market organization" as a way of assisting the less-developed countries. Presumably, this is an adaptation of their earlier price-support machinery. Such a scheme is relatively easy to operate bilaterally; it is much more difficult to apply the same technique to a product with a number of national producers and an even larger number of consuming countries, except through an international commodity agreement. Although commodity agreements are ostensibly intended to stabilize rather than raise prices, they do represent a possible technique for doing the latter, providing the consumer countries are willing to pay the higher prices. The chief difficulty in this approach is to make certain that price supports do not lead to such an increase in the supply as to destroy the plan through the accumulation of surpluses, or the encouragement of substitutes or synthetics. Where there is a relatively large number of small producing countries, it is particularly difficult to operate a scheme limiting supply. Where a single country is involved (Nigeria or Ghana, for example), the situation has been met in the past by not permitting the price rise to go to the individual producer, but by drawing off any margin because of high world prices through an intermediary marketing board and presumably using the proceeds to keep domestic prices up if and when world prices should fall. The French way of increasing the level of certain commodity prices was to levy an import tax, the proceeds of which were turned over to the less-developed country.

The problems underlying commodity price behavior in the less-developed countries are much like those which led to the agricultural price-support programs. In an effort to increase personal income, the farmer expands his production. If, as a result of his action and parallel action by other farmers, the supply is increased, the price may fall. With lower prices, he may redouble his efforts to maintain his income. Presumably, the situation finally corrects itself by forcing many of the less-efficient producers out of business. Rather than have this happen, governments have set up price supports and direct or indirect production controls. Although the technique can work in a single country, it is much more difficult to operate on an international basis, as has been shown all too clearly in the efforts of the European Economic Community to deal with agriculture. And as in that case, since the price-support program leads almost certainly to attempts to liquidate the high-cost producers and to encourage diversification, the probable impact is to require more rather than less aid, at least in the short run.

* * *

A third complaint is related not so much to the long-term trend of export earnings as to their wide fluctuations from year to year. Economic planning, it is argued, is impossible for a less-developed country if income is unpredictable, and export earnings have a sufficient multiplier effect so that wide fluctuations in them will disturb the entire economy. While cases can be found where single products dominate exports to the point where general instability results from export fluctuation, it is an open question whether this is generalized and disturbing enough to call for new and complex machinery.[10]

The most usual device aimed at stabilizing prices is the commodity agreement; several international agreements are now in operation, while many commodities also have national support schemes. The record of commodity agreements thus far is not very encouraging. The International Wheat Agreement, which sets maximum and minimum prices, has no export or production controls and has been unable to maintain prices during periods of increasing stocks. The International Tin Agreement, based upon the purchase and sale of buffer stocks, proved ineffectual in keeping prices from rising from 1963 to mid-1966 after the stocks were exhausted. The International Agreement on Olive Oil arranges exchanges between surplus and deficit countries but has built up sizable stockpiles; it has no price objectives. A new five-year International Sugar Agreement went into effect at the beginning of 1969, but covers only about 40 per cent of world sugar trade, has a target price-range, and uses export restrictions to regulate the market. The International Coffee Agreement is probably the most successful, having 66 members, price targets, and adjustable export quota restrictions. It is concerned with curtailing world coffee production capacity through diversification programs of its producing members. The UNCTAD is endeavoring to establish a cocoa agreement.

Since over 80 per cent of less-developed country exports are primary commodities, it is not surprising that this was a major subject at the UNCTAD I in 1964. The less-developed countries were joined by France in arguing that world markets should be so organized as to increase and stabilize prices for these products. The opponents raised technical difficulties, primarily the problems of adjusting supply and the body of principles associated with the concept of free world trade.

Later in that year, the U.N. General Assembly assigned responsibility for action in this field to the UNCTAD. Since then, all five agreements have been renegotiated, although the sugar agreement was in a sense new, the 1958 agreement having been inoperative since the end of 1961. Three UNCTAD Cocoa Conferences tried to work out an agreement, but by mid-1969 the only result was a bilateral agreement between the United States and Ghana. The UNCTAD II in 1968 was less ambitious about reaching formal international agreements, laid down some general guidelines, and urged that there be permanent study groups to deal informally with such problems as might appear.

Even where there is no permanent organization, a crisis may lead to common action. When tea production increased in 1968 and 1969 to a level considerably above that of consumption, and prices for plain tea were halved, delegates from 14 tea-exporting countries agreed to propose a 7 per cent cut in exports in 1970.

Since then a Consultation Committee on Tea has been established under the sponsorship of the FAO. Unfortunately, the situation is complicated by the fact that tea cultivation is being expanded in some developing countries in Latin America and Africa in their search for export possibilities.[11] With respect to coconut, the Ceylonese government has proposed to the Asian Coconut Community that a buffer stock scheme be established and that there be an agreement on prices of desiccated coconut.

An international agreement on tuna fishing in the Atlantic Ocean was drawn up in May 1960 in Rio de Janeiro under FAO sponsorship. It finally entered into force March 21, 1969, with seven ratifications, although ten other countries had originally declared their intention to participate. Agreements concerning seals, salmon, and whales have existed for many years.

As pointed out above, one central difficulty is that one cannot deal with prices without being concerned with quantities. Thus, the extended Coffee Agreement (effective October 1, 1963) provides for a Coffee Diversification Fund, based upon a charge of 60 cents for each 132-pound bag of coffee exported annually over the quota of 100,000 bags, plus voluntary contributions by importing countries. The United States has indicated that it would lend $15 million and match another $15 million in loans or contributions from other coffee-consuming countries. The Fund may therefore have resources in excess of $150 million to finance agricultural diversification programs intended to prevent surplus accumulations of coffee. On the other hand, the new five-year sugar agreement promoted by UNCTAD (with neither the United States nor the Common Market as participants) merely provides for progressive reductions in export quotas whenever the price drops to 3.5 cents per pound, thus passing the problem of adjustment of supply back to the members.

* * *

Export instability may come from many different factors within the producing country (weather or disorder) or in the external market (substitutes or general recession). And variation in the availability of foreign exchange may be caused by nontrade factors in the balance of payments. Therefore, more recently, the idea that the problem of instability in export proceeds should be handled through financial machinery was put forward in UNCTAD I, studied by the staff of the IBRD, and debated and returned for further study by the UNCTAD II.

This approach involves setting up a fund to be available to assist a country if its foreign exchange earnings should fall, for reasons beyond the country's control, below a level previously determined to be that which might be reasonably expected. Most of the advanced countries have not supported this proposal, although it was originally put forward by the United Kingdom and Sweden. In addition to various technical difficulties, they do not favor earmarking funds for such a limited purpose and see no reason why the problem, if and when it appears for any individual country, should not be handled by the International Monetary Fund as a temporary balance-of-payments difficulty. For example, in April 1968 Ceylon made a drawing from the IMF of $19.3 million under the Fund's policy of compensatory financial assistance to countries experiencing a temporary shortfall in total export earnings when attributable to circumstances beyond their control. In the Ceylon case, the guilty parties were tea and rubber, which constitute 75 per cent of its total exports. A similar drawing was made by Afghanistan, suffering from a reduction in earnings from karakul skins and carpets due to a fall in demand, and from cotton because of a poor crop.

In July 1969, the International Monetary Fund set up a new financial arrangement to contribute to commodity stabilization. In addition to the existing procedures of the IMF for compensatory financing, drawings up to 50 per cent of quota are authorized for the purpose of financing buffer stocks accumulated in compliance with international commodity agreements. At the same time, the World Bank announced increased activity in helping countries to diversify their production, strengthen the competitiveness of primary products in world trade, and participate more effectively in international commodity agreements.[12]

An interesting special arrangement to meet one aspect of this problem has been suggested as part of the effort by the Common Market to assist its dairy industry, namely to place a tax on all margarine, domestic and foreign. The significant point for this discussion is the proposal that the proceeds of the tax would be distributed to the associated African countries which, together with the United States, are the main suppliers of the raw materials for margarine.

* * *

Quite apart from the notion that development can be accelerated by innovations in the field of trade are a number of suggestions in the financial field. One such approach is put forward by those who are eager to increase the resources available for assistance without having to go through the repetitive process of legislative appropriation. They have suggested that a large part of the new monetary reserves to be created through the IMF be allocated to the less-developed countries.

The newly invented Special Drawing Rights (SDR) have been distributed to members of the International Monetary Fund in the same proportions as their quotas in the Fund. Since the share of less-developed countries in the total quotas of Fund members is well in excess of their share either in existing world reserves or in international trade, the less-developed countries have been somewhat favored in the distribution of the special drawing rights under the established formula. While the amount of new liquidity to be added each year remains to be determined, it has been forecast to be at least $2 billion per year. Various methods have been suggested which could be used to make a larger share of this new international purchasing power available to the less-developed countries.

The initial suggestion of making the original distribution only to less-developed countries raised the difficulty that this automatic distribution would not give any recognition to need or to ability to use it effectively. Another proposal received some approbation when a subcommittee of the Joint Congressional Economic Committee proposed in August 1969 that the member countries of the IMF should agree to earmark 25 per cent of their SDR allocations to help less-developed nations. By turning over this amount to the IDA, its lending capacity would be increased to $1 billion a year without placing a burden on any country's balance of payments.[13]

Although this general idea was presented by a group representing UNCTAD to the sponsors of the new SDR program (the eleven members of the so-called Group of Ten), the central bankers with their usual caution were fearful that the need for development finance was so great it might lead to an undue extension of SDR's beyond the amount required to maintain liquidity, and that such an expansion of the international monetary base might have inflationary results. Probably one should not endeavor to alter the agreed basis for the extension of SDR's in this early stage of the new means of settling international payments. Nevertheless, the suggestion represents a relatively painless way of moving added goods and services to the less-developed countries which may be worthy of keeping in the "active" file. It could accomplish a great deal with a minimum disturbance of established budgetary procedures, tariff arrangements, or machinery to support foreign earnings.

* * *

A second suggestion in the field of finance which has had considerable discussion, called the Horowitz proposal after its originator, is to raise funds in the private market at whatever yields are necessary, and use public monies to pay the difference between borrowing hard and lending soft. This is the normal procedure within a government when it provides loan funds for a specific purpose at rates below those under which it does its current borrowing or refunding. If such a procedure were applied to the World Bank, for example, it would mean that government financing of the IDA would not consist so much in contributing principal as in assuming a commitment over a number of years to pay the unrequited part of the interest charges as they fall due. The principal amount of foreign aid made available to less-developed countries in any year would come out of the private market, while the public contribution would be a commitment for a much smaller annual payment over the period covered by the private borrowing.

This approach would reduce the budgetary burden on governments in the particular years when the loan was made. However, if continued year after year, the supplementing interest payments might have accumulated to a sum equal to, or perhaps more than, one year's payment on principal. For example, suppose that the assistance being given is $100 million for 25 years at 2 per cent interest and that the money is raised through public borrowing at 6.5 per cent. Under the Horowitz proposal, the public commitment would be to provide $4.5 million per year for twenty-five years to make up the interest gap. Under the more usual practice, the budget would pay out $100 million in the first year, and then collect interest of $2 million per year for twenty-five years. In both cases, the amortization would be the same. Theoretically, the ultimate cost should be the same if one discounts the future as the market does. In fact, however, with the great emphasis placed by governments on short-run 'budget balancing, it may well be that the series of smaller future payments would be much more acceptable.

A variant on the Horowitz proposal has been suggested by the Pearson Commission, that "donor countries commit the equivalent of one-half or more of the interest payments due them on official bilateral loans from developing countries to the World Bank to subsidize the interest rates on some Bank lending." [14] In 1968, this would have amounted to slightly over $300 million. If this were used on a funding basis, it would permit the bank to borrow $600 million in the private market at 7 per cent and relend it at 3 per cent. If it were not on a funding basis, but was regarded as an assured annual contribution, it could support a 4 per cent annual payment on $15 billion. To be sure, giving up half their interest inflow would be a cost to the suppliers, and the distribution of the contribution would fall largely on the United States, Germany, and the United Kingdom. However, it would permit the raising of capital in the private markets without the necessity of saddling the ultimate borrowers with such high rates or taking the principal amount out of national treasuries.

An interesting suggestion made by Robert Roosa [15] is that donors should make a combined commitment to the various international development banks to be allocated among the supporting countries from year to year in accordance with their surplus or deficit positions. A country would make a larger contribution in a year when it was in surplus. Much of these funds might come back to the supplier if it were successful in competitive bidding on projects, while in general the raising of new money would be allocated to countries where the burden on the national economy would be least. Though simple enough, the concept has technical difficulties since the reserves held in central banks are not necessarily government funds freely available for its use. To some extent, the multilateral agencies do operate on this principle, as illustrated by their heavy borrowing in Germany in 1968–69. The World Bank, for example, placed no bonds in Germany in fiscal years 1965–67, only $25 million in 1967–68, but $360 million in 1968–69, when the German surplus was very large. In such cases, of course, the contributions are not permanent since the bonds will either be sold or held until maturity.

Quite a different proposal, described as tentative, has been made by Albert O. Hirschman and Richard M. Bird.[16] The essence of their plan is to involve the individual taxpayer of the donor countries in the foreign aid program and to establish a flow of assistance independent of government control and interference. For payment made to one or several competing, independent, private World Development Funds, the individual would receive an income-tax credit up to 5 per cent of his income tax liability but not more than $10,000. Presumably this would shift the judgment concerning the support of foreign aid away from legislative halls to individual decisions. The individual would receive an appropriate number of "Shares in Development" which might earn a small return. The Fund or Funds would contribute to, but not fully finance development projects, thus encouraging less-developed country investment and the flow of private capital.

The estimate given by the authors is that full participation in this scheme in the United States would have yielded about $1.5 billion in 1965 or about 40 per cent of U.S. official assistance in that year, slightly more than double the amount estimated to be contributed to private voluntary agencies for foreign assistance where the tax benefits depend upon one's income bracket.

Whether or not the individual's interest would increase with the knowledge that his money was going for development purposes is not entirely clear. Norway has a Development Assistance Tax amounting to 0.25 per cent of taxable income, and is near the bottom in the relative level of its official aid. It could be that such a direct procedure is felt by the participants to provide enough for the purpose. It might be an interesting experiment to use the tax incentive device to encourage contributions to the existing multilateral institutions. However, tax incentives are uncertain and uneven in their effectiveness. Even if the proposal led to substantial flows, it is difficult to see how it could do more than add more channels to the flow of resources to less-developed countries. And enthusiasm for a new channel would have the danger of encouraging a reduction in those already established.

* * *

The proposals described above do not cover the full range of possibilities, but demonstrate their variety. Many ingenious individuals, unhappy over the declines in appropriations for foreign aid, have produced various suggestions for recovering American vigor and leadership in the foreign aid field. However useful the ideas for improving the situation, the great danger is that in the process of establishing something new, gains in organization, knowledge, and practice painfully accumulated in the past will be lost.

15 · The Learning Process

From an examination of the various policy and operational problems of assistance programs, it is evident that changes have taken place in the 1960s that are of basic importance to the nature and organization of the assistance effort. First is the progress of the less-developed countries themselves. In 1960, one-third of the present members of the United Nations were still colonies. They had not yet faced the manifold responsibilities and difficulties of functioning as independent nations. Most of the other less-developed countries were only beginning to organize their thinking and their efforts toward development objectives. Thus, at the beginning of the decade, most of the less-developed countries were little prepared to deal with the relatively sophisticated issues of domestic and foreign policy and with the complex operational problems inherent in the process of moving toward modernization.

So much needed to be done that they hardly knew where to begin. As a result, the developed countries often provided needed initiative and direction along with enthusiasm and insistence, supplying operators and advisers, helping in developing plans, and urging various institutional changes. Contacts with the outside world grew rapidly and advice became plentiful. The United States in general, and France in areas of its particular interest, were especially active.

Experience naturally came to replace naïveté in the recipient countries. Technical problems required answers; policy choices had to be made. Civil services were gradually built up, contributing to a marked improvement in the quality and competence of most governments in the less-developed countries, particularly with reference to development matters.

Such an evolution was probably natural, given time and experience, but it was greatly hastened by the pressure of events and by technical assistance and training activities. Assistant Secretary of State Charles A. Meyer, testifying before the House Committee on Foreign Affairs on May 8, 1969, summarized the situation in Latin America as follows:

> Within the framework of the Alliance for Progress, our sister Republics have made notable gains in many areas. . . . wide recognition that the energies, talents, and resources available. . . must be even more vigorously directed toward accelerated development. There are a number of increasingly effective multilateral and bilateral mechanisms. . . . Much has been done to create the climate, train the talent, and to tool up for the demands of the decade ahead.

There still are great differences in the competence of the governments of the less-developed countries, reflecting in considerable part their general stage of development and the extent to which they have had earlier experience in policy-making. As far as external assistance is concerned, these differences mean that a much larger proportion of technical assistance and basic infrastructure is needed by the poorer of the less-developed countries, which might be described as being in a pre-investment stage.

As a country becomes more able to handle its own affairs, foreign agencies can take on more of an assistance than a leadership role. The more intimate and paternalistic bilateral relationships of earlier days are becoming less and less appropriate, which does not mean a break in relations but a change in kind. The manner in which assistance is given can either circumscribe or encourage the growth of self-reliance. Even the developed countries discuss and criticize each other's policies at the OECD, nor are these sessions limited exclusively to economic matters. The United Nations and its specialized agencies provide many opportunities for considering different policy alternatives. And the multilateral institutions, particularly the financial institutions like the World Bank and the IMF, are, as President McNamara described it, more and more helping the developing countries to establish an over-all development strategy.

Although the changing relationship does not lessen the need for resources—quite the contrary—it does mean for the supplying governments a shift in attitude from that of resident director to a sort of limited partnership. The change is indirectly illustrated by the growth of program aid. Under the procedure of program aid, there is no specific project jointly developed with feasibility surveys and detailed specifications. Assistance would not be given for program aid, however, unless the supplier had confidence that the recipient government has an adequate development plan and carries on a relatively effective and disciplined operation.

For the supplier countries and the United States in particular, the general trend—the increasing competence of the less-developed countries—means that the suppliers can take a less prescriptive position. Much smaller resident staffs are required. The less-developed countries must make their own decisions and be allowed to learn from mistakes as well as from advice.

* * *

Of similar importance in revising the pattern of economic assistance is the increasing activity of multilateral agencies. Not only are there many more of them, but their professional staffs have grown, and their disbursements have increased much more rapidly than those of the bilateral agencies. Without going into the details again (see Chapter 9), it is important to recall how great the change has been since 1960. At that time, the IBRD was the only agency with a substantial resource flow. Neither the IDA nor the IADB had begun to make disbursements, and the Asian and African Development Banks had not even been conceived. The U.N. Expanded Program for Technical Assistance had a budget of less than $30 million. According to the estimates for 1968, new commitments by multilateral agencies were $2,146 million although net disbursements were only $814 million. A considerable part of these funds was raised in private capital markets and might otherwise not have gone into projects in less-developed countries.

The activity of the multilateral agencies goes far beyond the flow of people and resources. Some agencies, like ECOSOC, the UNCTAD, the Alliance for Progress or the U.N. regional commissions, are not channels through which assistance actually moves, but represent central points for common review and evaluation. In individual cases, the staffs of the specialized agencies and the financial institutions act as expert advisers, particularly where there are consortia and consultative groups. The new

schedule of expert reviews by the World Bank, the expanded annual consultations by the IMF, and the corps of UNDP resident
representatives will provide an even closer contact.

The position of the multilateral agencies is strengthened by the
fact that the less-developed countries play an active role in their
governance, contribute personnel to their secretariats, and sometimes even provide the executive head. Although many of the
agencies are supposed to be global in their responsibilities, they
have come more and more to focus their activities on assistance
to the less-developed countries. To be sure, the agencies are not
without political problems, since they continually deal with governments, but they do not have the multiplicity of interests in
nondevelopmental matters which sometimes intrude into bilateral
relationships.

While various further steps for reorganization of the agencies
have been suggested, the major contribution which they have already made and will continue to make should not be minimized.
Their growing activity not only increases the emphasis given to
feasibility studies and carefully planned programs, but it clearly
broadens the sources from which aid can be drawn and spreads
more widely the responsibility for devising wise programs and
policies.

*   *   *

A third gradual change in the 1960s has been the rediscovery of
an obvious truth that was too often ignored because of the subdividing of knowledge and expertise into specialized disciplines—
namely, that development is a total process, that national life
should not be defined and measured only in economic terms, especially if a country is in the less-developed category. Of course,
economic data frequently have been the only available indicators
of change, although often of very poor quality by statistical standards. Furthermore, the level of economic life is exceedingly important, being a necessary though not a sufficient element in
measuring progress.

Even economic progress is not easily evaluated. Although he
was discussing the American economy, Solomon Fabricant was
making a statement of general application when he said that the
"trouble" with a dynamic, growing economy is that it is a system
of parts that are continually undergoing adjustment.[1] Economic
development leads to, requires, and forces adjustments in innu-

merable ways. Although the national aggregates may appear to move along smoothly, the sectors have widely differing rates of growth. The capital-labor mix may change. The introduction of new products and new processes is almost certain to be erratic. There may be changed requirements in organization. Economic growth, says Fabricant, is never balanced.

But the economic growth rate is not the only index to look at. Employment, rural improvement, redistribution of income, social welfare, family planning, education, regional development, decent and competent government on the local as well as the national level, freedom of speech, a functioning system of law, and national self-support all have their importance. Any addition to the list of objectives beyond simple economic productivity greatly expands the number of considerations and variety of actions which enter into the policy choices involved in the development process.

Social aspects of development include not only the functioning of institutions like the family, but imbedded social attitudes toward such widely varied elements of life as work, public and private celebrations, wealth and its most desirable form, gifts and charity, thrift, relatives, children, strangers, risk-taking, the earth and natural phenomena, honesty, the taking of life, occupational status, promptness and the value of time, the desire to please, and the importance of the individual. The shape which these attitudes take creates a social organization, usually unique, which has become firmly established over generations in a world of its own. While these social habits of thought vary widely from country to country, usually they are not sympathetic to technical change or the requirements of modern life. Ghandi was expressing his scale of values in life when he gave priority to the spinning wheel and the hand loom over more productive factory production with power machinery.

Attitudes toward change itself are of strategic importance for development. And inertia and resistance to change may be inbred, maintained by institutions which themselves are long and firmly established and concerned with their own survival, not to mention the resistance of those individuals who are at or near the top of the existing power structure.

Social considerations include attitudes and institutions, as well as a host of special problems, such as the care and feeding of children; the treatment of delinquents, disabled and old persons; and the position of women. Every society has its own way of handling these problems, but social and economic change may challenge the established mores. Thus, the migration of individuals to the cities has shifted the problems of support and discipline away from the family, and into the economic and political realm.

To the economic and social conditions must be added the political behavior of the nation. With independence for the former colonies, a new political entity replaces the old one, the top of which has suddenly been amputated. Since the new status is based on unfamiliar concepts of nationalism and sovereignty, the new government is very likely to be authoritarian, as was the political structure which preceded it, and individual leaders are dominant.

The political structures of the less-developed countries show great variety.[2] As of January 1, 1968, some 15 countries had hereditary rulers, or a reasonable facsimile thereof. Their presumed powers ranged from the absolute, as in Saudi Arabia, to the very limited, as in Cambodia. In nearly all these cases, there are constitutions (sometimes on the shelf) and legislative bodies, the members of which are sometimes appointed and sometimes elected. The rulers of another 18 national governments had been established by some form of coup d'état, and often derived their power as head of a self-selected National Revolutionary, Liberation, or Reformation Council, or a Council of Ministers. In such cases, the constitution, if any, usually was set aside and the legislature dissolved. In a few instances (President Nasser in the United Arab Republic and Ayub Khan in Pakistan, who took over through military coups), new constitutions were put into effect and the heads of government were confirmed in their positions by elections.

In the rest of the non-Communist world, governments derive their authority through some form of election. Suffrage is not necessarily universal, and in many countries there is a one-party system so that the final election is merely a formal ratification of whatever selection process exists within the party. Frequently there are bicameral legislatures of which one body at least is chosen on some representative basis.

It is interesting to note that, with exceptions and not including the Communist countries, there is a tendency for small countries to be more authoritarian than large ones. Perhaps dictatorial machinery is better able to sustain itself in small countries; perhaps the small area is less likely to have divisive groups which must be controlled in some way by the government; perhaps it is merely that over-all they tend to be poorer and less well-educated. Political instability manifests itself most conspicuously through internal controversies, which can take the extreme form of revolution and civil war (not an unusual experience in any government) and through changes in leadership, whether by election or coup d'état. At first, American attitudes to these manifestations were greatly colored by the cold war. There was strong opposition to any tendency toward communism, and hearty endorsement of democracy, which was often identified as a procedural matter. Wherever there were elections, a constitution and a two- or multi-party system, democracy was assumed to exist. But it is now evident that form is much less important than behavior.

Perhaps because it has become a truism to say that the political, social, and economic aspects of any society are mutually interlocking and interacting, its full implications are too often overlooked. A most interesting effort to relate economic conditions to non-economic forces, using modern statistical techniques, was published in 1967 by Irma Adelman and Cynthia Taft Morris.[3] Their analysis demonstrates, among many other things, that social forces are of the greatest importance where there is the lowest level of socioeconomic development and that the political element under such circumstances seems to have little impact. However, as one moves to higher economic levels, the social factors exercise less and less influence and the political become increasingly important, reflecting the expansion of the market economy and the increase in requisite public action. This cross-section analysis corresponds to the history of the developed countries, whereby higher economic levels of living have resulted in more social mobility and greater political involvement.

Two important implications follow from the recognition that development is many-sided. The first relates to making a judgment on progress. It is all too easy to look at a percentage rate of growth in national income and decide that a country is or is not a success story. The United Nations Secretariat, in referring to the 5 per cent rate set as a growth target for the Development Decade, warned that "the growth target is too absolute and too simplistic to be used for appraising achievements in the complicated process of development."[4] Similarly, one should not necessarily be disappointed with slow motion in social reform. Political progress is less meaningful when assessed in terms of the manner in which leadership changes, or whether it is in civilian or military hands, than in terms of the underlying objectives, the competence of the civil service, efforts to achieve justice, and the relationship of the political structure to the common people.

A 5 per cent annual growth has been achieved in the 1960s by about three less-developed countries out of ten. If, starting at $100 annual per capita income, a 5 per cent growth rate is offset by a 2.5 per cent annual growth in population, the gain would amount to seven-tenths of a penny per person per day. One can hardly expect such slow beginnings to make any impression. Far more meaningful is the progress being made in terms of more children going to school, the eradication of malaria, or a new road to the next town. A measure which would recognize changes in the quality of life would have much more meaning than a numerical datum of economic productivity.

The second implication is the importance of the time dimension. The pace of the modernized world tends to destroy the quality of patience, and modern men are ill-suited to be inactive bystanders. Even a date in the next decade seems far away. In looking at the total requirements of development, one can see why patience is needed, since the process is bound to be long-run. To be sure, some freak economic event, like the discovery of oil in Libya, can result in a fantastic economic growth rate, but that raises many new problems, as would the sudden, unexpected inheritance of wealth by a poor, uneducated child. Libya is an extreme example of the social and political strains which such imbalance creates. The adjustments will take time.

*　*　*

Not only are there multiple dimensions within a society, but there is a growing recognition of the relationship between growth and foreign economic relations. One of the earliest complaints of the less-developed countries concerned the adverse terms of trade— that their primary-product exports could buy less and less of industrial goods. Along with this have come mounting demands for preferential tariff arrangements to facilitate entrance into markets in the more developed countries. Concern over price fluctuations has led to efforts to extend the number of commodity agreements, and to establish some form of supplementary financing for any country in trouble because of unexpectedly low proceeds from its exports. And the perennial problem of how to expand foreign private investment has moved forward on the stage since further increases in the total official flow of aid are not assured.

Actually, exports from the less-developed countries have been increasing, though at a slower rate than those of the developed countries. Their declining share in world trade is often presented as a distressing figure, but in reality that particular percentage figure is not very meaningful. The total trade figure consists largely of trade among the richer countries. If each should build its own airplanes, for example, all the trade percentages would change: total exports would be smaller, and the exports of the less-developed countries would then be a larger percentage of the total although their trade would not have changed at all.

Obviously, the less-developed countries must have foreign exchange for a number of reasons. In addition to the foreign exchange any government needs for diplomatic and travel costs and the like, their development requires many items which they cannot possibly produce for themselves, and their debt-service obligations are growing rapidly. Since both are subjects of interest to the developed countries in their position as exporters and as creditors, the problem of the long-run financial pattern of each less-developed country with the outside world is assuming ever-increasing importance. The obvious solution, intellectually, is to work out arrangements that will increase the developed world's imports from them, but the demand for protection from foreign competition is a powerful force in every country. Unless ways are found to increase foreign earnings by the less-developed countries, however, the alternatives would seem to be either to provide increasing amounts of assistance to meet the growing debt burden or to force them to cut back on their rate of progress.

A convincing demonstration of the relationship between external assistance and the prospective rate of growth has been presented by Professor John P. Lewis in his analysis of the Indian situation.[5] He describes the very promising program adopted by India in 1965–66 with a new agricultural strategy, the liberalization of imports and devaluation of the rupee, a new emphasis on export promotion, and real implementation of its family planning program. Extraordinary progress has been made along these lines, and per capita income can readily be increased by 3 per cent per year per capita instead of the 1 per cent averaged through the years 1950–65. Whether it will be more or less than that figure depends on many domestic and foreign factors, but Professor

Lewis argues that a major determinant will be the amount and reliability of external assistance. He sees the possibility of India being "the most successful developing economy in sight."

* * *

Not only does recognition of the total character of development make it much more difficult to assess how things are going, but it raises basic issues as to the process of change and, particularly, the part which foreign economic assistance can play.

It is easy to decry resistance to change as being either the result of some ancient traditions or taboos imbedded in a society, or the behavior of vested interests whereby established individuals wish to protect their power or their prestige. But in many if not most cases, there already has been a major political change, a massive urban migration, a new road network breaking down village isolation, and greatly expanded contacts with the outside world.

From the point of view of influencing and accelerating change, the economic aspects of life can probably be most easily reoriented. Furthermore, the provision of foreign assistance has been easiest in the economic field. Many projects—roads, electric power, port facilities, and government buildings—can be carried out without requiring any considerable cooperation, nor do they appear to displace or conflict with some existing structure.

Social change is much more difficult to engineer from outside. The social structure, inbred, traditional, and resistant to change, involves more people and a clearer break with tradition. Often there is little in tangible form which can be imported. There can be outside assistance for a family planning project, but its success is much more dependent on local effort than would be the establishment of a new steel mill! The social objective of widespread land ownership, as envisioned by the Alliance for Progress, becomes entangled with established patterns of inheritance, different production techniques necessary because of the change in scale, alterations in the class structure, and a whole set of new institutions for credit, marketing, and extension services. These institutional changes can be helped through technical assistance, but they depend essentially upon domestic action.

Political change is the aspect least susceptible to direct foreign influence and pressure, except on the how-to-do-it level. Foreign agencies can help with problems such as how to take a census, or make a budget, or establish a central bank, and can sometimes support action in the policy field. The reduction of centralized and direct controls over trade by Korea and Pakistan was encouraged by prolonged discussions with aid suppliers, who were prepared to back their arguments for reduced import restrictions by promising to meet any new trade deficit which might develop.

In cases dealing more directly with political structure and political behavior, the less-developed countries are very sensitive as a result of their newly-found independence and find it necessary to demonstrate that they are free at last from foreign domination. Changing events in the political world, particularly the short-run change of personalities, are the result of many, often unpredictable, factors, few of which come from outside the country. One cannot say that, in the political field, the United Nations agencies and individual governments have no influence, but it is usually not related to aid, and is likely to be effective only if it does not challenge either the independence or the sovereignty of the country concerned.

Economic programs are relatively specific and while one may not be able to envision their ultimate effect, the immediate activity is readily seen. Social change is much less distinct, though one can usually see the directions in which it is moving. It is political change which is most difficult to evaluate. Failure to make noticeable economic and social progress may lead to political disorder which can have either good or bad results. On the other hand, order may merely be a camouflage for rigidity and injustice.

Thus, as a general proposition, foreign assistance can contribute more to economic change than to social reform, and more to social reform than to political development, though each has some impact on the other. The shift from subsistence living to a market economy not only opens up economic opportunity but broadens the horizon, for feudal systems are built on ignorance and isolation. There is some slight evidence that social and economic development encourages governments to be more responsive to people's social and economic needs, if not their civil liberties.

Some years ago, there was a very active controversy among economists as to whether a given economic target would be reached more rapidly by planning for balanced or unbalanced growth. On the one side were those who feared that bottlenecks would slow down the whole process. On the other were those who felt that the pressure of bottlenecks would cause a stronger and larger effort to be made. Both recognized that in the end there was a limit to the amount of imbalance which could be tolerated. The same argument with the same conclusion can be made concerning the different aspects of society. Those who feel that assistance is too much economic and that not enough is being done on the social and political side may well argue for more balanced programs, but progress in the economic area is one way of forcing change in the others.

* * *

A consequence of increasing experience with development problems is the growing awareness of the differences among the less-developed countries and of the inadequacy of the state of knowledge about the process of change. At first the problem seemed simple: it merely required the transfer of skill and capital. Later it seemed relatively hopeless as various obstacles showed themselves to be recalcitrant, or a most promising case suddenly lost its momentum because of internal or external violence, or some country's insistence on an uncongenial policy in other areas was interpreted as demonstrating the ineffectiveness of foreign assistance. But more experience encourages the taking of a long-term view regarding the setbacks as conditions to be overcome. Both less-developed and developed countries have learned from their mistakes as well as their successes.

Many of the central problems are found in the developed as well as the underdeveloped countries. What to do about urban concentration? How to provide increased employment when machines are replacing workers and modern methods, especially in agriculture, are greatly increasing yields? How to balance a government's budget as its functions expand and multiply? How to build an adequate education system when population is growing so fast? One difficulty is that the answers found in the developed countries, if any, do not necessarily apply to less-developed countries. The approach that makes sense and is feasible in Latin America cannot also be expected to work in Africa or Asia. Almost as much as in physiology, there seems to be a social phenomenon called transplant rejection.

Even the seemingly simple economic projects in the transport and electric power fields have their special problems. The experience of the World Bank has shown that there is an inherent optimism in estimating cost, length of time required, and even technical feasibility, not very different from the easy optimism with which the Panama Canal and the St. Lawrence Seaway were undertaken.[6] Recent years have seen marked improvement in feasibility studies, although as Professor Hirschman has shown, a number of situations have worked out well in spite of unexpected troubles because of subsequent revision in the presumably carefully developed but inadequate blueprint.

However, the point to be made is that while a great deal has been learned, much more study and research is still needed. Much of the ground to be covered falls within specialized fields, but an important requirement is for interdisciplinary study. The history of economics shows frequent recognition of noneconomic factors, but all too often as something to be noted and then assumed away. But the rising fences at the boundaries between intellectual disciplines tended to prevent any over-all study of development until it became a necessity. In 1955, W. Arthur Lewis advanced the thesis that "the factors which determine growth are very numerous, and each has its own set of theories" and he demonstrated it with a profusion of illustrations.[7] But when it came down to actual operations, economic assistance started as a matter of specific projects, usually evaluated on the basis of economic criteria.

The increase in understanding has come from many sources. Thirty years ago, books about the less-developed countries were almost entirely colorful descriptions by travelers or reports by anthropologists. Most economists, political scientists, and sociologists were concerned only with the Western world. In the colleges and universities, one could find academic courses about the moon and stars more easily than about Brazil or India. Today the widespread interest in the less-developed world is impressive. Centers for area studies, the massive output of published material, and the multiplicity of meetings and conferences all testify to an immense effort to learn more about these nations and their development.

At the same time that private study and research in the field has greatly expanded and achieved status, the governments with assistance programs have also been involved in the learning process. For obvious reasons, administrators do not like to record mistakes, and governments are no exception. Why study a project when completed, since nothing can be done to change it? In spite of this bias, it is encouraging that a number of governments, particularly the United States, have made major efforts at evaluating their activities in the assistance field.

Another factor contributing to the learning process is that there has been less insulation between the scholar and operator than is usually the case, largely because the technical assistance and educational development programs have utilized many academics, and foundations have enabled scholars to make on-the-spot studies. However, like operators, the scholars have sometimes tended to generalize too broadly from a limited exposure in time and area. This situation might be eased somewhat if the extensive records of experiences now collected were more systematically available. Nevertheless, the growing mass of descriptive material about the consequences of using this or that policy or method of operation, the greatly improved though still inadequate statistical data, many reports of personal experience, and efforts at general analysis are all contributing to improved performance by both developed and less-developed countries.

Also to be mentioned is the growth in the kind of experience beyond that recorded in the written word—the development of a substantial number of persons who can be regarded as professionals. Many such people are now employed full-time—and some have been for years—in the multilateral and bilateral agencies. Professional societies have developed; consulting and engineering firms have built special staffs and skills; and the universities have become important operators of technical assistance projects.

The results of the learning process are evident throughout the development field. For example, at one time, the introduction of national planning was given very high priority. The early efforts to introduce advance planning into the less-developed countries usually produced grand middle-term development plans, which were then disregarded in actual practice. In part, plans were neglected because of their unreality, in part because of the special interests of particular ministries, and in part because they were incomplete blueprints without recognition of such problems as incentives and cost-benefits. Now after the experience of several generations of planning, most experts would argue that plans and planners are useful, but only when their work is interlocked and supported by politicians and administrators. Proper planning is not merely a rough sketch for constructing a producing economy. It must be broadened from the initial blueprints so that partial planning by functional subdivisions of government, such as treasury, agriculture, and foreign-exchange control, is made consistent not only for the middle-term but can also be reduced to annual programs. The planning process needs to take into account such matters as urbanization, income distribution, taxes, private foreign investment, and economic integration with neighbors. One particular value of the process—putting all the pieces together in a single pattern—is that it has given fresh emphasis to the dominant part played by domestic resources and domestic policies. It has made clear the essential though secondary role of foreign assistance, and has given more credence to the doctrine that assistance should be related to the efforts being made by the less-developed country itself.

Another aspect of the learning process already noted has been the reconsideration of emphasis. While each country presents different problems, certain general shifts have taken place in priorities. Only since the middle 1960s have agricultural development and population problems been given high importance. The usefulness of pre-investment studies has been strongly recognized by the United Nations Development Program and by some bilateral agencies. Technical assistance has become more and more regarded as an essential part of development, and as something where quality and continuity are required. The quick trip of a few weeks by some expert may on occasion be the appropriate means, but more often the transfer of knowledge and skills is a much more complicated and continuing operation.

Similarly, new problems have come to the fore in the financial field. At first, terms and conditions of assistance were of secondary interest, but they have become much more sensitive subjects. Both developed and less-developed countries are more aware of the growing foreign-exchange burden of debt service. The rapid expansion of high-cost export credits is of increasing concern. Strong feelings over the unnecessary costs imposed by tied aid have been eased by the options of program loans but were exacerbated by the concept of additionality. And the extension of the idea of tying to the support of international institutions has had little support outside the U.S. government.

The result of this learning process is the promise of the growing effectiveness of economic assistance. Such mistakes of the past as poorly prepared projects, lack of skilled management and manpower, the acceptance of prestige projects, the disregard of local costs, and the expectation of immediate results, are being avoided by experience on the part of both supplier and recipient. Much solid work has been done in making foreign assistance more productive and in finding better answers to the many specific problems that have appeared in what was uncharted territory. Along with this progress has gone the realization that there is still much to learn, and that even the best-laid plans are subject to the multiplicity of forces, natural and human, which are found with wide variations in every country.

* * *

Another evolutionary change is the much greater sense that development is a common effort and not a series of scattered and unrelated national and international activities. The growth in the organizational pattern bringing together suppliers, recipients, and both groups is extraordinary. Neither the development nor the assistance process is fully integrated, and probably should not be. The separate national programs serve to increase not only the sense of participation, but also the possible sources of imaginative management and significant analysis. Thus, appreciation for the potential food shortage was forced on the world largely by the United States, while Sweden should be given credit for its persistent sponsorship of international action in the field of family planning.

It is frequently suggested that a Marshall Plan for economic development is needed. But the phrase means different things to different people, and it is difficult to see many parallels. The Marshall Plan was only a four-year program, and was entirely an economic operation. It was possible to estimate the requirements because it was essentially a repair job, replacing parts of a previously existing economic machine which had been badly damaged. All countries involved were developed technologically and institutionally. The recipients were numerous while the United States, with an assist from Canada, was the supplier. In every respect, the situation with the less-developed countries is quite different. In fact, the supplier-recipient situation is almost a mirror-image, for in development it involves single recipients each with numerous suppliers.

It is easy to say that the existence of both functional and geographical agencies among multilateral organizations as well as in the various supplier governments makes for considerable duplication of effort. However, there has been great improvement as the result of growing cooperation among the agencies and greater concern about using the available resources most effectively. If the path to world community leads through an increasing series of common cooperative endeavors, the joint effort of rich and poor countries to accelerate development deserves strong support. But one of the implications of any joint effort is a fair sharing in the costs. Studies in greater depth need to be made as to what the less-developed countries might reasonably and properly be expected to do to help themselves, although this poses almost philosophical questions concerning consumption and saving, the present and the future, and the relative importance of various objectives.

As to how the requirements, if they could be determined, should be shared among suppliers, there have been innumerable studies and discussions. Certain percentages have been fixed for support of the multilateral agencies. Again, there is a philosophical question as to whether or not the richer rich countries should contribute a more than proportional share. If they should, the United States' share in the 1960s becomes even less defensible, as it ranks ninth among DAC members in its official aid, and eleventh if the private flow is counted. Since the American gross national product was 52.7 per cent of the total for all sixteen DAC members in 1968, it is crucial to the common effort that it take the lead in increasing its contribution.

In summary, the last two decades have brought out into the open a wide array of problems, uncertainties, and obstacles to the acceleration of the process of development in the less-developed countries. The recognition that progress is neither automatic nor simple has led to changes in emphasis, priorities, and procedures. These changes have occurred in many of the less-developed countries themselves, some of which are struggling for the first time to meet the whole complicated responsibility of operating as an independent nation. Despite the difficulties, many of the developing countries report economic growth at faster rates than the industrialized countries ever enjoyed at a similar stage in their history. More important is the gradual but essential development of new public and private institutions appropriate to their changing world.

The two decades have also seen major changes in the assistance programs of the developed countries. Not only have they found ways and means of being more effective in terms of priorities and methods, but they have been gradually shifting responsibility to international agencies and to the less-developed countries themselves. The learning process has been taking effect.

16·Why?

With the growth of economic assistance to the point where it is a sizable budget item, the question of "why" has become more insistent. While there are many points where improvement is possible, a careful study makes it clear that foreign aid is generally well managed and effective. There is no question about the need and hope of the less-developed countries. Nor is there any question that the governments in advanced countries have recognized the propriety of assistance and are making it more and more a common effort. Whether or not to provide help to the less-developed countries is not the question of the present and future, but rather how much effort should be put forward. Doing something about poverty was established as an international goal with the adoption of the United Nations Charter. In the United Nations, a 54-member committee is preparing a strategy acceptable to both rich and poor for "a decade of international economic and social development," to begin in 1971. When the question arose in the United Nations of setting 1972 as the date by which all the wealthier countries should meet the target of providing 1 per cent of GNP as aid, no country voted against the resolution although nine abstained, including France, the United Kingdom, and the United States.

Assistance is not without strong support, though its strongest advocates often have improvements to suggest in present practices and organization. The President's General Advisory Committee on Foreign Assistance Programs, in its first public declaration since its establishment in March 1965, protested against "the tide of withdrawal" and strongly recommended that President Nixon "take steps to reorganize and revitalize U.S. development assistance," as an "essential instrument for our country's foreign policy."

The leadership of the Catholic and Protestant churches has joined in a common program of World Cooperation for Development. Catholic activity is to some degree a reflection of Pope Paul VI's encyclical "On the Development of Peoples" (March 26, 1967): "Development demands bold transformation, innovations that go deep. It is for each one to take his share in them with generosity. . . . Advanced nations have a very heavy obligation to help the developing peoples." The General Board of the National Council of Churches declared, in a recent policy statement, "The U.S. contribution to development should be increased and maintained because of the need of people, and not in order to secure lesser objectives. . . . should be designed to produce needed and rapid social change."

The Commission on International Development, headed by Lester B. Pearson, reporting in October 1969, contrasted the progress of many developing countries and their increased capacity to utilize additional resources efficiently with the flagging international support for development. It concluded that "a considerably larger amount of foreign resources could be used effectively in the development effort," and endorsed not only the target of 1 per cent of gross national product for public and private flows (the 1968 figure for DAC members was .78 per cent), but added a level of .70 per cent for official development assistance (1968 was .42 per cent).[1]

The U.N. Panel on Foreign Investment in Developing Countries, meeting in Amsterdam in February 1969, called for "a massive increase in the rate at which capital is flowing into the developing nations from outside sources."

With particular respect to the situation in the United States, the report of the Peterson Task Force (March 1970) summarized the situation as follows:

> Many with whom we consulted are deeply troubled by particular aspects of U.S. foreign assistance programs and by the apathy and misunderstanding that seems [sic] to surround the issues. Nevertheless, virtually all believe that the United States has a large stake and serious responsibilities in international development.[2]

While the Task Force repudiated any formula for the volume of aid like the 1 per cent set by the United Nations, it did say that "the downward trend in United States development assistance appropriations should be reversed. . . . Additional resources, primarily in support of international lending institutions, are needed now."

Influential private American groups have also reviewed the aid situation. The Committee for Economic Development, consisting of 200 leading businessmen and educators in the United States, in its 1969 Statement on Development Assistance, proposed increased and more effective assistance, declaring that "Unless this trend [declining appropriations for official assistance] is reversed, and unless public assistance can be augmented by increased private investment, we will have lost an historic opportunity to achieve what could well become a decisive advance in the economic and social modernization of the emerging nations."

The National Planning Association, an independent, private, nonprofit, nonpolitical organization in the United States with a Board of Trustees representing all sectors of the American economy, urged in March 1969 that the U.S. foreign aid effort be restructured "in a way that will ensure continuity, adequate funding, and greater responsiveness to the changing needs of an effective development assistance relationship with the recipient countries."

The League of Women Voters of the United States has taken a strong position against curtailment: "The need for development aid is overwhelming. The momentum of growth in the developing countries must be maintained last all past efforts be wasted. . . . U.S. contributions can help make the difference between a margin of hope and utter despair."

* * *

While there may be considerable agreement as to what national policy should be, many different reasons have been given for providing aid and sympathetic encouragement to the less-developed countries. Nothing shows this more clearly than the statement of policy in recent U.S. foreign assistance acts, which declares that

the freedom, security, and prosperity of the United States are best sustained in a community of free, secure, and prospering nations . . . and ignorance, want, and despair breed the extremism and violence which lead to aggression and subversion. . . . It is not only expressive of our sense of freedom, justice, and compassion

but also important to our national security. . . . It is the policy of
the United States to support the principles of increased economic
cooperation and trade.

The policy declaration further suggests a number of specific objectives to be supported, such as freedom of the press, civil liberties, democratic participation, and multilateral and regional cooperation. Thus, political, economic, and humanitarian reasons
are all included.

To the list of official objectives, one must also add those of
voluntary agencies which either are strictly humanitarian, such as
the many American-sponsored educational institutions abroad
(like American University in Beirut, American University in
Cairo, and Robert College in Istanbul), or are supporting some
particular activity, such as cooperatives. The remaining private
flow is based on business motives, to ensure a source of supply,
to take advantage of a low-cost area, or to protect or establish a
foreign market.

To diagnose the motivation of governments is always difficult.
For example, it is certain that the interest of France and that of
Austria in less-developed countries are by no means the same.
Furthermore, in some cases there are virtually no official voices
speaking on the subject, while in others, there is a multitude often
giving different reasons for their position. When there is an official position, it is likely to be presented in extremely broad terms,
as in the preamble to legislation.

The British government has said that the basis of its aid program is a moral one, but that at the same time it can be defined
in political terms as an important part of international politics.
As secondary considerations, aid also is in Britain's long-term economic advantage by expanding markets, and by safeguarding the
supply of imports and returns on investments.[3] Rather surprising
testimony, because of its source, was given by Reginald Maudling, British Chancellor of the Exchequer, commenting on the
British White Paper just cited:

> It is to my mind impossible for the industrial societies to live
> easily with their consciences while the indigent societies are just
> over their garden fence. . . . We must recognize that overseas aid
> is a great and growing burden on our resources. Our reactions
> should not be . . . to cut back on aid, but rather to regard this as
> a source of inspiration in our efforts to expand our own economy
> and so increase the level of our aid achievement.[4]

The official justification of French foreign aid stresses humanitarian considerations, the dissemination of French culture, and the promotion of France's overseas interests.[5] The Dutch government regards foreign aid as an essential part of its foreign policy, since the prosperity gap is a threat to good relations between advanced and developing countries and a possible source of international conflicts. The central aim should be less to benefit the advanced states than to raise the standard of living for the largest possible number of people.[6]

The Pearson Commission declares that war against poverty and deprivation begins at home but it must not end there. Building on the concept of the moral responsibility of those who have to share with those who have not, it finds in the modern world community a political and social imperative upon governments to cooperate in international development. In addition, it sees a respectable and valid basis in terms of enlightened and constructive self-interest in a general increase in international trade and of stronger and friendlier political relationships. Its suggestion of a substantial increase in aid is tempered by the suggestion that developing aid should be self-liquidating and that it may be possible to reduce it substantially in twenty to thirty years.

Distinct from the infrequent statements in other countries, the American record of public debate is much more voluminous. The preamble to the Foreign Assistance Act quoted above hardly reflects the shifts that have taken place or the rationale of differing groups. Since the beginning, there has been steady support from religious and secular groups on the basis of moral responsibility. Ideas of brotherhood, stewardship, and the social gospel have long expressed themselves in contributions to overseas activities. The official position, however, has never relied heavily upon the moral approach, although President Kennedy did say that we should do it "because it is right."

Some who accept the moral argument use it to claim that "charity should begin at home," and argue that foreign aid funds should rather be given to domestic poverty programs. But the programs are not alternatives, and one can insist on a major effort to deal with the causes of poverty and social injustice at home without abandoning concern for even less fortunate people in other countries. Nor is it at all clear that reducing the one will increase the other.

Some moralists argue that aid in its present form misses the point, that what we should be really concerned with is people and not things. While this may appear to be the situation with individual transactions, the results of economic change may well be not only a higher living standard but a lowering of social barriers and an increase in social mobility. Since economic growth requires the development of new institutions, and institutions are inherently political—they must deal with and be confirmed by government—changes follow in the political structure. People are inevitably involved.

* * *

The earlier programs of the United States, though not those most immediately after World War II, were justified largely on the basis of the threat of Communism, which will continue to be an important consideration so long as Communism is combined with aggression. The United States has long enjoyed the sense of security engendered by the expanses of the Atlantic and Pacific, although the protection afforded by the sea has greatly lessened in recent years. But are the oceans plus deterrent power sufficient in the future? What if much of the underdeveloped world should align itself with Russia or China or both? Nightmares like these are still cited each year as one reason for supporting foreign aid.

While foreign policy necessarily concerns itself with security matters and the balance of power, the nineteenth-century preoccupation with these aspects of international life has been superseded in the twentieth century by a more complex set of foreign relations, paralleling the expanded national concerns of governments. As for political objectives, instead of simple anti-Communism—a position always difficult to define—the goal has become much more one of endeavoring to strengthen a less-developed country so that it is better able to protect itself from any outside domination. In the process, the West seeks to encourage open, progressive, accessible societies.[7] What kinds of political structure and attitude will eventually result are quite unpredictable. But, at least, keeping in mind the initial drive for independence, a less-developed country is not likely to return voluntarily to a condition of political subordination. It is in our interest to do what can be done to encourage more open societies and stronger international institutions.

This line of argument, while tied in with a basic American prin-

ciple of supporting independence, has grown somewhat less effective because of the reduced intensity of anti-Communist feeling,
and because of less certainty about the relationship of assistance
to political events. Assistance for education may serve to increase
discontent, which may weaken the existing power structure. In
today's world, military assistance intended to strengthen an existing regime may provide the means for its overthrow. A concern
with the "development of peoples" requires extraordinary discrimination to evaluate political change, at least in the short run.
Revolutionary action is not necessarily a product of Communism;
it may well be a protest against mass poverty and the debasement
of the individual. A repressive but orderly administration may
only lead to a more violent reaction later.

Dissatisfaction and rebellion seem to flourish in areas of poverty, hopelessness, and repression. There is some chance, though
no assurance, that economic growth and social development will
move fast enough to provide some hope and make easier the process of transition. Without economic and social development,
there seems to be little prospect of avoiding outbursts and explo-
sions, of encouraging evolution rather than revolution. Galo
Plaza, Secretary General of the OAS, said in a speech at the National Press Club in Washington late in 1968 that any U.S. ne-
glect of the Alliance for Progress was extremely short-sighted and
dangerous. In order to forestall other Cubas and Vietnams in
Latin America, it was essential that "the quiet revolution" be won
to eliminate the conditions that invite violent revolution. Furthermore, there is an economic reason because "the greatest trade
potential in the developing world lies in the Latin American
countries." [8]

Some criticize foreign assistance on the basis that it bolsters
existing regimes, many of which fall far short of American ideals.
How much economic assistance can directly affect the political
situation in a country is open to question. It seems clear that negative action in denying aid gives support most often to an in-
cumbent regime by permitting it to claim that it resists being
pushed around by any foreign power. Short-run shifts among the
holders of political power, as are so frequent in Latin America,
have little relation to the volume or character of assistance. But,
over a longer time span, the extent and character of economic
change will have an impact on political life. The expansion of a

middle class, the improved means of communication, and the development of a wide variety of public and private institutions all tend to reduce the possibility of centralized, arbitrary power. In the meantime, the flow of economic assistance can itself be related to projects and programs that are directed not at the enrichment of a few but at more widely based economic and social development.

Assistance does have a narrower political value in quite a different sense. In today's world, an effective foreign policy involves relations on many subjects with all nations, and assistance flows provide working contact. They do not necessarily win friends, create gratitude, affect U.N. votes, create democracies, or prevent rhetorical or worse attacks on the United States, its citizens, or their property. But they do have a major bearing on the opportunity to consult with the governments of many countries, such as India, Indonesia, and those south of the U.S. border. Without an aid program, any of the richer countries would be greatly handicapped in conducting its foreign affairs.

Some argue on quite a different basis—that the economic development of the less-developed countries will strengthen the world economy. More productive activities in the rest of the world will increase the volume of trade in commodities and services between countries, not to mention the expanded sources of raw materials with a limited world supply. Foreign trade, like all exchange, is a means of obtaining a greater return for the effort made on both sides. There is, moreover, the important matter of foreign investment. Already the sum is substantial, and its value will increase with the economic growth of the less-developed countries. Similar arguments can be advanced for enriching a country's culture by expanding the variety of sources contributing to it. This general line of argument, be it economic or cultural, suggests that development of countries with different backgrounds and natural resources may provide an enrichment of unknown dimensions to the affluent societies.

The Peterson Task Force, in summarizing many considerations in its report, mentioned the common interest of all people in peace, in the eradication of poverty and disease, in a healthful environment, and in better living conditions. It spoke of the U.S. interest in building an equitable political and economic order in which resources and knowledge are shared. And it closed its statement on objectives by saying:

What the United States should expect from participation in international development is steady progress toward its long-term goals: The building of self-reliant and healthy societies in developing countries, an expanding world economy from which all will benefit, and improved prospects for world peace.

Perhaps most important of all considerations is the basic fact that the world is growing smaller. The shrinkage in terms of transport and communication is incredible. The process of growth within any one country is more and more international. There may be efforts to withdraw into one's own bailiwick, but this is impossible for the larger powers, particularly for the United States. Barring the use of nuclear weapons, world population and world productivity may both double by the year 2000. But there will still be the problems of inequality, instability, and international friction, and there will still be mass poverty in many areas. Although military and economic power may put a country in a position of leadership, power does not ensure followers. Influence depends in large part on demonstration, persuasion, and evident interest in the problems of the other countries. The role the United States can and will play in shaping the world of the future will depend in considerable part on the way it is viewed by other nations: as a wealthy, selfish, calculating country, concerned almost entirely with security and the increase and internal distribution of its affluence, or as a country concerned about the condition of all people everywhere, using part of its affluence to help the poor beyond its borders. Foreign assistance grudgingly given loses much of the political value of the act. Nor is the image important only to the foreigner. Problems are created individually and collectively if there is too wide a gap between the American ideal and American performance. One basic element of the ideal is generosity.

Foreign aid has come a long way in two decades. The rich countries are all giving substantial assistance, but there are many ways in which the foreign aid programs can be strengthened. So far as the United States is concerned, the legislative arrangements should be improved to give more stability to the program. The executive administration should be more centralized, possibly with clearer functional responsibilities defined for subsidiary units. Much heavier investment should be encouraged. Consortia and consultative groups should be strengthened. The variety of conditions should be reduced and cumbersome procedures should be streamlined. Wherever possible, less-developed-country initiative with developed-country encouragement should be the basis for action. The amount of resources available must be much larger and based on much more generous terms. A more intensive effort is called for to open up ways to increase foreign earnings, particularly through trade policy. And every effort should be made to put development assistance into a more realistic time perspective.

One cannot predict the ultimate result, which will depend in large part on the less-developed countries themselves. Will they make the necessary investment of their own resources in capital and in manpower training? Will they succeed in eliminating inherited obstacles to modernization? Will their energies be diverted by dreams of military glory, or by internal divisive forces, or by political instability? The answers to dozens of questions like these will decide the outcome, but it would be unfortunate if it were decided by the failure of the rich to give the poor countries strong support in their search for a brighter future.

Appendix:
The Foreign Aid
Numbers Game

History. Prior to 1960, the United Nations Secretariat responded to various ECOSOC and General Assembly resolutions with reports on the international flow of private capital and on official economic assistance to less-developed countries.[1] Its estimates were based primarily on balance-of-payments data from the International Monetary Fund and on replies to questionnaires. With the target for aid of 1 per cent of national income, set in December 1960, a new importance attached to annual reports on the flow of capital and technical assistance. Various U.N. resolutions directed the Secretariat to provide more precise estimates.

Several years before the new emphasis in the United Nations, the main suppliers of assistance began to meet irregularly in various capitals as the Development Assistance Group (DAG). One of their first projects was to improve the statistical record in order to put their national statistics on as comparable a basis as possible and better evaluate the total flow. Surprisingly enough, up to that time most countries had not assembled their various forms of assistance to less-developed countries in any single tabulation. The work was carried out in collaboration with the Organization for European Economic Cooperation, which published in April 1961 its first summary of data collected from the members and Japan.[2]

In September 1961, the OEEC became the Organization for Economic Cooperation and Development (OECD), including the United States and Canada as full members. The DAG became the Development Assistance Committee (DAC) of the OECD. Since then, an annual report by the Chairman of DAC has presented and discussed the increasingly detailed data provided by

329

DAC members. As the membership of DAC has increased, the past record for each new member has been duly included back to 1956 to make the coverage constant.

At the present time, two summary tabulations of development assistance are published—one by the United Nations, the other by the DAC/OECD. The principal sources for the United Nations estimates are the DAC data, the IMF *Balance of Payments Yearbook*, and special questionnaires. The DAC estimates are based on data submitted by governments after joint examination with members of the OECD secretariat, plus some estimates made by the secretariat itself.

As might be expected, the results are quite similar because the estimators rely on much the same basic data. The main differences between the two grand totals are easily traced. The DAC figures include certain European less-developed countries such as Turkey, and also net private export credits of more than one year maturity, while the U.N. record did not until recently.

Definitions. The definition that the first UNCTAD adopted in 1964 with no adverse votes and nine abstentions listed what had come to be generally included in estimates of development assistance:

> Official cash grants and grants in kind (including grants for technical assistance); sales of commodities against local currencies; government lending for periods exceeding one year (net of repayments of principal); grants and capital subscriptions to multilateral aid agencies, and net purchases of bonds, loans and participations from those agencies.
>
> Private capital on the basis of net long-term movements, originating with residents of the capital-exporting countries. They are thus net of repatriation of principal, disinvestment, and retirement of long-term loans, portfolio assets and commercial debt. They are not net of reverse flows of capital originating with residents of the less-developed countries, nor of investment income.[3]

Virtually the same concept is found in the DAC definitions:

> This "net flow" consists of gross official aid disbursements and private investment and commercial flows from DAC Member countries bilaterally to less-developed countries, less amortization receipts, plus net flows from DAC Member countries to multilateral aid agencies. Grants made by private non-profit groups, such as foundations, voluntary agencies, or churches are not included for lack of reliable data. . . . Income from private investment and

changes in DAC countries' liabilities to developing countries (i.e. investments by developing countries in donor countries) are other categories of flow not covered by the statistics.[4]

In making its estimates of the total net financing flows received by less-developed countries from *all* sources, the DAC adds the flows from the multilateral aid agencies (deducting, however, the contributions of DAC members to these agencies to eliminate double counting), from the centrally planned countries, and from other developed nations not members of the DAC. This global estimate also does not include the flow of assistance among the less-developed countries themselves.

Figures of quite a different order are preferred by others. Thus, for example, Congressman Otto Passman talks about a figure of $10.8 billion for U.S. official assistance alone. This figure is so large because it represents the President's requests from Congress for 1969–70 for all contributions to foreign countries. One-quarter of the total is military aid and is included in the defense budget. Another quarter is a request for permanent increased authority to lend by the Export-Import Bank. The total, as he sees it, is what the taxpayer might have to pay sooner or later for assistance of all kinds to foreign countries if Congress approved all the aid requests made by the President during the year. There is no way to develop comparable figures for other countries, even if there were any desire to do so.

In contrast, there are those who would argue for much lower figures by leaving out certain items such as all private flows, or reducing the figures included by recognizing only the grant element in loans, or omitting all export credits even if guaranteed by the government, and even omitting all commodities which are regarded as surplus in the donor country. Still others would reduce the flows by regarding as offsets certain reverse flows from the less-developed countries, either all interest and dividend payments from the less-developed country, or any capital flow to the developed countries, or both.

The problem of what to include in measuring the flow of economic assistance to less-developed countries depends on the specific question one wishes to answer: What new resources are specially provided to assist the less-developed countries? What is the volume of the outflow of financial resources to less-developed countries? This is best answered by gross figures of both public and private flow.

What is the net contribution to the less-developed countries? Here one deducts certain back-flows and approximates a balance-of-payments concept. Ideally, one should include some measure of external benefits.

What is the assistance provided as actual donations, or to use more technical terms, the relative concessionary element? Here one should use a measure of gifts and grants, plus an allowance for credits at appropriately less-than-market rates.

What is the economic burden on the providing country? Here one needs to make allowance for the extent to which the economy has idle capacity, how much of the assistance takes the form of giving away surpluses, and what the alternative uses would be.

What is the burden on the taxpayer? This would omit most private flows and would have to take debt service on official loans into account, plus some allowance for whether or not the whole operation was helpful or harmful to the domestic economy.

How does assistance provided by Country X compare with that by Country Y? This question opens up other dimensions because the relative sizes and perhaps income levels of the two countries must be taken into consideration, as well as the terms and characteristics of the assistance given by each. And there is the troublesome problem of expressing them in a common currency.

In addition to any of these measures, the answer sought may require the inclusion of various indirect costs and benefits which are not recorded in the flow data: for example, costs involved in government actions such as special tax treatment, subsidies and guarantee schemes, pre-investment studies, and increased bureaucracy at home and abroad. On the side of benefits, one might include trade concessions, expanded trade, settlements of property disputes, and the release of impounded funds.

There are still other values, primarily in the moral or ethical area, which some would like to include in measuring aid and assistance. They feel that one should count only those flows which are motivated by philanthropy, i.e., gifts without an immediate or definite *quid pro quo*, or which represent sacrifice. But motivation is seldom specific and clear, especially on the part of governments, for a number of objectives may be included, ranging from a sense of obligation on the part of the rich to resistance to Communism, the nonrecognition of a third country, or the opening up of a potential market. National sacrifice is even more difficult to measure because it requires some sort of evaluation of the alternatives that are being given up. While no specific estimates have been made in terms of philanthropy or sacrifice, one can bring these considerations to bear in deciding how to adjust and interpret the existing figures.

Once there is agreement as to the general question to be asked, there would still be much room for argument as to how specific transactions should be treated. In order to make possible some of the adjustments which may be needed, more and more detail is being provided in the data. However, any summation of numbers has one basic weakness in that it fails to recognize differences in aspects which represent quality rather than quantity. The most usual figures used—public and private net disbursements—change substantially over time in their make-up between public and private flows, grants and credits, tied and untied aid, bilateral and multilateral transfers, etc. To answer certain questions about aid among those listed above, the qualitative elements should be taken into account.

Aid Received. At present, the record of flows is based on data from the supplier countries and the multilateral agencies. It would be desirable to have a cross-check by measuring the flow in terms of receipts by less-developed countries rather than outflows from the developed. For this purpose one would need different data, presumably provided by the less-developed countries themselves. Unfortunately, many of them do not have satisfactory balance-of-payments figures. However, even when they do, foreign assistance in grant form would not necessarily appear as an import in their records; many projects would involve a mixture of foreign and domestic contribution; and import valuations, especially of services, would not always be realistic. Furthermore, expenditures in foreign countries, such as scholarships for foreign students, would not appear as inflows to the less-developed country.

A U.N. group of experts examining the measurement problem tried to carry out such a cross-check on DAC and IMF data for 1964 by comparing the net flow of official resources as reported by recipients and donors.[5] The inflow estimates, based largely on balance-of-payments data, and the total net flow of official resources to developing countries were only about 7 per cent apart:

Reported by recipients $3,941 million
Reported by donors $4,221 million

For Latin America, however, recipients reported the year's flow
of official resources as $458 million while donors reported $804
million. For Africa, the two figures were about the same, while
the recipients' figures for West Asia and both South and Southeast Asia were somewhat larger than the donors'. The differences
in the figures for individual countries were much greater, as might
be expected by the size of their "errors and omissions" item as
well as the difficulties in the valuation of resources-in-kind and
technical assistance. The DAC has tried to approximate an "aid
received" figure by using bilateral disbursements plus multilateral disbursement figures.

Country Classification. One of the first problems is how the
countries are to be divided between the developed and the less-
developed. If one were measuring the global flow of aid directly,
there would be no need for any country classification; the record
of particular activities would suffice. Technical assistance from
India or Israel would be included in the recorded flows as well
as loans by the richer Middle East oil-producing countries. Since
there are capital flows among the richer countries as well as
flows to less-developed countries for various purposes, the problem
would then be one of defining more exactly which flows would
be counted as assistance for "economic development," regardless
of source or recipient. However, data on international transactions are all in national terms, and both the United Nations
and the Development Assistance Committee base their statistics
on country classifications of suppliers and recipients. The difficulty is that there is no dividing line which neatly separates the
rich from the poor, the industrial from the nonindustrial, or the
developed from the less-developed. On any of these bases, a
ranking from top to bottom can be made, but there is no point
of clear discontinuity.

If a dividing line were established on some arbitrary basis—
for example, some level of per capita income, some percentage
of employment in industry, or the ability to borrow capital in
the private capital market—sooner or later some countries now
regarded as less-developed would have to be reclassified as developed. In a sense, the U.S. government has done this in regarding Taiwan, for example, as no longer eligible for assistance

from AID because of its foreign trade position. Taiwan's per capita income is still very low, and it may still receive assistance under PL 480, from the Export-Import Bank, and from any of the other national or multilateral programs which would then be included in the reported U.S. assistance flow to less-developed countries.

For statistical purposes both the United Nations and the DAC have an unchanging list of developed and less-developed countries. For most of them, the appropriate classification is obvious. But because of the problem of the intermediate cases and the desire to maintain a consistent statistical base, both the United Nations and the DAC have established fixed membership in each group. Slightly different groupings are used for other purposes by UNCTAD and the IDA.

The United Nations classifies countries into four categories:

Group I. Developed market-economy countries providing resources (Europe except for Group II and III, Canada and the United States, Australia and New Zealand, Japan, and South Africa)

Group II. Centrally planned economies, including Yugoslavia, all of which are regarded as providers of resources

Group III. Less-developed market economies that are regarded as neither provider nor recipients of resources (Cyprus, Gibraltar, Greece, Malta, Spain and Turkey)

Group IV. Recipient, less-developed countries (the Americas below the Rio Grande, Africa, and Asia and the Pacific, except for countries noted above as being in other groups). Groups I and II therefore comprise the donor or developed countries and Group IV the recipient or developing countries.

Most DAC statistics relate to the outflow of assistance from DAC members, although, when the DAC presents global figures, it extends its coverage of suppliers to match that of the United Nations by including estimates for nonmember supplying countries. However, in accordance with the actual practice of its members, it includes as less-developed the European countries which the United Nations places in its Group III. The DAC, and also UNCTAD, regard Yugoslavia as a recipient country rather than as a provider of assistance in the U.N. Group II category along with the other centrally planned economies.

The difference between the total flow of assistance given by the United Nations and the DAC resulting from the different treatment of the Group III European countries and Yugoslavia is sizable, and even affects the trend since assistance to European less-developed countries has declined relative to flows to other areas. In fact, the net official flow to them declined from $434 million in 1965 to $384.5 million in 1968. The greatest reduction was in aid to Yugoslavia, the greatest increase to Spain.

When comparing the performance of individual supplier countries, it is important to remember that the suppliers of assistance have made their own selection as to the treatment of overseas territories (see Chapter 8). For example, the Netherlands includes as foreign aid its economic assistance to Curaçao; France does the same with its various overseas territories; as does Portugal with Angola and Mozambique. On the other hand, Denmark does not report flows to Greenland nor the United States to Puerto Rico, even though they are "overseas" territories. The statistical record has been based on the same geographical coverage over the entire period, not being affected by the many shifts in status from colony to independent nation.

Omission. If one could state exactly what one wished to measure, there would still be the problem of gaps and imperfections in the available data. Probably the most important omissions are certain flows in the private sector which surely belong in the calculations. Since the record for private capital covers only items which appear in the capital account of the balance of payments, it excludes the private transfer payment of charitable donations, activities of voluntary agencies, foundation grants, private contributions to technical assistance, and private remittances.

Beginning with the DAC Chairman's Report in 1966, the omissions were called to people's attention by means of a memorandum item at the bottom of the main table, "Grants by private institutions for development purposes, etc." It was not until 1967 that the coverage was of any real significance when the DAC report gave figures for nine countries, totalling $661.4 million. Some important areas were still missing—Canada, France, Italy, Netherlands, and Sweden. In 1968 the reported figure dropped to $586 million largely as the result of a drop in the United States contribution. The DAC defines this item as including grants made by private nonprofit groups such as foundations, voluntary agencies, or churches. The figures are described as rough estimates and are excluded from the total flow "for lack of reliable data." Where government assistance is given to such activities—for example, a contribution toward shipping costs—it would be included as part of the official flow. It is particularly unfortunate that these private activities are excluded from the estimates since the foreign, nonproselytizing activities of churches, foundations, trade unions, cooperatives, and other voluntary agencies usually represent assistance without strings or requirement of repayment.

Private foreign investment abroad also provides substantial unrecorded contributions in the form of continuing training and technical assistance programs, and there also may be considerable construction of roads, hospitals, schools, and housing. Such activities would usually be regarded as operating costs and for the most part are not included in the figures unless they are a part of some specific capital project or are accounted for as re-invested earnings.

Another contribution, which might be included but is not, is an allowance for the hidden subsidies to visiting foreign students and trainees through less-than-cost charges in educational institutions in the developed countries. This would be a very large figure, especially since such an estimate presumably would cover all students from less-developed countries and not merely those on fellowships or scholarships under official or multilateral programs.

Several other items apparently included in the total are only partially recorded. Thus, the record of export credits is limited to guaranteed credits, including the small unguaranteed portions. Export credits are omitted which are extended by the seller without government guarantee, either financed directly or through a commercial bank. The net flow is the net increase, measured by some countries as the change in the outstanding amounts guaranteed, by others as the change in outstanding amounts on disbursed credits. Such credits are often handled on a discounted basis so that interest is included in the sums regarded as outstanding, thus tending to overstate the net flow if gross new guarantees are rising, and vice versa.

Still another block of assistance which is not included is the contribution to development made by the United Nations and its specialized agencies from their regular budgets. When their activities are financed by the UNDP, they would appear in the totals as contributions to and disbursements by UNDP. Activities which are financed by the IBRD would be included in IBRD's outflow only if it were incorporated in a loan agreement with a less-developed country. To be sure, the activities of the United Nations itself and/or the specialized agencies would be difficult to untangle; since the less-developed member countries contribute to the regular budgets, and the activities of the specialized agencies are not limited to less-developed countries. Nevertheless, their programs have increasingly tended to serve the less-developed countries, which undoubtedly have a greater share of the benefits than of the cost.

There also is a problem of securing an exact figure for development assistance as such, since it is often impossible to distinguish among contributions for development, for welfare, or for relief purposes. Since the allocation of domestic expenditures within a country is easily changed, assistance provided for one purpose may in fact release funds for some other purpose. Thus the shipment of wheat to India not only helped to feed the starving, but it reduced the expenditure of foreign exchange which otherwise would have had to be made for foodstuffs and thus made possible a larger purchase of development goods. On the other hand, what appears to be development assistance may permit expenditures by the government on nondevelopment activities. Some expenditures may serve a dual purpose—a road may be of both economic and military value. Over the period covered by the statistics direct military aid has probably been more and more clearly separated from economic expenditures, particularly since the techniques of budget-making and intermediate-term budget planning have been improving.

Although the trend in most developed countries has been toward consolidating the budget items and appropriations for development assistance, there always will be many points where items may be shown in either functional or agency appropriations and the contribution made by the functional department may not be included in the national report. Luckily, there is a tendency for such accounting practices to persist so that trends are accurately portrayed, even though the level may be understated.

Sources and Timing. There are various sources from which one may select data. Nations had little reason to standardize their national accounting until the United Nations began to collect national income data and the IMF set forth a system for recording balance-of-payments data. The balance-of-payments material is helpful in answering many questions, but it also raises a number of uncertainties. In the first place, not only are many items based on estimates, but there is likely to be a large residual unexplained item of "errors and omissions," which may be due either to incomplete records of current transactions or unrecorded credit items and unreported capital flows. In addition, some items needed for measuring foreign aid may not be recorded as foreign payments—for example the related domestic costs of contractors and administration, travel and shipping costs, payments to experts and others working abroad that are deposited in the home country, and domestic costs of trainees and students on fellowships. Furthermore, few suppliers of assistance compile all the elements in their payments data according to receiving region or country, and commodity export figures may be based on intermediate rather than ultimate destination.

At the present time, both the U.N. and DAC estimates are based upon data provided by the various donor governments. Official foreign aid can be measured at several stages in the process—appropriation, commitment, and disbursement. The first stage, appropriation, represents the share allocated for aid by the parliament or Congress. It usually does not include the use of revolving funds (the Export-Import Bank, for example). Nor does appropriation assure that the sums available will all be spent; they may fall short either because of program difficulties or executive retrenchment. There is variation among nations in the extent to which unspent funds lapse or are carried over.

There also can be supplemental appropriations or assistance financing hidden in what might appear to be unrelated subsections of the budget. However, if comparable figures are kept over a period, appropriations will reflect more quickly than any other figure the relative treatment accorded to foreign assistance activities as of that moment in time. At present, no international source publishes national foreign aid appropriation figures regularly.

Commitments data are collected and published by the DAC. They constitute firm obligations supported by the availability of funds. They are shown on a gross basis, with no deduction for the current cancellation of commitments made in earlier years.

In a few countries, notably Australia, Austria, Belgium, and France, the bulk of assistance does not go through a formal commitment procedure, and data for gross disbursements are used by the DAC in commitments tabulations. Commitments represent only a potential transfer but are indicative of current government policies on volume, structure of terms, and country allocation. The commitment may be for a project which will take a number of years to complete. For a country with a small program, annual variations in commitments are likely to be much wider than in disbursements, which would not lump the cost of a multi-year project into a single year. However, for all countries, year-to-year comparisons are affected by whether or not any large commitments made near the end of the year happen to fall in December or January.

One special use for the commitment figure is in measuring the terms of aid which are currently in use by the different donors. There are no comparable data for the private sector, where flows relate to disbursements, and are largely taken from balance-of-payments records.

The figures usually given for the volume of aid are net disbursements: that is, grants plus loan disbursements minus amortization on past loans. While the net figures do reflect the change in the capital position of the less-developed country, i.e., its capital liabilities, the annual amortization figure is the result of past flows. Probably more attention should be given to gross disbursement figures than they usually receive. Except in the case of revolving funds, and sometimes even there, the gross amount is closer to that which is appropriated and thus is the amount which the government might have put to other uses. The gross figure is most likely to represent foreign aid in the minds of legislators and the public, in which form it competes with other demands upon the Treasury. Furthermore, the gross amount is the sum to be expended, which therefore involves all the policy issues and procedures associated with the provision of aid. While the net figure is obviously a better measure of the real burden on the taxpayer, the gross figure may better indicate the attitude, intention, administrative burden, and image abroad of the country concerned.

The level of amortization varies considerably from country to country according to the cumulated historical importance of official loans. In 1968, amortization received by all DAC countries was 24.2 per cent of new loans made and 12.8 per cent of their total gross official bilateral disbursements. It was highest for Italy, Portugal, and Germany, largely the result of relatively short-term credits.

In addition to amortization on loans, official transfers from less-developed countries to developed countries are deducted in calculating net disbursements. This is currently significant only in the cases of France, where tax receipts from overseas dependencies are deducted from gross bilateral flows, and of the United States, which retains certain local currency payments for its own use. In the balance of payments, transfer payments are recorded on a gross basis, and receipts such as these are shown as reverse grants.

The administrative costs of aid operations are excluded by the DAC in principle, although for some countries, notably the United States, part of such cost, chiefly AID expenses, is indistinguishably included in its figures from bilateral disbursements. These payments are regarded by the U.S. authorities to be an integral part of the aid operation and represent a cost to the taxpayer for this purpose. On this theory, a full costing would have to include a share of other government costs (and perhaps it should), such as those of the Budget Bureau, various departments, and even of Congress.

Grants and Loans. The allocation of official disbursements between grants and loans also raises various questions. For example, under grants are included cancelled debt repayments when the equivalent amount is to be applied by the debtor government to mutually agreed development purposes. Japan did this in 1965, and the practice will probably spread in the future. On the other hand, official interest-rate subsidies for past loans to less-developed countries are not included anywhere in the net disbursement totals.

Related problems within the official flow classification are how to categorize loans for which repayment is not required in the lender's currency, and how to treat such use as there may be of local currencies, obtained from the sale of commodities in a recipient country, which are regarded as the legal property of the donor. For such loans, a category has been created called "grant-like contributions," usually included under the general heading of "grants" because it does not create an external indebtedness of the recipient country payable in convertible currency. As to the second point, if some part of the local currency is reserved for use by the donor for its own use within the recipient country, this part of the flow is not included as assistance.

Bilateral grants also include intergovernmental reparations and indemnification payments. An immediate reaction is that such payments should not count as foreign aid since they are hardly voluntary. However, the definitions on which the statistics are based do not raise questions of motivation but relate to a flow of goods and services to the less-developed countries. Furthermore, in the German case, the payments listed were not imposed but technically represented voluntary payments to Israel. The Japanese reparations were negotiated under a general commitment in the Japanese Peace Treaty. From 1960 to 1965, German payments in this category averaged $67 million per year, with 1965 the last year of such payments. Italian reparations exceeded $20 million in 1957 and 1962, but averaged only $3.7 million in 1965–66. Japanese reparations jumped to $67 million in 1957, and to $46 million in 1968. The flow from the three countries averaged $143 million from 1960 to 1965, but dropped to $60 million in 1966 when such German payments ended. Italian reparations were $7 million in 1967 and $8 million in 1968.

A further refinement in classifying official flows was introduced by the DAC in connection with the 1968 figures, and made available back to 1960. This involved subdividing official disbursements into "Official Development Assistance" and "Other Official Flows." The first and much the larger category is defined as "flows which are intended primarily to promote the economic development and welfare of developing countries, and which are intended to be concessional in character." The second category includes commercial rather than developmental items, such as transactions of the U.S. Export-Import Bank and the U.S. Commodity Credit Corporation, the Japanese Export-Import Bank and Japanese OECF suppliers' credits which were previously recorded as private transactions, the German *Kreditanstalt für Wiederaufbau* when operating on its own account, and buyers' credits of the Canadian ECIC. It also includes the purchase and sale of bonds of multilateral agencies by central banks. The new Official Development Assistance category provides the base on which the revised targets for the terms of aid are calculated.

Valuation. Since the DAC records depend upon information from the donor, they represent the values set by the donor. Donations consisting of contributions in kind, mainly foodstuffs and other commodities, are in principle valued at world market prices plus the cost of ocean freight, unless the latter is provided by the recipient. However, the bulk of such contributions by the United States have been from surplus holdings by the government and are valued at the domestic support price, which is what the government paid for it. Such prices are substantially above world market prices.

Technical assistance is valued at cost, and is therefore related to wage levels in the developed country from which it comes. Accordingly, international comparisons in monetary terms do not reflect the number of individuals or the man-months involved.

It should be noted that these problems of valuation would be even more difficult if one included private transfer payments, since much of the activity of voluntary organizations is carried on by individuals who are compensated, if at all, considerably below the going wage rates.

Treatment of Loans. A number of problems arise in the area of loans and credits; some experts would not include flows in this form at all. Speaking in Buenos Aires in October 1968, Carlos Sanz de Santamaria, Chairman of the Inter-American Committee on the Alliance for Progress, insisted that official development loans that are to be repaid are not "aid," at least in the Marshall Plan sense, but might better be separately reported as "loans" or "external financial cooperation."

The usual practice is to record loans in the form of net flows— that is, the volume of new loans to less-developed countries with maturities in excess of one year, minus all amortization payments received. This is essentially an item which can be derived from the balance of payments. In that framework, it might be described as the net change in the capital account reflecting the outstanding obligations of the less-developed country.

For some years, the DAC statistics have shown interest payments received on official loans outstanding as a Memorandum Item. Some have argued that this interest payment should also be deducted, creating what is called the "net transfer." The World Bank, in presenting data concerning less-developed country indebtedness in its annual reports, lumps interest and amortization together as "debt service."

One may think of the interest payment either as an offset to the fact that the lender lost the use of the capital at home, or as a payment for productivity achieved in the less-developed country. Since neither of these appears in the balance-of-payments or the economic assistance provided, the deduction of interest becomes a single entry in what ought to be a double-entry bookkeeping system.

The net transfer concept creates a misleading picture over time. Since, over the life of the loan, the amortization would equal the original amount and since interest would be in addition to that, it would appear that assistance over the total period was negative. The explanation for this misleading conclusion is that the product of the capital in the country which is paying interest for its use is not included as aid. In the current practice of not deducting interest, it is assumed that the unrecorded product equals the interest and therefore both can be disregarded.

The net transfer concept is often justified as showing the impact of the loan on the balance of payments. However, in that case one ought to look at the extent to which the whole process has created new payments problems—not merely interest payments but requirements for raw materials, replacement parts, technical assistance, and the like—and the extent to which it has created new means of payments—increased exports, both visible such as copper, or rubber footwear, or invisible such as new resort facilities.

There is considerable interest in still another approach, namely, that loans should be considered only to the extent that their terms are more favorable than commercial rates, an amount which is called the "grant element." Thus, of the official loan commitments in 1968 for all DAC members, 49 per cent is calculated to be the grant element. For the United States, with slightly softer terms than the average, the grant element was 53 per cent.

Even if the full details concerning interest rate, maturity, and grace period are available, the grant element is not easily determined. It may logically be calculated on the basis of either an estimate of what the characteristics would have been if the loan had been on a commercial basis or what the yield of the capital would have been if used at home. These two are not necessarily identical, and differences in the rate at which the future payments are discounted can create substantial differences in the resulting figure. The amount of the "grant element" is recorded as being made at the time of initial disbursement. No further consideration of amortization or interest is relevant, since the grant element has been fully recorded, and the continuing debt service presumably relates to the excluded, commercial part of the loan.

The grant element is a conceptual figure rather than a real one and gives a result which has no counterpart in actual fact. Nevertheless, it is useful in answering certain questions, particularly if one wishes to compare the performance of several countries, taking into account the terms under which aid is given. On this basis, countries giving most of their aid in the form of hard loans will suffer in the comparison with other countries giving a higher proportion of grants or soft loans.

From the point of view of measuring aid actually received, the most realistic method might be to disregard entirely the flow of the initial lump sum of capital and its gradual repayment and look at the continuing contribution of the added capital to the economy as against its current cost. However attractive this approach may be in theory, it is certainly impractical—especially since many projects are valuable because of externalities, and program loans are important as general contributions to the ongoing economy of the recipient. On the other hand, the current effort made by, and the burden on, the donor relate to the initial outflow, which is the same whether a grant or a loan. And one might say in that case that the aid to be measured is the immediately added command over resources, even though their benefits may come somewhat later.

The leading methods of recording loans would yield roughly the following results, using the example that $100 of aid is provided annually in the form of 20-year loans to be paid off on a straight line basis of $5 per year at 4 per cent interest (and disregarding the complication of grace periods):

Gross flow: $100 each year.
Net flow: $100 in the first year, $95 in the second, and so on, reaching zero in the twentieth year and continuing at zero thereafter, the accumulated amortization payments equalling the new loan each year.
Net transfer: $100 in the first year, $91 in the second, reaching minus $40 in the twentieth year, when amortization offsets the

new loan each year, but interest on the balance in the various loan accounts must be paid.

Grant element: about $60 each year, depending on the assumed nonconcessionary rate of interest.

Thus, under identical circumstances, the record would look very different in both the short run and the long run according to the method used for treating debt service, and each calculation is appropriate in answer to some question.

Using the DAC definitions and disregarding the extremes, the differences involved in these several methods are as follows for 1968:

	$ Million
Gross official flow	8,057
Net official flow	7,095
Net transfer	6,483
Grant element	5,359

Since amortization and interest are growing at a faster rate than the total, the spread among the figures is steadily widening.

Under current practice, if a loan already outstanding is rescheduled or extended, it affects the tabulation of terms but not the flow figures since two offsetting actions are taken. However, if a refinancing credit in the form of a government loan replaces a credit originally extended by the private sector, the amount is deducted from the private flow and added to government loans. Similarly, when official lending agencies sell obligations from their portfolio on the private capital market, the transaction is entered as an increase in the flow of long-term private capital and a reduction in official loans. For example, in 1967, Swiss government holdings of $7.6 million of IBRD bonds were taken over by the private sector, thus giving Switzerland a minus figure in official multilateral aid and an increased private flow, though nothing outside the country was involved.

Reverse Capital Flows. As has been pointed out, if one is focussing on the net amount added from outside to the less-developed country's resources, a number of other items need to be considered. One deduction which is suggested by balance-of-payments considerations but for which data are poorly reported is that of reverse capital flows, especially those of new investment made abroad by residents of the less-developed countries. Since such countries often have no organized capital market, it is not surprising that individuals should invest abroad, for foreign funds also represent insurance against domestic instability. The record of reverse flows is unclear because such activity often is carried out in disregard of exchange regulations and kept secret for tax purposes. It is likely to affect the official records of foreign transactions only in the composite "errors and omissions" item, if at all.

Interest in this matter was demonstrated in August 1966, when the U.N. Economic and Social Council supplemented earlier resolutions concerning the measurement of the flow of assistance and long-term capital by requesting the Secretary-General to report annually on "the reverse flow of capital and invisibles, as well as of interest and dividend repayments, from developing to developed countries so as to determine the net external resources available to the developing countries." [6] In an occasional or unusual situation, such as the flight of capital out of Algeria, estimates have been made of capital flight. However, the prospects are not bright for accuracy in deriving annual figures for this phase of international bookkeeping.

Private Capital. Private foreign investment is not always what it seems to be. When a U.S. company borrows abroad, as in the Euro-fund market, the proceeds are recorded in the U.S. accounts as a balance-of-payments inflow. If the funds are invested abroad or transferred to a foreign affiliate, they are included in direct investment capital outflows. Since the two offset each other, there is no net effect on the United States balance of payments. However, in the foreign assistance records, this would appear as an outflow of American capital even though it can be traced directly to the Euro-dollar market, in which only a part of the funds come from American sources.

The figure for U.S. direct investment abroad was high in 1965, for example, because of unusually large tax settlements by petroleum companies and large oil lease payments. In 1966, the majority share in two large American mining companies which operate in Latin America, amounting to $155 million, had to be transferred to local ownership in order to conform to local government regulations, and this amount was regarded as a decrease in direct investment. In 1967, these companies received in return $120 million in debt obligations which appeared in the figure for portfolio investment and other new bilateral lending. Interestingly enough, the U.S. annual figures for the net flow of direct investment have never taken into account the loss of properties in Cuba in 1959–60. Presumably, the United States has a claim against Cuba for compensation, so that no loss has actually occurred as yet. In fact, settlements in nationalization cases clearly are repayments of capital and ought to be deducted. However, if the payment should be less than the amount of capital plus reinvested earnings, one would have to record a loss in some manner, since there is no continuing investment. The problem seldom arises since, in most cases, the settlement is in the form of securities and must be treated as being an equitable transaction.

Multilateral Flows. Problems also arise in recording multilateral flows. The DAC record includes as multilateral agencies the IBRD, IDA, and IFC; the European Development Fund and the European Investment Bank; the Inter-American, Asian, and African Development Banks; the OAS; and the technical and welfare programs of the United Nations institutions—the Regular Programme of Technical Assistance (UNTA); the U.N. Development Program (UNDP), originally the Expanded Program for Technical Assistance and the Special Fund; the Children's Fund (UNICEF); the Relief and Works Agency for Palestine Refugees in the Near East (UNRWA); the High Commission for Refugees (UNHCR); the Fund for the Congo (UNFC); the Korean Relief Agency (UNKRA); the World Food Program (WFP); and the United Nations Temporary Authority in West Irian (UNTEA). The contributions by the United States to the Secretary-General of the U.N.'s Trust Fund for Population Problems is included because it comes from the AID appropriation and is administered by UNDP.

Omitted from the calculation are the various specialized agencies of the United Nations, except that they may administer funds originally contributed by governments to the above agencies. Transactions with the International Monetary Fund are excluded as representing purchases of currency (or drawings) rather than credit transactions in the usual sense. One might speculate about whether or not the new issue of Special Drawing Rights is a form of assistance when given to less-developed countries as their share in a global transaction. Also omitted, at least through the 1968 figures, are the more limited regional institutions, such as the Andean Development Corporation, the East African Development Bank, and the Caribbean Development Bank.

Presumably, the figures are limited to contributions earmarked for development and welfare purposes in less-developed countries, and do not include regular contributions to the administrative budgets of the agencies concerned. The calculation is complicated by the fact that less-developed countries also make contributions to most of these institutions. Furthermore, the global institutions may provide aid to developed countries. In fact, in the early years of its life, the IBRD made many reconstruction loans to war-devastated countries in Europe, and over the years, Japan has been its largest borrower. In 1968–69, the only developed countries to receive new loans were Finland and Ireland.

The problem of annual figures is complicated because of timing problems. There is the tiresome problem of differing fiscal years. Much more difficult is the fact that national practice varies as to the point in the process at which the transfer from national treasury to multilateral agency is recorded. Governments may provide non-interest-bearing, non-negotiable notes, which are considered as assets by the agency concerned, are included in its balance sheet, and are translated into cash when needed for current lending operations. However, when the United States became concerned with its balance-of-payments position in 1965, and $604 million was made available in the form of promissory notes to the IBRD and IDA but encashment totalled only $79 million in that year, it revised its record of multilateral contributions back to 1960 to be on the encashment basis and continues to do so.

Both commitments and disbursement figures are available for the multilateral agencies. Their flows show large gaps between the extension of loans and actual disbursements, especially in years of expansion. In 1968–69, for example, the IBRD made new loans totalling $1,399 million and disbursements of $762 million. As of June 30, 1969, the undisbursed portion of IBRD's effective loans was $2,373 million, and an additional $634 million represented signed agreements where further action was required to make the loans effective.

A recent development is that governments make use of multilateral institutions to arrange loans with less-developed countries in their behalf, using trust funds or some other arrangement.

This is a growing activity by the regional banks. Such transactions are recorded as bilateral.

* * *

As in any complicated statistical undertaking, many special problems of definition or estimation arise in trying to measure the flow of economic assistance. The DAC and the United Nations are both dependent upon the accuracy of the basic data compiled by individual governments. Governments often operate on a fiscal-year basis, and for them to produce data for calendar years has itself been a considerable complication. Since 1960, most governments have made a major effort to improve their records, particularly in recording the flows in the private sector, but there still is much room for reducing the probable error.

As one might expect, the record as it stands at the end of the 1960s is more accurate when measuring official flows than private. It is much better in indicating trends than in defining the actual volume for any one year. Since it is measured in current dollars, changes in the real volume over time cannot be estimated, for there is no satisfactory price index to use for deflating the figures. It reflects fairly accurately the relative efforts of different donor countries, although for this purpose one must take the quality of the assistance into account.

One of the biggest steps forward has been the greater availability of data, with some governments even publishing the full information which they submit to the DAC. This often makes it possible to make the adjustments needed to answer this or that specific question. Yet even then, as with most social and economic matters, the whole story can never be told in numbers.

Notes

CHAPTER 1

1. See Table 1 for present membership covered at the time of writing. Since then, Finland has joined, but revised figures including Finland are not yet available. For a description of the Development Assistance Committee, see Chapter 13.
2. Figures for official economic assistance involve a number of decisions as to what should or should not be included but the coverage is constant over the period. (For details about this, see Appendix, "The Foreign Aid Numbers Game.")
3. Herrenschmidt, J. R., "Planning for the Expansion of Development Aid," *OECD Observer*, Paris, February 1969, No. 38, p. 15.
4. Senate Committee on Foreign Relations, *Report No. 1479*, 90th Congress, 2nd Session, July 26, 1968, p. 3.
5. Frank M. Coffin, *Witness for Aid* (Boston: Houghton Mifflin, 1964).
6. Richard P. Stebbins, *The United States in World Affairs, 1967* (New York: Simon and Schuster for the Council on Foreign Relations, 1968), p. 353.
7. Commission on International Development, *Partners in Development* (New York: Praeger Publishers, 1969).

CHAPTER 2

1. Quoted by Martin C. Needler, "Mexico as a Case Study in Political Development," *International Development Review*, Washington, March 1968, Vol. X, p. 12.
2. Nelson A. Rockefeller, *The Rockefeller Report on the Americas* (Chicago: Quadrangle Books, 1969).
3. Dean Rusk, testimony before House Foreign Affairs Committee, May 2, 1968.

CHAPTER 3

1. Alliance for Progress, *Weekly Newsletter*, Washington, October 13, 1969.
2. John Maynard Keynes, *Essays in Persuasion* (New York: Harcourt Brace, 1932).

351

3. Reported in *Far East Trade and Development*, London, January 1969, p. 27.
4. Felipe Herrera, "Economic Development and Integration of Latin America," Address at the Vienna Institute of Development, November 18, 1968.
5. Reported in Alliance for Progress, *Weekly Newsletter*, Washington, April 28, 1969.

CHAPTER 4

1. For complete statement, see *The Department of State Bulletin*, August 4, 1969, p. 81.

CHAPTER 5

1. Angus Maddison, *Foreign Skills and Technical Assistance in Development* (Paris: OECD Development Centre, 1965).
2. Section 211-(d).
3. For a fuller discussion, see Philip H. Coombs, *The World Educational Crisis* (Oxford: Oxford University Press, 1968).

CHAPTER 6

1. For discussion of this point, see Simon Kuznets, "Notes on the Take-off," in W. W. Rostow, ed., *The Economics of Take-off into Sustained Growth* (London: Macmillan, 1963).
2. United Nations, Department of Economic and Social Affairs, *The Financing of Economic Development* (World Economic Survey, Part I). New York, 1966, p. 15.
3. Simon Kuznets, "Quantitative Aspects of the Economic Growth of Nations," *Economic Development and Cultural Change*, Chicago, July 1960.
4. Alexis Lachman, *The Local Currency Proceeds of Foreign Aid* (Paris: OECD Development Centre, 1968).
5. IBRD, *Annual Report*, 1969, Washington, p. 49.
6. See, for example, Albert O. Hirschman and Richard M. Bird, *Foreign Aid—A Critique and a Proposal*, Essays in International Finance, Princeton, No. 69, 1968.

CHAPTER 7

1. For much more detail, see the volumes in the Transport Research Program of the Brookings Institution, Washington.
2. U.N. doc. F/1546 [222(IX)]. Adopted August 14-15, 1949.
3. Reported in *Far East Trade and Development*, London, August 1969.
4. U.S. Department of Agriculture, *The World Agricultural Situation*, 1969, Washington.
5. Lester R. Brown, in a speech delivered at Kansas State University, December 3, 1968.

6. M. N. Harrison, "How Hybrid Seed is Revolutionizing Maize Growing in Kenya," *International Development Review*, Washington, September 1968, Vol. x, p. 9.
7. For a much more detailed discussion see Clifton R. Wharton, Jr., "The Green Revolution: Cornucopia or Pandora's Box," *Foreign Affairs*, New York, April 1969, Vol. 47, p. 464.
8. For a more detailed discussion see Frank Notestein, "Population Growth and its Control" in American Assembly, *Overcoming World Hunger*, New York, 1969.
9. UNA-USA National Policy Panel, *World Population*, New York, May 1969.

CHAPTER 8

1. *Congressional Record*, 1968, p. 6964.
2. E. M. Martin, *Development Assistance*, *1969 Review* (Paris: OECD, 1969), p. 178.
3. Inter-American Development Bank, *Proceedings*, *April 1968*, p. 63.
4. Percy Selwyn, "Should the Poorest Countries Get More Aid?," *International Development Review*, Washington, September 1969.
5. *Proposed Mutual Defense and Assistance Programs—FY 1964*, Washington, 1963.

CHAPTER 9

1. Robert Jackson, *A Study of the Capacity of the United Nations Development System*, Geneva, 1969.

CHAPTER 10

1. *Business Week*, New York, August 3, 1968.
2. U.S. Department of Commerce, *Survey of Current Business*, Washington, March 1970, Vol. 50, p. 21.
3. *Business Week*, New York, August 9, 1969.
4. Speech at Eighth Florida World Trade Conference, April 10, 1969. Reported in *Survey of International Development*, Washington, April 15, 1969.
5. *The Economist*, London, June 14, 1969.
6. Dirk U. Stikker lists treaties of the first type since 1945 involving the United States of America, 12; Japan, 4; U.K., 1; and of the second, Federal Republic of Germany, 36; Switzerland, 16; Netherlands, 4; Sweden, 3; Belgium and Luxembourg, 2; and U.K., 1. France also has a network of treaties with at least seven countries. In report to UNCTAD, *The role of private enterprise in investment and promotion of exports in developing countries*.
7. *The Economist*, London, June 14, 1969, p. 71.
8. *The Case for a U.S. Overseas Private Enterprise Development Corporation*, December 1968. Distributed by AID, Washington.

CHAPTER 11

1. Hollis Chenery and Alan Strout, "Foreign Assistance and Economic Development," *American Economic Review*, September 1966.
2. IBRD, *Annual Report*, 1964–65, p. 62.
3. Reported in Alliance for Progress, *Weekly Newsletter*, Washington, May 19, 1969.
4. Felipe Herrara, Speech before the Canadian Manufacturers' Association, Toronto, June 2, 1969.
5. For a detailed discussion of these issues, see Appendix, "The Foreign Aid Numbers Game."
6. For a full description of the new Recommendation, see OECD *Observer*, Paris, June 1969, No. 40, p. 16.

CHAPTER 12

1. *New York Times*, May 30, 1969, p. 4.
2. Quoted in David Wise, "Flies in the Honeypot," *Saturday Evening Post*, September 7, 1968.
3. *New York Times*, April 6, 1969, p. 16.
4. For a discussion of these legislative proposals, see New York State Bar Association, *Bulletin of the Committee on Federal Legislation.* January 1969, pp. 25-26.

CHAPTER 13

1. *The Department of State Bulletin*, August 4, 1969, p. 81.
2. IBRD *Press Release*, May 23, 1969.
3. Charles A. Meyer testifying before the Senate Committee on Foreign Relations concerning "Current U.S.–Peruvian Problems." *Department of State Bulletin*, May 12, 1969.

CHAPTER 14

1. For a detailed analysis, see Hal B. Lary, *Imports of Manufactures for Less Developed Countries* (New York: Columbia University Press, 1968).
2. Seiji Naya and Theodore Morgan, "The Accuracy of International Trade Data," *Journal of the American Statistical Association*, Washington, June 1969, Vol. 64, p. 452.
3. Quoted in Council of Economic Advisors, *Annual Report*, Washington, 1970.
4. Olivier Long. "International Trade—The Present Challenge." Address before the National Foreign Trade Convention, New York, November 19, 1969. GATT Press Release 1048. Geneva.
5. *The Department of State Bulletin*, December 15, 1969.
6. Hal B. Lary, *Imports of Manufactures from Less Developed Countries* (New York: Columbia University Press, 1968), p. 137.
7. Harry G. Johnson, "U.S. Economic Policy toward the Developing Countries," *Economic Development and Cultural Change*, Chicago, April 1968.

8. Judd Polk has estimated that American investment abroad of $133 billion has an annual production volume of $200 billion. *United States International Economic Policy* (New York: United States Council of the International Chamber of Commerce, Inc., March 1969).

9. Reported in IMF, *International Financial News Survey*, May 9, 1969, p. 141.

10. Alastair MacBean, *Export Instability and Economic Development* (Cambridge: Harvard University Press, 1966).

11. Reported in the *Wall Street Journal*, New York, September 15, 1969.

12. IMF *Press Release* No. 746, July 9, 1969, and IBRD *Press Release*, July 9, 1969. Washington.

13. Joint Economic Committee (U.S. Congress), *A Proposal to Link Reserve Creation and Development Assistance*, Washington, August 1969.

14. Commission on International Development, *Partners in Development* (New York: Praeger Publishers, 1969), p. 222.

15. Speech at Sun Valley, Idaho, reported in *The Economist*, September 28, 1968, p. 67.

16. Albert O. Hirschman and Richard M. Bird, *Foreign Aid—A Critique and a Proposal*. Essays in International Finance, Princeton, No. 69, 1968.

CHAPTER 15

1. Solomon Fabricant, "Wage, Price and Productivity Data for Economic Policy," American Statistical Association *Proceedings*, 1968, p. 146.

2. Statistics given are based on Walter H. Mallory, *Political Handbook and Atlas of the World*, 1968 (New York: Simon and Schuster for the Council on Foreign Relations, 1968).

3. Irma Adelman and Cynthia Taft Morris, *Society, Politics and Economic Development* (Baltimore: Johns Hopkins Press, 1967).

4. United Nations, *World Economic Survey*, 1967, New York, 1968, Part I, p. 2.

5. John P. Lewis, *Wanted in India: A Relevant Radicalism*, Center of International Studies, Princeton University, 1969, Policy Memorandum No. 36.

6. Ben King, *Economic Development Projects and Their Appraisal* (Baltimore: Johns Hopkins Press, 1967).

7. W. Arthur Lewis, *The Theory of Economic Growth* (London: George Allen and Unwin, Ltd., 1955).

CHAPTER 16

1. Commission on International Development, *Partners in Development* (New York: Praeger Publishers, 1969).

2. From text of letter to President Nixon, published in the *New York Times*, March 9, 1970, p. 12.

3. Ministry of Overseas Development, *Overseas Development: The Work of the New Ministry*, London, Cmnd. 2736, 1965.

4. Quoted by Sir John Maud, *Aid for Developing Countries*, Stamp Memorial Lecture, 1963.

5. Report of a Commission of Inquiry, *La Politique de Cooperation avec les pays en voie de Developpement*, Paris, 1963.
6. Ministry of Foreign Affairs, *Development Assistance Policies of the Netherlands*, The Hague, 1966.
7. See Charles Wolf, Jr., *United States Policy and the Third World* (Boston: Little, Brown, 1967).
8. Quoted from Society for International Development, *Survey of International Development*, November 15, 1968.

Appendix

1. See United Nations, *The International Flow of Private Capital, 1946-1952*, New York, 1954. Also United Nations, *International Flow of Long-Term Capital and Official Donations, 1951-1959*, New York, 1961, and subsequent publications of similar titles.
2. OEEC, *The Flow of Financial Resources to Countries in the Course of Economic Development, 1956-1959*. Paris, 1961.
3. United Nations Conference on Trade and Development, *Growth and Aid*, Recommendation a/IV/2.
4. Report of the Chairman of the Development Assistance Committee, *Development Assistance, 1968 Review* (Paris: OECD Development Centre, 1968), p. 25.
5. United Nations, *Measurement of the Flow of Resources to Developing Countries*, 1967, Table 8.
6. United Nations, Economic and Social Council, Resolution 1184 (XLI), August 5, 1966.

Index

Act for International Development, 8, 9, 12, 50, 54–55

Additionality, concept of, 215–16, 315

Adelman, Irma, 307

Afghanistan, 65, 88, 295

AFL-CIO, 245

Africa, 72, 90, 133; Chinese aid to, 65, 66; and Consultative Group of East Africa, 171; and East African consortium, 262; economic groupings in, 287; exports of, 275; growth rates of, 44; inflow estimates (1964) of, 334; private flows to, 142; regionalism in, 147, 171; U.S. aid to, 255

African-American Institute, 85

African Development Bank, 148, 158, 162

Agency for International Development (AID), 15, 51, 53, 229, 231, 232; assistance criteria of, 266; and agricultural aid, 121, see also Agriculture; educational assistance of, 87–88; and estimating aid requirements, 203; expenditures (1968–69) of, 165; industrial projects of, 115; priorities of, 116; survey assistance of, 236; technical assistance programs (1967–68) of, 74–76; see also United States aid

Agricultural Trade and Development Act (1954), see PL 480

Agriculture, 36, 116–22; and price support, 292; research activities in, 119; and transmission of knowledge, 118–19; yield increases in, 117–18, 119

Ahidjo, Ahmadou, 291

Aid-tying, 213–15, 250, 266, 315; see also Foreign Aid, and political prohibitions

Algeria, 17, 36, 104

Algiers Charter, 253

Alliance for Progress, 45, 51, 131, 152, 236, 263–65, 303, 325; aid allocation for, 133, 134; growth targets of, 42; Inter-American Committee for (CIAP), 148, 264, 343; and land ownership, 310; technical assistance to, 75

American University, Beirut and Cairo, 322

Amortization, 209, 341–42; see also Debt-servicing

Anaconda Copper Company, 188

Andean Common Market, 287

Andean Development Corp., 349

Angola, 336

Ankrah, J. A., 239

Argentina, 67, 98, 183

Asante, K. B., 151

Asia, 275, 334; see also individual countries

Asian Coconut Community, 294

Asian Development Bank, 53, 148, 158, 161, 162

Atlantic Committee Development Group for Latin America (ADELA), 196

Australia, 63, 286; and aid, 129; as capital importer, 217; grants by, 96; loans to, 67; technical assistance of, 74

Austria, 57, 59, 74; and export credits, 183; grants by, 96

Balance of payments, 212–13; accounting of, 339; and foreign investments, 192–94; and import substitution, 273; LDCs, 333; U.S., 192–94, 212, 213, 215–16, 349

Bank lending, 101, 179

Belgium, 28, 61, 238; and aid to ex-colonies, 129; as capital exporter, 217; and export credits, 183; grants by, 96; and technical assistance, 74; and trade preferences, 278; and volunteer programs, 81

Berne Union, 102

Bird, Richard M., 299

Bokaro Steel plant (India), 65

Bonds, 101, 154, 179

Less-developed countries (*cont.*):
movements in, 20–23, 31; and
management problems, 225; and
military expenditures, 241; military governments of, 23–24, 30;
one-party system in, 22, 23, 30,
306; and political stability, 25–29;
poverty in, 39–40; research interest
in 313; savings by, 91, 92; technical assistance by, 66–67; trade
among, 275, 286–88; trade proposals for, 278–79
Less-developed countries, aid to, 6,
33–34, 200; coordination of, 252–
53; estimating requirements of,
202–6; in food, 53, 93, 119–20,
121, 338; *see also* PL 480; financing of, from all sources (1959–
68), 68; in grants or loans (1964–
68), 95; and loans, 97–98; *see also*
Foreign aid; Technical assistance;
U.S. aid
Lewis, Arthur W., 313
Lewis, John P., 309–10
Liberty Lobby, 245
Libya, 36, 181, 185, 308
Loans, 96–98, 349; arguments for,
99, 100; classification of, 343–46;
coordination of, 211; development,
103; "dollar repayable," 96; funding of, 297–99; hard *vs.* soft, 94,
95–96; measurement of, 341–42;
terms of, 94, 95–96, 211–12

McGee, Gale, 14
McNamara, Robert S., 302; on aid
emphasis, 139; on lending, 161,
167, 168
Madagascar, 163
Maddison, Angus, 71
Malaysia, 88–89, 128, 212
Mali, 28, 65
Malthus, T. R., 116
Manufactures, 282
Markets, national, 37, 272; *see also*
Trade
Marshall Plan, 47, 49–50, 51, 93–94,
95, 100, 104, 133, 134, 144, 170,
226, 264, 265, 316
Martin, Edward, 179
Marx, Karl, 113
Maudling, Reginald, 322
Mauritania, 36, 170

Mexico, 98, 114; borrowing by, 183;
export credits to, 67; and *Nacional
Financiera*, 170; and U.S. oil expropriation, 188
Meyer, Charles A., 302
Middle East, 148, 170
Military assistance, 12, 14, 55, 228–
29, 230, 267–68, 325, 331; U.S.,
12, 228, 229–30
Morocco, 38
Morris, Cynthia Taft, 307
Morse, Wayne, 242–43
Most-favored-nation treatment, 280,
284
Mozambique, 336
Multilateral agencies, 67, 154, 164,
172–73, 331; assessments by, 163;
and bond purchases, 101; and capital flows, 104, 157, 159, 348; coordination among, 171–72, 175–
76; development activities, 302,
303–4; efficiency of, 156; financing
of, 154, 170, 260; fragmentation
of, 155; and loans, 98, 160, 298;
membership of, 130, 131; and
personnel drain, 173–74; and political influence, 156–57; *see also*
Technical assistance
Multinational corporations, 61, 62,
196, 198, 289
Multiplier effect, 90, 292
Mutual Security Act, 50, 51, 267
Mutual Security Agency, 227, 231

Nasser, Gamal Abdel, 306
National Council of Churches, 320
National Planning Association, 321
Nationalism, 26–27
Natural resources, 185, 186
Neocolonialism, 64; *see also* Colo-
nialism
Net transfer, foreign aid, 343–44,
345–46
Netherlands: and aid, 7, 57, 226,
323; as capital exporter, 217; and
Curaçao, 336; and ex-colonies, 28,
129, 131
New Guinea, 129
Nigeria, 26, 39, 222, 291
Nixon, Richard M., 53, 319–20; on
family planning, 125, 126; foreign
aid message of, to Congress
(1969), 13, 14; on Latin Ameri-

Recent Publications

FOREIGN AFFAIRS (quarterly), edited by Hamilton Fish Armstrong.
THE UNITED STATES IN WORLD AFFAIRS (annual), by Richard P. Stebbins.
DOCUMENTS ON AMERICAN FOREIGN RELATIONS (annual), by Richard P. Stebbins with the assistance of Elaine P. Adam.
POLITICAL HANDBOOK AND ATLAS OF THE WORLD, 1970, edited by Richard P. Stebbins and Alba Amoia (1970).
JAPAN IN POSTWAR ASIA, by Lawrence Olson (1970).
THE CRISIS OF DEVELOPMENT, by Lester B. Pearson (1970).
THE GREAT POWERS AND AFRICA, by Waldemar A. Nielsen (1969).
A NEW FOREIGN POLICY FOR THE UNITED STATES, by Hans J. Morgenthau (1969).
MIDDLE EAST POLITICS: THE MILITARY DIMENSION, by J. C. Hurewitz (1969).
THE ECONOMICS OF INTERDEPENDENCE: Economic Policy in the Atlantic Community, by Richard N. Cooper (1968).
HOW NATIONS BEHAVE: Law and Foreign Policy, by Louis Henkin (1968).
THE INSECURITY OF NATIONS, by Charles W. Yost (1968).
PROSPECTS FOR SOVIET SOCIETY, edited by Allen Kassof (1968).
THE AMERICAN APPROACH TO THE ARAB WORLD, by John S. Badeau (1968).

DATE DUE

10/30			
GAYLORD			PRINTED IN U.S.A